Christ Church
KU-026-784

Foreign-Language Printing in London 1500-1900

Edited by
Barry Taylor

THE BRITISH LIBRARY
Boston Spa & London 2002

First published in November 2002

ISBN 0 7123 1128 9

Typesetting and jacket design by Cynthia McKinley

Printed in Great Britain by Bookcraft, Midsomer Norton

Contents

Preface

For centuries London has been a truly cosmopolitan city, partly based upon its status as a centre of international trade, finance and diplomacy and partly upon its hospitability to successive waves of immigrants from abroad, in particular Europe. During the period studied in this book many refugees fled to London and some of the English provinces to escape religious and/or political persecution in their homelands, typically for their Protestant or liberal/radical beliefs. The presence of so many foreigners in Britain's capital city created a market for foreign-language publications, initially to serve the needs of the stranger communities themselves (or, in the case of grammars and vocabularies, to assist the small number of English people who needed the language for commercial reasons); but subsequently to satisfy the inquisitiveness of the indigenous population about the culture, history, politics, language and literature of the lands from which these immigrants came.

The fourteen substantive essays assembled in this volume represent the first systematic attempt to document and to analyse the tradition of foreign-language printing in London during the period 1500 to 1900. With five exceptions, they are based upon papers given at a highly successful one-day conference held in the British Library Conference Centre on 8 May 2000, masterminded by Graham Jefcoate (then Head of the British Library's Early Printed Collections and now Director of the Staatsbibliothek in Berlin) and chaired by Professor Theo Hermans of University College London.

The papers comprise a combination of general surveys covering one or more centuries and a series of case studies. The former include overviews of publishing in French (David Shaw), German (Graham Jefcoate and Susan Reed), Scandinavian (Peter Hogg), Italian (Stephen Parkin), Spanish and Portuguese (Barry Taylor), and Hungarian (Bridget Guzner). The case studies are of particular books (Morna Daniels) or printers/publishers (Denis Reidy, Kate Sealey Rahman and Janet Zmroczek). There are two hybrid chapters, part survey and part case study, by Anna Simoni and Chris Michaelides. Shaw concludes the volume with a statistical analysis of foreign-language publishing in London.

A variety of approaches are pursued by the several authors, from the perspective of the history of printing, of publishing, of bookselling, of readership (domestic and overseas), of the book as a cultural artefact, and of the reception of foreign languages in England. A complex picture is revealed whereby foreign printers based in London did not necessarily confine their efforts to printing in their native tongue, but also printed in English and other languages; many works published in London were still printed abroad; and English printers and publishers strayed increasingly into publishing foreign-language texts, sometimes, as with Richard Field (who traded as Ricardo del Campo), trying to disguise themselves as of foreign birth.

The scale of foreign-language printing in London during the period under review cannot be quantified with absolute precision. In part, this reflects the continuing unevenness of the bibliographies and databases which can furnish the evidence. Thus, although the *English Short-Title Catalogue* is fully searchable by language and place of imprint, it is still far from comprehensive in respect of the 1501-1700 period; for the eighteenth century it is more definitive. The *Nineteenth-Century Short-Title Catalogue* has no search capability by language and place, so recourse has to be had to other union catalogues such as those maintained by the Consortium of European Research Libraries and the Consortium of University Research Libraries. In part, of course, there is also the distorting effect of false imprints, the numerous publications claiming London as a place of imprint but which were actually published abroad, and which are not always easy to detect. This is a particular factor in French- and, to a much lesser extent, German- and Italian-language publications. Usually, these false imprints were intended to mask the responsibility of native printers and publishers for controversial or subversive works which could have resulted in their persecution. False imprints are generally out of scope for this collection. Another complication was publishing in Law French – a creole based upon Anglo-Norman French with English and used by English common lawyers – with 1,000 titles identified to 1800.

Within these limitations, Shaw has provided an estimate of 'genuine' foreign-language books in London of 2,945 editions (excluding Latin, Law French, Welsh, Irish and Gaelic) to 1800, just under one per cent of the total output of the London presses. The earliest and most numerous works were in French, which was the only foreign language to have been printed continuously in London from the fifteenth to the nineteenth centuries. French accounted for 81 per cent of all foreign-language books to 1800 and for one in every ninety of all editions printed in London. Italian, Spanish and Dutch books appear from the sixteenth century, German and Portuguese from the seventeenth century, and other languages only in the eighteenth (for example, Scandinavian) or nineteenth centuries (for instance, Polish). As

Parkin points out for Italian, printing in any language did not necessarily become an institutionalised feature of the publishing scene immediately from its commencement: 'the phenomenon is a highly discontinuous and episodic one. The map drawn by these bibliographic resources depicts an archipelago not a single landmass.' For some languages London was the dominant centre of publication outside the country concerned, but for others (for instance, Polish where Paris was the emigré publishing centre) this was not the case. Books predominated for most of the period studied, foreign-language periodicals and newspapers appearing during the nineteenth century.

All the authors of this book are serving or former members of the British Library's staff or voluntary assistants working on the Library's collections. Cumulatively, they testify to the significant value which the British Library adds to its internationally-prestigious collections through the research and expertise of its curators. This volume, like others they have produced individually or collectively, is a distinguished contribution to scholarship in its own right.

Dr Clive Field
Director of Scholarship and Collections
The British Library
10 March 2002

Graham Jefcoate [1]

German Printing and Bookselling in Eighteenth-Century London
evidence and interpretation

When Bernhard Fabian suggested over ten years ago that I should widen my researches into German printing and bookselling in eighteenth-century London, the scale of the task was hardly apparent. Some evidence had begun to emerge through early reports to the *Eighteenth-Century Short-Title Catalogue* (ESTC)[2] during the 1980s. Although many German-language imprints claiming 'London' as place of publication could easily be dismissed as deceptions by German printers and publishers intending to mask their responsibility for controversial or subversive texts, some were clearly genuine. The extent of German-language printing and bookselling in colonial America was becoming better known.[3] In addition, it was clear that printers and booksellers on the margins of the London trade with apparently German names were responsible for a considerable number of non-German titles. If some of these were indeed well known, the German contribution to their publication had been overlooked.

By 1988, when I joined the ESTC team at the British Library, only one or two substantial articles and a number of bibliographical notes about aspects of German printing and bookselling in eighteenth-century London had appeared. In the late 1970s a lively correspondence in *Factotum*, the ESTC's

1 This is a much revised and greatly expanded version of papers given at two conferences in May 2000: see my 'German Immigrants and the London Book Trade, 1700-70', in *From Strangers to Citizens: the integration of immigrant communities in Britain, Ireland and Colonial America, 1550-1750*, ed. R. Vigne and C. Littleton (Brighton: Sussex Academic Press, 2001), pp. 503-10.

2 Shortly after this, ESTC was to expand into the *English STC*, the online national bibliography of the English-speaking world from Caxton to 1800.

3 See especially Gerd-J. Bötte and Werner Tannhof, *The First Century of German Language Printing in the United States of America*, ed. K. J. R. Arndt and R. C. Eck (Göttingen: Niedersächsische Staats- und Universitätsbibliothek Göttingen, 1989).

newsletter, had attracted contributions from a number of scholars,[4] including Professor Fabian, the bibliographer of the reception of English books in the eighteenth century. The discussion in *Factotum* focused above all on John Haberkorn, the printer of a 1751 German New Testament, the first printed in London, whose personal misfortunes were revealed in an exchange of frankly bizarre anecdotes. One suspected that his name, somewhat comical for English-speaking readers, might have added to the interest.

My own first investigation into an aspect of German book trade activity in the eighteenth century had dealt with a much later period. In 1987 I published an account of the *Deutsche Lese-Bibliothek*, a German circulating library operating in the Strand during the 1790s.[5] During my work on the *Lese-Bibliothek*, the British Library acquired some of its very rare printed catalogues, allowing me to trace its progress in some detail and to reach some very preliminary conclusions about its significance in the context of the contemporary London trade. Even then it was apparent, however, that the evidence for German book trade activity in eighteenth-century London remained to be collected, let alone properly assessed.

Copies of German books printed in London tend to be scarce survivors, scattered through the world's collections both major and minor. Only the development of the ESTC, which by 1990 had over a quarter of a million records based on the collections of around 1,500 libraries world-wide, had begun to bring many of them together. Coverage of German libraries in the ESTC was and remains relatively poor, with the single exception of the University Library of Göttingen, the English holdings of which had been catalogued in collaboration with the ESTC.[6] Other catalogues had to be searched manually *in situ* as the opportunity arose. Single, unrecorded collections, such as the library of St George's, Little Alie Street (a Lutheran parish church founded in 1762), acquired by the British Library as recently as 1997, proved to contain unique copies of key works. Only in recent years has it been possible to gain easy access to the holdings of libraries in Halle which are rich in the printed evidence for early German printing in London.

In the last ten years, the catalogues of many more collections both in Germany and abroad have been retrospectively converted to machine-

4 See for example *Factotum*, nos 1, 2, 5 and 6, with articles and notes by V. A. Berch, F. J. Mosher, B. Fabian and R. J. Goulden.

5 'The Deutsche Lese-Bibliothek and the Distribution of German Books in London, 1794-1800', *The Library*, 6th ser., 9 (1987), 348-64.

6 *A Catalogue of English Books Printed Before 1801 Held in the University Library at Göttingen*, compiled by Graham Jefcoate and Karen Kloth; ed. Bernhard Fabian (Hildesheim: Olms-Weidmann, 1987-8).

readable form and placed online. More recently, search engines such as the *Karlsruher Virtueller Katalog* (KVK)[7] have opened up access to them through a single interface on the World Wide Web. By searching online databases using parameters such as language and keywords in imprints, patterns were revealed suggesting that German printing and bookselling in the eighteenth century were not confined to occasional and isolated examples but rather were considerable and sustained throughout much of the period. There are few published contemporary accounts and very little archival material relating to German printers or booksellers in the eighteenth century; further sources remain to be identified in libraries and archives in both Britain and Germany. Again, Internet search engines have proved invaluable in tracing biographical information about German immigrants.[8] The rarity of German names in an English context has of course aided the retrieval of relevant data.

Above all, any assessment of the significance and impact of Germans working in the London book trade needed to be based on the kind of evidence which Professor Fabian and Marie-Luise Spieckemann have assembled for their reception bibliography or which the compilers of the bibliography of early German-American imprints had assembled for theirs. My annotated bibliography of printing in German and of material printed or published by Germans in London from 1680 to 1811 (based on the ESTC and my own researches), now comprising over 600 entries, at last provides a basis for a proper account and an evaluation. I hope to publish the full bibliography in the course of the coming year.

Such bibliographical data, combined with the evidence of a few booksellers' catalogues and other archival sources, paints a rather surprising picture. Although almost all German book trade initiatives ended in commercial failure, German printers and booksellers can be shown to have been among the more enterprising and innovative members of the London trade in the period. A number can now be recognised as considerable figures in their own right and I am particularly pleased that two of them, at least, have been awarded the accolade of entries in the *New Dictionary of National Biography*.[9]

---

7 http://www.ubka.uni-karlsruhe.de/kvk.html

8 See the Public Record Office's online catalogues. The Church of Jesus Christ of Latter-day Saints's FamilySearch service is another obvious example, providing access to parish records that can then be checked and verified. See http://www.familysearch.com/Eng/Search/frameset_search.asp

9 Johann Christoph Haberkorn himself and Carl Heydinger (I have also contributed the entry on Joseph Downing). I believe that a strong argument could be made for the inclusion of two others: Johann Christian Jacobi and Constantin Geisweiler.

German-speaking communities in eighteenth-century London

If the surviving evidence for German printing and publishing has now indeed been comprehensively (if not definitively) assembled in a bibliography, the process of evaluation continues to be hampered by our lack of knowledge of its social and economic context. Both German and British historians have tended to focus either on the mercantile communities of the medieval and early modern periods or on the exile communities of the nineteenth and twentieth centuries. The eighteenth century remains relatively neglected and much archival evidence is still to be identified and assessed. Those few accounts that have been published often appear to be compiled largely from secondary sources and to be based on previously held perceptions of what is significant. With few exceptions, they have not provided a particularly useful insight into the presence of Germans or the development of German-speaking communities in eighteenth-century London, necessary background for a proper assessment of the role of German printers and booksellers.

German communities are attested in London from the medieval period. The Hanseatic settlement in the Steel Yard is well known. In the early modern period, the Strand area and the liberty of the Savoy were favoured by German-speaking residents of London as they were by other expatriate communities. Numbers appear to have increased rapidly after the Restoration and St Mary's in the Savoy, a Lutheran chapel (usually known in German as the *Marienkirche*), was founded in 1694 to meet the spiritual needs of a growing community, St Paul's in the Strand (*Paulskirche*) following in 1697. These were not the only Lutheran congregations in London at the beginning of the eighteenth century. Chapels had been founded to serve communities that flourished in the City (Holy Trinity or *Trinitätskirche*, 1669) and around the court at St James's (German Court Chapel or *Hofkapelle*, about 1700). In the course of the century, a further Lutheran chapel was opened in Goodman's Fields, east of the City, to serve the community of German sugar refiners in the area (St George's, Little Alie Street, or *Georgenkirche*, 1762). In addition to these Lutheran chapels, German-speaking Calvinists, Catholics and Jews all had their own meeting places in London at different periods throughout the century.[10]

These places of worship are evidence for a growing and sustained resident population of German speakers. The great majority of this immigration was from northern Germany and had economic causes,

10 See Susanne Steinmetz, 'The German Churches in London, 1669-1914', in *Germans in Britain since 1500*, ed. P. Panayi (London: Hambledon, 1996), pp. 49-71 at pp. 51 ff.

although refugees from Catholic repression in southern Germany (such as the well-known case of the Palatines who arrived in London in 1708) also swelled the numbers. The accession of a German dynasty to the British throne in 1714 played only a relatively indirect role in terms of German immigration. Rather, Germans were attracted to London as Europe's most vibrant commercial centre, providing opportunities for enterprise and entrepreneurship, and as a hub of a growing Atlantic trade, as even a cursory reading of contemporary London trade directories will attest. Links with the port cities of Hamburg and Bremen were especially strong and a number of German merchants and tradesmen took British nationality.[11] Germans became predominant in a number of trades in the course of the century (one thinks of bookbinding and music); other trades (such as sugar refining and baking) became near-monopolies for those of German immigrant origin.

If some Germans came to London as settlers, others were transitory visitors or temporary residents, for example apprentices sent to gain experience of commercial life and practice by merchants in the Hanseatic ports. Even allowing for this, one credible estimate suggests there were at least 20,000 Germans living in London by the end of the eighteenth century, the equivalent of a medium-sized contemporary German town. Information about this community does survive, at least partially, in parish registers and other archives. The outbreak of the First World War brought an end to the German-speaking community in London and little work as been done since to collect and collate the surviving evidence. Other language-based communities in eighteenth-century London (for example, the Huguenots) are much better known. Only when this historical groundwork is available will we be able to place German book trade activity in its wider context.

The main phases of German book trade activity

For the purposes of my research, I have defined 'the long eighteenth century' as starting about 1680 and continuing until 1811. This period begins with isolated examples of German-language printing in London and ends with the dissolution of the partnership of Vogel and Schulze, after

---

11 Of the 316 Germans naturalised in the eighteenth century, at least 263 were merchants. See Margrit Schulte Beerbühl, 'Naturalization and Economic Integration: the German merchant community in 18th-century London', in *From Strangers to Citizens*, pp. 511-18. Naturalisation appears to have been expensive and therefore quite rare, which explains the relatively low numbers of naturalised Germans. Beerbrühl's list of professions of naturalised Germans (p. 513) shows no booksellers.

which (very broadly speaking) we soon find ourselves properly in the nineteenth century.

I cover printing, bookselling and publishing, within our modern understanding of those terms, but generally exclude bookbinders, print- and music-sellers, engravers, stationers and paper-makers. We should note, however, that Germans were also active in all these trades, including some of the printers and booksellers considered here.[12] I also include English printers and publishers of German books but only to consider their activities relevant to the present topic.[13] My bibliography covers London printing of substantive German texts, including works not necessarily connected with the German trade; examples include grammars, language primers and privately printed German texts of all kinds. I exclude German 'false imprints', that is to say works printed in Germany but claiming to have been printed in London (or occasionally elsewhere in the British Isles). Finally, this is not a study of the reception of German language and literature in the English-speaking world, even if it might be read as a contribution to that topic. Translations of German authors or editions of works originally published in German-speaking countries are therefore excluded from the bibliography, unless printed or sold by Germans, and are only considered as relevant background in the study itself.

Accepting my narrow definition, German book trade activity in London from 1680 to 1811 can be now be recognised as falling into several distinct phases. Periods of sustained and connected activity were interrupted by periods of apparent inactivity and discontinuity. These phases might be characterised in the following terms:

[First Phase]

- Before 1705: Grammars and isolated examples of German-language printing in London publications.
- 1705-1725: German printing (often in English black letter) by Joseph **Downing**, printer to the Society for Promoting Christian Knowledge, under the influence of Halle Pietism represented in London by Anton Wilhelm Böhm.

---

12 Perhaps rather wilfully, I have excluded John (Johann) Bohn, a bookbinder who also appears to have sold second-hand books before 1811, and Christopher Frederick Seyfang, a printer who appears to have entered into a partnership with Thomas Hamblin in 1810. Neither is central to this topic.

13 Examples are Joseph Downing, William Faden and Charles Whittingham.

- 1709- c. 1717: The establishment of the first German retail outlet by the Pietist Johann Christian **Jacobi** in the Strand.
- c. 1725-1749: A period with no resident German printers or booksellers and only occasional examples of German-language printing.

[Second Phase]

- c. 1749-1767: The establishment of the first German press (with the capability of printing with *fraktur* types) by Johann Christoph **Haberkorn** (and, to 1753) Johann Nicodemus **Gussen** in Gerrard Street (later Grafton Street), Soho.
- The establishment of bookshops by Andreas **Linde** in Catherine Street, c. 1750-1759, and by Christlieb Gottreich **Seyffert** in Dean Street, Soho (later Pall Mall), 1757-1762.
- c. 1766-1784: Carl **Heydinger**, printer and bookseller at various locations in Soho, the Strand and Holborn; examples of German printing using *fraktur* types by William Faden, 1766-1776.
- c. 1785-1793: A further period without a resident German printer or bookseller and only isolated examples of German-language printing and German grammars.

[Third Phase]

- c. 1793-1800: Opening of a German circulating library, the **Deutsche Lese-Bibliothek**, in the Strand; James **Remnant** opens a German bookshop in West Smithfield (later, St Giles and High Holborn), c. 1793-1802; Henry **Escher** in Broad Street, Bloomsbury (later Piccadilly), c. 1794-1813.
- Increasing numbers of German grammars and primers for English readers from 1790; isolated examples of German-language printing for English readers, c. 1796-1801.
- c. 1799-1802: Constantin **Geisweiler**, publisher of the *German Museum* and bookseller in Parliament Street; Charles Whittingham printing with *fraktur* types.
- From c. 1802: A further period without an effective German bookshop.
- c. 1809-1811: Johann Benjamin Gottlieb **Vogel**, printer in Poland Street, Soho, from c. 1803; in partnership with Gottlieb **Schulze**. First German-language newspaper, *Der Treue Verkündiger*, 1810-1811.

Three periods of sustained activity can be distinguished here: a preliminary 'Pietist' phase associated with Anton Wilhelm Böhm and Johann Christian Jacobi, from c. 1705 to 1722; the period from 1749 to the mid-1780s during which a number of specialist German printers and booksellers focusing, inter alia, on the German-speaking community emerge (Haberkorn and Gussen; Linde; Seyffert; Heydinger); the period from the early 1790s to c. 1802 associated with a number of new specialist German booksellers seeking to profit from a new interest in German literature by for example importing German titles (Remnant; Escher; Geisweiler); and a 'final' period of more modest activity associated above all with the partnership of Vogel and Schulze.

One obvious pattern emerges: almost all the German book trade initiatives listed here were relatively short lived, typically ending with the printer or bookseller selling his stock and 'going into another way of business'. Certainly those few contemporary accounts that we have for this aspect of the London trade suggest a record of successive business failures.

Between the distinct phases of sustained and related activity lay at least three periods of apparent discontinuity: from the period following Böhm's death in 1722 to Haberkorn's establishment of a press c. 1749-1750; the period after Heydinger's withdrawal from the trade and death to the arrival of James Remnant and Henry Escher, c. 1784-1793; and the period after Geisweiler's business failure in the first decade of the nineteenth century. Although certain political and economic trends and patterns within the book trade itself may explain these periods of sustained activity and discontinuity, the ways in which they might relate to developments in the wider German community or to the business cycle need to be more thoroughly investigated.

Pietist beginnings

Before 1700, only very few examples of German-language printing in London have been identified. John Gain's printing of the German mystic Quirin Kuhlmann's *Lutetier- oder Pariserschreiben* of 1681 remains an isolated and bizarre example of an English printer attempting to set German text. The imprint (with the phrase 'drukkts vor') suggests that he – or someone in his shop – was more familiar with Dutch. *The High Dutch Minerva a-la-mode or a perfect grammar never extant before, whereby the English may both easily and exactly learne the neatest dialect of the German mother-language used throughout all Europe* appeared in 1680 and was reissued in 1685.[14] The German examples are printed using English black letter types as a substitute for true *fraktur*. William

14 British Library, C.95.a.24.

Freeman and Benjamin Barker issued Johann König's *Ein volkommener englischer Wegweiser für Hoch-Teutsche* in 1706 with the English title on a parallel title-page: *A Compleat English Guide for High-Germans*, with a dedication to the royal consort George, Prince of Denmark, implying that German-speaking immigrants (including members of George's own household) were by now numerous enough to represent a potentially lucrative market.

The earliest evidence for true German book trade activity is found in the first decade of the eighteenth century. I have described elsewhere the very considerable impact that Pietism had on the recently founded Society for Promoting Christian Knowledge and its printer/publisher Joseph Downing (d. 1734).[15] Anton Wilhelm Böhm (d. 1722) was the London representative of Hermann August Francke (d. 1727) at Halle, the leading contemporary figure in the Pietist reform movement within the Lutheran Church. Böhm was responsible for an ambitious programme of translating and preparing for publication a range of key Pietist texts, concentrating of course on the works of Francke himself. These texts were disseminated in editions printed and sold by Downing, many with the direct or implicit support of the SPCK itself.

The earliest example of Böhm's association with Downing bearing fruit in the form of a publication in German may be a prayer book for the use of Prince George's German Chapel issued in 1707. In 1709, Downing printed a bilingual catechism; a manuscript note in the Bodleian copy tells us it was 'translated and published for the use of the Palatine refugees by John Tribbeko [i.e. Johann Tribbechov, b. 1677] Chaplain to the late Prince George'.[16] The 'Palatines' were a well-known group of Protestant refugees from the Palatinate region who had come to England in 1708.[17] Downing printed a number of items in German for their use during this period, including (quite possibly) in 1710 an English primer: *A Short and Easy Way for the Palatines to Learn English. Oder eine kurze Anleitung zur englischen Sprach, zum Nutz der armen Pfälzer, nebst angehängten englischen und teutschen ABC.*[18]

It is within this context that we must understand the establishment of the first German bookshop by Johann Christian Jacobi (1670-1750) 'next door but one to Sommerset-House in the Strand'[19] about 1709. Jacobi appears to have

15 'Joseph Downing and the Publication of Pietist Literature in England, 1705-1734', in *The German Book, 1450-1750. Studies presented to David L. Paisey in his retirement*, ed. John L. Flood and William A. Kelly (London: British Library, 1995), pp. 319-32.

16 Oxford, Bodleian Library: Mar. 229.

17 Many later emigrated to Ireland or to the North American colonies.

18 British Library, 626.g.41.

19 Cf. the imprint to *Der christliche Wandermann* [...] (London: printed by J. D. [Joseph Downing] and sold by the German Bookseller's shop [Johann Christian Jacobi]).

developed a specialist retail outlet aimed at the growing German market and based largely on titles printed by Downing for the SPCK and items imported from the *Waisenhausbuchhandlung*, Heinrich Elers's Pietist bookshop at Halle, especially German Bibles, psalters and prayer books. An exception to this rule is the *Guide de Londres dediè aux voyageurs etrangers* he issued under the curious imprint 'le German Bookseller-shop' in 1710, an indication perhaps of an attempt to widen his market, in this case to the many French-speaking immigrants and visitors likely to be found in the Strand area.

In 1712, Jacobi's address appears as Southampton Court, Southampton Street, Covent Garden, but by 1717 he had premises in the Exeter Change on the Strand, which provided cheap retail space for a number of foreign booksellers in this period and was of course close to Germans living in the Savoy and the German chapel. His name occurs some fourteen times in imprints between 1710 and 1718, sometimes described simply as 'the German bookseller in the Strand'. The economic basis for Jacobi's bookshop is not entirely clear, but clearly it was not sustainable as a purely commercial enterprise.

After Jacobi's withdrawal from the trade around 1718, there is no evidence of German bookselling until the late 1740s although Downing continued printing Böhm's sermons, using roman (antiqua) types until the latter's death in 1722. Benedikt Beiler's *A New German Grammar [...] Especially useful for merchants and travellers*,[20] with a dedication to Frederick Louis, Prince of Wales, appeared in 1731 (second edition, 1736). Among the booksellers mentioned in the imprint is the Dutchman 'Abraham van den Hoek', then 'at Virgil's Head overagainst the New Church in the Strand' but later to move to Germany, finally settling at Göttingen as the new university's first official printer. James Bettenham's printing of satirical verses by Christian Friedrich Weichmann (1698-1770) in 1727 may stand as a very isolated example of a publication in German in this period, presumably privately sponsored. *Etwas Teutsches zur Verteidigung der Teutschen* complains about English ignorance of German literature and their preference for the French:

> 'In London Teutsch? – Verhasste Muse, still!
> Wer wird doch wol, bey Englands reichen Chören,
> Den harten Klang von fremden Liedern hören,
> Falls Welschlands sanfter Ton das Ohr nicht kützlen will?'[21]

---

20 British Library, 628.e.8.

21 British Library, C.20.f.2(241), p. 1. 'German in London? Hated Muse, be still! Who wants to hear, next to England's rich choirs, the harsh tones of foreign songs, if it is not soft Latin tones that seek to tickle the ear?'.

The disinclination of the English to learn German was to remain a theme throughout the century.

The first German press in London: Johann Christoph Haberkorn

Between March and June 1749, Johann Christoph Haberkorn, who had been present in London from at least 1746, acquired a property on the north side of Gerrard Street ('next *[sic]* zu Mills's Coffee-House')[22] and, with his partner Johann Nicodemus Gussen, set up the first German press using *fraktur* types, probably imported from Halle. In December 1750 they announced the publication of a duodecimo edition of Luther's translation of the New Testament, printed by them and also sold by Andreas Linde, a German bookseller recently established in Catherine Street. In the preface to the New Testament, Haberkorn and Gussen describe their motivation for setting up a press purely in religious terms: its purpose was 'entirely to print good, improving works that would promote true Christianity'.[23] As a comparison with contemporary editions printed in Germany itself or by Christoph Saur in Philadelphia will show, this is a very creditable production.[24] It was available on fine paper ('mit neuen Lettern und auf fein Papier gedruckt') for one shilling and sixpence.[25]

In the first years of the press's existence (1749-51), some twenty titles are known to bear Haberkorn's imprint in addition to the New Testament, including a German psalter (fig. 1) and such substantial items as Heinrich Rimius's pro-Hanoverian *Memoirs of the House of Brunswick* (1750), a quarto of nearly five hundred pages and one of their first productions in English using roman types. Among other important titles are a translation of the first part of *The Pilgrim's Progress* by Christoph Mattheus Seidel (1751) and Johann Jakob Bachmair's *Complete German Grammar* (also 1751) which was printed and sold by Haberkorn and by three other booksellers including Linde.

Haberkorn's distinctive ornaments allow us to identify other, unsigned, work from his press, for example a rare programme book for a French play

22 See the imprint to *Herrn Benjamin Schmolckens gott-geheiligte Andachten* (London, 1749).

23 'Weil es denn geschehen, daß nach dem Willen Gottes auch an diesem Ort allhier, nemlich in der Stadt London, vor kurtzer Zeit eine teutsche Druckerey veranstaltet worden, und zwar gäntzlich in der Absicht, gute, erbauliche und auf die Beförderung des wahren Christenthums abzielende Schriften zu drucken ...' (*Das Neue Testament* (London, 1751), p. [4]).

24 For example, Saur's own quarto New Testament of 1743. See Bötte and Tanhoff, pp. 23-25.

25 See the catalogue appended to *Girrendes Täublein* printed by Haberkorn and Gussen the same year.

performed by the girls of a school at Hoxton.[26] A majority of the German-language titles appearing in Gerrard Street in this period, however, are sermons by the court preacher Friederich Michael Ziegenhagen (1694-1776), apparently paid for by members of his congregation (the titles usually include the formula: 'zum Druck befördert auf Kosten einiger Freunde') and typically priced sixpence. Their appearance underlines the purported aim of the press and might imply support for the Pietist orthodoxy then prevalent among Lutherans in London.

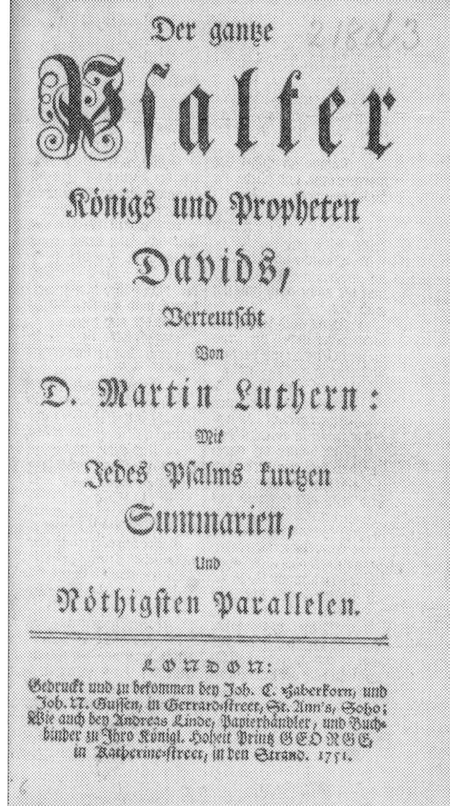

Der gantze
Psalter
Königs und Propheten
Davids,
Verteutscht
Von
D. Martin Luthern:
Mit
Jedes Psalms kurtzen
Summarien,
Und
Nöthigsten Parallelen.

LONDON:
Gedruckt und zu bekommen bey Joh. C. Haberkorn, und Joh. N. Gussen, in Gerrard-street, St. Ann's, Soho; Wie auch bey Andreas Linde, Papierhändler, und Buchbinder zu Ihro Königl. Hoheit Printz GEORGE, in Katherine-street, in den Strand. 1751.

Fig.1: *Der gantze Psalter Königs und Propheten Davids, verteuscht von D. Martin Luthern: ...* (London: gedruckt und zu bekommen bey Joh. C. Haberkorn, und Joh. N. Gussen, in Gerrard-Street, St. Ann's, Soho; wie auch bey Andreas Linde, Papierhändler, und Buchbinder zu Ihro Königl. Hoheit Printz George, in Katherine-street, in den Strand, 1751).
British Library pressmark: 218.d.3.

Haberkorn appears to have been a model of Lutheran propriety, and was certainly later closely associated with St George's in Goodman's Fields. A number of his productions, though unsigned, suggest a certain heterodoxy or at least flexibility in his religious scruples. The surreptitious printing of *A*

26 *Gabinie, tragédie chrétienne*, 1751. British Library, T.1605(1).

Manual of Devout Prayers,[27] a Catholic prayer book, for the Catholic bookseller James Marmaduke in St Martin's Lane is known to have led to the arrest of Haberkorn and Gussen, their temporary incarceration, a fine, and (according to a contemporary report) the destruction of their press, although this seems improbable in view of their continuing high rate of production.[28] More significant, perhaps, is their association with the Moravians, the sect led by Nicolaus Ludwig, Count Zinzendorf, which was gaining ground in England at the time of the founding of the Gerrard Street press and often found itself in bitter opposition to the Pietist orthodoxy represented, for example, by Ziegenhagen himself. Their association is attested both by their imprint on part of Zinzendorf's London hymnal of 1753 [29] and also by Haberkorn's ornaments in later, unsigned, Moravian works.[30]

Despite, or perhaps because of, the personal and business risks he was taking, Haberkorn (whose partner Gussen is no longer mentioned after 1753) appears to have built a substantial and successful printing business, with a little associated bookselling, into the early 1760s, which enabled him to move into larger premises in Grafton Street in Soho in 1761 and to employ at least one apprentice. This period of expansion is marked by the wholesale diversification of his programme. While continuing to print for the German-language market, and in the English vernacular, Haberkorn appears to have begun to specialise in foreign-language books (especially French and Italian) and also in the letterpress for prestigious plate books, including a number of the key titles in the development of architectural taste and interior design during the period.

In 1754, Haberkorn printed Thomas Chippendale's highly influential *The Gentleman and Cabinet-maker's Director*[31] (although his name only appears in the imprint of the reissue of 1755), demonstrating an ability to manage quite complex projects involving both letterpress, pages combining letterpress and engraving, and plates. Chippendale sold the work from his own premises in St Martin's Lane (it was also available from a number of booksellers in London,

---

27 Cf. F. Blom, J. Blom, F. Korsten, G. Scott, *English Catholic Books, 1701-1800: a bibliography* (Aldershot: Scolar, 1996), pp. xi, 191 (no. 1780).

28 Much of the correspondence in *Factotum* cited above concerns this incident. See F. J. Mosher's note in *Factotum*, no. 2 (June 1978), p. 9.

29 *Alt- und neuer Brüder-Gesang*. The imprint 'London: mit Haberkorn- und Gussischen Schriften' is found in that part headed *Etwas vom Liede Mosis*. British Library, 3437.ee.51.

30 The ornaments in *Hirten-Lieder von Bethlehem* probably allow us to identify Haberkorn behind the fictitious imprint: 'London: drukts, im Brüder-Hofe, Joh. Jacob Würz, 1754'.

31 British Library, C.119.k.4.

Edinburgh and Dublin at 'one pound ten shillings in sheets, or one pound fourteen shillings bound in calf'). In 1757, Haberkorn was entrusted with the production of English and French versions of *Designs of Chinese Buildings, Furniture, Dresses, Machines, and Utensils*, the first of a number of major projects by William Chambers, the architectural instructor of George III as Prince of Wales, and later the preferred court architect. Chambers's *A Treatise on Civil Architecture* appeared in 1759 under Haberkorn's imprint, the money having been raised by subscription; *Plans, Elevations, Sections, and Perspective Views of the Gardens and Buildings at Kew* followed in 1763.

Haberkorn's association with some key English architectural works of the eighteenth century has so far gone unremarked,[32] but he was also responsible for the production of the first volume of James Stuart's important *The Antiquities of Athens*, published in 1762, where letterpress and the engravings of Stuart's architectural drawings are particularly well integrated. The title-page uses a mock archaic design which is echoed in another extraordinary project of 1762, Vicenzio Martinelli's edition of Boccaccio's *Decamerone*.[33] Although the imprint on the title-page reads 'presso Giovanni Nourse libraio di S M Britannica', Haberkorn's involvement is revealed in a colophon to the preface.

A greater contrast can hardly be imagined than that between the *fraktur* sermons from the early days of Haberkorn's press and these neo-classical productions of some ten years later. It is a measure of the way he had innovated and diversified. Nevertheless, Haberkorn was apparently unable to sustain a successful business and returned to Germany by the late 1760s. His personal misfortunes before and after his move to Danish-ruled Altona near Hamburg need not concern us in detail here. There is evidence at the Public Record Office of a long Chancery case involving the family of his late second wife. At Altona, he appears to have taken one last risk, and with disastrous consequences: his reprinting of a London pamphlet in favour of the disgraced Danish queen landed him in prison, where the harsh régime appears to have led to his death, shortly after his release, in 1776.

---

32 See, for example, Eileen Harris, *British Architectural Books and Writers, 1556-1785* (Cambridge: Cambridge University Press, 1990).

33 British Library, 86.k.4.

Settlement and assimilation: German readers in eighteenth-century London

In the preface to their German New Testament of 1751, Johann Christoph Haberkorn and Johann Nicodemus Gussen describe the market they anticipate for their German publications. Essentially, this encompasses four audiences. Acknowledging that many German-speaking residents will have brought their own Bibles to London from Germany, they mention schoolchildren ('die hiesige Teutsche heranwachsende Schul-Jugend'). In addition, they refer to itinerant professionals and tradesmen ('solche Personen [...], die ihrer Professionen und Gewerbe halber von einem Orte zum andern reisen') who may have moved to London without a Bible, expecting to be able to find one there. A further clientele might be found among charitable persons ('wohltuende Hertzen') disposed to buy a number of copies with the intention of distributing them as gifts among the poor ('den Armen das Wort Gottes umsonst mitzutheilen'). Haberkorn and Gussen then turn to the potential of the many thousands of German-speaking Protestants in the British colonies in North America ('absonderlich in Pensylvanien *[sic]*, Carolina, Georgien, u.s.w.'), who, they believe, lack German Bibles. Once again, they hope that charitable persons will consider placing bulk orders for copies to send to those in need of God's word in the German tongue across the Atlantic. The price per copy would again be reduced in proportion to the numbers of copies such customers bought.

As we have seen, in terms of numbers, Haberkorn and Gussen may not have been unjustified in identifying German-speaking Londoners as a potential market. Nevertheless, the very 'itinerant' nature of much of that population, with merchants and tradesmen spending too little time in one location to settle, might have prevented them from acquiring goods (including books) in any quantity. More importantly, perhaps, there is considerable evidence for the increasing social and linguistic assimilation of longer-term German residents in this period, and especially of the second and third generations. Even the parish school of St Mary's in the Savoy was obliged to divide the school day into German and English sessions[34] and the question of holding Lutheran services in English for the children of Germans who were not fluent in their parents' language was to split the congregations of parishes such as St George's, Little Alie Street, later in the century.[35] There

34 *Grundris einer Schulordnung, bey der Deutschen Evangelischen St. Marien-Gemeinde, in der Savoy, in London* (London: gedruckt bey C. Heydinger, 1782), p. 12.

35 See J. G. Burckhardt, *Kirchen-Geschichte der Deutschen Gemeinden in London nebst historischen Beylagen und Predigten* (Tübingen, 1798), p. 112.

were certainly frequent complaints about the lack of 'patriotism' among London Germans. Mostly merchants and tradesmen, they often sought to shed their German roots as quickly as possible, preferring assimilation to being regarded as outsiders. In any case, they were often inexperienced or unenthusiastic readers. In general, as one close observer of the Germans resident in London noted: 'Was die Sitten der Londner Deutschen betrifft, so sind sie ein sonderbares Gemisch vom Englisch-Deutschen Character.'[36]

From the beginning, Haberkorn and Gussen had recognised the need to address this audience in English. One of their earliest known productions is itself of interest in this regard:

> *An Ode on the Happy Marriage of the Learned and Reverend Philip David Kræuter, D.D. Minister of the German Lutheran Church of St. Trinity in London, with Miss Eliz. Spellerberg Daughter of Joseph Ludolph Spellerberg, Esq; Composed and humbly exhibited by J. J. B.* (London: printed by J. Haberkorn & J. Gussen, in Gerrard Street St. Ann's Westminster, 1749).[37]

That the unidentified 'J. J. B.' had chosen to commemorate this essentially German occasion in the English vernacular is surely significant.

If the German-speaking population might not have presented quite the market opportunity Haberkorn and Gussen hoped for, what of the 'charitable persons' who might be induced to buy numbers of copies? This activity was one with a proven track record in the English book trade. Earlier in the century, Joseph Downing had exploited the mass market for cheap devotional literature for the SPCK, offering discounts for bulk orders by those who wished to distribute improving tracts among the poor and needy and other marginal groups. Contemporary German visitors remarked on the numbers of German poor in London;[38] they were clearly numerous enough to attract Haberkorn and Gussen's attention.

It is difficult to assess the success or failure of this marketing strategy. The very small numbers of surviving copies of Haberkorn and Gussen's German publications – and our knowledge that stock was still available from Carl Heydinger over twenty years later – does not necessarily suggest that small numbers of copies were actually circulated: for obvious reasons, many examples of cheap, popular printing are scarce. The assumption has to be, of course, that they did not find a ready market. The apparent absence of copies from North America, however, is probably explained by their inability to

---

36 Burckhardt, p. 65. 'As far as the manners of the London Germans are concerned, they are a curious mixture of English and German characteristics'.

37 Yale University Library, Ik Od215.749.

38 Burckhardt, p. 61.

break into a market already catered for by Christoph Saur of Germantown. 1,200 copies of his German New Testament of 1743 are known to have been printed and copies are not scarce today.[39] That the Germantown edition was fulfilling a need is confirmed by the numbers of editions issued by Saur and his successors. Saur brought out a second in 1745 and further editions appeared regularly in each decade: ESTC records some nineteen editions of German New Testaments alone printed in America before 1801.

Early German bookshops: Andreas Linde and Christlieb Gottreich Seyffert

Andreas Linde appears to have set up shop in the somewhat insalubrious Catherine Street between Covent Garden and the Strand shortly after Haberkorn and Gussen in Soho.[40] He had been in London since at least 1743. Like Haberkorn, Linde sought to diversify his business, combining bookselling with bookbinding and selling stationery, typically describing himself in imprints as 'Buchbinder und Papierhändler'. Indeed, in an early engraved trade card preserved at the Bodleian Library he describes him principally not as a bookseller but as a bookbinder:

> Andrew Linde, at the Bible in Catherine Street in the Stand, book-binder, to His Royal Highness Prince George, binds all sorts of books, gilt and letter'd. Also books bound in vellum, in the neatest manner, Dutch fashion. Likewise planiers, or size's, foreign books, fit to bear ink, & to write upon. He sells likewise all sorts of stationary [sic] ware at the best prices.[41]

The association with the household of the Prince of Wales is reinforced on the trade card by the familiar three-feather emblem and the motto 'Ich Dien' as well as by the formula 'bookseller to her Royal Highness the Princess Dowager of Wales' frequently found in his imprints. Although examples of bindings signed by him are found in George III's collection (for example, on the Haberkorn psalter of 1751),[42] the few references to Linde in the royal archives might suggest his claim to a close connection with the court to be somewhat exaggerated. Linde's description of himself as a bookbinder is

39 Bötte and Tannhof, no. 49.

40 I have not yet been able to verify the imprint date on a printed table held at the Bibliothèque nationale de France ('1749') which would pre-date other Linde imprints by two years.

41 Bodleian Library, John Johnson Collection, Trade Cards.

42 British Library 218.d.3. Linde's binding work is scarcely of the highest quality, but he was one of the first Germans working in a trade in which they were later to predominate.

dropped from imprints after 1753 in favour of 'bookseller' and 'stationer' and it is as a bookseller that he is assessed here.

Most of Linde's earliest appearances in imprints are associated, like the New Testament of 1751, with German books printed by Haberkorn and Gussen. In clear contrast to Haberkorn, however, Linde's process of diversification into printing in the vernacular is marked by opposition to the Moravians at a time when the sect was finding increasing acceptance in England. During 1753 and 1754, Linde issued a number of attacks on Zinzendorf and his followers, the Herrnhuter, by Heinrich Rimius or edited by him. These typically deride them as 'enthusiasts and fanaticks', suggesting that Linde was content to see his imprint associated with Lutheran and Pietist orthodoxy. A further collaboration saw Linde's imprint on works and translations by Christlob Mylius, a young German writer who died in London in 1754. One of these is possibly Linde's most celebrated publication, Mylius's highly influential German translation of William Hogarth's *Analysis of Beauty*.[43] This is one of two examples of Linde's connection with J. W. Schmidt in Hanover, the first such direct link between the London and German trades since Jacobi's with Elers over forty years previously.

Important evidence for Linde's bookselling activities is contained in *A Catalogue of Curious and Usefull Books in All Languages and Sciences, the most of them lately imported* to be sold by Linde 'very cheap' on 4 December 1754.[44] A note on the title-page ('Catalogues of the German books may be had separate') demonstrates the importance of German titles among the imports. Further evidence for Linde's connection with the German trade can be found in his inclusion by Gleditsch among the international purveyors of the Leipzig *Commentarii de rebus in scientia naturali et medicina gestis* from 1756 to 1758. The Royal Society at Göttingen also considered using Linde as the London agent for its *Transactions*.[45]

From 1759, however, the *Commentarii* were sold at London not by Linde but by Christlieb Gottreich Seyffert. Although Linde imprints continue occasionally into the next decade (at least one attributable to his widow), Linde himself gave up bookselling, selling his stock by auction in November 1758. Although the announcement of the auction (by Longman) tells us he

---

43 *Zergliederung der Schönheit* [...]) (London: bey Andreas Linde, J. K. H. der verwittweten Prinzessin von Wallis, Buchhändler, und in Hannover bey J. W. Schmidt, 1754). British Library, C.109.i.6.

44 Harvard, Houghton Library B1812.5*

45 See my 'Wilhelm Philipp Best und der Londoner Buchhandel', *Leipziger Jahrbuch zur Buchgeschichte*, 6 (1996), 199-210, at p. 204.

was 'going into another way of business' it seems probable that he died shortly after.

Seyffert, Linde's successor as the principal purveyor of German books in London, may himself have come to London originally from Leipzig. He is perhaps the least known of the German members of the London trade but was clearly a major importer of books from Germany. Unfortunately the only recorded copies of two catalogues (English and German) issued by him in 1757 are missing (presumed destroyed), but the evidence we have of them suggests a determined attempt to supplant Linde or at least to establish himself as a serious player in the foreign book market. For example, he is known to have distributed copies of the English catalogue to potential customers with a signed printed letter soliciting orders.[46]

Seyffert established himself during 1757 in a substantial property 'at the corner of Kings Street in Dean Street opposite St Anns Church Soho', an area associated above all with the French-speaking community, and soon acquired a wife and family. In the following year, he issued an English translation of Jan Swammerdam's *Book of Nature*, two substantial folio volumes with plates, financed by subscribers, as well as Madame de Fauques's topical allegory *La derniere Guerre des bêtes*, the popularity of which ensured several further editions and sequels, an English translation, and the accolade of foreign pirated editions masquerading as Seyffert's own.

It was this topical and satirical vein that Seyffert decided to mine rather than the kind of expensive scientific publication represented by the Swammerdam. About 1760, Seyffert moved from Soho to the more cosmopolitan and sophisticated Pall Mall; his publications (chiefly in French) continued in the same line. In 1762, however, he was obliged to sell his business and his entire stock.[47] Although the reasons for his 'going into another way of business' are unclear, documents in the Public Record Office show him in the unexpected role of attorney for Germans with claims on the British military resulting from the Seven Years' War.[48]

---

46 *Catalogue of New Books Lately Imported in [the] French, Latin, and German Languages.* Formerly held by the Staatsbibliothek zu Berlin – Preußischer Kulturbesitz. See also British Library MS. Add. 4475, fol. 207.

47 The sale was announced in the *Daily Advertiser* on four successive days, 17-20 May 1762.

48 Public Record Office, Treasury Papers, Papers of the Lords Commissioners for Settling German Demands, T 1/432/46, dated: 1 May 1764.

Carl Heydinger

By the end of the 1760s, Carl Heydinger had emerged as successor to Haberkorn, Linde and Seyffert. According to John Nichols 'he was unsuccessful in business; and died in distressed circumstances about 1778'.[49] The second of these two statements, however, is certainly untrue, and the first needs to be re-examined carefully in the light of sources now available to us. With Haberkorn, Carl Heydinger can now be recognised as the most significant of the German members of the London book trade in the eighteenth century.

The earliest date we have for Heydinger's activities is the dedication to a German translation of *The Pilgrim's Progress*, which is signed by him and dated: 'London, den 25. Julii 1766'.[50] Two further imprints are recorded from that year, including a French verse translation of Milton's *L'Allegro* and *Il Penseroso* in which his name is supplied uniquely as 'F. C. Heydinger'.[51] One of the German imprints links him with William Faden, 'Mr. W. Faden, printer of the Public-Ledger, in Peterborough-Court, Fleet-Street', suggesting perhaps an early business partnership; certainly a number of Faden imprints are recorded where, independently of Heydinger, he demonstrates the capability of printing with *fraktur* types.[52]

A growing family and an expanding business probably led to the acquisition in 1767 or 1768 of new premises in Grafton Street. There were further moves to No. 274, the Strand, 'opposite Essex Street', about 1771, and to No. 6, Bridges Street, Strand, 'opposite the Theatre Royal, Drury Lane', about 1776. By 1768 Heydinger was referring to himself in imprints as 'imprimeur et libraire' or 'Buchdrucker und Buchhändler'; from that year we have his first surviving advertisements on leaves forming part of the final gatherings of books printed and sold by him. One of these lists works in German, French and Latin, mostly imported; another includes a number of German and English items, some originally printed or sold by Heydinger's German predecessors in the London trade, offered at prices between fourpence and ten shillings and sixpence. He supplemented his work as a printer and bookseller with translations of German texts into English. From 1770 to 1773, Heydinger also attended the Leipzig Book Fairs, the first London-based

---

49 *Literary Anecdotes of the Eighteenth Century* (London, 1812), III, 644.

50 *Eines Christen Reise nach der seligen Ewigkeit, [...]* Neue und verbesserte Auflage (London: zu finden bey Carl Heydinger, in Moor-Street, St. Ann's, Soho; wie auch bey Mr. W. Faden, printer of the Public-Ledger, in Peterborough-Court, Fleet-Street, 1766).

51 The first of these initials is not mentioned again.

52 Faden's name occurs in a number of imprints with Heydinger's and also independently as the printer of German texts. Among the most curious of these are two new editions of sermons by Ziegenhagen. Halle University Library, AB 10 50 A h, 24.

bookseller to do so.[53] He used his visits to establish contacts with booksellers in German-speaking Europe and his presence at Leipzig certainly explains the high number of German books imported into England in those years.[54]

Heydinger issued *A Catalogue of Books in All Arts and Sciences in the German, Latin, French and English Language* in 1769, although no copy appears to have survived. According to Nichols, Heydinger issued further catalogues of the books he printed and sold in 1771, 1773 and again in 1777 (this latter with two supplements), though copies survive only of the 1773 catalogue. He appears to have reduced his publishing activities after 1777 and no imprints bearing his name have so far been recorded for the years between 1778 and 1782. A letter from Georg Forster to his friend Johann Karl Philipp Spener dated 17 February 1778 hints at financial difficulties in this period: apparently 'der arme Heydinger' ('poor Heydinger') was among the London creditors of the notorious Rudolf Erich Raspe.[55]

A final move to No. 7, Queen's Court, Great Queen Street, Lincoln's Inn Fields, must have taken place in the summer of 1780, as Heydinger took out an insurance policy with the Sun Fire Office on 7 June that year.[56] The policy describes a not insubstantial establishment valuing the 'household goods', including 'utensils & stock', and 'wearing apparel' both at £60. Moreover the house is described in the policy as a 'new dwelling house only brick'. None of this exactly suggests the 'distressed circumstances' reported by Nichols (who believed Heydinger had died some two years previously).[57] Premiums on this property continued to be paid until at least 1783; Heydinger's last recorded imprints are from the following year. The frontispiece to one of these provides the very latest date which can with certainty be associated with him: 'Septr. 14th. 1784'.[58] It may have been shortly after this that he died. The

53 See the Book Fair catalogues for these years.

54 See Giles Barber, 'Book Imports and Exports in the Eighteenth Century', in *Sale and Distribution of Books from 1700*, ed. R. Myers and M. Harris (Oxford: Oxford Polytechnic Press, 1982), p. 88. Barber was of course unaware of the link with Heydinger.

55 Georg Forster, *Sämtliche Schriften, Tagebücher, Briefe*, ed. S. Scheibe, XIII (Berlin: Akademie-Verlag, 1978): '... Ich weis es ist hart auf Zahlung zu warten. Er wußte es auch; der arme Heydinger dem er noch von Cassel aus schuldig ist, weis es leider auch! ...'.

56 Guildhall Library MS. 11,936/284, fol. 51.

57 Nichols, p. 644.

58 *An Exact and Authentic Narrative of M. Blanchard's Third Aerial Voyage, from Rouen in Normandy, on the 18th of July, 1784. [...]* (London: printed by and for C. Heydinger, in Queen's-Court, Great Queen Street, Lincoln's-Inn-Fields. Sold by R. Baldwin, No. 47. Paternoster-Row; J. Debret, opposite Burlington-House, Piccadilly; R. Faulder, New Bond-Street; and W. Babbs, Oxford-Street, 1784). The frontispiece engraving ('A representation of M. Blanchards balloon, & apparatus.') is dated: 'Publish'd Septr. 14th. 1784 by C. Heydinger Queen's Court Great Queen St. Lincolns Inn Fields'.

occasional revival of the 'bey Carl Heydinger' imprint into the 1790s can probably be attributed to one or both of his sons (Charles and John). Whatever the date or circumstances of Heydinger's death, there was certainly a contemporary perception that he, like Haberkorn, Linde and Seyffert, had been unsuccessful in business.

Of Heydinger's known titles, the largest single category is theology or devotional literature, mostly in German and associated with the Lutheran congregations in London. The second largest category is medical and scientific literature. The edition of Albrecht von Haller's *Bibliotheca botanica* (1771-2) is of particular interest: it is a reissue of the Zurich edition of the same years with cancel title-pages. Heydinger's 1773 catalogue shows it was sold for '£1 14s. *in boards*'.[59] As letters preserved among Haller's correspondence in the City Library at Bern confirm, Heydinger wrote to him in 1772 and 1773 proposing a number of projects.

After the mid-1770s, Heydinger normally appears in imprints as the sole printer and bookseller. This phase is also marked by his increasing use of a personal ornamental device (fig. 2). An early example is found on the title-page to *L'Impie démasqué* printed by Heydinger in 1773. It shows a conventional allegory of the book trade as an alliance of scholarship and commerce. Heydinger's use of it suggests, perhaps, a growing self-confidence in a year in which he issued a major catalogue. The same catalogue also shows that he was diversifying his business further in ways typical of booksellers in this period by importing patent medicines from Halle and offering them for sale in London.

As a specialist German printer, Heydinger enjoyed a near-monopoly after Haberkorn's departure in the late 1760s. As an importer of German titles (and Latin titles printed in Germany) no other London bookseller could rival his links with the German trade. The demand for German-language books, however, remained small in this period and for Heydinger, as for his precursors, diversification meant printing and selling books in foreign languages other than German (principally, of course, French) and establishing a niche for himself in the publication of books in English.

After Heydinger's final imprints in 1784, there is no evidence for German printing or bookselling activity before the early years of the next decade. Despite a still growing German-speaking population, it had apparently proved impossible to sustain even a single book trade outlet specialising in German materials. Indeed, so serious was this period of

---

59 *Catalogus librorum latinorum, graecorum, hebraicorum, &c .... Qui venales prostant Londini apud C. Heydinger, bibliopol. in platea vulgo dicta the Strand* (Londini, 1773), p. iii.

Fig. 2: Device of Carl Heydinger, from Jacob von Staehlin, *An account of the new northern archipelago, ...* (London: printed for C. Heydinger, in the Strand, 1774). British Library pressmark: 304.i.17.

discontinuity that memory of the period of sustained activity from Haberkorn to Heydinger appears to have been lost; later commentators appear to have been unaware of the presence of Germans in the London book trade before the 1790s. German books, if they were required at all, were obtained from English booksellers specialising in foreign imports such as Joseph de Boffe in Gerrard Street. In 1789 Prince and Cooke at Oxford issued *A Select Catalogue of German Books; with the subject of each in English*, which was also sold by the Rivingtons and Elmsly in London. To understand why and how a German element in the London book trade nevertheless re-emerged in the following decade, we shall need to consider the reception of German language and literature in eighteenth-century England in a little more detail.

The reception of German language and literature in England

If most German-speaking Londoners do not appear to have been conspicuous consumers of German books, English-speaking Londoners were very unlikely to replace them at the bookseller's counter. Despite a vogue for the German language and its literature late in the century, the English-speaking world remained almost completely immune to their pleasures. German authors, even the most celebrated, remained almost unknown in England and relatively few German works of any kind were translated into English. Moreover, German books were widely regarded as poorly produced and expensive.

The historian Jonathan Israel has recently pointed out that English-speaking intellectuals were 'virtually completely devoid of acquaintance with books and periodicals in other Germanic languages'.[60] There was a marked absence of German-language books from contemporary English and Scottish libraries. To say English-speaking readers of German hardly existed in the mid-eighteenth century would be an exaggeration, but probably not a serious one. If German was widely spoken and read in northern and eastern Europe, the English took very little interest in either the language or its literature until at least the end of the eighteenth century, and even then only superficially. As with the German element within London's population in the eighteenth century, this aspect of reception studies remains relatively neglected by scholars and the only discursive account of the subject in English was published as long ago as 1929.[61]

One problem for literary historians, whether German- or English- speaking, is probably the nature of the works that were translated and received. Few canonical German literary authors were read or regarded in eighteenth-century England. The great majority of works translated from German into English or published in England during the century were in fact devotional (with Pietist works playing an important role earlier in the century). Only a few hundred titles were translated in total, in contrast with the many thousands known to have been translated into German from English. A search of ESTC for the keywords 'translated from the German' or 'translated from the High Dutch', for example, currently retrieves 709 and 177 titles respectively. This suggests a total corresponding to less than ten per cent of the number of English titles translated into German.[62] If in the course of the eighteenth century German readers were able to access most significant literary and non-literary texts in German translation, the English, until the end of the century at least, were largely excluded from intellectual and literary developments in the German-speaking world. If German books were largely absent from English and Scottish libraries, English books found a prominent place in the greatest contemporary German research library, the University Library at Göttingen.

Of the German texts that were translated and read, Salomon Gessner's *Der Tod Abels*, published in English in an adaptation by Mary Collyer in 1761, was one of the best known and most successful, going through numerous

60 Jonathan I. Israel, *Radical Enlightenment* (Oxford: Oxford University Press, 2001), pp. 137-8.

61 V. Stockley, *German Literature as Known in England, 1750-1830* (London: Routledge, 1929).

62 As so far identified by Bernhard Fabian and Marie-Luise Spieckemann for their bibliography of English works received in Germany in roughly the same period.

editions before 1800. Klopstock's *Messias*, first published by the Dodsleys in an English translation in 1763, enjoyed a comparable success. The *succès de scandale* of Goethe's *Werther* is familiar; less well known is that the first version published in English (1779) was based on a French verse translation. Few other works by Goethe were so well known before the turn of the century. Apart from the rather special phenomenon of Pietism (and later of Moravianism), German-language culture made very little impact on the great majority of London's inhabitants before 1790, despite the presence of considerable numbers of Germans in their midst.

As the European reputation of German scholars and writers grew, English critics became increasingly aware of the knowledge gap. Indeed, it began to be regarded in some circles as a serious problem. As one commentator noted: 'the brilliance of the Litterature in Germany is obscured by prejudice, and ignorance'.[63] A contemporary reviewer admitted that 'there is a great deal of useful literature conveyed in the German language we have no doubt' but went on to complain about the lack of translations into English.[64] That English readers might attempt to tackle German literature in the original was clearly not regarded as a serious option.

Nevertheless, the 1790s saw a sudden and rather unexpected rise in the level of interest in the German language and its literature in Britain. German literature came to be compared favourably with that of Revolutionary France. A quotation from one issue of the *Monthly Magazine* (February 1796) may give some idea of the extent of the change:

> We know not even if it be saying too much, to affirm, that more German books are annually published than in one half of the world besides: they are not all excellent, to be sure, but most of them are good, and few intollerable *[sic]*. [...] Their poetry is greatly improved, and every day improving. In novel-writing, they are more natural than we. [...] In mathematics, natural history, physic, experimental philosophy, they are second to none. In rational theology, they have made great progress; and in biblical criticism, hold the very first rank.[65]

The process by which German scholarship and imaginative literature began to enter the consciousness of the British cannot be described in detail here[66]

63 Letter from James Johnstone to J. J. Eschenburg, dated: London, 25 August 1783. Herzog August Bibliothek, Wolfenbüttel, Cod. Guelf. 619 Novi.

64 *Gentleman's Magazine*, 59 (1789), p. 834.

65 p. 35.

66 See Rosemary Ashton, *The German Idea* (Cambridge: Cambridge University Press, 1980), and my summary of contemporary reviews in 'The Deutsche Lese-Bibliothek', pp. 358-9.

but a number of important aspects should be highlighted. The British remained stubbornly attached to literary authors or works now regarded as non-canonical or at best second rate. A short-lived vogue for Romantic ballads led to a number of imitations of G. A. Bürger's *Lenore* (six alone in 1796, some printed with parallel German texts). It is well known that one of Walter Scott's first published works was a translation of Goethe's *Götz von Berchlingen* (1799). Certainly the most popular and successful of these German authors was the dramatist August von Kotzebue whose bourgeois dramas dominated the London theatre for several seasons around the turn of the century and were published. By 1800, the *Allgemeine Zeitung* was describing him as 'der Liebling der engl[ischen] Bühnen' ('the darling of the English stage') and bemoaning that his pieces were driving out worthier English productions.[67]

English specialists in German literature began to emerge, above all William Taylor of Norwich (1765-1836) who translated Lessing's *Nathan der Weise* (1793) and Goethe's *Iphigenie auf Tauris* before contributing a version of Bürger's *Lenore* to the flood of translations appearing in 1796. Samuel Taylor Coleridge's early interest in German literature is even better known, leading him to travel to Germany in 1797 with William and Dorothy Wordsworth in order to learn the language and study German literature. It is often overlooked that Coleridge's interest in German literature was following rather than setting a trend. At least at this early stage, English authors were interested almost exclusively in a particular genre of German literature, and ironically one derived from English and Scottish models. As Rosemary Ashton has pointed out:

> Coleridge's interest in Germany had begun with the widespread enthusiasm in Britain for single works by German authors. The German literature which was noticed in England was itself largely influenced by English models. Percy's *Reliques of Ancient English Poetry* (1765) inspired imitation by Bürger; the melancholy 'Ossian' and Young's poetry excited the young Goethe. [...] When Coleridge read Schiller's *Räuber* in November 1794, it chimed in perfectly with his beliefs.[68]

Book trade responses to the new awareness of German literature in England

This unprecedented interest in German books inevitably had a resonance in the London book trade. A modern grammar was an early desideratum and

67 1800, p. 470.

68 Ashton, pp. 4-5.

Gebhard Friedrich August Wendeborn's *An Introduction to German Grammar* was issued in 1790 and sold by the Robinsons in Paternoster Row. Wendeborn, a German cleric long resident in London whose contribution to Anglo-German cultural relations in the latter half of the eighteenth century deserves closer examination, published a number of accounts of England for German readers. A third edition of the *Introduction* accompanied by a volume of *Exercises* followed in 1797. Two years later, William Render published *A Concise Practical Grammar of the German Tongue* in direct competition with Wendeborn, after which a number of guides to the German language began to appear on the English market. In 1800, George Crabb issued not only his own *Exercises*, followed by an adaptation for the English of his *Deutsche Sprachlehre für Schulen* (Berlin 1795), but also *Elements of German Conversation* and *An Easy and Entertaining Selection of German Prose and Poetry.*

Crabb's linguistic works were printed by Charles Whittingham (d. 1840), an English printer in Fetter Lane who, like William Faden in earlier decades, appears to have developed a capacity to print in *fraktur* during the period 1799 to 1803, a clear signal that there were those in the trade who once again saw a potential market for German books in London.

In response to the unprecedented interest in German literature and its presumed market potential, two booksellers opened up shop in London, both referring to themselves specifically as 'German booksellers'.[69] In contrast to German book trade initiatives of earlier decades, printing and publishing German books in London was to prove less important than importing them. Diversification away from dealing exclusively in German books also meant importing books from other language areas. This new kind of specialisation brought with it a new kind of risk at a time when trade with the Continent was to be made increasingly difficult by the French Revolutionary and Napoleonic Wars.

James Remnant, the brother of William Remnant, the English bookseller at Hamburg,[70] set up shop in West Smithfield in 1793, later moving to High Holborn about 1795 and St Giles in 1800. In an 'Advertisement' to a catalogue he issued in 1794 he notes:

> Little having been imported from Germany other than very expensive articles which comprise a great value in small compass, chiefly on account of the very heavy duty, and the custom-house expenses, the numerous, smaller, and most

69 John Feltham's *Picture of London for 1802* also lists Vaughan Griffiths in Paternoster Row among the 'German booksellers' for reasons not entirely clear. Griffiths was finally declared bankrupt in 1803.

70 See Bernhard Fabian, 'Die erste englische Buchhandlung auf dem Kontinent', in *Festschrift für Rainer Gruenter* (Heidelberg: Winter, 1978), pp. 122-45.

> useful works published in that country [...] have been nearly totally lost to the learned and curious in Great Britain.[71]

Remnant explains that four years' residence in Germany has provided him with the contacts he needs to procure 'any books, journals, maps, prints, &c.' for the 'public in general' but in particular 'the trade'. He has not brought across a stock of German-language books as the language is probably 'too little understood to warrant the undertaking'. Rather he will act on commission, making available 'the most modern German catalogues' from which titles can be chosen and ordered. In other words, he was hoping to make a living as a specialist supplier and wholesaler importing materials from the Continent.

In 1795 Remnant encountered a competitor in his niche market when the Swiss Henry Escher opened a shop in Broad Street, Bloomsbury, later moving to Gerrard Street and Piccadilly about 1807. His *A Catalogue of German, Latin, French, Italian, and English Books*,[72] which appeared in 1796, lists over 300 German titles. A cautionary note tells us that orders for other publications in Germany or Switzerland will be 'gratefully accepted, and executed as expeditiously, and at as cheap a rate, as the present unfavourable circumstances will allow'.

As Remnant and Escher were establishing themselves, a German circulating library opened on the Strand. The *Deutsche Lese-Bibliothek*,[73] which issued a number of catalogues between 1794 and 1797, appears to have opened with idealistic aims, for example excluding fiction from its stock, but latterly became more overtly commercial under one J. L. W. Gebhart, a new proprietor. The *Lese-Bibliothek*, which appears to have enjoyed close links with a bookseller at Braunschweig (Brunswick) encountered the same problems with supply as Remnant and Escher. It had folded by the turn of the century.

The 'circumstances' caused by naval action in the North Sea were, of course, to become even less favourable over the next decade until Napoleon's Continental System of 1806 made legal trade with the north German ports very difficult. They must have contributed to Remnant's business failure in 1804 when his stock was sold at auction. When Escher issued a catalogue in November 1807, he announced he would accept orders for foreign books and

---

71 *A Catalogue of Ancient and Modern Books, English and Foreign; particularly those published in and near Germany; now selling, for ready money by James Remnant, No. 6, St. John's-Lane, West-Smithfield, London.* John Rylands University Library, Manchester, R152594.3.

72 British Library, S.C.730(1).

73 See my 'The Deutsche Lese-Bibliothek'.

fulfil them when 'free communication with the Continent' permitted it, which, in practical terms, meant they could not be fulfilled indefinitely.

Constantin Geisweiler

This final phase of German book trade activity in eighteenth-century London culminates, however, in the person of Constantin Geisweiler. Geisweiler, another Swiss, who had appeared in London about 1792, initially made a living selling prints, setting up shop as a bookseller in Frith Street, Soho, in 1796. He moved to Pall Mall and then to No. 42, Parliament Street in 1799. Geisweiler is one of the very few German booksellers working in London during the eighteenth century to have attracted scholarly attention before the advent of the ESTC.[74]

Like Heydinger, he combined considerable ambition with great energy, seeking to establish contacts with German booksellers (including Hoffmann at Hamburg) and prominent literary authors (including Wieland, Goethe and Schiller at Weimar). From 1798, his own imprints reflect the growing taste for translations of German plays (particularly those of Kotzebue), often translated by his wife Maria. In 1801, he used the opportunity of a brief period of peace to visit Weimar itself, travelling on to the Leipzig Book Fair where he attempted, apparently unsuccessfully, to sell prints, to establish direct contact with members of the German trade, and to discuss various publishing schemes with prominent authors.[75] On returning to London, he claimed to be able to supply any title available at the Leipzig Book Fair, even reprinting the entire catalogue as a supplement to his periodical.

The Geisweilers' literary ambitions and proselytising zeal attracted considerable attention in Germany itself, as a report in one literary periodical attests:

> Unter die vorzüglichsten Beförderer derselben rechnet man den Buchhändler, Herrn C. Geisweiler, und dessen Frau, Maria Geisweiler. Er hat in London eine deutsche Buchhandlung angelegt, und dabei, seiner eignen Angabe nach, vorzüglich den Zweck die deutsche Litteratur den Engländern bekannter zu machen. (Among its foremost promoters [i.e. of German literature in London] must be counted Herr C. Geisweiler and his wife Maria Geisweiler. He has set up a German bookshop in London and states that his principal aim in doing so is to make German literature better known among the English.)[76]

---

74 See Lieselotte Blumenthal, 'Geisweiler und Weimar', *Jahrbuch der Deutschen Schillergesellschaft*, 11 (1967), 14-46.

75 Blumenthal, p. 40.

76 *Eunomia: Eine Zeitschrift des neunzehnten Jahrhunderts* (June 1801), 484.

In view of their sense of their own importance, the commentator notes that 'much depends' on the pair's 'literary taste' in selecting texts for translation, taking them to task for publishing such stuff as Kotzebue's dramas.

Geisweiler's best-known contribution to the reception of German literature in England, however, was to take another form. In 1800 he started the *German Museum*, an ambitious monthly periodical intended to tap the growing interest in German literature among the British. *The German Museum, or monthly repository of the literature of Germany*,[77] which cost one shilling and sixpence an issue, was edited by Peter Will (1764-1839), the pastor of St Mary's in the Savoy, and Anton Florian Madinger Willich, a German language teacher (fig. 3). The occasional texts in the original German carried by the periodical were printed by Charles Whittingham using authentic *fraktur* types.

By abandoning the likes of Kotzebue and seeking to promote better German authors, Geisweiler was taking a considerable risk. Despite his best efforts at promoting the title, the *German Museum* proved enormously expensive to produce and ultimately unsustainable. In the middle of 1801, the journalist Johann Christian Hüttner reported that, although the bookshop was becoming more significant ('zusehends bedeutender'), the periodical was no longer appearing monthly. Geisweiler was putting the best gloss on this, arguing that a quarterly publication would be easier to manage, cheaper to produce and easier to market.[78] Nevertheless, he was forced to close the title during 1801 and, with it, his fortunes as a bookseller also began to decline. By 1803 he appears to have given up bookselling entirely. By this time, Thomas Boosey in Old Bond Street had established himself as the leading purveyor of foreign books in London, his lack of German being compensated for somewhat by advice on what to stock from the Hamburg bookseller Perthes.[79]

The failure of German book trade initiatives in London at the turn of the nineteenth century

If hopes had been high at the turn of the century for the development of a German element within the London book trade, these hopes had already been dashed by 1803, by which time almost all the initiatives of the 1790s had foundered. Philip August Nemnich, the Hamburg writer on commercial affairs, had visited London in 1799 and was able to compare the hopeful situation then with the complete absence of a German bookshop five years

77 British Library, 226.l.24.

78 *Englische Miscellen*, 2 (1801), p. 66.

79 'The Deutsche Lese-Bibliothek', p. 361.

The
GERMAN MUSEUM,
OR
Monthly Repository
OF THE
LITERATURE of GERMANY,
the North
and the Continent in general.

VOL. I for the YEAR 1800.

London.
Printed for C. Geisweiler & the
PROPRIETORS,
N. 42. Parliament Street,
by C. Whittingham, Dean Street, Fetter Lane.

Fig. 3: *The German museum, or monthly repository of the literature of Germany, the North, and the continent in general. Vol. I for the year 1800* (London: printed for C. Geisweiler & the proprietors, No. 42. Parliament Street, by C. Whittingham, Dean Street, Fetter Lane). British Library pressmark: 226.l.24-26.

later.[80] All the book trade initiatives he had found at the turn of the century had sunk ('haben Schiffbruch erlitten'). Nemnich castigates Remnant, Escher and Geisweiler individually, blaming their supposed personal failings (Geisweiler) and business incompetence (Remnant) for the renewed lack of a sustainable German element in the London book trade. The apparently

80 See *Beschreibung einer im Sommer 1799 von Hamburg nach und durch England geschehenen Reise* (Tübingen, 1800), p. 456, and *Neueste Reise durch England* (Tübingen, 1807), p. 169.

never-ending conflict in Europe, with its increasingly unfavourable impact on maritime trade with the Continent, was clearly a further factor, inhibiting booksellers in the fulfilment of promises to deliver titles through their German book trade connections.

The decisive factor, however, was almost certainly the failure of a sustained market for German books to develop. In June 1800, a Dr Hoffmann wrote to Jeremias David Reuss, professor and librarian at Göttingen:

> Die deutsche Litteratur ist in England außerordentlich geschätzt und das nicht bloß bey Gelehrten – ich habe eine große Menge davon kommen lassen, welche alle Deutsch verstanden und in unserer schönen Litteratur weiter besser zu Hause waren, als ich, im Deutschen. (German literature is most highly esteemed in England, and not only by scholars – I summoned a great many of them, all of whom understood German and were far better acquainted with our literature in German than I am myself.)[81]

In fact, first signs of a critical reaction against the popularity of German literature had already begun to appear some years previously. The periodical *Anti-Jacobin Review* had attacked the over-emotionalism of German writers and their English imitators as early as 1797-8. As Rosemary Ashton notes:

> Whether as a direct result of the Anti-Jacobin ridicule of 'German drama' or not, English interest in German dramas ceased abruptly around 1800. Periodicals like the *Monthly Review* and *Monthly Magazine* had published regular notices of translations and productions of German plays in the 1790s, but by 1800 the reviewers were complaining of the 'trash' they had been 'obliged to swallow' in the form of more plays by Kotzebue. In October 1800, after a year of increasingly unfavourable reviews of plays by Kotzebue, Schiller, and Iffland, Coleridge's translation of Schiller's *Wallenstein* was reviewed negatively in the *Monthly Review*.[82]

The influential *Edinburgh Review* was to carry only one notice of a German book between 1803 and 1813. The fears of German commentators appear to have been confirmed: interest in German plays and poetry had proved to be a passing fashion. The type of German imaginative literature received appealed to the almost morbid sensibility characteristic of contemporary 'Gothick' novels. This appetite could be satisfied by locally made literary productions, however, without the need to learn the difficult German language or to penetrate the complexities of its best authors. It was William Lane of the Minerva Press, the publisher of so many English horror novels, who was to

---

81 Dated: 'Herstmonceux Place, 18. Juni 1800'. Göttingen University Library, MS. Cod. Mich. 257.

82 Ashton, pp. 8-9.

benefit from this fashion in the longer term, rather than the likes of Remnant, Escher and the Geisweilers.

Only after 1820 did critics such as De Quincey and Carlyle attempt a new evaluation of German imaginative literature, opening a new chapter in the history of the reception of German-language culture in Britain in the nineteenth century.

Postlude: Vogel and Schulze

By 1810, when direct communication between London and Hamburg and Bremen had become extremely difficult, the only Germans active in the London book trade (within my definition of the term) appear to have been the printers Vogel and Schulze in Poland Street, off Oxford Street, in Soho. Johann Benjamin Gottlieb Vogel first appears in 1804 as a partner of P. Daponte at No. 15, Poland Street, emerging as an independent printer at No. 13 in 1806. It was at this address that he printed Henry Escher's *A Catalogue of German Books, and Prints* in November of the following year. In 1805, he had printed the first of a series of pamphlets in English and French on the economic consequences of the Napoleonic War by Sir Francis d'Ivernois (1757-1842). This was to prove a more typical production than his printing of Eliza Ratcliffe's *The Mysterious Baron, or the castle in the forest, a Gothic story* of 1808, when Vogel ventured into territory more usually associated with the Minerva Press. Imprints dated 1809 attest to a new partnership, with the fellow German Gottlieb Schulze.

Much of Vogel and Schulze's work in the years 1809-11 remains to be uncovered as retrospectively converted catalogues for nineteenth-century publications do not generally carry as much imprint information as, for example, the ESTC. Also, their responsibility for particular publications, typically for this period, is often concealed in colophons. Nevertheless, it is clear that they retained the capacity and capability of printing in a variety of languages, including English, French, German, Italian and Swedish. Although most of their work so far identified could be classified as topical pamphlet literature, a number of significant German works should be mentioned here. In 1810 they printed for Thomas Boosey *Die deutsche Blumenlese*, an anthology for English readers of German selected 'aus den besten Schriftstellern Deutschlands'.[83] In the following year they printed the *Kirchen-Ordnung der Evangelisch Lutherischen St. Marien- oder Savoy-Gemeine*, originally issued in 1743,

83 British Library, 12253.dd.14.

with a *Grundriß einer Schul-Ordnung bey der Deutschen Evangelischen St. Marien-Gemeine*, a new edition of a work originally printed by Heydinger in 1782.[84]

The most significant fruit of Vogel and Schulze's partnership, however, is the first German newspaper printed in London, *Der Treue Verkündiger*,[85] which appeared fortnightly from January 1810 to June 1811, price sixpence (and 'threepence halfpenny' duty) or five pounds for an annual subscription. It is not clear who may have been responsible for the newspaper editorially; the printers certainly appear to have carried the full cost of its production and distribution. That it was intended primarily for export is clear from the editorial matter which is not addressed to German residents in London but rather to Germans in states under Napoleonic occupation. Indeed, the title may have been encouraged if not directly commissioned by the government. A very few advertisements do appear, including one for Boosey's *Blumenlese* (on 24 April 1810).

The project appears to have been accompanied by practical and financial difficulties from its inception, as an announcement in the issue for 1 January 1811 makes clear. Among the problems they describe is the lack of German typesetters in London ('Mangel an deutschen Setzern'), presumably caused by the Continental System preventing easy travel from Germany. It had been necessary to engage English typesetters, inevitably unacquainted with the German language, which had led to a large number of errors. More serious was the limited number of subscribers which essentially meant that the newspaper was far from breaking even, let alone making a profit. The evil day could only be postponed for a further six months before we learn (on 25 June 1811) that the title is to be discontinued, or rather replaced by *Der Verkündiger. Eine Zeitung politischen, literarischen und vermischten Inhalts.* This relaunched title was apparently to offer less politics and more accounts of literature, as well as more 'Züge zur Charateristik des brittischen Volks', all of which was intended to make the content more interesting. It is as yet unclear if the failure of this project led directly to the breakup of the partnership of Vogel and Schulze during the same year.

Benjamin Vogel and Gottlieb Schulze did not disappear from the London book trade after the failure of their newspaper in 1811: both firms continued in various forms into the century.[86] Their future progress as independent printers, or in partnership with others, however, is beyond the temporal scope of this present study. The failure of their newspaper project in

84 British Library, 3425.dd.2.

85 British Library, Newspaper Library (formerly Foreign Office Library).

86 See P. A. H. Brown, *London Publishers and Printers, c. 1800-1870* (London: British Library, 1982), pp.170-1, 210.

1810-11 can be seen as the final German initiative in the eighteenth-century London book trade.

Summary and conclusions

German printers and booksellers appear to have been motivated as much by idealism and optimism as by a calculated assessment of a market opportunity. Ostensibly the conditions for a distinctly German element in the London book trade did exist: a large and growing German-speaking population both in London and in the wider Atlantic world and, latterly, a new interest among English-speakers in German language and literature. The line between success and failure in the eighteenth-century London book trade was a narrow one, however, and it seems clear that most German initiatives in this area were indeed relatively short-lived. Although I do not think we should necessarily take contemporary perceptions of failure at face value, no sustainable model of a successful book trade outlet with distinctly German characteristics appears to have emerged before 1810. We certainly need to understand much more about contemporary retailing and the market beyond the book trade before we can evaluate properly the evidence we have.

To survive and prosper, German members of the London book trade clearly needed to diversify their businesses in response to demand in the market place. German printers and booksellers, such as almost all of those reviewed here, can be shown to have seized the initiative and taken risks in order to expand their opportunity in the market. Printing in German and English could be expanded into other languages. Specialist areas of publishing, such as plate books, 'fancy' printing, religious controversy, topical satire, political pamphlets and foreign-language publications, might profitably be explored. Bookselling was often supplemented by offering other services and products, such as bookbinding, stationery and paper retailing or importing patent medicines. Some took to translating and editing texts. Even if no sustainable model for a German book trade in eighteenth-century London was to emerge, the evidence suggests a succession of enterprising individuals prepared to innovate and diversify in order to succeed. In the process, they produced lasting work of great interest and high quality.

When I first set out to identify the precise location of Haberkorn and Gussen's press in Gerrard Street, I followed the route of the rate collector for the Parish of St Anne's, Soho, as recorded quarterly in the parish rate books at the City of Westminster Archives. I found that their shop was probably on the site of today's Aroma Chinese Restaurant. On the first floor of the building, above the restaurant, was the Gerrard Press, a Chinese printers serving the local community. The Press now appears to have closed or moved, but its presence on this site in the late 1990s was a remarkable sign of continuity and change in London society over three centuries. The books which Germans printed and sold in the eighteenth century are not merely of interest in themselves. They provide significant evidence for a continuing process, the interrelation of indigenous and non-indigenous languages and cultures in a rapidly developing society.

Susan Reed

Printers, Publishers and Proletarians
some aspects of German book trades in nineteenth-century London

To come to the history of German book trades in nineteenth-century London with any preconceptions is to see those preconceptions, if not dashed, then strangely distorted. Knowing that by the late nineteenth century Germans formed London's biggest immigrant community, with a wide range of clubs, societies and religious and educational foundations, one might expect to find a thriving book trade based on the needs of this community and its institutions. Knowing that in the late 1840s England saw an influx of educated and articulate German political refugees, and that Karl Marx famously spent over half his life living and working here, one might expect a forceful German radical press to have grown up for the exchange of ideas among the exiles and for the avoidance of the censors back in Germany.[1] In fact, neither of these assumptions is fully borne out by the evidence, although there are elements of truth in both.

A true picture of German book trades in London from the early nineteenth century to 1914 is harder to define. What I aim to present here is not an exhaustive account of all firms with German origins or with an interest in German-language publishing, but rather an overview of particular trends in the course of the 'long nineteenth century', highlighting selected German firms and individuals and their work for the German community (or communities) in London. This necessarily presents a partial view, but it also provides a more specifically German focus than would a wider perspective.

---

1 The best single source of information on Germans in nineteenth-century Britain is Panikos Panayi, *German Immigrants in Britain during the Nineteenth Century, 1815-1914* (Oxford: Berg, 1995); Rosemary Ashton, *Little Germany: exile and asylum in Victorian England* (Oxford: Oxford University Press, 1986) focuses more narrowly on political exiles, but provides an excellent picture of literary German London.

In the early part of the period, the picture remained much as Graham Jefcoate has described it.[2] Indeed, some eighteenth-century German publishing firms or their offshoots continued in business. Thus after the separation of Vogel and Schulze, members of both families continued to work in the book trade. The Schulzes remained in their Poland Street premises where a firm of Schulze and Burt was active into the 1880s, while the Vogels gradually moved away from the centre of London to Camberwell, where they disappear from view in the middle of the century.[3]

Like their eighteenth-century predecessors, these German publishers were not necessarily producing German-language material. Indeed, apart from a few literary works in the original language, and with the consistent exception of material for the German churches, any German publishing activity they undertook tended to involve language textbooks for English students or translations of German literary and philosophical works. Nor was German the only foreign language in which they published; like other 'foreign booksellers' of the day they published material in a range of European languages. These foreign booksellers were not necessarily of foreign birth. Indeed, a major publisher of German books at this time was David Nutt, a native Londoner. As well as publishing German (and other foreign) literature in his own right, Nutt was for over thirty years the London agent for the Berlin bookseller Adolph Asher, whose work was so important in the building of the British Museum Library's collections, and whose firm retained a London connection until 1914.[4] Although Nutt's main business was taken over by his partner, Nikolaus Trübner, on his death in 1863, his own descendants continued as publishers and booksellers, and retained a connection with foreign-language material, mainly in the form of grammars and textbooks, until well into the twentieth century. From the German perspective, it is also interesting to note that a firm called Haas and Nutt was trading in Langham Place until the mid-1890s.[5]

---

2 See Graham Jefcoate, 'German Printing and Bookselling in Eighteenth-Century London: evidence and interpretation' in this volume.

3 P. A. H. Brown, *London Publishers and Printers, c. 1800-1870* (London: British Library, 1982).

4 On Asher's relationship with Nutt see David Paisey, 'Adolphus Asher (1800-1853): Berlin Bookseller, Anglophile, and Friend to Panizzi', *British Library Journal*, 23 (1997), 131-53. I have traced only one German-language item published in London in Asher's own name, the *Deutsches Taschenbuch* of 1837, printed by Trowitsch and Son in Berlin.

5 *Kelly's Directory* for 1896 has an entry for Haas and Nutt; advertisements from the following year's issues of *Der Vereinsbote*, a journal for German governesses in London, show that the firm briefly became simply Haas & Co. and was then taken over by August Siegle.

Nutt was both a bookseller, importing foreign works for sale, and a publisher in his own right, often collaborating with others in the same business. His ventures into the field of German-language publishing were usually printed by the firm of Wertheimer, founded by Joseph Wertheimer in Leman Street. This was one of the centres of the East End's German community, where the printers were near neighbours to some of London's poorest German immigrants and to St George's German Lutheran Church in Little Alie Street, which provided some of Wertheimer's earliest business printing liturgies and religious works. The firm later moved to a more up-market address in Finsbury Circus where, as Wertheimer, Lea & Company, they would continue into the twentieth century, although without a specifically German emphasis.

The Wertheimers were unusual in being a successful firm printing German books in England. Indeed, for a period in the mid-nineteenth century they appear to have had something of a monopoly, producing literature, liturgical works (for both Christian and Jewish communities), and periodicals. As a rule, however, publishers of German works in England tended to look abroad for printers. Many German works with a London address on the title-page are revealed by their colophons to be printed in Germany. This was clearly not a convenient state of affairs for the authors, publishers or readers. In the May 1855 issue of the London literary journal *Deutsches Athenäum*, the editors explain that printing errors are inevitable because they cannot efficiently check proofs printed in Leipzig. Nearly thirty years later we find the editor of the London-published and Berlin-printed *Jahrbuch der Deutschen in England* making a similar apology.[6] The publishers of these works, Franz Thimm and August Siegle, were both well-established London booksellers (Thimm also ran a German circulating library), and it seems strange that they did not turn to existing London printers, but they were not alone in this.

There may have been advantages in using printers in Germany; difficulties in obtaining German type in Britain may have influenced the decision, or booksellers and publishers may have preferred to exploit existing German contacts with an eye to distribution in Germany as well as in Britain. The last possibility certainly seems to have carried weight with the educated middle-class radicals who settled in England after the 1848 Revolution. Although many of these wrote, often prolifically, in exile, they tended to

---

6 *Deutsches Athenäum: Zeitschrift für deutsche Literatur und Kunst* (London: Franz Thimm, 1853-6), Nr. 29 (May 1855), 8; *Jahrbuch der Deutschen in England.* Herausgegeben von Heinrich Dorgeel (London: A. Siegle, 1882), p. vi.

publish their works in Germany wherever possible, preferring to share their ideas and experiences with the compatriots they had left behind rather than with fellow exiles. Thus, for example, Karl Marx, although both he and his main supporter Engels were resident in England, generally published original German works here only as a last resort, as in the case of the aggressive *Herr Vogt*, which no German publisher would accept.[7] (However, as we shall see, there was one important exception to this rule where Marx and Engels were concerned.)

Likewise, Germans in England, whether exiles or voluntary immigrants, tended to rely on imported German books and periodicals to provide them with reading-matter in their own language. The fact that many, especially among the educated middle classes who were most likely to form a reading public, were keen to adapt to the culture and language of their new home also reduced the need for a German-language press and the opportunities for Anglo-German publishing ventures to flourish. Of course many such assimilated Germans were involved in the communication of German culture to their British neighbours; for example, Germans played a major role alongside British enthusiasts in the founding of the British Goethe and Wagner societies (although by contrast the London 'Schillerfest' of 1859 was organised chiefly by and for Germans). This kind of communication naturally had an impact on German-language publishing, leading to an increase in types of material familiar from earlier in the century – literary criticism, language textbooks and study editions of literary works. Some such works were issued by publishers with a German background, but these firms often had a more general academic focus rather than a specifically German one. Moreover, the new interest in foreign literature and culture was not restricted to German studies, and the market for foreign-language books was thus just as tempting to established English publishers as to those with a foreign background or bias.

Just as German writers and scholars in Britain often chose to write for the British market, so Germans who came to Britain with a background in the book trade were likely to work in British firms or the English-language market. Printing, publishing and bookselling were not in any case trades strongly represented among the German immigrant community. A rare

---

7 Karl Marx, *Herr Vogt* (London: A. Petsch & Co., 1860). An address in Fenchurch Street is given on the title-page for Petsch, but I have been unable to trace a publisher or bookseller of this name in any other source. The printer was R. Hirschfeld of Clifton Street, Finsbury Square, who also produced a short-lived Communist journal, *Neue Zeit*, in 1858-9, and was responsible for a German edition of the Communist Manifesto in the late 1850s or early 1860s.

example – both in terms of a well-documented life and of his very existence – was Nikolaus Trübner, one of the few Germans to make a truly successful career in the British book trade in his own right. Indeed, his business survives today in a somewhat ghostly form as an ancestor of the modern firm of Routledge.[8]

Fig. 1: Nikolaus Trübner, from *Trübner's American, European, & Oriental Literary Record.* N.S., vol. 5, nos. 3-4 (Apr. 1884), facing p. 36.
British Library pressmark: PP.6490.c.

---

8 A chapter is devoted to Trübner and his firm in F. A. Mumby, *The House of Routledge, 1834-1934: with a history of Kegan Paul, Trench, Trübner and other associate firms* (London: Routledge, 1934). This, along with the many obituaries reprinted in the commemorative issue of *Trübner's American, European and Oriental Record,* N.S. 5:3-4 (April 1884), is the major source for the following summary of Trübner's life.

Trübner (fig. 1) was a native of Heidelberg whose apprenticeship at fifteen to a bookseller was apparently intended as a substitute for the university education his family could not afford. He went on to work for publishing houses such as Vandenhoeck & Ruprecht and Hoffmann und Campe, both of which survive as well-respected firms in Germany today. At the same time, he became involved with the liberal ideas of the 'Young Germany' movement, and, although not himself a political refugee, his decision in 1843 to take a job with Longmans and settle in London may have been influenced by the greater political freedom to be found in Britain. In 1852 he left Longmans to set up his own business, but his partner, Thomas Delf, was a feckless character, and the venture was only rescued by a new partnership, this time with David Nutt, which was to last until Nutt's death in 1863. Trübner gradually moved away from Nutt's traditional specialism in European literature and into the areas where his own scholarly and ideological interests lay. American literature and oriental studies were chief among these, and were the fields in which Trübner & Company's excellence came to be acknowledged. However, he maintained a foothold in the German-language market largely through his sympathy for liberal causes.

Although barely mentioned by his many fulsome obituarists, this sympathy was reflected throughout Trübner's publishing career. He not only co-published literary works by revolutionary writers such as Paul Harro-Harring and Adolf Strodtman in the 1850s and early 1860s but also produced more purely political works on the state of Germany. Most notably, he was the publisher of *Der deutsche Eidgenosse*, a short-lived but briefly influential periodical of the mid-1860s produced by the Verein 'Deutsche Freiheit und Einheit'.[9] Trübner himself was a member of this society which brought together like-minded German intellectuals with shared ideals of a unified and democratic German republic, and which had already published a series of pamphlets on political questions in both English and German. Trübner was certainly responsible for some of the English editions of these pamphlets, but the German versions were generally published in Hamburg, where much of Trübner's own German output was printed (and where he seems to have first become closely involved with democratic movements in the late 1830s). It is interesting to note that Trübner's name disappears from the imprint of the *Eidgenosse* in its later issues. The first issue to bear only the imprint 'Expedition des *Eidgenossen*' is that of 15 June 1866 which contains a rather extravagant fifteen pages of mourning for Ferdinand Blind, the

9 *Der deutsche Eidgenosse* Jg. I/II, No. 1-12 (London: Trübner & Co., 1865-7; facsimile reprint: Glashütten im Taunus: Auvermann, 1973).

stepson of the journal's editor, who had committed suicide in prison after a failed attempt to assassinate Bismarck. Trübner continued to be involved with both the journal and the society; the address given for the 'Expedition des *Eidgenossen*' is still Paternoster Row, where he had his premises, and his account books show that he was still dealing with back issues in 1869, two years after the journal had ceased publication.[10] However, he may have wanted to distance himself from Blind's implied support for violent revolutionary action. Although there is no reason to doubt that his support for republican causes was genuine, as a businessman and member of respectable society he must also have been aware of the need for caution in his political expressions. After the collapse of the *Eidgenosse* in 1867 Trübner's German output became more sporadic and his production of German political works seems to have ceased altogether.

This period, the late 1860s, was on the whole a quiet one for German political activity in London, but it fell between two significant peaks. The first of these had, of course, been the 1840s, culminating in the revolutionary years of 1848 and 1849. As early as 1837, a group of German workers in London had formed a mutual support society, with the motto 'Alle Menschen sind Brüder'. This was to develop into the body which I will refer to as the 'Bildungsverein' for convenience, although its exact name varied over the course of time.[11] For groups such as this, self-help and education were as important as political radicalism and no doubt many German workers attended the classes and social events they organised without becoming involved, or even interested, in political activity. However, politics were an ever-present background, and loomed especially large in the late 1840s as social and political unrest grew throughout Europe. The Bildungsverein in particular became closely connected with the newly-founded Communist League, and in 1847 debated setting up an in-house press in connection with the League's attempts to found a journal.

In the event, only a sample issue of the planned *Kommunistische Zeitschrift* was ever produced, and although the 'Bildungsverein für Arbeiter' was named as its publisher, the printers were Meldola, Cahn and Company.[12] This firm has proved hard to trace through any source other than the works they

---

10 Trübner & Co. account books, in *Archives of Kegan Paul, Trench, Trübner & Henry S. King 1858-1912* [Microfilm] (Bishops Stortford: Chadwyck-Healey, 1974).

11 The earliest name seems to have been 'Bildungs- und Gegenseitige Unterstützungs-Gesellschaft für Arbeiter in London', later changing to 'Londoner Deutscher Arbeiter-Verein', 'Londoner Arbeiter-Bildungs-Verein' and finally 'Communistischer Arbeiter-Bildungs-Verein'. However, the record of these changes does not take into account the various schisms and breakaway groups.

printed, but Meldola was probably Samuel Meldola, son of a Portuguese rabbi settled in London; he appears, both with and without Cahn, chiefly as a printer of Jewish service books. Their partnership began in 1845, a year when Cahn had independently printed the statutes of the Bildungsverein and the first issues of the *Deutsche Londoner Zeitung*, a curious instance of a radical newspaper funded by a deposed Grand Duke. It thus seems likely that it was Cahn's connections rather than those of his partner that brought the firm work for the Bildungsverein and the Communist League.

Manifest

der

Kommunistischen Partei.

Veröffentlicht im Februar 1848.

London.

Gedruckt in der Office der „Bildungs-Gesellschaft für Arbeiter" von J. E. Burghard.

46, Liverpool Street, Bishopsgate.

Fig. 2: Title-page of the Communist Manifesto, from Karl Marx, *Manifest der Kommunistischen Partei: originalgetreue Reproduktion der Erstausgabe 1848* (Berlin: Dietz, 1986). British Library pressmark: YA.1990.a.16409.

By early 1848 the Bildungsverein may have moved further towards having a self-sufficient press, or at least its own printer, for its most famous publication was not printed by Meldola and Cahn, but instead bears the imprint 'Gedruckt in der Office der "Bildungs-Gesellschaft für Arbeiter" von J. E. Burghard'. This was the first edition of the Communist Manifesto prepared by Marx and Engels and published in late February 1848 (fig. 2).[13]

12 *Kommunistische Zeitschrift*. Probeblatt (London: Bildungsverein für Arbeiter, 1847; facsimile reprint: Leipzig: Hirschfeld, 1921).

Although it is one of very few works by the 'fathers of socialism' to be published in London in its original German, this slim, yellow-bound pamphlet has a strong claim to be the most influential original document ever published in a foreign language in this country.

Fifty years later, Friedrich Lessner, a veteran of the Bildungsverein, still proudly recalled playing a 'modest role in the publication of this epoch-making work'; his task was to take the manuscript to the printer and bring the proof-sheets back for correction.[14] However, exactly where Lessner's journey took him has been a cause for some debate. Burghard's address is given as 46 Liverpool Street, but some writers have speculated that his premises were actually in Warren Street, where the *Deutsche Londoner Zeitung* was printed in the late 1840s. The Bildungsverein must have had close links with the *Deutsche Londoner Zeitung*, which began serialising the Communist Manifesto as early as March 1848. However, the paper's Warren Street printer and publisher was John Harrison, not J. E. Burghard.[15] Significance has been read into the fact that Burghard's name is not in contemporary directories, but this does not necessarily mean that he was operating clandestinely. It is more likely that both he and Harrison simply ran small operations from premises which were not their own, and that their work for the Bildungsverein came about through personal contacts and shared convictions rather than being the result of the search for a press through commercial channels. In fact several of the German publishing and printing firms active in nineteenth-century London are not to be found in directories of the time, and their absence may not necessarily even imply a small or short-lived firm, let alone a clandestine one. For example, Adolf Vogel of Camberwell, the last of the long-established printing dynasty, printed the 1842 edition of *Robson's London Directory* but his own firm does not appear in its trade or street listings.

---

13 *Manifest der Kommunistischen Partei* (London: Gedruckt in der Office der 'Bildungs-Gesellschaft für Arbeiter' von J. E. Burghard, 1848; facsimile reprint: Berlin: Dietz, 1986).

14 Friedrich Lessner, 'Vor 1848 und nachher: Erinnerungen eines alten Kommunisten', *Deutsche Worte*, 18 (1898), 97-112, 145-61, 193-295, at pp. 108-9. A modern German edition of Lessner's memoirs (Berlin, 1975) was given the title *Ich brachte das 'Kommunistische Manifest' zum Drucker*, emphasising his 'modest role' in Communist (and printing) history.

15 Thomas Kuczynski, *Das kommunistische Manifest (Manifest der Kommunistischen Partei) von Karl Marx and Friedrich Engels: von der Erstausgabe zur Leseausgabe, mit einer Editionsbericht* (Trier: Karl-Marx-Haus, 1995) gives a detailed summary of the disputes surrounding the printing history of the Manifesto and of the variant impressions of its first edition (pp. 58-94). A quotation from the diary of the *Deutsche Londoner Zeitung*'s editor (p. 70, footnote) suggests that Burghard was printing the paper in 1847.

The influx of refugees from the revolutions of 1848, rather than reinforcing groups like the Bildungsverein, led to internal battles, schisms and the foundation of new and rival groups. This lack of unity was one of the factors preventing the growth of any successful radical exile press, despite a small boom of attempts to found journals. In the event few of these lasted more than a year, if that. Many, along with the details of their publication, must now be completely lost to posterity simply because no recorded copies survive. For example, we would know little if anything of *Der Kosmos*, which ran to three issues in early 1851, were it not for a number of references in the letters of Marx and Engels expressing a degree of vitriol wholly disproportionate to the journal's impact.[16] The only periodical founded by a 'forty-eighter' to enjoy a long life was Gottfried Kinkel's *Hermann*, printed by the ubiquitous Wertheimers, and this owed its long-term success less to its politics than to the fact that it gradually became a focus for reports of German clubs and societies in London and thus the semi-official newspaper of the city's German community. As the *Londoner Zeitung* it survived until 1914.[17] More purely political journals such as *Das Volk*, which was set up by Marx and Engels specifically to compete with *Hermann* (Kinkel being one of their many pet hates), aroused little enthusiasm among the wider public.[18]

There was another small upsurge of radical activity and radical publishing among London's Germans from the 1880s onwards, largely due to the arrival of more refugees following the passing of new anti-socialist laws in Germany. Series of pamphlets with titles like *Sozialdemokratische Bibliothek* and *Bibliothek der Solidarität* and firms such as the German Co-operative Publishing Company appeared around this time. Meanwhile existing associations such as the Bildungsverein continued to publish their own material, occasionally using it to fight internal battles in public. The new radical press, like the workers' movement itself, became more international in scope, a change illustrated in its idealised form by a book published in 1906 which contains revolutionary songs in no fewer than nine languages, including Russian and

---

16 Julius H. Schoeps, '*Der Kosmos*: ein Wochenblatt der bürgerlich-demokratischen Emigration in London im Frühjahr 1851', *Jahrbuch des Instituts für Deutsche Geschichte* [Tel Aviv], 5 (1976), 212-26.

17 *Hermann: deutsches Wochenblatt aus London*, Nr. 1-573 (London: Wertheimer, 1859-69); continued as: *Londoner Zeitung*, Nr. 574-Nr. 2903 (London: Wertheimer, 1870-1914).

18 A comprehensive list of the British Library's holdings of London German newspapers, compiled by Dorothea Miehe and Christopher Skelton-Foord, can be found on the British Library website <http://www.bl.uk/collections/newspaper> and provides a useful bibliography of titles; a general article on the Newspaper Library's German-language holdings by the same authors appeared in *Newspaper Library News*, no. 27 (Winter 1999/2000), available at the same web address.

Yiddish.[19] Anarchist groups added a new element to the revolutionary mix in this period. Johann Most's anarchist journal *Freiheit* was published in London during the early 1880s, even being produced in Most's own kitchen at one point.[20]

It is hard to say what kind of audience these publications reached. It was probably not a large one, but socialistic workers' organisations were perceived as a definite threat and their influence was regularly deplored by more conservative writers who probably better represented the German reading public in London. Printing condemnations of radical political groups clearly had an element of sound business sense for the publishers of works such as the 1882 *Jahrbuch der Deutschen in England* since it tacitly endorsed their own non-political publications and the non-political associations behind them. These were firms such as that of August Siegle, actual publisher of the *Jahrbuch*, and Henry Detloff who printed the *Londoner General-Anzeiger*, the city's second-longest running German newspaper. Both are typical of the firms that successfully served the large and confident German community in Britain in the decades before the First World War.

August Siegle was born in Stuttgart, and must have started his London business in the early 1860s since advertisements from 1913 and 1914 boast that the firm has been 'established half-a-century'. By the 1870s he was active as a publisher of general works for and about the German community. He was also involved in German associations such as the rather exclusive 'German Athenaeum' literary society, and the Masonic lodge 'Der Pilger', connections he exploited by publishing material for both. Like Nutt and his fellows seventy years before, Siegle was a 'foreign' rather than exclusively German bookseller and printer, and a charming image from 1914 advertises the range of languages on offer (fig. 3). It shows an elegantly-dressed young woman holding a bunch of balloons, each bearing the name of one of the languages in the firm's repertoire, with 'English' and 'German' flying significantly higher than the rest. By this time the firm seems to have been divided into a printing operation in the City and a publishing and bookselling business at 2 Langham Place (premises previously occupied by two earlier German booksellers: Kolckmann, and Haas & Nutt). The Langham Place concern also appears as 'Siegle and Hill' from 1906 onwards; after 1914 the

19 *Le Chansonnier International du Révolte = Internationales Rebellen-Liederbuch* ... (London: Broschüren-Gruppe des Comm. A.B.V, 1906).

20 Frederic Trautmann, *The Voice of Terror: a biography of Johann Most* (Westport, Conn.: Greenwood Press, 1980), p. 40. Trautmann names Henry Tusson and John Bale & Sons as the main London printers of *Freiheit* and also describes the latter firm as long-time printers to the Bildungsverein (pp. 70-1).

Fig. 3: Advertisement for August Siegle, from *Deutscher Kalender für Grossbritannien* (1914), 63. British Library pressmark: PP.2423.y.

name Siegle disappears from their imprints. The Siegle family may have lost their share in the business or found it safer to shelter behind the name of their English partners when German property was confiscated on the outbreak of the First World War; alternatively, they may simply have ceased to play an active role in the firm by this time.

The outbreak of war in 1914 and the accompanying surge of anti-German feeling effectively put an end to London's German community as a major ethnic group and cultural force.[21] In the previous three decades there had actually been something of an increase in German-language publishing for Germans in Britain. Although earlier middle-class immigrants had often preferred to import their reading-matter from their old homeland or to become assimilated into the cultural life of their new one, the later nineteenth century seems to have witnessed a growing feeling of German-ness among London's German community. One reason for this was surely the growth of German national pride and self-confidence following unification in 1871 and the consequent desire of Germans abroad to reassert their cultural identity. Increasing literacy also meant that poorer immigrants

21 An account both of growing anti-German sentiment in the years before 1914 and of the fate of Britain's German residents during the war can be found in Panikos Panayi, *The Enemy in Our Midst: Germans in Britain during the First World War* (New York: Berg, 1991).

now constituted a reading public without necessarily sharing the middle-class aspirations towards cultural assimilation or exchange. Finally, more Germans were coming to England to work for a few years rather than to settle permanently, waiters and clerks being the most common groups in this category. All these factors also contributed to the growth of German clubs and societies during this period, which is again inextricably linked to the expansion in German-language publishing.

This culture survived the growing anti-German feeling of the years leading up to 1914, but when war at last broke out German associations were quickly banned and German-language periodicals closed down; printers could legally have their presses impounded if they failed to comply. It is rather poignant now to note that the 'Anglo-German Publishing Company' was founded in 1913 and began to publish at least two journals in the year war broke out.[22] Of the nineteenth-century firms I have traced in this paper, only one appears to have survived into the post-war years bearing its own name, that of Henry Detloff. As late as 1937, Detloff's name appears in the imprint of a festschrift in German celebrating the anniversary of the German Hospital in London;[23] the firm, now referred to as 'The Finsbury Press (Henry Detloff Ltd.)', was still based in Sun Street near Finsbury Square where it had been since at least 1896.

Of course by 1937 there was a new community of German exiles in London with its own publishing activity. That is another story, and a very different one, but the survival of a nineteenth-century German institution and a nineteenth-century foreign printing firm shows how slender threads of continuity link the two. As for the full story of German book trades in nineteenth-century London, there is much more that could be told, and much more that remains to be discovered. Undoubtedly, such research will shed interesting light not only on the London book trade, but also on the history of one of the city's major foreign communities of the time.

---

22 *Deutscher Kalender für Großbritannien*, 1914; *Der Kolonist: Monatsschrift für koloniale Siedlung, Kolonialwirtschaft und Finanz*, Nr. 1- 6 (Jan.-June 1914). The firm also published a guide to 'German London', *Die Deutsche Kolonie in London*, in 1913, and, rather more unexpectedly, a work entitled *Concrete Products* in 1914.

23 *Freiherr Bruno von Schröder. Zum siebzigsten Geburtstag in Dankbarkeit und Verehrung*, ed. G. Schönberger (London: Finsbury Press, 1937).

Anna E. C. Simoni[1]

Dutch Printing in London

I. A survey

Printing in Dutch arose in London following the persecution of Protestants in the Low Countries in the early sixteenth century. Britain in general and London in particular, then as now, became a place of refuge for the exiles. These refugees then clung together for mutual support, they created their own religious congregation and for this more than any other cause they began to print. Printers and other members of the book trade among them worked for English masters,[2] some established themselves independently and in both capacities they produced works in English, Latin, French and also in Dutch. Such printed material, whether purely religious or with a political dimension, could also be exported to their country of origin to give comfort and help to friends left behind.

---

1 My chief sources have been P. Valkema Blouw, *Typographia Batava 1541-1600*, ed. A. C. Schuytvlot (Nieuwkoop, 1998), henceforth TB; A. W. Pollard and G. R. Redgrave, *A Short-Title Catalogue of Books Printed in England, Scotland, & Ireland and of English Books Printed Abroad 1470-1640*, 2nd edn rev. & enl., begun by W. F. Jackson and F. S. Ferguson, completed by K. F. Pantzer (London, 1976-91), henceforth STC. My sincere thanks are due to Ms Susan Reed for assistance given to the internet-illiterate with the *English Short-Title Catalogue*, henceforth ESTC. Other colleagues gave welcome expert advice. My special gratitude goes to Dr J. A. Gruys of the Royal Library, The Hague, who patiently and repeatedly answered my queries, and to Dr Paul Hoftijzer who sent me a copy of his article (see n. 31).

2 Cf. J. G. C. A. Briels, *Zuidnederlandse boekdrukkers en boekverkopers in de Republiek der Verenigde Nederlanden omstreeks 1570-1630. Een bijdrage tot de kennis van de geschiedenis van het boek* (Nieuwkoop, 1974), p. 13, for a list of 21 refugees from the Southern Netherlands who came to London between 1533 and 1583, including eleven bookbinders, two probable compositors, six printers and two booksellers, one of them uncertain. According to Briels one 'stationer' also came to Oxford from Antwerp and two settled in Norwich. This list is not complete, excluding as it does a number of important printers such as Richard Schilders who came to London in 1567 and paid his fee to the Stationers' Company in 1568, nor does it include members of the book trade who either arrived from the Northern Provinces or for some reason did not register properly.

A number of distinguished scholars and learned merchants among the Protestant refugees from the Netherlands in England maintained a flourishing intellectual life.[3] The works they wrote and published were however mainly in Latin or French and those that were in Dutch, if they were printed at all, were not all printed in England. A case in point is Emanuel van Meteren's famous history of the Dutch wars, whose 1609 and 1610 revised editions proclaim London as place of publication, but declare having been printed 'in Schotlandt buyten Danswijck'. The author was no doubt happy to sell as many copies as he could from his home in London; the books were printed, not 'outside Danzig', but by Salomon de Roy at Utrecht (STC 17845.3, 17845.7).

Printing Protestant texts had become extremely dangerous not only in the Low Countries, but also in pre-Reformation England: to mention only two instances, the printer Jacob van Liesvelt was beheaded in Antwerp in 1545 for having persistently printed the Bible in Dutch and produced other offending, mainly Lutheran, items; his fellow countryman and colleague Christoffel van Ruremonde, who had similarly offended against the strict laws of the land, came to England only to be imprisoned in Westminster where he died in 1531.[4] Nor were they the only victims. Nevertheless, Protestant material in various languages, including English, was printed particularly in Antwerp and exported to fellow Protestants in other countries.

Of course, when Catholics were persecuted in England, a stream of refugees, with printers among them, arrived similarly on the Continent, including the Spanish-ruled provinces of the Low Countries, and soon began printing there too, not only in English but also in Latin and very much for export to England. So each country lost and each country gained. The situation was reversed during the reign of Queen Mary, but returned to what it had been on the accession of Elizabeth.

The first book to appear in London in Dutch was a translation by Jan Utenhove of Joannes a Lasco's catechism. *De catechismus, oft kinder leere, diemen te Londen is ghebruyckende* was printed in London in 1551 by Steven Mierdman, a

---

3 See L. Forster, *Janus Gruter's English Years: studies in the continuity of Dutch literature in exile in Elizabethan England* (Leiden & London: The Sir Thomas Browne Institute, 1967), pp. 25-68. Also useful for a general picture of the early years is J. A. van Dorsten, *Poets, Patrons and Professors: an outline of some literary connexions between England and the University of Leiden, 1575-1586* (Leiden: The Sir Thomas Browne Institute, 1962). I thank Dr Barry Taylor for drawing my attention to the book by Forster and lending me his own copy.

4 For brief accounts of these printers' lives see Anne Rouzet, *Dictionnaire des imprimeurs, libraires et éditeurs des XVe et XVIe siècles dans les limites de la Belgique actuelle*, Collection du Centre national de l'archéologie et de l'histoire du livre. Publications, 3 (Nieuwkoop, 1975).

refugee from Antwerp,[5] and was a quick response to the foundation, as allowed in 1550 by a statute of Edward VI, of the Dutch Church at Austin Friars.

This work was reprinted in 1553 and an abridged version, entitled *De cleyne catechismus*, first published in 1552, saw at least three reprints, two in 1561, when John Day issued one edition printed in gothic type and another printed in roman, and one in 1566, again brought out by John Day.[6]

Other texts, equally related to worship and mainly serving ritual and the instruction of the faithful, came from the presses for the expanding community as waves of Protestants arrived, invited to exercise their skills such as weaving, or just fleeing when their particular town or region changed hands from the 'rebels' back to the Spaniards.

The reconquest by Spain of Antwerp in 1585 sent forth a flood of its Protestant citizens who preferred emigration to abandoning their belief. But by then the Northern Provinces had, in 1579, formed the Union of Utrecht for mutual assistance and, in 1581, abjured Philip II, thus declaring their independence from Spanish rule. In consequence, not only did the Antwerp Protestants leave chiefly for the north, but also many of the Dutch exiles from the Southern Provinces left London to begin a new life in the United Provinces.[7] But others stayed and the Dutch Church survived and has done so ever since, not even ceasing its activities when the church itself was bombed in 1941 and its services were transferred to a West End church until rebuilding was completed in 1954.[8]

Outside London, Dutch communities were founded in the sixteenth and early seventeenth centuries, partly as overflow from the London congregation, partly established by new arrivals. They existed mainly in Kent and East Anglia and thrived more or less for a time, vanishing from the records in the early eighteenth century or being absorbed into the Church of England, as happened in Norwich by the early nineteenth century. It was only at Norwich, however, that any printing in Dutch occurred, again in the service of the Dutch Reformed faith.[9]

---

5 Joannes a Lasco, *De catechismus, oft kinderleere, diemen te Londen, in de Duytsche ghemeynte, is ghebruyckende.* [Tr. Jan Utenhove.] Londen, Steven Mierdmans, 1551. STC 15260, TB 1013. The 1553 edition: STC 15260.5, TB 1014.

6 Joannes a Lasco, *De cleyne catechismus, oft kinderleere.* Ghemaeckt [i.e. abridged] doer M. Microen. Londen, Nicolaes vanden Berghe, 1552. STC 15260.7, TB 3463. Later London editions: STC 15260.7 pt. 2, 2739.5, 15251, 15262, TB 3468-3471.

7 Cf. Briels (n. 2), p. 14 and passim under the names of printers.

8 Cf. J. Lindeboom, *Austin Friars, History of the Reformed Church in London 1550-1950* (The Hague, 1950), pp. 191-3. A view of the old Austin Friars is shown on pl. II in the same book; the rebuilt Austin Friars is copiously illustrated in the church guide, *The Dutch Church, Templum Domini Jesu* (London, 1954).

9 Cf. Lindeboom, op. cit. (n. 8), pp. 104-11.

Early London-Dutch printing, which is responsible for some forty editions at least, to which can be added another three or four at Norwich,[10] can be divided into various categories. These are (1) straightforward books in Dutch with normal imprints, which are the majority; (2) books without imprint, but known to come from London; (3) books with a London or Norwich imprint, but known to have come from the Netherlands or from Germany, in particular from Emden. The reasons for such subterfuges had all to do with politics.[11] A possible fourth category could be added, of books in English printed in London, but containing quotations in Dutch; however, although some publications of this kind might be obvious, such as works dealing with Dutch history or literature, and certainly those devoted to the Dutch church in London, an attempt to find special groups limited by time or subject matter would go far beyond the scope of this survey.

In the first category are the catechisms mentioned above. But Marten Micron and Jan Utenhove provided further religious texts for the Dutch congregation, including several editions of the Psalms translated by

---

10 On Antonius de Solempne see STC, vol. III, p. 158. STC assigns or tentatively assigns seven editions to him, but queries one, which is sometimes attributed to him (5600.5), attributed in TB (5749) to a different author and to no named printer or place. One in French (5792) and two in English (3835, 16510.5) are of course not listed in TB. TB, vol. II, p. 554 lists seven editions by him, all in Dutch, three of which (TB 523, 524, 2443) are definitely and one (TB 4355), bearing the imprint 'Buyten Colen', 'outside Cologne', is tentatively attributed to Solempne. Forster also mentions a broadside by the Spaniard Antonio de Corro, produced by Antonius de Solempne in Norwich in a Latin, a French and a Dutch version, copies of the Latin and French editions being preserved in Cambridge University Library (STC 5792, 5793), while no copy of the Dutch version has survived (op. cit., pp. 30-1). No such lost Dutch printed text is listed in TB. Forster's account of a second Norwich printer of Dutch texts, Albertus Christiani operating 'outside Norwich' (op. cit., pp. 32-5), proves once again that even Homer can nod: the name is a pseudonym, the place of publication, 'buyten Noirdvvitz', is a favourite false imprint (the title with place-name only STC 151, the title also with printer's name STC 17450 and, with further identification, TB 2354).

11 The simplest way to hide the printer's identity was to issue a book or pamphlet without his name and/or place and this was constantly done with 'dangerous' material. But in countries where an imprint was required by law, as was the case both in England and the Spanish-ruled Netherlands, a book without such information was immediately suspect; a false imprint could, with luck, be mistaken for a true one and allow the book at least a short spell of relatively safe circulation. But often the false imprint would be an open gesture of defiance, with or without added mockery. Such means have been adopted through time and, so far as Dutch printing is concerned, were used especially for the clandestine publications in the Netherlands during the German occupation in World War II (cf. the publishers' index in A. E. C. Simoni, *Publish and Be Free* (The Hague, 1975), pp. 230-69, passim).

Utenhove.[12] A writer using the pseudonym of Reginaldus Gonsalvius Montanus had two editions of his book against the Spanish Inquisition, originally written in French, printed in Dutch translation by John Day in London in 1569 and 1581.[13] And more of this sort. A very substantial work, in verse, deserving a mention in this category, is the Dutch minister in London Symeon Ruytinck's *De gulden legende vande Roomsche Kercke*, which includes a 'Historisch lied' on the Gunpowder Plot.[14] But there were wholly secular books too, such as Claude Hollyband's *The French schoolemaister*, translated into Dutch under the not wholly certain title of *Instruksie om draa en goed Frans te leeren*, published by Thomas Vautrollier, London, 1581,[15] or the translation of Plutarch's *Coniugalia praecepta*, published, presumably by Richard Schilders, under the title of *Den spieghel des houwelicks*, in 1575.[16]

The seventeenth century, not free from religious persecution either, saw much less printing in Dutch outside Dutch-speaking areas. The division between the North, where the Calvinist Church was dominant and members of other faiths, whether Protestant or Catholic, not to mention the Jews, had

---

12 E.g. Marten Micron, *Een claer bewijs, van het recht gebruyck des nachtmaels Christi*. Lonnen, S. Mierdma*n*, 1552 (STC 17863.3, TB 3460); *Een corte ondersoeckinghe des gheloofs*. [London? Nicolaes van den Berghe?] 1553 (TB 2922, with literature for an edition of which no copy is now known); *Een korte ondersoeckinghe des gheloofs, over de ghene die sick [*sic, for *'sich'] tot der ghemeyntte begheven willen*. Londen, Jan Daye, 1561 (STC 18812, TB 2926); [Psalms 23, 101, 115, 128, in an early version of Jan Utenhove's translation. London, Nicolaes van den Berghe, 1552] (STC 2738.7, TB 5285); *Hondert Psalmen Davids* [with other matter. Tr. Jan Utenhove] (STC 2739, TB 2514); *De Psalmen Dauidis, in Nederlandischer sangs-ryme door Jan Wtenhoue*. Londen, Jan Daye, 1566 (STC 2740.3, TB 4129): *Die Psalmen Davids, ende ander lofsangen, wt den francoysen dichte ouerghesedtt door Petrum Dathenum*. Buyten Londen, Merten Wendelen [or rather, Deventer, Simon Steen], 1566 (STC 2740.5, without identification of printer, TB 4126 [without reference to STC]). Some of the above were reprints of editions printed elsewhere and further reprints were produced both in London and abroad.

13 Reginaldus Gonsalvius Montanus, *De heylighe Spaensche inquisitie, met haer loosheyt, valscheyt ende argelisten ontdect*. Tr. [allegedly from the Latin] Mauluspertus Taphaer. Londen, John Day, 1569 (STC 12000 [without calling both names pseudonyms]; TB 2125); *Historie der Spaenscher inquisitie*. [London, John Day], 1581 (STC 12000.5, TB 2127).

14 S. Ruytinck, *De Gulden legende vande Roomsche Kercke. Aenden toet-steen der waerheyd beproeft*. Londen, Thomas Snodham, 1612 (STC 21471, A. E. C. Simoni, *Catalogue of Books from the Low Countries 1601-1621 in the British Library* (London, 1991) (henceforth, Sim), R124).

15 Claude Hollyband, *Instruksie om draa en goed Frans te leeren, en Engels*. Londen, Thomas Vautrollier, 1581 (TB 2490 [described from the sale catalogue of the library of Petrus Scriverius, *Bibliotheca Scriveriana*, Amstelodami, 1663]).

16 Plutarch, *Den spieghel des houwelicks*. [Tr. Richard Schilders?] [London], Richard Schilders, 1575. (STC Addenda 200051.5, TB 4038).

freedom of conscience although they were treated as second or third class citizens, and the South, where the Catholic Church was very successful in banishing all the rest, no longer required the production of Dutch books abroad as had occurred before. Only those exiles who still remained in their new country and their descendants might want to read new Dutch books, but they could procure these in the main from the Low Countries themselves.

In fact, as time went on, with few exceptions even the books specially produced for use by the London Dutch, other than perhaps advertisements or other ephemeral matter, would be sent in manuscript to a printer in the Netherlands. This was the procedure, for instance, still observed in the twentieth century with the book commemorating the jubilee of the London Dutch Society in 1923. Intended for private circulation only and consisting mainly of the photographs of its officers and members, it was published by the Society and therefore in London, but it was printed by Roeloffzen-Hübner & Van Santen and Gebr. Binger in Amsterdam.[17]

Very occasionally however an ephemeral, or not so ephemeral, Dutch text turns up with a London imprint, for example the two funeral sermons of 1806 and 1834,[18] a Dutch hymn-book and a catechism of 1813 and 1820, with their descendants,[19] and a Dutch Bible of 1812,[20] followed, though beyond

---

17 *De Nederlandsche Vereeniging te Londen, 1873-1923.* Aangeboden door den President van de Nederlandsche Vereeniging te Londen bij gelegenheid van haar vijftigjarig bestaan. [London; Amsterdam printed, 1923]. Copy in BL.

18 H. Potter, *Lykrede op L. H. Schippers Paal.* Londen, T. Bensley, 1806 [source: *Catalogus van het boekenbezit van de Dutch Church Austin Friars. Kasten A-F* [typescript, copy in BL]; Hendrik Gehle, *Lijkrede bij den dood van den heere Jan Werninck.* Londen, P. P. Thomas, 1834 [source: ibid.].

19 *De Evangelische gezangen.* London, 1813 [source: *Catalogus van het boekenbezit* (n. 18)]; *De Heidelbergsche Catechismus.* London, 1813 [source: *Catalogus van het boekenbezit*]; *De Evangelische gezangen om nevens het boek der Psalmen by den openbaren Godsdienst in de Nederduitsche Hervormde gemeenten gebruikt te worden.* Londen, Gedrukt door T. Hamblin, 1820, followed by *De Heidelbergsche Catechismus, benevens eenige Christelyke gebeden en formulieren, die in de Nederduitsche Gereformeerde kerken gebruikt worden.* Gedrukt door T. Hamblin, Op Garlick Hill, Thames Street. Te Londen. 1820 [copies in the BL. The two books are not only bound together, the sequence of signatures, those of the *Evangelische Gezangen* being lower, those of the *Catechismus* upper case, show they were intended to be issued together. I have not seen the 1813 editions belonging to Austin Friars, but expect they were equally produced as a single book]; *Gezangen ten gebruike bij den openbaren Godsdienst der kerk. Nieuwe en vergroote uitgave.* London, Society for Promoting Christian Knowledge, 1892 [in fact based on Anglican hymns, copy of this, but none of an earlier edition in BL]; *Gezangen*, etc., London, Society for Promoting Christian Knowledge; printed at Bungay, 1906 [copy in the BL].

20 *Biblia, dat is de gantsche H. Schriftuur.* Londen, Hamblin & Seyfang, 1812 [source: *Catalogus van het boekenbezit* (n. 18)].

the chronological limit set for this survey, by another hymn-book in 1952,[21] and further Bibles in 1909 and 1910, the Bibles published in London, but printed elsewhere in England.[22]

The second category, of books without imprint, but known or believed to have been printed in London, contains translations of English pieces considered to be of topical interest also to Dutch-speaking inhabitants of this country or the Netherlands, like that of Lord Willoughby's anonymously published *A short and true discourse*, in its Dutch form entitled *Cort verhael om te vreden te stellen*,[23] or Johannes Engelram's *De collectuer des nieuwen boeckskens geintituleert uutsprake van der kercken*, which only reveals its author's name by means of an acrostic and evidently wished to conceal its origin even more securely.[24] Lacking an imprint, perhaps to protect its distributors in the Republic, is a denunciation of the atrocities committed by representatives of the Dutch East India Company against English subjects in Amboina, translated from the English and published as *Een waer verhael vande procedure teghen de Enghelsche tot Amboyna*.[25] That the poet Jan van der Noot had two books, *Het theatre* and *Het bosken*, printed in London without an imprint may perhaps be attributed only to his eccentricity.[26]

The third category, of books with misleading English or English-sounding imprints, can itself be divided into two groups: one not intentionally

---

21 *Gezangen ten gebruike by den openbaren godsdienst der kerk*. London, Society for the Promotion of Christian Knowledge; Bungay printed, 1952 [source: *Catalogus van het boekenbezit* (n. 18)].

22 *Bijbel, dat is de gansche heilige schriftuur*. Londen, Britsche en Buitenlandse Bijbelgenootschap, [1909] [source: *Catalogus van het boekenbezit* (n. 18)].

23 *Cort verhael om te vreden te stellen ende vernoegen alle de gene, die de waerheit niet wetende, ondiscretelicke spreken vande coninginne van Engeland*. [London, Richard Field], 1589. (TB 2855 [attribution to Field on typographical grounds]).

24 Johannes Engelram, *De collectuer des nieuwen boeckskens geintituleert uutsprake van der kercken bevesticht ende bewyst breeder t'gene dat hy van het ampt en officie der overheit geschreven heeft in den voornoemden boecksken*. [London, John Day], 1567 (TB 1165, not in STC where a Latin work by the same author, published in London in 1587, is entered under Johannes Aengelramus).

25 [Sir John Skinner], *Een waer verhael vande onlanckxsche ongerechte, wreede, ende onmenschelijcke procedure teghen de Enghelsche tot Amboyna in Oost-Indien, door de Nederlanlanders* [sic]. [London, J. Beale], 1624. Translated from *A True Relation of the Unjust, Cruell, and Barbarous Proceedings against the English at Amboyna* (STC 7451) (STC 7455, W. P. C. Knuttel, *Catalogus der pamfletten-verzameling berustende in de Koninklijke Bibliotheek te 'sGravenhage* ('sGravenhage, 1899-1920), henceforth Kn, 3459).

26 Jan van der Noot, *Het theatre oft toonneel, waer in ter eender de ongelucken ende elenden, op dander syde 't gheluck vertoont worden*. [London, John Day, 1568] (STC 18061; TB 3781); *Het bosken, inhoudende verscheyden poëtixe werken*. [London, Henry Bynneman, 1570-71] (STC 18600.5; TB 3780).

deceitful and another certainly meant to hoodwink opponents of the views expressed. The former consists of reprints and translations of pieces first printed in London, where the original imprint is given on the title-page rather as proof of authenticity, but has sometimes been misunderstood as denoting actual London production. Such 'copy' imprints occur especially, but not exclusively, on official publications, like Queen Elizabeth's proclamation against piracy of 8 Feb. 1559.[27] The intentionally misleading method met with varied success in its own time and can still confuse the unwary.[28]

The placename '[London?]' has been suggested for several Dutch-language publications listed in *The English Short-Title Catalogue*,[29] which I myself do not consider credible. There are, for example, three descriptions by a certain L. Cohen of goods, apparently textiles and skins, shipped from Bengal to be sold on 7 January 1795.[30] These commercial documents in Dutch can hardly have been wanted by potential English buyers. If they were meant for Dutch merchants, would they not have been printed in the Netherlands for local distribution? Similarly, an edition in Dutch of Anthony Daffy's *Elixir salutis*, which bears the author's London address and has been given the date [1762?], cannot easily be considered of much use to possible purchasers in London. In fact, this paean in praise of his concoction is known to have been on sale in Amsterdam, where Elizabeth Ainsworth sold the elixir in 1673 in the coffee house she ran with her husband Benjamin May. In 1700 her sister-in-law Abigael Swart advertised in the Leiden newspaper that she had taken over the sale of the elixir which could be bought in her own Amsterdam bookshop. Another Amsterdam bookseller, Jacob van de Velde, who had learned the trade with Mercy Arnold, widow of Joseph Bruyning, and at one time had John Locke living in his house, translated medical and medicinal literature. It would be natural to seek the translator and therefore also the printer of Daffy's advertisement in this circle of English dissenter booksellers in Amsterdam. A printed edition in Dutch of Daffy's leaflet and manuscript recipes for Daffy's panacea, said to cure everything from gout to

---

27 *Proclamatie vande coninghinne van Enghelandt om te verbieden van te offendeeren oft beschadigen op de zee persoonen, schepen ende goederen van staten, wesende in vrientschappen met de coninghinne.* Londen, Christoffel Barker [or rather, Amsterdam, Cornelis Claesz], 1599. (TB 4076-7, translation of STC 8267).

28 See for instance n. 10: 'Buyten Colen' and especially n. 12: 'Merten Wendelen buyten Londen'.

29 *The English Short-Title Catalogue* <http://www.rlg.org/estc.html>.

30 L. Cohen, *Bevinding over de cossaes & callicoes van de aenstaende Bengaelse verkooping (over de volgende kist goederen, over de kist bont goederen), vast gesteld voor den 7. Jan. 1795.*

women's diseases and even the plague, survive in Amsterdam Municipal Archive, the latest of them dated 1817.[31]

ESTC gives a '[London? 1797?]' imprint to an eighteenth-century document which, although I have my doubts about a possible origin in the capital, must at least have been printed in England. It is a list of the weekly provisions per head for prisoners of war, in this instance Dutch.[32] One can imagine a prison governor faced with half-starved Dutch prisoners asking for more, like so many Oliver Twists, but unable to explain to them that they were not entitled to more. If one of the prisoners knew enough English to translate the English list supplied to the prison, the governor could send the manuscript to the local jobbing printer. Assuming that the date is more or less correct, one would need to discover where Dutch prisoners were then held. In my opinion London is unlikely.

In contrast, in 1799 the exiled William V attempted, with the help of British troops, to return to what was by then called the Batavian Republic to regain his former stadholdership. The attempt ended in defeat, but to assist his cause a document, signed by him and dated Hampton Court, 28 July 1799, was printed to be scattered among the population. Bearing no title other than William's greetings to his fellow-countrymen, it encourages them to come to the aid of the 'liberators' and throw off the yoke imposed on them by the French. It was very probably printed in London, if not in the Hampton Court area.[33]

---

31 Anthony Daffy, *Elixir salutis*: (van myn huys in Prujans Court, in den Oude Bayle, London). The English advertisement was published several times with dates ranging from [1670?] to 1700, the last of them issued by his widow Elio Daffy [copy in BL]. An eight-page leaflet entitled *Onderrigtingen gegeven van Dr. Antony Daffy: tot het gebruik van zyne ongevaarlyke, onschadelyke en voor veele menschen gelukkige cordialen drank, genaamt Elixir salutis, welke an [= na?] zyn dood gecontinueerd is te maken* ..., printed in Amsterdam in the nineteenth century, presumably reprinted from a seventeenth-century original, has been notified to me by Dr Gruys as held in the library of the Wellcome Institution, while a copy of what could be the original is in Amsterdam University Library. Dr Gruys also informed me that Eleanor Daffy survived her husband until 1732. Parts of *Onderrechtingen Gegeeven van Dr. Antony Daffy Tot het gebruik van zyne ongevaarlyke, onschadelyke en voor veel menschen gelukkige cordialen dranck, genaamt Elixir Salutis, welke na zyn Dood gecontinueert is te maken, by zyne nagelate Wed: Elio Daffy*, an advertisement for the medicine on sale by the widow of Joseph Piecock [sic] at the English Orphanage, are reproduced in P. G. Hoftijzer, 'Het Elixir Salutis. Verkoop en bereiding van een Engels medicijn in Amsterdam', *Amstelodamum. Maandblad voor de kennis van Amsterdam*, 72 (1985), 73-8. The edition listed in ESTC may of course not be that of either of the above, but is doubtless of similar origin.

32 *Weeks provisie voor de gevangenen per man.* [London? 1797?]

33 The piece is variously referred to in the literature as *Manifest* or *Publicatie;* Cornelis van der Aa, *Geschiedenis van het leven, character, en lotgevallen van* ... *Willem den Vijfden, IV* (Amsterdam, 1808), pp. 542-6, mentions a 'Proclamatie aan de Nederlanders' of the

Some occasional pieces, orders of special church services, notices of births or deaths, new addresses and the like, may have been printed in Dutch for friends and relations by the nearest printer in London, but are now lost or kept privately by the descendants of those who had them done. Although such items might throw welcome light on the life of the Dutch who lived in London, they would hardly add important matter to our knowledge of Dutch printing in London or the history of printing as a whole.

The above is a first attempt at mapping the printing of books and other pieces in Dutch in London. It does not pretend to be complete, nor can such conclusions as I have reached be definitive. My hope is that curiosity will lead one of its readers to devote a more thorough investigation to this subject.

II. The strange case of Double-Dutch double vision: bilingual pamphlets of 1615

To find a bilingual edition combining English and Dutch, produced in London in the sixteenth or seventeenth century is, to say the least, unusual. While bilingual editions of biblical texts and of the classics have a long and international tradition, not even dictionaries or grammars, which would attempt to teach the English Dutch or the Dutch English, are known from that period from London printers. An ephemeral edition like the London produced pamphlet, which in fact comprises several Dutch ones, could not fail to arouse curiosity: what exactly is it and why was it produced?

The full title of the pamphlet I am going to discuss here is:

> A Vision or dreame contayning the whole state of the Netherland warres, as it appeared to a louer of the Netherlands lying in his bed, vpon the 7. of Nouember, betweene 3. and 4. of the clocke in the morning, wherein was presented vnto him a goodly country, and therein a fayre comely horse well brideled and sadled, whereat being much amazed, he sayde, Behold the Horse, but where is the Rider? This horse is compared to the Netherland; his chiefe owner the King of Spaine, who with riding thereof, had cruelly spurgalled him; hereupon appeared a cunning rider out of Orange, and took on him to manage

same date and place. Dr J. A. Gruys first kindly notified me of the copy of this piece in Leiden University Library, then sent me a photocopy of the item in the Royal Library, Kn 23037, which together with his arguments convinced me of the document's English origin. Among other characteristics, the terrible misprint 'voedspoor' for 'voetspoor' could hardly have been committed by a Dutchman. Various issues exist, see Kn 23037-51. The episode is reminiscent of a more recent event, when the Government in Exile of Queen Wilhelmina of the Netherlands had leaflets printed in England, this time not for distribution by the soldiers on the ground, but to be dropped over the country by the RAF.

the horse gently: this horse was by policy & great subtilty of the Pope sought to be betraied, as it lately appeared, who by his bishops can when he pleaseth change the names of men, and so they haue giuen another name vnto the warres making the King's warres the Emperours warres, thereby with more ease, to lay holde vpon the horses bridle, by that meanes the better to inclose the Netherlands. [woodcut] Imprinted at London for Edward Marchant, 1615 (fig. 1).[34]

The explanatory title 'Who shall ride mee?' given to the woodcut as it were summarises the rather overlong title. Between them they would have made matters perfectly clear to the reader in the Dutch Republic; the English reader, unless well versed in contemporary history and politics, might have

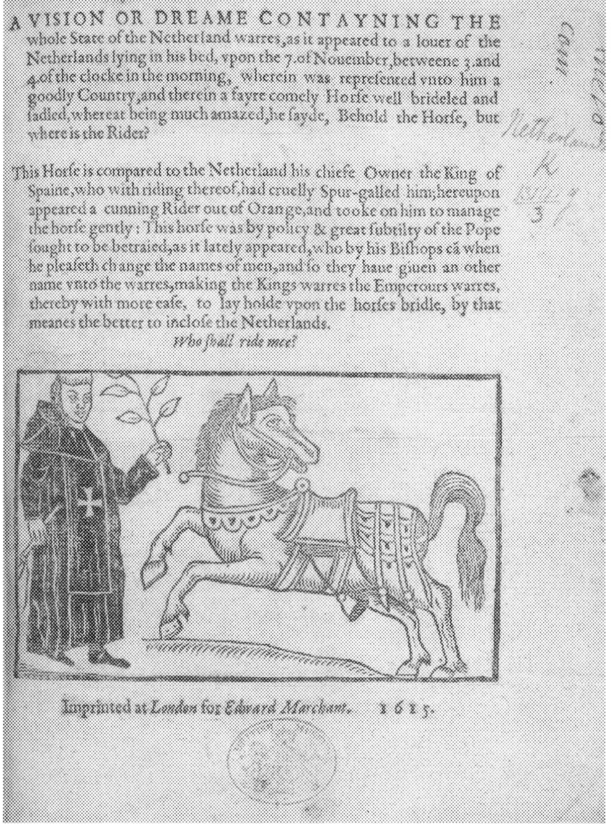

A VISION OR DREAME CONTAYNING THE whole State of the Netherland warres,as it appeared to a louer of the Netherlands lying in his bed, vpon the 7.of Nouember,betweene 3.and 4.of the clocke in the morning, wherein was represented vnto him a goodly Country,and therein a fayre comely Horse well brideled and sadled,whereat being much amazed,he sayde, Behold the Horse, but where is the Rider?

This Horse is compared to the Netherland his chiefe Owner the King of Spaine,who with riding thereof,had cruelly Spur-galled him;hereupon appeared a cunning Rider out of Orange,and tooke on him to manage the horse gently: This horse was by policy & great subtilty of the Pope sought to be betraied,as it lately appeared,who by his Bishops cã when he pleaseth change the names of men,and so they haue giuen an other name vnto the warres,making the Kings warres the Emperours warres, thereby with more ease, to lay holde vpon the horses bridle, by that meanes the better to inclose the Netherlands.

Who shall ride mee?

Imprinted at *London* for *Edward Marchant*. 1615.

Fig. 1: *A Vision or dreame contayning the whole state of the Netherland warres ...* (London: printed for Edward Marchant, 1615), title-page.
British Library pressmark: 1314.g.16(3).

34 STC 18445.7; Sim V200; BL: 1314.g.16(3, 4).

been somewhat puzzled and his modern counterpart is quite possibly at a complete loss.

In the following I shall try to provide a brief account of the situation in the Netherlands as it had come to be by 1615. King Philip II of Spain, who on the abdication of the Emperor Charles V inherited all seventeen provinces of the Netherlands, continued his father's policy against the Protestants, if anything, more ferociously and more efficiently. This, together with increased taxation and what the inhabitants considered infringements of their old privileges, led to the Revolt which began in 1568 with a war that was to end only in 1648. The early stage of the Eighty Years' War brought Prince William of Orange to prominence as a military leader and statesman. He was assassinated in 1584 and his son Maurice succeeded him as stadholder. After lengthy negotiations a truce to last twelve years was proclaimed in 1609. Peace of a sort, but an uneasy one. In the Southern Provinces Catholicism was thoroughly enforced. In the Northern Provinces, which had formed the Republic of the United Netherlands and declared independence, the Reformed Church was recognised as the official ecclesiastical institution, but Catholicism persisted among large strata of the population and other Protestant denominations had many adherents. This was seen as a threat by members of the dominant Reformed Church from whose ranks came all the political leadership. Furthermore, a split occurred within the Reformed Church between the strictly orthodox and the less orthodox, the latter being easily accused by the former of favouring Catholicism and Spain. An international troublespot showed itself with the problem of the succession to the dukedom of Juliers, Cleves and Berg, which covers several areas along the Lower Rhine. The last duke's daughters were excluded from the succession under Salic law. Various princes made claims, especially the Margrave of Brandenburg, a Lutheran, the Count of Pfalz-Neuburg, a Calvinist, and the Archduke Leopold, a Catholic and the Emperor's favourite. The population was of mixed beliefs and was not consulted. The neighbouring countries took sides according to the prevailing religion and the situation became explosive. Neither the Dutch nor the Spaniards wanted to be seen as breaking the truce, but warlike stances were taken. Spanish armed excursions into Germany under the command of the Italian general Ambrogio Spinola caused great alarm in the Republic, which was collectively ruled up to a point by the States General and defended by the Stadholder.

So much for the background to the 'Vision'. The English title given above precedes the English text which is then followed by the Dutch original from which it has been translated. The Dutch text had been published already in 1614 under an earlier title and with a number of illustrations, among them a very small woodcut showing the riderless horse being deceived by a monk holding an olive branch and whip.[35] This image was then used in various forms in a number of editions of 1615 which bore a new title corresponding to that of the English edition. Although none of the editions I was able to consult agrees totally with the Dutch text as reproduced in the London edition, the one nearest to it is that printed by B. J., identified as Broer Jansz of Amsterdam.[36] Comparison of the texts shows differences in spelling and also in the text, e.g. the date in the Amsterdam title is 9 November, in the London edition it is 7 November. As the Dutch title has not been reproduced in the 'Vision', one cannot say that a copy of this particular pamphlet served as a model for the London production whose printers, according to STC, were George Purslowe for the first part and Nicholas Okes for the second. Nevertheless, it is the illustration of Broer Jansz's edition which inspired the English artist who copied it and made rather a better job of it.

Another issue, though its text pages are exactly like those of the preceding piece, has a different, engraved title-page.[37] This image combines the small woodcuts of the 1614 edition, with the horse shown twice: lying down before William, freed from Spanish Inquisition and Spanish Tyranny, and standing warily between the deceitful monk and the sleeping Oldenbarneveld. This elder statesman's great services to the Republic counted for nothing since he was a prominent figure in the Remonstrant, less orthodox, faction in the Dutch Calvinist Church. He wanted an honourable peace with Spain after the truce, but many pamphlets of the time pictured him as in the pay of Philip II. He was soon to be executed as a traitor. The horse is wary because at its feet, ready to be imposed on him, lies the 'tenth penny', the tax levied by the Duke of Alva which was believed to have sparked off the Eighty Years' War. The hills in the background must be those of the Rhineland. The title on the engraving is written in verse: 'Verklaert dit vijsioen, en wilt het wel besien | het is gedroomt seer coen, sestien hondert vijftien' [Explain this vision and study it well; it was dreamt proudly in sixteen hundred-fifteen]. There is the same short title at the head of page A2r as is found in the previously described issue and as in the Dutch text printed by Purslowe on his p. 9, sig. B1r: 'Een Visioen in den droom, inhoudende den voorleden ende teghenwoordighen staet der vereenichde Nederlanden' [A vision in a dream, containing the past and present state of the United Netherlands]. Had the title-page of the original issue been removed and given to the artist? Or did he and the printer

---

35 Kn 2107b.
36 Kn 2175.
37 Kn 2176.

each have a complete copy to work from? The English and Dutch versions of the London edition take up pp. 1-17, sig. A-C1v.

The various editions and issues of the Dutch 'Visioen' all stand alone. Not so Marchant's publication, which after this tour de force adds as many as three other pieces, equally bilingual and similarly propounding warnings against Spain and the Catholic Church.

Thus, after the dream horse, we get a merry dance. It begins on p. 17, sig. C2r, and is entitled 'Looke out, good countrimen, while you have time and tide, | Behold a strange dance made about the Holland bride'. This pamphlet tells of the princes of Europe, including the Pope, each in his own way wooing the Dutch Maid. She only trusts Maurice, while the others make music and dance trying to entice her. Later the dance is described as Moorish or Moresco, i.e. a 'morris dance'. It is a not very subtle warning against those who wished to have the truce eventually extended or, better, transmuted into peace, meaning especially Oldenbarneveld.

The original Dutch pamphlet again exists in a number of different editions and issues, the one of which the British Library owns a copy being entitled *Ghy Patriotten thans,, kijck uut, kijck uut, kijck uut. Siet vvat een vreemden Dans,, om de Hollandtsche Bruut.* Its colophon claims that it was printed 'buyten Antvverpen, in de Druckerije van een Lief-hebber des Vaderlants' [outside Antwerp, in the printing shop of a lover of his fatherland], 1615.[38] A copy of this edition can safely be stated to have been used by the English printer. The evidence is an initial at the very beginning of the text where the first word is 'onlanghs', meaning recently. The other Dutch editions have the correct capital letter O in this place, but the edition represented in the British Library has a large ornamental initial V instead, which could begin the word in the unusual spelling 'unlanghs' (fig. 2).[39] Or it could be read as D and make no sense. Purslowe's compositor read it as a V (fig. 3).[40] This could imply that this compositor was an Englishman rather than a man of Dutch descent, but either could have just copied blindly as compositors tended to do very often anyhow. But what are we to make of the description 'Hollandtsche Bruut'/ 'Holland Bride' in the title, which makes the lady the Maid of the province of Holland rather than of the whole of the Netherlands, while the text only speaks of 'Neerlandt', the 'Netherland', a much wider geographical and political term then as now. Each town and province had its own 'Maid', as did the whole Union. True, the action is set near the sea in a rich and fertile

38 Kn 2177; Sim G90; BL: 11555.e.44(3).

39 p. 3, sig. A2.

40 p. 24, sig. D1v.

3

Ghy Patriotten thans ,, kijck uut, kijck uut, kijck uut,
Siet vvat een vreemden Dans ,, om de Hollandtsche Bruut.

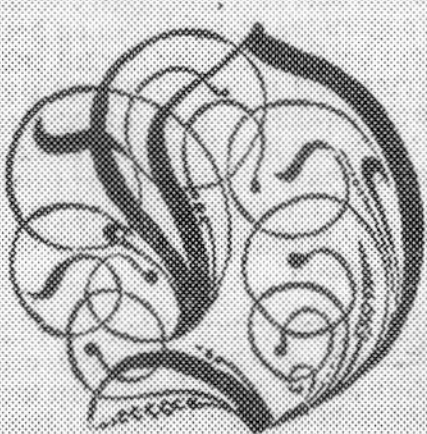

Nlanghs was ick reysende (met myn ghedachten) ende quam in een schoon / vruchtbaer (doch een leegh ofte) Neerlandt, waer in dat stonde acht bezondere Hoven, elck vast betuunt / ende verciert met door-loopende Visch- ende Scheep-rijcke Rivieren; eenighe van dese Hoven oostwaerdts / waren gheleghen ontrent hoogh ende berghachtich Landt / zeer Bosch- ende Vee-rijck: Maer de voorste / voornamelick het eene Hof, was een groene lieflicke Lantsbouwe / aen de noordt-zijde met een vvijdt VVater bezet: Desen Hof scheen de rijckste van ghewas te zijn / ende de cierlickste door de menich-vuldighe Goudt-gheele Bloemen / oock alder-vruchtbarichst van nutte ende proffijtelicke Vruchten / nochtans ghesteelt op een water-achtich ende Hol-landt, niet-te-min als een schoon Prieel ofte Lust-hof / met een edele wel-lustighen Haegh beplant / in welck Prieel een Maeghdelicke Jonckvrouw haer-selven hielde / die men zeyde dat de Bruudt was: Dese Maghet zat op een vaste wel ghemaeckte Stoel / welcke Stoel Eendracht ghenaemt was / hebbende in hare rechter-handt een door-schijnende verd-siende Glas Voorsichticheydt ghenaemt / op hare slincker-handt een Kraen-voghel VVackerheydt ghenaemt / ende sy wierdt om-helst van haer Minnaer / een edel-moedich-manlick persoon / hebbende syne rechter-handt steunen

A ij op

Fig. 2: *Ghy Patriotten thans,, kijck uut, kijck uut, kijck uut* (buyten Antvverpen, in de Druckerije van een Lief-hebber des Vaderlants' [outside Antwerp, in the printing shop of a lover of his fatherland], 1615), p. 3, sig. A2.
British Library pressmark: 11555.e.44(3).

24

Ghy Patriotten , kijck uut , kijck uut , kijck uut,
Siet wat een vreemden Dans,, om de Hollandt-sche Bruut.

VNlanghs was ick reysende (met myn ghedachten) ende quam in een schoon , vruchtbaer) doch een leegh ofte) Neerlandt, waer in dat stonden acht bezondere Hoven , elck vast betuunt , ende verciert met door-loopende Visch ende Scheep-rijcke Rivieren ; eenighe van dese Hoven oostwaerdts , waren gheleghen ontrent hoogh ende berghachtich Landt, zeer Boschende Vee-rijck: Maer de voorste , voornamelick het eene Hof, was een groene lieflicke Lantsbouwe, aen de noordt-zijde, met een wijdt Water bezet: Desen Hof scheen de rijckste van ghewas te zijn, ende de cier-lickste door de menich-vuldighe Goudt-gheele Bloemen, ooch alder vruchtbarichst van nutte ende proffijtelicke Vruchten, nochtans ghesteelt op een water-achtich ende Hol-landt, niet-te min als een schoon Prieel ofte Lusthof, met een edele wel-lustighen Haegh beplant , in welck Prieel een Maeghdelicke Jonckvrouw haer selven hielt , die men zeyde dat de Bruudt was : Dese Maghet zat op een vaste wel ghemaeckte Stoel, welcke Stoel Eendracht ghenaemt was , hebbende in hare rechter-handt een door-schi nende verd-siende Glas Voorsichticheydt ghenaemt, op hare slincker handt een Kraen-voghel Wackerheydt ghenaemt , ende sy wierdt om-helst van-haer Minnaer , een edelmoedich-manlick persoon , hebbende syne rechter handt steunen op syn Swaerdt , ghenaemt Trouwicheydt , ghevest aen een Orangie Wimpel : Rondt om zaten haer Maeghschap,Ghebueren,ende Ghenooten, onder welcke dat waren machtighe Personen, met Kroonen op hare Hoofden,

Fig. 3: *A Vision or dreame contayning the whole state of the Netherland warres ...* (London: printed for Edward Marchant, 1615), p. 24, sig. D1v.
British Library pressmark: 1314.g.16(3).

region, immediately suggesting Holland, the richest, most important and most powerful province of the Republic. But Holland is not named in the text. It seems that the specific adjective of the title not so much confuses as conflates the terms. A strange case indeed.

The dance pamphlet ends on p. 30, sig. D4v, and completes Purslowe's part of the production. A new pagination starts on sig. E1r with a second title-page: *A Short and Faithfull Narration from certaine Citizens of note of the Towne of Goch, concerning the abhominable and wicked Treasons attempted and concluded by eighteene persons to haue beene executed vpon the Townes of Goch, Cleef, Emmeryck, and Rees, discouered by Gods prouidence the last of Februarie. 1615.* At London Printed. 1615. The next leaf is correctly signed E2, but p. 5 bears the erroneous signature A3. E4r appears to be yet another title-page, with the corresponding Dutch text *Corten* [sic] *waerachtich verhael wt de mont van eenighe loffweerdighe Borghers van Goch, vant abominabel ende boos verraet by seeckere achthien persoonen geintenteert ende besloten op de Steden Goch, Cleef, Emmerick ende Rees, door de voorsichtigheyt des alder hoochsten Godts uyt ghecomen op lesten Februwarie, Anno 1615.* TOT VTRECHT, Ghedruckt by Ian Amelissz woonende onder de Laeckensnijders, in vergulde ABC. Anno 1615. This looks at first sight as if an original Dutch-printed edition had been inserted into the London edition of the pamphlets, but it is of course nothing of the sort. Okes had simply copied his model's whole title-page, including its full imprint. The verso of this pseudo-title-page is blank. The text takes up pp. 9-11, sig. F1r-F2r.

This piece in its original Dutch version is once again known in more than one issue.[41] It reports the arrest and trial, not without torture, of citizens of the fortified town of Goch in the northern part of the disputed territory, now in Germany, who are alleged to have conspired to betray it to the Spanish army, with similar plots in the other places mentioned in the title. By painting the terrifying picture of Catholics to the north-east of the Republic, had the conspiracy succeeded, the pamphlet adds yet another dimension to the preceding warnings. It does not yet mention the outcome of the trial, though it promises to provide such information at a later time: there could really be no doubt of what the verdict and sentence would be.

The timely apprehension of the Goch traitors and their trial ends the first piece of Okes's part. The final piece, his second and the fourth in this collection, begins on p. 12, sig. F2v: 'Pope Paul the fift [*sic*] his tenne commaundements giuen to Marquis Spinola, his Sonne' in English, filling pp. 12-13, sig. F2v-F3r, and 'De Spaensche gheboode ingestelt door Paus Paulus

41 Kn 2164, 2165.

V' in Dutch, on pp. 14-16, sig. F3v-F4v. While the occasional couplet or longer rhymed passage occurs in the preceding prose texts, this piece is entirely in verse. I have been unable to find an original Dutch edition of this poem, nor has a copy yet come to light in the *Short-Title Catalogue Netherlands* which, when completed, will describe the holdings of Dutch books in the major Dutch and some foreign libraries, including those of the British Library.[42] Such an original, if it existed independently in print, may have been completely lost, not surprising as it would have consisted of two leaves at best or a broadsheet printed on one side only, or it may be included in another work, as here, and so far not have been described separately, or it circulated only in manuscript. But Edward Marchant had a copy and gave it to Nicholas Okes to print together with its English translation. It is a powerful piece of crude anti-Catholic propaganda, a fitting climax to the whole booklet. The Pope is made to encourage Spinola and his army to misbehave most brutally, e.g.:

> With neighbours house, wife, mayd and man,
> T'your hearts desire, doe what you can,
> Or will: for all their goods and lands
> I freely giue into your hands,

of which the Dutch text reads:

> Met 'snaesten huys, wyf, knecht, end maecht,
> Doet stoutlyck wat v hert behaecht,
> Haer geldt end goet, end wat meer is,
> Toecom 'uwen soldaten fris.

In one stanza Spinola is told to make it appear that he is fighting for the Emperor who must be obeyed: a link here with one of the phrases explaining the illustration of the riderless horse on the main title-page of the London pamphlet, where it is stated that the pope and bishops can change names and call the king's war the emperor's war. The Dutch text of the Pope's Ten Commandments ends each stanza with the injunction to Spinola 'Breeckt de Unie' [break the Union], i.e. the result of the treaty of 1579 binding the rebellious provinces together, thus creating the United Provinces. In the English version this refrain occurs only after the tenth commandment: 'And see you break the Vnion', which here comes like a thunderclap. Both versions end with a 'Conclusion', which in the English version is separated from the Pope's words by a rule, in the Dutch version by a typographical border. Now

42 STCN <http://www.kb.nl/kb/zoek/zoekext.htm#sten>.

the poet himself utters a prayer for the preservation and strengthening of that very Union, which very effectively sums up and ends the whole collection of pamphlets:

> Oh God that art in Heauen aboue,
> Conuert these blind mens hearts to loue,
> that onely on their strength rely,
> Or else destroy them utterly.
> And strengthen still the Vnion.

The question, whether the English reader would really get the same information – or disinformation – from this work as did the Dutch reader, has to be answered without hesitation in the affirmative. The translation is of a high quality, it is faithful without being slavish, it often uses a happier turn of phrase than the Dutch text taken literally would have provided. This applies to both the prose and the verse. The translator is not named and there were quite a number of capable people in London at the time, like Edward Grimestone, to mention only one. But there remains the problem of why the 'Vision' was produced at all in a joint English-Dutch edition. Surely, for the Dutch community in London either copies of the originals imported from the Netherlands or reprinted in London would have served equally well and for English readers the Dutch versions would have been superfluous, even if some of them were able to read them.

The following suggestion is based purely on speculation and has to be taken for what it is worth. In my view it is perfectly clear what the Dutch pamphlets were intended to do in the Republic: to present the perceived danger of renewed Spanish/Catholic domination, even if disguised as imperial power, and rally the opinion of the people in support of Maurice rather than Oldenbarneveld. At the same time the assistance of foreign powers was vital. France was on the Republic's side, though rather lukewarm, while England had a definite interest in preserving this Protestant state and not to let Spain reoccupy what was now the Dutch coastline. But James wanted peace and the present truce was good enough for him. He did allow English and Scottish troops already in the United Provinces to be deployed at the frontier, but it was not a very large contingent and these duties removed them from a possible defence of other areas.

I see in the existence of so many editions and issues of the Dutch pamphlets the desire of their propagator to distribute this material as quickly and as widely as possible. Other pieces of a similar character were also reissued and reprinted and some were translated into English. These and the 'Vision' itself in its bilingual form were reissued in England as well which again suggests the wish to achieve wide distribution.[43] A need for speed can be detected in the shared printing and the possible use of more than one copy of the original to be used concurrently by the translator or printer and the woodcutter. But would not single-language production have been faster as well as cheaper? Here I see again a possible political motive: English readers presented with the Dutch original after the translation were thereby enabled to check the accuracy of the translation and even if unable or unwilling to avail themselves of this opportunity, it was reassurance of a sort that they had been sold the genuine article and not a pretence. But what English reader would have been aimed at? The man in the street could not influence his king's foreign policy one way or another, while concern among the political elite for the maintenance of Protestantism in the Republic could perhaps have an effect on James's advisers, or such might have been the hope of the man or men who paid for this production. I do not believe that Edward Marchant, or William Welbie who put his name on the 'Vision' issue now in the Bodleian Library, were such ardent fans of Prince Maurice that they published this booklet at their own expense. It might rather have been one of Maurice's political adherents who came to England to plead for James's help, who at the same time conducted a little private propaganda campaign, leaving future generations to ponder the strange case of Double-Dutch double vision.

---

43 For another pamphlet explaining the situation in the Republic, much in Maurice's favour, translated into English and also published in 1615, see STC 18437, 18437.5. For other issues of the 'Vision' see ibid., 18446, 18446a.

Peter Hogg

Scandinavian Printing in London in the Eighteenth Century and its Social Background

A mere twenty-five items in Scandinavian languages have so far been identified as printed in London during the eighteenth century. Nine of these are in Danish, published between 1705 and 1793; one is in Icelandic, printed in 1788; while the rest are ephemera in Swedish that appeared during the years 1780-1800. All are directly related to the activities of the Scandinavian community that had emerged in London during the decades after the Great Fire of 1666, when imports of timber and metals expanded, first in order to rebuild the city and subsequently to meet the needs of the expanding British economy.

The printed items identified, by language[1]

In Danish:

1. Penn, William: [A Key Opening the Way to Every Common Understanding] Een liden Nôgel, til at aabne Veyen for alle, som sôge derefter … Schrevet i det engelske Spraag af W. Penn. Oc siden oversat paa Fransk, Hôytydsk, Hollandsk, oc nu paa Dansk, af C. Meidel. [*London*]: *findis til kiôbs hos T. Sowle, i White-Hart-Court i Gracious-street*, 1705. [12], 55, [1]p. 8vo.[2]
2. Dell, William: Βαπτισμων διδαχη: eller Lærdom om Daabe, adskilt fra forrige oc itzige Tiders Misbrug; oc igien bragt til den fôrste Sundhed oc Eenfoldighed … Ved William Dell … *London: tryckt iblant andre hands Prædickener, paa Engelsk, 1652; oc nu oversat paa Dansk af Christopher Meidel*, 1706. [24], 55, [1]p. 8vo.[3]

---

1 Of the items listed below only nos. 1, 2, 4-6 and 10-15 are recorded in the ESTC.

2 British Library (BL), Sloane copy: 856.f.30.(8.) With a dedication 'Til Printz Georg af Dannemark, &c.' – This work was reprinted in 1736 with the imprint: *Tryckt i London hos J. Sowles Arvinger, i George-Yard i Lombard-street*, 1736. 16mo. (J. Smith, *A Descriptive Catalogue of Friends' Books*, vol. I (London, 1867), p. 308.) There is a copy of the reprint in Det Kongelige Bibliotek, Copenhagen (KB, Copenhagen), and it is listed in the ESTC.

3 BL copy: RB.23.a.9899. With an address by Meidel 'Til den Danske og Norske Lutherske Menighed, i London i Engeland' (B1-4, C1-4).

3. R. B. [Barclay, Robert]: [A Catechism and Confession of Faith] En Catechismus oc Trois Bekiendelse … Hvilchen indeholder en sand oc troværdig Summa paa de Principia oc Lærdomme, som hierteligen trois af de Christi Kircher i Engeland oc Irland, som forachteligen kaldis Qvæchere … Ved R. B. … *Tryckt i London: hos J. Sowles Arvinger*, 1717. viii, 182, [2]p. 8vo.[4]

4. Barclay, Robert: [An Apology for the True Christian Divinity] Forsvar for den sande christelige Theologi, som den kundgiôris og prædikis af det Folk, som, af Foragt, kaldis Quækere … Skreven paa Latin og Engelsk ved Robert Barclay, og siden oversat paa Tydsk, Hollandsk, Fransk, Spansk, og nu paa Dansk, af C. Meidel, til Fremmedis underviisning … *London: trykt hos T. Sowle Raylton, i George-Yard, i Lombard-street*, 1738. xviii [i.e. xxvi], 556, [8]p. 8vo.[5]

5. Berthelson, Andreas: An English and Danish Dictionary … Vol. I. *London: printed for the author by John Haberkorn, and sold by A. Linde, bookseller to Her Royal Highness the Princess of Wales, in Catherine-Street in the Strand, and W. Baker, stationer, next the post-office, in Lombard-Street*, 1754. [638]p. 4to.[6]

6. Wolff, Ernst: En dansk og engelsk Ord-Bog … *Trykt udi London: af Frys, Couchman, og Collier, paa Forfatterens egen Bekostning*, 1779. [562]p. 4to.[7]

7. [Wolff, Ernst]: Den Norske-Last-Drager, eller Bord-Reduction, indeholdende Tabeller, der ved förste Öyekast viiser dobbelte og tykkere Bords og Battens Indhold fra 9 til 20 foed lange, fra eet Bord til 10 Tusinde udregnet til det almindelige Maal, eller de saa kaldte Enkelte Bord, hvor efter Fragten af en Ladning retter sig imellem Norge og Engeland. *Trykt udi London: af Frys, Couchman, og Collier*, 1780. [3], 137p. 4to.[8]

---

4 Description from a copy in KB, Copenhagen. (*Bibliotheca Norvegica*, III, 1193; NUC.) Translated by C. Meidel.

5 BL, Sloane copy: 855.i.7; with two leaves of errata. – According to *Bibliotheca Luxdorphiana*, pt. I (Havniae, 1789), p. 287, B. W. Luxdorph (1716-88) owned two copies of a London 1738 reprint of (1) and a 1705 issue in addition to the 1706 issue of (2), apart from a copy each of (3) and (4). (The first two may be ghosts, however, as neither a 1738 reprint of Penn nor a 1705 issue of Dell is now known.)
J. Worm, in his *Forsøg til et Lexicon over danske, norske og islandske lærde Mænd*, Dl. II (Kiøbenhavn, 1773), under 'Meidel, Christopher', refers only to items (1), (2) and (4) above. R. Nyerup and J. E. Kraft, *Almindeligt Litteraturlexicon for Danmark, Norge, og Island* (Kjøbenhavn, 1820), list Meidel's first translation as: '*William Penn*'s liden Nøgel for at aabne Vejen for Alle til Qvækernes Religion … London 1706', but no reissue with that title has been traced.

6 BL (King's Library and Hannås) copies: 69.e.2; Han. 8. – The orthography of the Danish text in the dictionary, printed in roman, is non-standard, using lower case initials for nouns (including 'prinds') and ö instead of ø. (*Bibliotheca Norvegica*, III, 828.)

7 BL (Old Library, General Library, Banks and King's Library copies): 1333.h.19; 12972.q.3; 434.c.6; 69.e.3. – The Banks copy contains the note (in English): 'A present from the Author for Aron Mathesius. London 9th Oct. 1779.' Mathesius (see below) may have given the volume to Banks before he left London in 1784. (*Bibliotheca Norvegica*, III, 528.)

8 Description from a copy in KB, Copenhagen. (*Bibliotheca*, II, 4681.)

8. [Wolff, Ernst]: The Norway Wood Carrier, or Reduction of Norway deals, containing curious tables, which show in a moment the contents of 1¼, 1½, 2, 2½, 3, and 4 inch deals and battens, from 9 feet long and upwards to 20 feet long, calculated from one deal to ten thousand, and reduced to the usual standard measure or single deals; after which the freight between the southern part of Norway and England is regulated. By the author of the Danish and English dictionary. The second edition. *London: printed by Frys and Couchman*, 1785. 135p. 4to.[9]

9. [Wolff, Ernst]: Den Norske-Last-Drager, eller Bord-Reduction ... Udgivet af Author af det förste danske og engelske Dictionair. Den tredie Edition. *London: trykt af W. Hales, stationer, Fenchurch Street*, 1793. [12], 145, [1]p. 4to.[10]

In Icelandic:

10. Fragments of English and Irish history in the ninth and tenth century. In two parts. Translated from the original Icelandic, and illustrated with some notes, by Grimr Johnson Thorkelin ... *London: printed by and for John Nichols; printer to the Society of Antiquaries*, 1788. xi, [1], 59, [1]; 95, [1]p., [1] leaf of plates (map). 4to.[11]

In Swedish:

11. Wesley, John: [The Cure of Evil-speaking] Bot emot förtal. En predikan öfver Matth. xviii. 15, 16, 17. Öfversatt ifrån engelskan. *London: trykt hos Frys, Couchman och Collier*, 1780. x,18p. 12mo.[12]

12. Mathesius, Aron: Guds besynnerliga omsorg för sjömannen uti stormen. En predikan öfver Psal. CVII. 23-32. Hållen, uti Portsmouth hamn, den 31 jan. 1781. *London: tryckt hos Frys, Couchman, och Collier*, 1781. 30, [2]p. 12mo.[13]

---

9 Description from a copy in KB, Copenhagen. (*Bibliotheca Danica*, III, 898.) Parallel text in Danish and English; Danish title: *Den Norske-Last-Drager, eller Bord- Reduction ... Udgivet af Author af det förste danske og engelske Dictionair. Anden Edition.* Trykt udi London: af Frys og Couchman, 1785.

10 Description from *Bibliotheca Norvegica*, II, 4682. Parallel text in Danish and English.

11 BL (General Library, Banks, King's and Grenville) copies: 1572/471; 454.d.3; 454.e.6; 188.a.9; G.3303; G.5399(8). Parallel text in Icelandic and English. – The work forms no. XLVIII (part VIII of the sixth volume) of the collection 'Bibliotheca topographica britannica'. The preface is dated 'London, November 2, 1788'.

12 Kungliga Biblioteket, Stockholm (KB, Stockholm): Rar 584. Translated by 'A. M.' (i.e. Aron Mathesius). – Reprinted in Göteborg in 1819.

13 KB, Stockholm: Rar 581. – Reprinted without changes in Göteborg 1782 and 1786, Stockholm 1783 and 1827 and Gävle 1785. (A copy in Uppsala University Library was once owned by Mathesius's successor in London, S. C. Nisser, who clearly intended to publish a second edition of it, as he made various ms. amendments and additions, including the words 'Andra Uplagan' on the title-page.)

13. Vid herr doctor Daniel Solanders grift, den 13, [*sic*] maj, 1782. Af dess sörjande landsmän och vänner i London. [*S. l.: s. n.*, 1782.] [4]p. 4to.[14]

14. Wid doctor Daniel Solanders graf, den 19, maj, 1782. [*S. l.: s. n.*, 1782.] [4]p. 4to.[15]

15. Mathesius, Aron: Reglor, at förnya vårt förbund med Gud, öfversatte från engelskan, af Lars Peter Schenmark. *London: tryckt hos Frys och Couchman*, 1783. 34, [2]p. 12mo.[16]

16. [Trustees for Ramsgate Harbour:] The Bye Laws of Ramsgate Harbour. Swedish. [*S. l.: s. n.*, 1793?] 24, [4]p. 8vo.[17]

17. American Agency Office: To the Inhabitants of Europe. Aux habitans de l'Europe. Till alla folkslag i Europa. An die Einwohner von Europa. [*London: s. n.*, 1795.] [2]p. 1o.[18]

18. London Missionary Society: Vänlig erinran från Mission-Samfundet uti London, til alla christendoms bröder, så präster som lekmän uti konungariket Sverige. [*S. l.: s. n.*, 1798?] [4]p. 2o.[19]

19. Nordiska Sällskapet: *Begins:* Det Nordiska Sällskapet uti London önskar göra sig påmint hos alla dess frånvarande ledamöter … [*London: s. n.*, 1798.] [2]p. 4to.[20]

20. [Nisser, Samuel C.]: *Begins:* Det nya engelska Mission-Samfundet förmodar jag vara långt för detta kändt uti Sverige ehuru icke så noga och allmännt som det förtjenar … [*S. l.: s. n.*, 1798.] 6, [2]p. 4to.[21]

---

14 BL: 1871.e.1(17). An epitaph. – A manuscript 'Epitaph for Daniel Solander' by 'B[aron] Nolcken' is preserved among the Banks papers at California State University in San Francisco (*Daniel Solander 1733-1782* (Piteå, 1983), p. 169), indicating that the text was composed by the Swedish envoy in London, G. A. von Nolcken, and that Banks arranged for its printing.

15 BL: 1871.e.1(16). In verse.

16 KB, Stockholm: Rar 583; Teol., Uppbygg., (Br.), 4.

17 KB, Stockholm: Rar. 609. Cover title. Final leaf pasted to back cover. – Text in Swedish, including: 'Utdrag af Parlaments acten, fastständ uti det 32, aret of [*sic*] Hans Konglige Mayestät af Stora Britannien, konung George den III. regering, rôrande underhàllandet och fôrbättrandet af Ramsgates hamn, uti grefskapet Kent, och fôr Sandwichs hamns rensande, fôrbättrande, och wid magt hàllande, belägen i samma grefskap'.

18 KB, Stockholm: Rar. 624. Caption title. Single sheet, folded twice. – Dated in ms. 'London 25 August 1795', signed 'Barrell & Servanté', sealed and addressed on the back to 'P. Lindahl Junr. Esqr. Norkioping'. (The English text begins: 'The Era of Reason is now dawning upon Mankind …')

19 KB, Stockholm: Sv. Saml., Teol., Sällsk., Mission, Utl., (Br.), Fol. 1700-1829. Caption title. Printed in Gothic type, which was still common in Sweden.

20 KB, Stockholm: Sällsk., Int. o. utl., (Br), Okat. Single sheet, folded; last two pages blank. Copy dated London, 12 April 1798 and signed in ms. by S. C. Nisser (as 'Ordförande'), Claes Grill and Ernst Wolff.

21 KB, Stockholm: Rar. 649 and three other copies. – Includes: 'Korrt berättelse om Mission-Samfundet uti London' (pp. [5-6]). All four copies are signed in ms. 'S. C. Nisser' and dated 1 May 1798.

21. [Nisser, Samuel C.]: Skål af swenska coopvardie-farare, talrikt samlade på Paul's Head Tavern, uti London, den 21 november, 1798. [*S. l.: s. n.*, 1798.] 4p. 4to.[22]

22. [Hackson, H.]: Sånger vid middags måltiden då Nordiska Sälskapet i London den 21 december 1799 firade födelsen af Sveriges kron-prins. [*London*:] *printed by J. Skirven, Ratcliff-Highway*, [1799]. 12p. 8vo.[23]

23. [Nisser, Samuel C.]: De förtrogna systrarnas skål högtids-dagen, 1799. [*S. l.: s. n.*, 1799.] [2]p. 8vo.[24]

24. [Nisser, Samuel C.]: Afskeds-skål. [*S. l.: s. n.*, 1800?] [4]p. 8vo.[25]

25. [Nisser, Samuel C.]: *Begins:* Vid Svenska församlingens allmänna kyrkomöte den 20de sistledne april gjordes proposition: om ett hus i Princes Square, Ratcliff-Highway, til säkert boställe för svenske pastorn uti London. ... [*London: Skirven, typr. Ratcliff-Highway*, 1800.] [2]p. 8vo.[26]

The London printers

All four of the tracts translated by Christopher Meidel (1-4) were printed by T. Sowle, the first two at White-Hart-Court in 'Gracious-street' (Gracechurch Street), the last two at George Yard in Lombard Street. They were presumably paid for by the Society of Friends.[27] Tace Sowle (1667-1749) was a remarkable Quaker woman who began her career in 1691 as an assistant to her father and took over his printing and bookselling business in 1695. After her marriage in 1706 to Thomas Raylton (d. 1723), a printer in Lombard Street, her name was replaced on the works that she produced by that of her widowed mother Jayne and, after the latter's death in 1711, by her 'assigns'. In 1736 she reappeared under her own name as T. Sowle Raylton and continued to be the main London printer for the Society of Friends until her death.[28]

---

22 KB, Stockholm: Rar. 650.

23 KB, Stockholm: Rar. 654. Signed: H – . The author, H. Hackson, became a 'trustee' of the Swedish church in 1801.

24 KB, Stockholm: Rar. 653. Caption title.

25 KB, Stockholm: Rar. 648. Caption title. – Printed by J. Skirven in London between 1798 and 1800.

26 KB, Stockholm: Kyrko, Sv., (Br.), 1800, Okat. Copy dated from No. 13, Princes Square, 7 May 1800, signed (in ms.) 'S. C. Nisser' and addressed to 'Mr G. Carsberg, Great Windmill St'. Circulated to 'Svenska församlingens trustees, kyrkovärdar och contribuerande ledamöter'.

27 The Norwegian iron magnate and collector Carl Deichman (c. 1705-1780), who owned copies of items (1) and (4) (*Catalog over det Deichmanske Bibliothek* (Christiania, 1850), pp. 10, 64), wondered in the case of the latter who could have financed the printing of such a substantial work to promote the cause of the Quakers (A. Arnesen, *Boken om bøker*, I (Oslo, 1926), p. 151).

28 H. R. Plomer, *A Dictionary of Printers and Booksellers ... from 1668 to 1725* (Oxford, 1922), pp. 277-8; P. H. Muir, *The Library*, 4th ser., 14 (1933), 150-70; R. S. Mortimer,

The printer of Berthelson's dictionary (5), Johann Christoph Haberkorn (fl. 1749-67), was a German who had originally set himself up in 1749 as a bookseller in Gerrard Street, Soho, but then acquired a printing press on which he printed books in English, German, French and Italian from 1751 onward.[29] Many of the German titles were religious works produced for the Lutheran and Moravian communities in London, whereas most of his output in English and other languages consisted of secular works.

An advertisement in German for Andreas Linde at the end of Berthelson's dictionary shows that he supplied books in English, French, Latin and German and indicates that it was he who acted as the main distributor of this item. Linde was a German bookseller and bookbinder who established himself in Catherine Street north of the Strand around 1751. In 1753 he collaborated with Haberkorn in publishing a German translation of Bunyan's *The Pilgrim's Progress* and in 1755 he published *The Natural History of Norway*, translated by Berthelson, but on 28 November 1758 he sold his stock, as he was 'going into another way of business'.[30]

The second distributor, William Baker, was a stationer in Lombard Street on his own during 1753-4, having been in a partnership with George Dawson at the same address during the previous decade. He was to form a new one there as Baker and Fourdrinier (1755-65) and may also have been the man of that name who was a partner of the bookseller Daniel Baker at Stationers Court, Ludgate Street 1752-5 and occasionally acted as a joint publisher with him between 1746 and 1764.[31]

The printers of the dictionary published by Wolff in 1779 (6) – Joseph Fry (1728-87), Stephen Couchman (fl. 1779-1824) and Collier – had only formed their partnership in that year at 8 Queen Street, Moorfields, where Fry had been in business since he moved from Bristol to London in 1766.[32] They also printed the first edition of Wolff's timber trade manual (7) in the following year, as well as the first two items associated with Mathesius (11-12) during 1780-1.[33] In 1782 Fry's sons Edmund (1754-1835) and Henry (fl. 1782- 1808)

'Biographical Notices of Printers and Publishers of Friends' books up to 1750', *Journal of Documentation*, vol. 111, no. 2 (London, 1947), p. 121.

29 He is listed as a printer in Gerrard Street 1755-65 (H. R. Plomer, *A Dictionary of the Printers and Booksellers ... from 1726 to 1775* (Oxford, 1932), p. 112) and also in Grafton Street, Soho, in 1763 (I. Maxted, *The London Book Trades 1735-1775* (Exeter, 1984), p. 15).

30 Plomer (1932), p. 156; ESTC.

31 Plomer (1932), p. 13; Maxted (1984), p. 2; ESTC.

32 I. Maxted, *The London Book Trades 1775-1800* (Folkestone, 1977), pp. 54, 86.

became partners with their father and a year later Collier withdrew, leaving only the Frys and Couchman as printers of the third Mathesius item (15) in 1783 and the second edition of Wolff's manual (8) in 1785.

John Nichols (1745-1826), who acted as both printer and publisher of Thorkelin's work (10) in 1788, had been an independent printer in Red Lion Passage, Fleet Street (as well as an author in his own right), since 1778, when he also became editor of the *Gentleman's Magazine*.[34] His premises had been destroyed by fire only two years earlier,[35] but he was able to print the Icelandic texts quite elegantly, using special types for *þ* but lower-case *d* for *ð*. As early as 1773 Nichols had collaborated as an apprentice with his master William Bowyer in printing the typographically far more complex Anglo-Saxon version of Orosius.

The third edition of Wolff's manual (9) was printed in 1793 by William Hales, a stationer and bookseller in Fenchurch Street 1782-1825.[36] On the other hand, the printers of most of the Swedish-language items from the years 1793-8 are not identified. The regulations for Ramsgate harbour (16) are badly set, whereas the prospectus from the American Land Agency (16) and the two items relating to the London Missionary Society (18, 20) are reasonably well produced but lack many of the requisite special characters.

For at least seven years from 1798 onward John Skirven (d. 1817), who was in business as a printer from 1781 at the corner of Old Gravel Lane and Ratcliffe Highway in Wapping, was the one favoured by the Swedish community.[37] Although his name only appears on two of the listed items, dating from 1799 and 1800 (22, 25), his style is recognisable in some others from that period.[38]

---

33 The fact that Joseph Fry, who was a Quaker, had printed a number of works for Wesley in 1777, including his five-volume *Survey of the Wisdom of God in the Creation*, may have brought him to the attention of Mathesius even before Ernst Wolff gave the latter a copy of his dictionary in October 1779 (see n. 7 above). – The two Solander items (12-13) may also have been printed by Frys, Couchman and Collier.

34 Plomer (1932), p. 180. See also the article on Nichols in *DNB*.

35 W. B. Todd, *A Directory of Printers ... London and Vicinity 1800-1840* (London, 1972), p. 139.

36 Maxted (1977), p. 98. Hales had commissioned printing work as early as 1774 and acted as a printer himself since at least 1784.

37 Maxted (1977), p. 206; Todd, op. cit., p. 176.

38 Nos. 19, 21, 23-24. In 1805 Skirven printed *A Short Introduction to Swedish Grammar, adapted for the Use of Englishmen* (ii, 96, iii, 40p. 12mo) by the incumbent Swedish pastor in London 1802-14, Gustaf Brunnmark (see n. 117).

The social contexts of the publications

The two dozen printed items described above are divided between those written by clergymen with a religious purpose, works of a practical nature and items, mostly ephemeral, associated with the social activities of the Scandinavian élite in London. The two dictionaries printed in 1754 and 1779 (5-6) were both linked with the Norwegian timber trade, while the Swedish-language regulations for Ramsgate harbour (16) and the prospectus for settlers in North America (17) were produced for English and American businessmen connected with the Swedish community. The single academic publication in this group is the collection of historical texts edited by Thorkelin (10). Only the Quaker tracts translated into Danish by Meidel (1-4) and the sermons and mission tracts (11-12, 15, 18, 20) produced by the Swedish pastors Aron Mathesius (1771-84) and Samuel Nisser (1791-1802) were intended for a wider readership than the small middle-class element in London.

The Scandinavian Lutheran community had built its own church in 1696 in Wellclose Square, Wapping, but in 1710, after the outbreak of war between their countries, the Swedish minority separated itself from the Danes and Norwegians and rented a chapel in Ratcliffe Highway, next to St George in the East. Their second pastor (1712-23) was Olof Nordborg (1681-1745). Soon after taking over, in 1713 or 1714, he printed and distributed a circular to the Swedish congregation, urging it to contribute more for the upkeep of its chapel. That is the earliest recorded Swedish item to be printed in London, but no copy of it appears to survive.[39]

Nordborg's successor Jakob Serenius (1723-33), a friend of Sir Hans Sloane, a lexicographer and a member of the Royal Society from 1731, was able to collect enough money to build a new Swedish church in Princes Square, now Swedenborg Square, in Stepney, in 1728.[40] By then, however, he was already involved in a conflict of authority with the Swedish envoy in London.[41] The clash between ecclesiastical and state interests in the London

---

39 S. Evander, *Londonsvenskarnas kyrka genom 250 år* (Lund, 1960), pp. 31, 46.

40 One reason for his success was the favour he gained with the Swedish Parliament by publishing a work on English agriculture and sheep-farming, *Engelska åker-mannen och fåra-herden* (Stockholm, 1727), based on John Mortimer's *Whole Art of Husbandry*, 5th edn (London, 1721).

41 As early as 1724 Serenius clashed with the Swedish envoy Count Sparre, who wanted one of his children (whom Serenius had already christened) to be re-baptised, with King George I as its godfather. When Serenius refused the count is said to have drawn his sword against him.

In July 1733 Serenius wished to travel to Hamburg to print the English-Swedish

churches was to flare up again in both Scandinavian congregations during the 1760s and 1770s, in each case being resolved in favour of the home government.[42]

Lutherans and Quakers

The four earliest Scandinavian-language items printed in London (1-4) were translations into Danish of works by English non-conformists. The translator of all of them was the Norwegian ex-clergyman Christopher Meidel, whose life provides an early example of the influence of English non-conformity in Scandinavia. Born around 1660 at Langesund in southern Norway, where his father became a timber trader, he attended a school at Roskilde in Denmark until 1677 and then the University of Copenhagen before being called by the Scandinavian merchants in London to serve as their pastor from the autumn of 1687.[43] Until then all the Lutherans in London had attended the German church in Little Trinity Lane in the City, but in that year a number of Scandinavians who did not understand German and lived east of the City decided to form a separate congregation, acquired premises in Old Gravel Lane in Wapping and invited Meidel to take charge of the new church.

When the Toleration Act was passed in 1689 Meidel began to introduce some non-conformist doctrines and practices into his services. Complaints about these 'divisive innovations (*schismatische Neuerungen*)' were investigated by the Danish envoy H. H. von Ahlefeld.[44] Meidel was obliged to resign his office in 1690 but continued for a time to hold private services (described as '*ein eigenes Conuenticulam*' [sic]) in his own house, while some members of the congregation returned to the German church. Ahlefeld tried to bring him to order, first by friendly persuasion and then by a harsher approach ('*auf meine*

dictionary that he had compiled with the encouragement of Bishop Gibson of London, *Dictionarium anglo-suetico-latinum* (Hamburg, 1734), in the preface to which he asserted that English was a 'daughter language' of Swedish. Sparre had ordered Serenius to apply for permission whenever he left London and when the instruction was ignored the envoy lost his temper and publicly struck the pastor in the face in St James's Park. Serenius then left for Hamburg and Sweden, where he was to end his career as a bishop (S. Evander, op. cit., pp. 48-69). He published a second part of the dictionary in Sweden in 1741 as well as a second edition of the first part (as *An English and Swedish Dictionary*) in 1757.

42 See n. 86.

43 See the entry on 'Meidel, Christopher Gertsen' by L. Selmer in *Norsk biografisk leksikon* (Oslo, 1939).

44 He was in London 1690-1 to discuss the defensive alliance under which Danish troops had been supplied for the Irish campaign of William III in 1689.

theils gütliche und scharfe erinnerung'), after which Meidel promised to discontinue the house meetings.[45] It was then decided to draw up a set of rules for the Danish-Norwegian congregation and to employ another Norwegian pastor, Iver Brink (1665-1728).[46]

Meidel was subsequently employed as a preacher and schoolmaster by one of the many London congregations of Calvinist-inspired Independents, located in Nightingale Lane, East Smithfield, Wapping, where he married an Englishwoman and had several children. He was gradually attracted to the Society of Friends, but for a long time his family responsibilities prevented him from leaving the Independents. Around 1699, however, he did finally join the Society,[47] became acquainted with its leaders, including William Penn (1644-1718), and was employed as a missionary.

In 1702 Meidel returned to his homeland, allegedly bringing with him 'some sackfuls of Quaker tracts which he distributed among his countrymen, but, having been reported by the clergy, they were all banned and confiscated',[48] although there is no evidence that any of the Danish translations of such publications were printed before 1705. He stayed at Skien, where he had many relatives, including the local postmaster, and then with his older brother Gerhard, who was the parish priest at Holden (Holla) in Telemarken. He is said to have engaged in arguments with other local clergymen,[49] which so worried the rector of Skien, Nyeborg, that he approached his bishop, Hans Munch. On 16 November 1702 the latter appealed to the governor for assistance against a threat worse than that of Catholicism, as the Quakers 'wish to overturn all authority in the republic as well as all order in the kingdom of

---

45 Ahlefeld's report to King Christian V of 27 Feb. 1691, reproduced in E. F. Wolff, *Samlinger til Historien af den danske og norske evangelisk-lutherske Kirke i London* (Kiøbenhavn: Sebastian Popp, 1802), p. 395.
In the address that Meidel wrote for Dell's tract in 1706 he claims to have been deposed because he had, for reasons of conscience, denied communion to certain members of the congregation. See also H. Faber, *Danske og Norske i London og deres Kirker* (København, 1915), pp. 45-47.

46 Brink had been a chaplain with the Danish regiment in Ireland and arrived in London from Limerick in August 1691.

47 J. G. Bevan, *Piety Promoted … The tenth part*, 2nd edn (London, 1811), p. v. – Nyerup and Kraft, op. cit. (1820), stated that Meidel was only dismissed after joining the Quakers (which is incorrect) and subsequently lived in poverty. The source for their claim that he 'finally converted to the Catholic religion and went to Ireland' is unknown.

48 B. W. Luxdorph, *Luxdorphiana*, pt. 1 (Kiøbenhavn, 1791), p. 284.

49 Including a three-day debate with Halvor Nielsen Gjerpen (pastor at Eidanger 1685-1712), according to a note by Carl Deichman in his copy of Worm's *Forsøg* (Dl. II, 32; see n. 5) reproduced by A. Arnesen (n. 27).

God'.[50] Meidel was arrested in December and convicted of religious subversion by an ecclesiastical court at Skien the following February, when he was deprived of his clerical status and deported back to England.[51]

It was probably after his return to London in 1703 that Meidel translated the tracts by Penn and Dell (1-2).[52] For the Danish version of his *Key*, the English original of which had been published in 1693, Penn wrote a dedication to Prince George of Denmark (d. 1708), the consort of Queen Anne, expressing the hope that 'Denmark, among other countries, will come to know a people who are so misrepresented'. The translation of Dell's tract contains an address to the Danish and Norwegian Lutheran congregation in London, dated from Chelmsford prison on 5 June 1706, in which Meidel explained his gradual conversion to Quakerism.[53]

In 1708 he travelled to France, where he was also imprisoned for a time in Paris, according to a letter dated 22 August 1708 that he wrote from there to his fellow-Quaker William Sewel (1654-1720) in Amsterdam.[54] He had been arrested two weeks earlier at 'Pont'[55] on his way to Lille and 'brought, chained

---

50 Terje Christensen, *Gjerpen bygds historie*, II (Skien, 1978), pp. 286-7.

51 E. F. Wolff, op. cit., p. 4. – For the Danish-Norwegian legislation on religious dissenters 1690-1772 see 'Den norske Dissenter-Lov', *Theologisk Tidskrift*, 1 (Christiania, 1846), pp. [47]-164.

52 William Dell (d. 1664) became an antinomian during the English civil war; his work on baptism was first issued in 1648.

53 In the same year Meidel contributed a learned theological preface to the third part of John Tomkin's *Piety Promoted* (London: T. Sowle, 1706, 12mo), a collection of writings by persecuted Quakers. It was later said that he had been jailed for publicly contradicting the pastor of the Danish church in London, who at the time (1702-13) was Jørgen Lauridsen Ursin.
According to John Whiting's bibliography *A Catalogue of Friends Books* (London, 1708; with descriptions completed from J. Smith, op. cit., vol. II, 172) two English texts by Meidel were printed in folio in 1706: (1) *To My Neighbours, and Others, in and about Stratford, near Bow in Essex, assembled to dance on the 1st of the 3rd month, called May-Day, 1706.* ([London]: printed by T. Sowle, in White-Hart-Court, in Gracious Street; 4p.) and (2) *Directions to Collect Matters for a General History of the Entrance and Progress of Truth in this Age: by way of annals.* ([S. l.: s. n.]; [2p.]). The first of these was also printed by T. Sowle in a small octavo in 1706, but only the folio edition of that title is listed in ESTC.

54 The letter was reproduced in the 'Historical account' prefixed to J. G. Bevan, op. cit., pp. v-vi. (It is presumably the 'Narrative' of 1708 referred to by J. Smith, loc. cit.)
The French translation of Penn's *Key*, entitled *La Clef pour ouvrir la voye* (Londres: T. Sowle, 1701) [856.f.26], was attributed to C. Meidel in the British Museum Library catalogue, but the attribution is doubtful, as a long list of errors (on 21 of the 42 pages of text) had to be inserted with the explanation that 'le traducteur, n'étant pas bien imformé [sic] des principes de ceux que l'on appelle Trembleurs, a fait quelques méprises, qui ont donné occasion à un errata'.

55 Perhaps Pont-Audemer or Pont-à-Vendin in northwestern France.

to other prisoners', to the Grand Châtelet prison in Paris where, despite haranguing the bystanders ('Repentez vous de vos péchés, o vous Parisiens', and so forth), he was treated 'civilly and kindly'. The greetings in the letter indicate that Meidel himself had earlier visited Amsterdam, Rotterdam and Haarlem. In 1717 his translation of Barclay's *Catechism* (3) was published and in 1738 that of the *Apology* (4).[56]

An attempt to distribute a consignment of Quaker tracts in Norway in 1739 was described by Hans Gram (1685-1748) in a letter written from Copenhagen on 29 April 1740 to the Swedish bishop Eric Benzelius about religious dissidence in Denmark:

> From Norway a parcel of books that had arrived from England was sent down here to the General Church Inspectorate. It contained many copies of the small Quaker books and their catechisms translated into Danish from the writings of Penn and others and printed in England in roman type. The translator and distributor of these books is an old Norwegian Quaker by the name of Christen Meidel, who fifty years ago was the Danish pastor of the Lutheran church in London. Abandoning that office, he joined the Quakers, indeed before the turn of this century he had the same kind of Quaker tracts distributed in his homeland. Among these is an item on baptism, from which our shoemakers and furriers may learn what they did not know before.[57]

Meidel and his family are known to have lived at Stratford in east London in the early years of the eighteenth century.[58] Deichman and Gram assumed that he was still alive as late as 1738 or even 1740, but in fact nothing certain is known about him during the three preceding decades.[59]

---

56 Robert Barclay (1648-90), a Quaker leader, published his *Catechism* in 1673 and the English version of his *Apology* in 1678.

57 *Breve fra Hans Gram* ... (Kiøbenhavn, 1907), p. 189. Gram explained that dissidents were visited by Lutheran clergy and that unrepentant ones were offered the choice of emigrating or of moving to one of two specified towns: Fredericia in Jutland or Friedrichstadt in Schleswig-Holstein.

58 Perhaps at Maryland Point near Stratford, where Meidel's friend John Tomkins died in September 1706 (J. G. Bevan, op. cit., p. v).

59 For Deichman see n. 27. Selmer (n. 43) believed that Meidel had died before July 1715. See also Dagfinn Kvale, 'Norges første kveker og hans dramatiske skjebne', *Kirke og kultur*, 98 (1993), 43-4.
Remaining copies of Meidel's 1738 Danish translation of Barclay's *Apology* were given by local Friends to Norwegian prisoners of war at Chatham between 1807 and 1814. A number of them were converted and in 1818 founded the first Norwegian branch of the Society of Friends at Stavanger (B. Furre, *Kirke og kultur*, 98 (1993), 404), where Meidel was commemorated two decades later by a publication entitled *Om den danske Præst i London, Christopher Meidels Overgang til Vennernes (eller de saakaldte Qvækernes) Samfund* (Stavanger, 1837).

Danish dictionaries and Norwegian timber

The five remaining Danish items consist of two dictionaries and three editions of a commercial manual, produced by two other Norwegians resident in London. The English-Danish dictionary compiled by Andreas Berthelson (5) (fig. 1)[60] bears a dedication to Christian, Crown Prince of Denmark and Norway, and an address to the readers, the first in both English and Danish, the second only in Danish. The bilingual dedication to the Danish royal family emphasises 'the novelty of the attempt' of producing a Danish-English dictionary and refers to the author's intention that it should be of 'specific use to those who may wish to study either of the languages, whether to improve their education and knowledge or for convenience and profit in trade and commerce'. The subscription list shows that of the 218 subscribers 154 lived in Norway, thirty each in Great Britain and Denmark and four in Sweden. The commercial usefulness of the work is attested to by the fact that the subscribers included forty-eight Norwegian captains and fifteen merchants.[61]

The author of the Danish-English dictionary of 1779 (6), Ernst Fredrik Wolff (1734-1808), was engaged from 1767 onward in the timber and shipping business in London together with his younger brother Georg Wolff (1736-1828). Both were born in Christiania (Oslo), from where Georg moved to London in 1759, to be joined there later by Ernst. For many years they lived near the Danish church in Wellclose Square, but with the growing success of the firm of Wolff & Dorville, which they established in 1783, they eventually moved to Balham, where they resided for the rest of their lives.

In the preface to his dictionary, which was dedicated to the new Danish Crown Prince Frederik, Ernst Wolff explained that the timber trade between Norway and England made it necessary for many Norwegians to learn English.[62] Rather than spending up to £300 doing so in England, however, he suggested that they should be able to learn the language either by using his

---

60 Berthelson (originally Bertelsen) was born in Kristiansand around 1716. As a theology student he had assisted at the Danish church in London during the illness of its pastor 1746-8.

61 One of the subscribers was the incumbent Swedish pastor in London 1749-61, Carl Noring. – Berthelson intended to produce a second, Danish-English volume, which was never completed. He did, however, translate *Det første Forsøg paa Norges naturlige Historie* (Kiøbenhavn, 1752-3) by Erik Pontoppidan, which was published in folio by Andreas Linde as *The Natural History of Norway* (London, 1755).

62 The preface is dated London, 1 Sept. 1779. Wolff had used the English dictionaries of Abel Boyer, Nathan Bailey (published by W. and D. Baker in 1764) and Samuel Johnson in compiling his own.

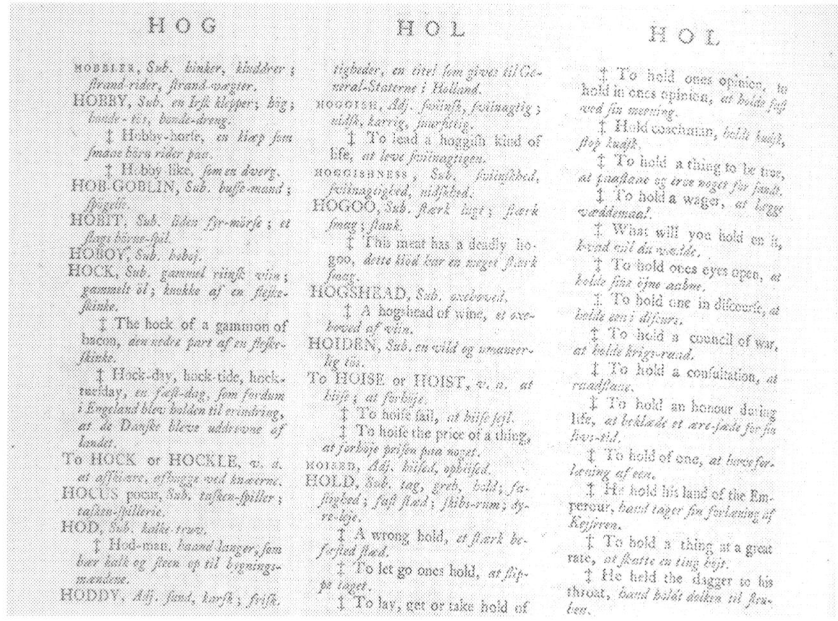

HOG

HOBBLER, *Sub. hinker, kludrer; ſtrand-rider, ſtrand-vægter.*
HOBBY, *Sub. en Irſk klepper; bög; bonde-tös, bonde-dreng.*
‡ Hobby-horſe, *en hæp ſom ſmaae börn rider paa.*
‡ Hobby like, *ſom en dværg.*
HOB-GOBLIN, *Sub. bufſe-mand; ſpögelſe.*
HOBIT, *Sub. liden fyr-mörſe; et ſlags börne-ſpil.*
HOBOY, *Sub. hoboj.*
HOCK, *Sub. gammel rinſk viin; gammelt öl; knokke af en fleſke-ſkinke.*
‡ The hock of a gammon of bacon, *den nedre part af en fleſke-ſkinke.*
‡ Hock-day, hock-tide, hock-tueſday, *en feſt-dag, ſom fordum i Engeland blev holden til erindring, at de Danſke bleve uddrevne af landet.*
To HOCK or HOCKLE, *v. a. at affkiære, afhugge ved knæerne.*
HOCUS pocus, *Sub. taſken-ſpiller; taſken-ſpillerie.*
HOD, *Sub. kalke-trug.*
‡ Hod-man, *haand-langer, ſom bær kalk og ſteen op til bygnings-mændene.*
HODDY, *Adj. ſund, karſk; friſk.*

HOL

tigheder, en titel ſom gives til General-Staterne i Holland.
HOGGISH, *Adj. ſviinſk, ſviinagtig; nidſk, karrig, ſmerſtig.*
‡ To lead a hoggiſh kind of life, *at leve ſviinagtigen.*
HOGGISHNESS, *Sub. ſviinſkhed, ſviinagtighed, nidſkhed.*
HOGOO, *Sub. ſtærk lugt; ſtærk ſmag; ſtank.*
‡ This meat has a deadly hogoo, *dette kiød har en meget ſtærk ſmag.*
HOGSHEAD, *Sub. oxehoved.*
‡ A hogshead of wine, *et oxehoved af viin.*
HOIDEN, *Sub. en vild og umanerlig tös.*
To HOISE or HOIST, *v. a. at hiſe; at forhöje.*
‡ To hoiſe ſail, *at hiſe ſejl.*
‡ To hoiſe the price of a thing, *at forhöje priſen paa noget.*
HOISED, *Adj. hiſed, ophiſed.*
HOLD, *Sub. tag, greb, hold; faſthed; faſt ſted; ſkibs-rum; ſyre-löje.*
‡ A wrong hold, *et ſtærk beſeſted ſted.*
‡ To let go ones hold, *at ſlippe taget.*
‡ To lay, get or take hold of

HOL

‡ To hold ones opinion, to hold in ones opinion, *at holde faſt ved ſin meening.*
‡ Hold coachman, *hold kudſk, ſtop kudſk.*
‡ To hold a thing to be true, *at ſtaaſtaae og troe noget for ſandt.*
‡ To hold a wager, *at lægge væddemaal.*
‡ What will you hold on it, *hvad vil du vædde.*
‡ To hold ones eyes open, *at holde ſine öjne aabne.*
‡ To hold one in diſcourſe, *at holde een i diſcurs.*
‡ To hold a council of war, *at holde krigs-raad.*
‡ To hold a conſultation, *at raadſlaae.*
‡ To hold an honour during life, *at beklæde et ære-ſæde for ſin livs-tid.*
‡ To hold of one, *at have forlæning af een.*
‡ He hold his land of the Emperour, *hand tager ſin forlæning af Keiſeren.*
‡ To hold a thing at a great rate, *at ſkatte en ting höjt.*
‡ He held the dagger to his throat, *hand holdt dolken til ſtruben.*

Fig. 1: Andreas Berthelson, *An English and Danish Dictionary* … (London: printed for the author by John Haberkorn, and sold by A. Linde, bookseller to Her Royal Highness the Princess of Wales, in Catherine-Street in the Strand, and W. Baker, stationer, next the post-office, in Lombard-Street, 1754), vol. I. British Library pressmark: 69.e.2.

dictionary or else by attending a school that could be established in Norway with annual fees of no more than twenty *rixdaler*. Wolff next produced the manual for timber traders (7-9) of which four editions were printed in London, the second (1785), third (1793) and fourth (1804) being bilingual, with parallel English text. His final service to his adoptive community was to compile a history of the Danish-Norwegian church in London until 1775, which was published in Copenhagen in 1802.[63]

Scandinavian scholars and their patrons

Of the many Scandinavian scholars who spent some time in London during the eighteenth century only two are associated with items printed there in their vernaculars. One was a Swede, the other an Icelander.

63 See notes 45 and 117.

Daniel Solander (1735-82) came from Piteå in the far north of Sweden, studied from 1750 at the University of Uppsala, where he became an amanuensis of Carl Linnaeus, and arrived in London in June 1760. From 1763 he was employed in the Natural History department of the newly opened British Museum, became a friend of Joseph Banks and accompanied him as botanist on the first voyage to the Pacific with Cook during the years 1768-71. On his return Solander brought with him lime saplings from the Cape of Good Hope that were planted around the Swedish church in Stepney, as well as grass seed that was sown on the surrounding green.

During the following decade he served as Banks's librarian in Soho Square while also resuming work at the Museum from 1773.[64] He died suddenly on 13 May 1782 and was buried a week later beside his countryman

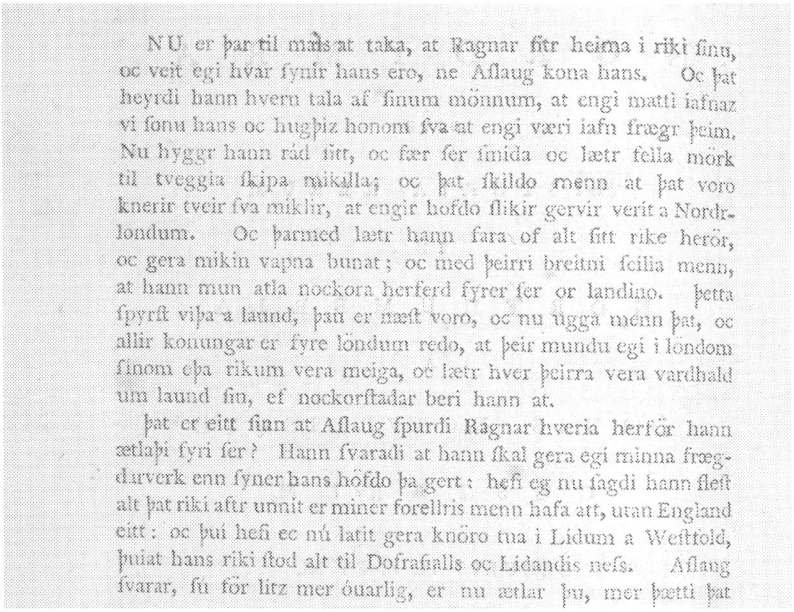

NU er þar til máls at taka, at Ragnar ſitr heima i riki ſinu, oc veit egi hvar ſynir hans ero, ne Aſlaug kona hans. Oc þat heyrdi hann hvern tala af ſinum mönnum, at engi matti iafnaz vi ſonu hans oc hugþiz honom ſva at engi væri iafn frægr þeim. Nu hyggr hann rád ſitt, oc fær ſer ſmida oc lætr fella mörk til tveggia ſkipa mikilla; oc þat ſkildo menn at þat voro knerir tveir ſva miklir, at engir hofdo ſlikir gervir verit a Nordr-londum. Oc þarmed lætr hann fara of alt ſitt rike herör, oc gera mikin vapna bunat; oc med þeirri breitni ſcilia menn, at hann mun atla nockora herferd fyrer ſer or landino. Þetta ſpyrſt viþa a lannd, þau er næſt voro, oc nu ugga menn þat, oc allir konungar er fyre löndum redo, at þeir mundu egi i löndom ſinom eþa rikum vera meiga, oc lætr hver þeirra vera vardhald um laund ſin, ef nockorſtadar beri hann at.

Þat er eitt ſinn at Aſlaug ſpurdi Ragnar hveria herför hann ætlaþi fyri ſer? Hann ſvaradi at hann ſkal gera egi minna frægdarverk enn ſyner hans höfdo þa gert: heſi eg nu ſagdi hann fleſt alt þat riki aftr unnit er miner forellris menn hafa att, utan England eitt: oc þui heſi ec nú latit gera knöro tua i Lidum a Weſtfold, þuiat hans riki ſtod alt til Dofrafialls oc Lidandis neſs. Aſlaug ſvarar, ſu för litz mer óuarlig, er nu ætlar þu, mer þætti þat

Fig. 2: *Fragments of English and Irish history in the Ninth and Tenth Century. In two parts. Translated from the original Icelandic, and illustrated with some notes, by Grimr Johnson Thorkelin …* (London: printed by and for John Nichols; printer to the Society of Antiquaries, 1788), p. 2 (detail).
British Library pressmark: G.5399(8).

64 He is remembered there as the designer of 'Solander boxes'.

Swedenborg[65] in the crypt of the Swedish church. It was presumably the Banks family that organised the funeral and paid for the lapidary epitaph and the sheet of commemorative verse in Swedish (13-14), both anonymous, that were hurriedly printed during the intervening days.[66]

Four years later the Icelandic scholar Grímur Jónsson Thorkelin (1752-1829) arrived in London. After a few years of study at Copenhagen University from 1773 onward Thorkelin began his academic career by editing half a dozen medieval texts before 1786, when he travelled to Britain with a commission from his government to search out and copy documents relating to the history of the Danish realm. During his time in London Thorkelin produced two works of his own – the anonymous pamphlet *An Essay on the Slave Trade* (London: G. Nicol, 1788)[67] and *Fragments of English and Irish History* (10)[68] – as well as editing E. R. Mores's *De Ælfrico, Dorobernensi archiepiscopo, commentarius* (London, 1789)[69] The *Fragments* was included in the series 'Bibliotheca topographica britannica' which the printer John Nichols edited and published in 52 parts between 1780 and 1790 (fig. 2).

The texts selected by Thorkelin for the *Fragments* were two Icelandic prose narratives regarding Northumbria in the viking era, namely 'Nordymra' (a version of *Ragnars saga loðbrókar*) and a section of *Laxdæla saga*, which form the bulk of the first and second parts of the work (apart from Thorkelin's

---

65 Emanuel Swedenborg (1688-1772) produced four substantial works (including the 8-volume *Arcana cœlestia*, 1749-56) and four pamphlets in London between 1745 and 1758, as well as a leaflet in 1769, but all of these were printed in Latin, mostly by John Lewis of Bartholomew Close in the City. (The second edition of Linnaeus's *Flora lapponica* was likewise printed in London in 1792, in Latin.)

66 The epitaph appears to have been composed by the Swedish envoy in London, Baron Nolcken (see n. 14). The printed verse is written in the first person plural to represent the Swedish community as a whole, presumably by one of its leading members. – These items have probably only survived because they were paid for by Solander's employer Sir Joseph Banks and were kept as mementos by the latter's sister Sophia Sarah Banks (1744-1818); after her death they passed with the rest of her collections to the British Museum.

67 The Banks copy in the BL [B.491(3)] bears the ms. dedication 'To Sir Joseph Banks Baron President of the R. S. from the author.' In the *Essay* Thorkelin made use of the same passage from *Laxdæla* that he was to use in the *Fragments*, adding the flattering footnote (p. 4): 'This curious manuscript is now, among many other, in the possession of the British Museum, owing to the public spirit and unrivalled liberality of Sir Joseph Banks, baronet, president of the Royal Society, &c.'

68 The *Fragments* was printed in a style (using *þ* but not *ð*) similar to that adopted for the three Icelandic texts published in Copenhagen in 1780 and 1782, in collaboration with Thorkelin, by James Johnstone, chaplain to the British embassy there (*Anecdotes of Olave Black*; *Lodbrokar-quida*; and *The Norwegian Account of Haco's Expedition against Scotland*).

69 For Anglo-Saxon names in Mores's work the printer (Charles Clarke) used *ð* but not *þ*.

notes), two short extracts from *Eyrbyggja saga* and *Landnáma* describing voyages to Ireland in the tenth century and some Norwegian ecclesiastical documents of 1319-29, mostly in Latin, relating to the Orkneys.[70] All the Icelandic texts are accompanied by parallel English translations, while 'Nordymra' is also followed by a Latin translation.[71] The engraved frontispiece map shows the British Isles between the ninth and thirteenth century as they were described by Icelandic historians.

Thorkelin dedicated his work to Francis Lord Rawdon (1754-1826), which he explained in a letter to his Danish patron Johan von Bülow on 5 June 1789: 'My decision to dedicate the book to Lord R. arises from his respect for our nation; his friendliness towards me, and the fact that he descends from the ancient Danish princes through the Counts of Huntingdon.' More to the point, he added: 'It is from his father, the Earl of Moira, that I can expect to receive the best reception in Dublin and throughout Ireland, where I hope to be during the months of July and August.'[72] On 21 May 1790 Thorkelin told Bülow that he had declined an offer, made three days earlier through the Archbishop of Canterbury, of a position in the British Museum as successor to Dr Woide. In the spring of 1791 he returned to Copenhagen, where he finally fulfilled his long-pursued ambition of being appointed head of the Royal Archives.[73]

---

70 A century earlier George Hickes (1642-1715) had included an Icelandic vocabulary in his *Institutiones grammaticæ anglo-saxonicæ et mæso-gothicæ* (Oxford, 1689), pt. II, 97-132. In the first volume of his *Thesaurus linguarum septentrionalium* (1703-5) Hickes replaced that vocabulary with a different one (pt. III, 73-91), while adding a facsimile of a Swedish 'runic' text (pt. IV, 123-47) that unfortunately turned out to be a forgery.

71 The translator of the English version of the 'Nordymra' text was the Scots antiquarian John Pinkerton (1758-1826). According to Thorkelin he was associated with the publisher John Bell (1745-1831), but he could have been recommended to Thorkelin by George Nicol or John Nichols, who produced works for both men. (The latter had printed Pinkerton's 'Hardykanute, an heroic ballad' in 1783.)
Writing on 2 January 1787 to Johan von Bülow – whom he informed that he was working on 'an Icelandic account of the invasion of England by the Danes, in particular in Northumberland in the eighth century' – Thorkelin referred to 'Mr Pinkerton' as an 'enthusiastic Nordic-Dane' (A. Glahn, 'Mæcen og Klient: af en Brev Veksling mellem to Bogvenner 1785-1790', *Aarbog for Bogvenner*, 9 (1925), 61-2). He may, however, have fallen out with him after the appearance of Pinkerton's *Dissertation on the Origin and Progress of the Scythians or Goths* later that year in London ('printed by John Nichols, for George Nicol'), for Thorkelin provided his own English translations for the second part of the *Fragments*.

72 Glahn, op. cit., p. 73.

73 He held that post for the rest of his life, his main achievement being to produce the first edition of the text of the Beowulf poem that he had found in the British Museum, *De Danorum rebus gestis ... poema* (Copenhagen, 1815). See K. S. Kiernan, *The Thorkelin Transcripts*, Anglistica, 25 (Copenhagen, 1986).

Methodism and authority in the Swedish church

Aron Mathesius (1736-1808), the Swedish pastor in London who officiated at the funerals of both Swedenborg and Solander, was born at Pyhäjoki in Ostrobothnia in Finland as the youngest of twenty-five children of the local clergyman.[74] Two of his brothers were already involved in radical politics in the early 1760s while he was still a student at Uppsala University. He left in 1764 with a master's degree and spent the next three years as a tutor in the household of the dean Carl Noring (1717-86), who had been pastor of the Swedish church in London until 1761 before returning to Sweden to teach theology in Uppsala.[75] It was probably Noring who found a position in London for Mathesius, who was priested at Åbo (Turku) in Finland in December 1767 and travelled to England the following spring to become assistant to the Swedish pastor there, Noring's successor Arvid Ferelius.

Not long after his arrival in London Mathesius met a former landlord of Emanuel Swedenborg, Mr Brockmer, whom he 'led off to the house of Mr Burgman, the Minister of the German Church in the Savoy', in whose presence he took a statement from Brockmer concerning the religious crisis that Swedenborg had undergone in London in 1744.[76] Some years later Mathesius gave a copy of this account to John Wesley, who published a translation of it in his journal.[77] He must have become attracted by

---

74 See the article by Thure Månsson on Mathesius in *Svenska män och kvinnor* (Stockholm, 1949). The British Library possesses three books once owned by Mathesius, his copy of the Swedish Bible (a reissue of the 1703 edition), a Finnish-language Lutheran hymn-book and the copy of Wolff's dictionary presented to him by the author: (1) *Biblia, thet är: All then helga skrift* … (Stockholm, 1720) [3041.b.2] (purchased in 1877); (2) *Uusi suomenkielinen wirsi-kirja* … (Turusa, 1772) [868.h.22] (donated by Mathesius to the British Museum in November 1775); and (3) E. Wolff, *En dansk og engelsk Ord-Bog* (London, 1779) [434.c.6] (see n. 7).

75 With money inherited in 1753 from his uncle Lars Victorin, a wealthy iron trader in London, Noring bought an estate in Sweden in 1765. (Victorin had come to London in 1709 with the returning British envoy, John Robinson, 1650-1723, who had served in Sweden since 1689 and became Bishop of London in 1713.)

76 W. White, *Emanuel Swedenborg* (London, 1867), pp. 220-5. As Mathesius had allegedly stated that Swedenborg had retracted his views on his deathbed, or even that he was a 'lunatic', some of Swedenborg's followers retaliated by insinuating that Mathesius, on his departure from London in 1784, was himself mentally ill. White summarises the controversy (pp. 231-2); but see also R. L. Tafel, *Documents Concerning the Life and Character of Emanuel Swedenborg*, II (London, 1877), pp. 586-604, 1304-7.

77 'An account of Baron Swedenborg', *Arminian Magazine*, 4 (Jan. 1781), 46-9. – After suffering a stroke at his lodgings in Clerkenwell in December 1771 Swedenborg was advised to send for Mathesius, who was then acting pastor. The old man objected so much to the latter's views, however, that Ferelius (who was still in London) had to be called instead, as he was again before Swedenborg died in March 1772, though it was Mathesius who conducted Swedenborg's funeral.

Methodism very soon after his arrival in London, for as early as July 1769 a Swedish visitor, J. H. Lidén, reported in a letter home that Mathesius and the young diplomat Malte Ramel were 'commonly referred to as Methodists'.[78]

Unfortunately for Mathesius, Pastor Ferelius had become involved in a bitter dispute with the Swedish envoy Baron Gustaf Adam von Nolcken (1733-1812), who had arrived in London in 1763 and was to retain his position there for three decades. The envoy was determined to establish control over the Swedish church, which had come to be dominated by its lower-class members in Wapping who outnumbered the merchants in the City. In Nolcken's view the former – mostly seamen, but 'partly publicans and partly the so-called crimps' – were a social rabble.[79] Their spokesman at that time was the expatriate radical Christopher Springer.[80]

In October 1769 Nolcken attempted to impose a new set of rules on the church but failed and sent a highly critical report to Sweden the following year. To counter that, Ferelius and his supporters wrote in 1771 both to the archbishop and to the new king, Gustaf III. At that time Mathesius was regarded in Wapping as Nolcken's man. In November 1771 Ferelius resigned and left his assistant in charge of the church,[81] and when the succession was confirmed two years later Mathesius was deliberately appointed both as legation chaplain and pastor in order to place him under the authority of the envoy.

---

78 S. Rydberg, *Svenska studieresor till England under frihetstiden* (Uppsala, 1951), p. 391. Johan Hinric Lidén (1741-93), a friend of C. B. Wadström (see below), was the author of the anonymous letters from abroad that C. C. Gjörwell published in his *Tidningar om lärda saker* in Stockholm during 1768-70. In one of them, sent from London in December 1769, he described a tour through the library galleries of the British Museum, following the order of his guidebook, *A Companion to Every Place of Curiosity … in … London* (London, 1767), but adding his own comments.
Malte Ramel (1747-1824) had only been in London since 1767 and was to be transferred to the Swedish legation in Paris in 1770.

79 Nolcken's report to the Swedish government 20 Feb. 1768, quoted in G. W. Carlsson, *Anteckningar rörande svenska kyrkan i London* (Stockholm, 1852), p. 56. – For the dispute see also C. V. Jacobowsky, *Svenskar i främmande land under gångna tider* (Göteborg, 1930), pp. 121-6.

80 In October 1765 Aron's brother Johan Mathesius (1709-65) had been sent from Stockholm to London with a message for the exiled Christopher Springer (1704-88), who had just been pardoned, but he died on board his ship in the Thames before they met: see D. Tilas, *Anteckningar och brev från riksdagen 1765-1766* (Stockholm, 1974), p. 146.

81 Mathesius covered vacancies in the Danish church during 1770-1 and 1773-4 (Wolff, op. cit., pp. 359, 383).

During the following years the situation appeared to be returning to normal. The traveller J. J. Björnståhl, who was in England during 1775-6, described a dinner to celebrate the birthday of the Swedish king given in February 1776 by the wealthy young merchant Claes Grill (1750-1816)[82] at the London Tavern, 'the largest inn in London', for sixteen prominent Swedes. The guests included Pastor Mathesius, the chargé d'affaires P. O. von Asp, Christopher Springer, Daniel Solander and the leading businessmen in London.[83]

Two weeks later, however, the conflict was rekindled when a meeting of the parish council at 'Mrs Brandt's coffee house'[84] near the Exchange decided to buy the house in Princes Square where Mathesius lived. Springer, who now sided with Baron Nolcken against the 'Wapping crowd', blocked the plan by refusing, as a trustee, to authorise the payment.[85] At the end of the year Nolcken himself clashed with Mathesius, who resisted a renewed attempt to introduce the proposed constitution for the church. In April 1777 the envoy reported to Stockholm, charging the pastor with a long list of irregularities and offences, including that of 'creating disunity within the congregation by which the lower classes are incited against their superiors and led to believe that they possess rights that do not belong to them'.

With government support the envoy suspended Mathesius in February 1778, introduced the new church rules in November and then reinstated him in March 1779. The establishment had won the last round.[86] A year later Mathesius translated Wesley's *Cure of Evil-speaking* into Swedish (11) and followed that up during the next two years by publishing a sermon that he had preached to the crews of three Swedish ships in Portsmouth (12) and a religious tract (15). The latter was originally written in English,[87] as if for use outside the Lutheran congregation – though many of the Swedish families

82 Grill's family had acted as Swedenborg's bankers in Amsterdam.

83 Jacob Jonas Björnståhl, *Resa til Frankrike, Italien, Sweitz, Tyskland, Holland, Ängland, Turkiet och Grekland*, dl. II (Stockholm, 1780), p. 217. – In May 1775 Solander had arranged for Björnståhl to visit the Department of Manuscripts in the British Museum, and in 1776 he showed C. B. Wadström and A. U. Grill (who were on a Continental tour) round the museum, where he then resided.

84 Also known as 'Swenska Caffehuset' (the Swedish coffee house).

85 Springer, who was a Swedenborgian, may have turned against Mathesius because of the latter's hostility to Swedenborg's doctrines.

86 A similar crisis arose in the Danish church at that time (1778-80), ending with the dismissal of the pastor, Alexander Holm, for attempting to give the congregation a larger role in the affairs of the church. That led to a serious conflict with the treasurer Georg Wolff, brother of Ernst, who refused to pay Holm's salary (H. Faber, op. cit., pp. 113-16).

87 Its title means 'Rules to renew our covenant with God'.

established in London were bilingual by the 1780s – and was translated for publication by the twenty-five-year-old Swede L. P. Schenmark.

By then Mathesius was clearly exhausted, however. 'After working and preaching for sixteen years in the smoke of the east of London his health failed.'[88] When he fell ill in the summer of 1783 Nolcken arranged for a replacement, and after the arrival of the new pastor in the following spring Mathesius returned to Sweden.[89]

Maritime trade, Swedenborgianism and colonial utopias

Some time after March 1793 a Swedish version of the by-laws for Ramsgate harbour (16) was printed. Ramsgate served the Baltic trade, and many of the 500 ships a year that entered its harbour during the 1790s came from Sweden. The booklet covers such matters as customs inspections, tonnage, ballast, anchorage, docking and fines and includes an account of a meeting in London on 7 November 1792 of the commissioners who were responsible for the harbours of Ramsgate and Sandwich as well as an abstract of a recent parliamentary act concerning them.[90] An advertisement on the recto of the last leaf for the stockbroker Nicholas Lutyens of 5 Martin's Lane, Cannon Street, a member of Lloyds and of the Hamburg division of the Exchange, suggests that it was he who sponsored the printing of the regulations in Swedish.

There is clear evidence, however, for a direct connection between the emigration prospectus in four languages, including Swedish, produced in August 1795 by the American Agency Office at 24 Threadneedle Street (17) and some of the Swedes in London. It was issued by the American Colborn Barrell and the Englishman Henry Servanté[91] and was aimed at 'such as may be inclined to associate for settling a Commonwealth on their own Code of Laws, on a spot of the Globe no where surpassed in delightful and healthy

---

88 W. White, op. cit., p. 232.

89 He spent the next two decades teaching in Västergötland, married in 1789, published another sermon in 1799 and was finally appointed rector of another parish in the same diocese in 1805. A collection of moral texts translated from English by Mathesius appeared as *Warningar emot dryckenskap, spel och sabbathens wanhelgande* ... (Skara, 1807).

90 See *An Act for the Maintenance and Improvement of the Harbour of Ramsgate* [32 Geo. II. c. 74] (London, 1795), effective from 27 June 1792.

91 For Henry Servanté (1742-1817), a close associate of the Swedenborgians Robert Hindmarsh, A. Nordenskiöld and C. B. Wadström, see R. L. Tafel, op. cit, II, 1187-9, and R. Hindmarsh, *Rise and Progress of the New Jerusalem Church* (London, 1861).

Climate and fertile Soil; claimed by no civilized Nation and purchased under a sacred treaty of Peace and Commerce … of the friendly natives'.[92]

The territory in question, supposedly 'comprehending 4 degrees of latitude, or 240 miles square' in an unspecified part of North America, had been acquired by Captain J. Kendrick, who had been sent there in 1787 by the Boston merchant Joseph Barrell and others to open up a trade in furs to China.[93] The prospectus referred to an account of that venture in *An Essay on Colonization* recently published in London by the Swedenborgian 'philanthropist' Carl Bernhard Wadström (1746-99) and noted that the deeds for the purchased land had been registered with the American consul in China.[94]

Captain Kendrick had reported to Joseph Barrell from Canton on 28 March 1792 that he had bought 'five tracts of land' on the northwest coast of America, but he never returned to Boston or sent the deeds to his employer.[95] The latter must, however, have obtained information about the purchases from other captains, for in January 1793 he wrote to Kendrick that the lands

---

92 In May and July 1794 the American Agency had issued several circulars relating to land at Franklinville, Kentucky from 31 Threadneedle Street. In October 1796 Barrell and Servanté were conducting their American land agency from Ingram Court, Fenchurch Street (ESTC).
The English text of the 1795 prospectus (from a copy in the library of the Massachusetts Historical Society, with the ms. date 'London 18 August 1795') is reproduced on pp. 60-2 of F. W. Howay, 'An Early Colonization Scheme in British Columbia', *British Columbia Historical Quarterly*, 3 (Jan. 1939), 51-63.

93 Kendrick's instructions of 1787 included the phrase that 'it would not be amiss if you purchased some advantageous tract of land in the name of the owners'.
Logbooks and correspondence relating to the earliest American voyages to British Columbia are printed in *Voyages of the 'Columbia' to the Northwest Coast 1787-1790 and 1790-1793*, ed. F. W. Howay, Massachusetts Historical Society collections, 79 (Boston, 1941). See also F. W. Howay, 'John Kendrick and His Sons', *Quarterly of the Oregon Historical Society*, 23, no. 4 (Dec. 1922), 288-9. (In the summer of 1792 Kendrick and his crew killed some fifty Haida people during an incident off the Queen Caroline Islands.)

94 C. B. Wadström, *An Essay on Colonization*, II (1795), pp. 6, 363.

95 The five deeds were summarised in *House of Representatives Document No. 43* (26th Congress, 1st session, 1840; 14p.) and printed in full with associated documents in *Senate Committee Report No. 335* (32nd Congress, 1st session, 1852; 32p.). They show that John Kendrick had 'bought' the tracts of land from Ahausath and La'o'qwath (Wakashan) chiefs at various points on the Pacific coast of Vancouver Island (Nootka and Clayoquot Sound) between 20 July and 11 August 1791 for 18 muskets, three sails, some gunpowder and an American flag. In reality they amounted altogether to only about 50 miles square, much of that being water, and extended over less than one degree of latitude, 49°10′-50′ N. (A Swedish-owned ship, *Gustavus III*, Capt. Thomas Barnett, traded on the same coast in the summer of 1791.)

'appear to be of little value, but in some future time they may possibly be worth possessing.'[96]

Joseph Barrell had still not received the original deeds when he wrote from Boston to his brother Colborn in London on 1 December 1794, a few days before Kendrick was killed in Hawaii: 'If you wish for large employ, I can give you commission to sell upwards of six millions of acres on the north-west coast of America, better land and better climate than Kentucky.' On 18 June 1795 he wrote again to Colborn that the deeds were 'registered in the office of the American consul' in China and covered 'four degrees of latitude, or two hundred and forty miles square' – the very phrases that were to be used in the London prospectus two months later.

The wording of the prospectus itself indicates a close association of Barrell and Servanté with Wadström, who was a dedicated advocate of colonisation as a means to improve the world morally.[97] That is confirmed by the fact that they and their relatives appear in 1794 among the subscribers to his *Essay* for eleven copies, more than the nine copies ordered by the 'Northern Society, Cateaton St.' in London, though far surpassed by the 100 copies subscribed for by Claes Grill.[98] Their association with the Swedenborgians in London can indeed be traced back to the founding by Wadström, Robert Hindmarsh and others of the New Jerusalem Church in Cheapside in 1788.

---

96 At about the same time (1 March 1793) Kendrick sent copies of the deeds from Hong Kong to Thomas Jefferson suggesting an act 'to secure the property of these purchases to me, and the government thereof to the United States'. (It was these copies that were published in 1840 and 1852, the originals having been lost in the East Indies around 1798.)

97 Wadström included in his *Essay* (II, 182) 'Outlines of a plan for forming an Association, in order to establish a new and free Community out of Europe, and beyond the sphere of its political, financial and (especially) commercial influence'.

98 Joseph Barrell in Boston subscribed personally for three copies. The other 284 subscribers to the *Essay* included many Britons associated with the abolition movement, the Sierra Leone colony and the exploration of Africa, from Sir Joseph Banks to 'Gustavus Vassa, a native of Africa'; members of the Scandinavian establishment, such as the Swedish ambassadors in London and Paris (L. von Engeström and C. Staël von Holstein); the Danish and Swedish pastors in London and the Swedish archbishop Uno von Troil; the Norwegian timber merchant Ernst Wolff; the Swedish botanists Anders Sparrman (who had travelled to West Africa with Wadström in 1787) and Adam Afzelius (who was then in Sierra Leone); and many other individuals, including P. Lindahl (the addressee of the copy of the prospectus in KB, Stockholm) and eight other Swedes resident in Wadström's home town of Norrköping.

A year after that event August Nordenskiöld (1754-92), who was to die in Sierra Leone, had published a *Plan for a Free Community upon the Coast of Africa, under the Protection of Great Britain* (London: R. Hindmarsh, 1789) which would simultaneously benefit the Africans and realise Swedenborg's social ideal of a 'New Jerusalem'. It was signed by the Swedes Nordenskiöld and Wadström, Colborn Barrell ('from America') and the Prussian Johan Gottfried Simpson.[99] Nordenskiöld became a member of the editorial board of *The New-Jerusalem Magazine* (London, 1790), the managing editor of which was Henry Servanté. It is clear, therefore, that in 1794-5 Joseph Barrell was making use of the Swedenborgian connections of his relative Colborn in a cynical but, as it turned out, fruitless attempt to sell his Pacific 'tracts' in Europe.[100]

Evangelicalism, patriotism and drinking songs

The remaining items (18-25) are connected in various ways with the Swedish pastor in London, Samuel Nisser (1760-1814), who served there for eleven years from 1791.[101] The first and third of these provide evidence of Nisser's personal interest in the English missionary societies. As early as 1793

99 E. W. Dahlgren, 'Carl Bernhard Wadström ...', *Nordisk Tidskrift för Bok- och Biblioteksväsen* (1915), 24.
In 1789 the Swedish artist C. F. von Breda exhibited two portraits at the Royal Academy in London: one of Baron Nolcken and the other of Wadström instructing an African youth in Swedenborg's doctrines (E. Hagen, *En frihetstidens son* (Stockholm, 1946), p. 158). In the same year Wadström published an abolitionist pamphlet called *Observations on the Slave Trade* (London: James Phillips, 1789). When he was obliged to auction his possessions in London in November 1790 he bought back a copy of Nordenskiöld's *Plan*, together with copies of Barclay's *Apology* and Swedenborg's *Heaven and Hell* (Dahlgren, op. cit., p. 33).
An attempt to establish a British colony on Bulama Island close to Sierra Leone was made by the Bulam Association formed in 1791. At the same time a Sierra Leone Association (to which several members of the Grill family belonged) was founded in London, and a year later it began sending settlers to the Freetown colony, founded in 1787, including a number of Swedes, among them Nordenskiöld (who died there), Adam Afzelius and Daniel Wilhelm Padenheim. Georg Wolff, a leading member of the Northern Society, was also a director of the Sierra Leone Company, which held a meeting in March 1794 at the Paul's Head Tavern, Cateaton Street, where the Society had its headquarters.

100 Wadström moved to Paris in 1795 to continue his endeavours there and is said to have lent his only remaining copy of the *Essay* to Bonaparte, who took it with him on the expedition to Egypt in 1797 (Hagen, op. cit., p. 183).

101 See the note on Nisser by Hans Gillingstam in *Svenskt biografiskt lexikon*, XXVII (Stockholm, 1990-1), 75.

he had written an account of the Society for Promoting Christian Knowledge and of the Society for the Propagation of the Gospel in Foreign Countries for the journal of the Swedish society Pro Fide et Christianismo (PFC),[102] which had been established in 1771 by Carl Magnus Wrangel and Malte Ramel on the model of the SPCK but under strong Methodist influence.[103]

In 1795 the London Missionary Society was founded, and at its meeting on 7 November 1797 it decided to print a short address to other Protestant churches, urging them to support missions among the heathen on a non-sectarian basis. Nisser was approached to provide a Swedish translation of the address, which he did (18),[104] adding a separate appeal of his own to the Lutherans in Sweden, dated 1 May 1798 (20), with a brief account of the first missions of the Society to Tahiti, Sierra Leone and the Cape of Good Hope. He transmitted the printed addresses to PFC in Sweden, which elected the two signatories of the LMS statement as foreign members on 1 December 1798.[105]

---

102 'Berättelse om tvänne de betydligaste religions-samfund uti London, och några missioners närvarande tilstånd …', *Svenska Samfundets Pro Fide et Christianismo Samlingar*, bd. I, st. 3 (Stockholm, 1795), pp. [193]-230, dated London, 1793. He probably also wrote the report of the same date on the Society for Promoting Religious Knowledge among the Poor (ibid., bd. I, st. 4, 1798, pp. [299]-318).

103 S. J. Nilson, *Samfundet Pro Fide et Christianismo* (Stockholm, 1921), pp. 18-19; R. Murray, *Samfundet Pro Fide et Christianismo under 200 år* (Stockholm, 1971).
During 1759-68 C. M. Wrangel had served as pastor of the Swedish congregations in North America, where he heard George Whitefield preach, and on his way home he also met John Wesley in England. Among the chairmen of PFC during its early years, apart from Wrangel and Ramel, was the future archbishop von Troil, who had taken part in Joseph Banks's trip from London to Iceland in 1772. By 1788 its members included both the former London pastor Aron Mathesius (who had also joined the SPCK) and his successor Andreas Leufvenius (1784-90).

104 It was reprinted in Göteborg in 1798 as *Wänlig erinran från Mission-Samfundet uti London.* – In 1796 Nisser married Sara Margaretha Brunnmark during a visit to Sweden. On 30 May the same year he wrote to the Swedish government, suggesting that the pastor in London should also act as a cultural attaché in England and as an agent ('commissionaire littéraire') for supplying books from there to the research libraries in Sweden, but his proposals were not accepted (Evander, op. cit., p. 134; O. H. Selling, *Svenska Linnésällskapets årsskrift* (Uppsala, 1960), p. 135).

105 Rowland Hill (1744-1833) and John Love (1757-1825), chairman and foreign secretary of the LMS. – When Nisser reported the failure of the Tahitian mission in the autumn of 1799 the PFC published his letter and an appeal for donations to be sent to England in the newspaper *Stockholms-Posten* on 1 November 1799. It also published an account of the LMS, *Missions-Societeten i Ängland*, 2 vols (Stockholm, 1799-1801), as well as circulars in support of the missions in West Africa and the Pacific, dated 1 Jan. 1800, and in South Africa, dated 26 Jan. 1803 (Nilson, op. cit., pp. 19, 21).

In April 1798 the Northern Society in London issued a circular (19), signed by the committee members S. C. Nisser (as chairman), Claes Grill and Ernst Wolff, urging members abroad to write letters to the 'brotherhood' through the Swedish consul once a year on any subject of their choice.[106] The Society had been established a dozen years earlier by the Norwegian timber merchant John Collett (1758-1810), who from 1780 to 1793 lived in London, where his house in Wellclose Square provided a focus for the Scandinavian social élite. In 1786, having been elected superintendent of the Danish-Norwegian church, Collett founded 'Det Nordiske Selskab i London' with the aim of maintaining contacts with Scandinavia and promoting patriotic enterprises.[107] In a letter sent to Bülow on 3 November 1786, Thorkelin commented: 'Three nations lived in London, unacquainted with one another, each avoiding the other: by an amicable tie they are now united and will try to extend useful knowledge by means of publications.'[108]

Of the series of publications begun by the Society only two appeared, however. The first issue of *Samling af Skrifter, udgivne fra det Nordiske Selskab i London* (Kiøbenhavn, 1788) contained a prize-winning essay on patriotism by the Norwegian pastor Johan Nordahl Brun, together with his poem 'Fiskerierne'.[109] The second and last issue in 1790 included an address ('Indtrædelses Tale') given in London by the Norwegian timber merchant Bernt Anker and a patriotic poem by his fellow-countryman Andreas Bull.[110]

After Collett's departure from London in 1793 the society came to be dominated by its Swedish members,[111] although the presence of the

---

106 Claes Grill was Swedish consul general in London 1786-1815.

107 See the article on Collett by S. H. Finne-Grønn in *Norsk biografisk leksikon* (Oslo, 1926). Twenty-five Scandinavian publications published between 1785 and 1792 and stamped 'Nordisk Selskab (1792)' or 'Nordiska Sällskapet' have been identified among the holdings of the BL. These (and presumably some, not yet identified, in other languages) may represent the remnants of a former library of the Northern Society in London, most likely housed until 1800 in its Cateaton Street premises. Most of the items are Danish polemical tracts, but they also include Danish translations of Milton's *Paradise Lost* and Goethe's *Erwin und Elmire* and a copy of Swedenborg's *Om nya Jerusalem och des himmelska lära* (Stockholm, 1787).

108 Glahn, op. cit., p. 58. Thorkelin, who was also a freemason, added that the society was a fraternal order and that, as a member, he would propose that it extend honorary membership to Bülow, as it had already done to the Danish historian Suhm.

109 BL copy: 12260.b.8. (*Bibliotheca Danica*, IV, 533.) – The prize had been advertised in June 1786 and was awarded in 1787.

110 Faber, op. cit. (1915), pp. 118-19; A. Collett, *Familien Collett og Christianialiv i gamle dage* (Kristiania, 1915), p. 167. – Both Collett and Anker visited Paris in December 1789.

111 In January 1794 the Northern Society published *The Dreadful and Calamitous Effects of Fire* … ([London, 1794]; 8p.), a fund-raising advertisement – reproduced from *The*

Norwegian Wolff on its committee in 1798 and the attendance of a Danish diplomat in 1799 indicates that it remained genuinely 'Nordic' in spirit.[112]

The last few items listed here (21-25) are ephemera connected with social events in the Scandinavian community in London between 1798 and 1800. In November 1798 a number of Swedish ships' captains (and no doubt merchants) gathered at the Paul's Head Tavern in Cateaton Street, where the Northern Society had its premises, the host being 'our Consul', Claes Grill. For the occasion Pastor Nisser, who is said to have had a certain talent for poetry and a 'charming voice', composed a drinking song in Bellmanesque style (21).

On 22 December the following year the Northern Society met there again to celebrate the birth of Crown Prince Gustaf in Stockholm on 9 November.[113] A collection of songs had been printed (22), one for each of three toasts. The first was 'to the fatherland', sung to the melody of 'God Save the King'; the second to the crown prince, to the melody of 'Gustafs skål, den bäste kung &c.'; and the third to the ladies,[114] to the tune of 'Om Bacchus! Du är gud'. A separately printed song honouring the female members of the Society (23), and apparently sung to the tune of 'Rule Britannia', is attributed to Nisser.

A report of 'the celebration of the birth of the heir apparent to the Swedish throne by the *Nordiska Salskapet*, or Northern Society' appeared in *The Times* on 10 January 1800. It begins:

True Briton – for a fire-fighting technique invented by the Swede Franz Joachim von Aken (1738-98), with a concluding note by the Society's secretary, the Rev. Nisser. (A full account of von Aken's 'discovery' was published in Stockholm in 1797.)

112 Pastor Nisser eventually acted as both chairman and secretary of the Society in London, in which capacity he invited Adam Afzelius to join its 'Enlightened Degree' on 5 November 1798 (Selling, loc. cit.).

113 Nisser's own first son Per was born in London only ten days earlier, on 31 October. – On 28 October 1799 Nisser had written a report to the Swedish chargé d'affaires, Baron Silverhielm, to explain his contacts with the exiled Finnish officer J. A. Jägerhorn, who had arrived in London from Hamburg in April 1797 on a secret mission on behalf of the French government to meet Lord Edward Fitzgerald, leader of the United Irishmen. (Jägerhorn was assisted in that task by the two Swedes Adam Afzelius and D. W. Padenheim, both of whom had lived in Sierra Leone during 1792-6.) When Jägerhorn returned to London with his family in 1799 he was arrested and imprisoned in the Tower for two years. Nisser had found him lodgings on the first occasion, and during his incarceration his wife and children were looked after by Mrs Nisser, not only as her Christian duty but also because she lacked 'Swedish female company in London' (B. Lesch, *Jan Anders Jägerhorn* (Helsingfors, 1941), pp. 359, 384; with reference to P.R.O. file H.O.42/47).

114 'Sällskapets Ordens-Systrar.'

> This Society, which is so called, as being solely composed of Swedish, Danish, and Norwegian gentlemen, was instituted for the purposes of facilitating social intercourse, reviving and preserving early friendships, and extending their benevolent aid to the indigent of their respective nations in this country. They hold their meetings at the Paul's Head,[115] and on the 22nd ult. gave an entertainment in honour of the birth of the Crown Prince of Sweden, at which were present the two Swedish Ministers, Barons Nolcken and Silverhjelm; Baron Robeck, the Secretary to the Danish Embassy in London, several British merchants, who are engaged in Swedish commerce, and a numerous meeting of the Society's members.

The Danish ambassador and Sir Joseph Banks sent their apologies, both being previously engaged. The account continues:

> The entertainment was conducted throughout with the greatest propriety; the rooms of the Society, as well as the Ball-room where they dined, being elegantly illuminated by coloured lamps, arranged in devices suitable to the occasion, and an excellent band of music added zest to the general hilarity. Four beautiful little odes and songs composed for the day, in the Swedish language, by Mr. Hackson,[116] two of which were set to the music of 'God Save the King', and 'Rule Britannia', were sung with infinite taste and spirit; and it was a high gratification to the Englishmen present to hear their own favourite melodies feelingly appropriated by the individuals of other nations … on this *their* day of rejoicing.

In addition to the songs Gustaf Brunnmark, the pastor's young brother-in-law and assistant, recited a prose oration and the pastor himself a 'beautiful and most appropriate ode … both written in honour of the day'.

An undated farewell song (24) apostrophising 'Friendship', on the occasion of a friend leaving London, is also thought to be by Nisser. After that, the final item (25) is something of an anti-climax. It is a printed summons to a parish meeting at the Swedish church on 18 May 1800 to discuss the acquisition of the pastor's residence at 13 Princes Square. The proposal was evidently rejected again, as no such purchase took place. Nisser appears to have become disillusioned with his work in England, for in May 1801 he asked the Trustees to replace him. A year later he could announce that he had been appointed to a parish in Sweden and left the London congregation in the care of his assistant.[117]

---

115 The Society must have had to find a new address when the Paul's Head Tavern closed in 1800 (B. Lillywhite, *London Coffee Houses* (London: George Allen and Unwin, 1963), p. 441).

116 Only the first three were by Hackson, the fourth probably by Nisser.

117 Gustaf Brunnmark (1773-1814), who served in London from 1799 until his death (from 1802 as pastor), continued the literary tradition of his predecessors, publishing a Swedish grammar (London, 1805; see n. 38) and a sermon preached on Christmas Eve

Conclusion

The publications in Danish, Swedish and Icelandic printed in London between 1705 and 1800 reflect particular aspects of the Scandinavian community there. It was an essentially commercial population, with a wealthy minority of timber and iron merchants, insurers and financiers working in the City and a few diplomats; craftsmen of every kind escaping the guild restrictions in their homelands; a miscellaneous stratum of artists, innkeepers, tailors and servants; and a large but seasonally fluctuating number of seamen and captains, mostly resident in Wapping and Stepney.[118] To these largely voiceless residents were added occasional visiting scholars, among whom Banks's Swedish librarians Daniel Solander and Jonas Dryander were exceptional in choosing to settle permanently in London.

During the century after 1688 the liberalism of England in both religious and secular matters attracted growing numbers of Scandinavians, as did its achievements in science, technology and literature. At times, however, it caused serious concern to the diplomatic representatives of both Denmark and Sweden, who saw it as not only unsettling the social relations within the Scandinavian communities there – especially in London, where it infected even some of the local pastors – but also as providing a source of potentially corrosive influences on the political and religious institutions of their home countries.

1809, *En betraktelse öfver ljuset* (London, 1810), as well as translating into English a work by the Swedish chemist J. J. Berzelius, *A View of the Progress of Animal Chemistry* (London, 1813).
Brunnmark, Claes Grill and the Danish pastor Ulrik Frederik Rosing (1801-11) became founder-members in 1804 of the British and Foreign Bible Society, which was to print a large proportion of the items in Scandinavian languages produced in London during the nineteenth century, as well as of the Society of Friends of Foreigners in Distress (1806). – When Rosing was about to leave Copenhagen for England in 1801 Ernst Wolff asked him to bring him certain books and to approach Thorkelin about the printing of his history of the Danish church in London (Faber, op. cit., p. 125; cf. n. 45).

118 Many Scandinavian seamen served on British ships. In 1804 the Swedish congregation received £200 for the families of sailors who had died in the battle of the Nile and a couple of years later another £100 for those who had fallen at Trafalgar (Evander, op. cit., p. 125). Of 7,000 Danish and Norwegian prisoners of war from 1807 only 300 joined the British navy (Faber, op. cit., p. 132), but in 1814 there were over 5,000 unemployed Swedish and Finnish seamen in London, whom Pastor Brunnmark succeeded in getting repatriated by the Swedish government.

David J. Shaw

French-Language Publishing in London to 1900

Describing the output of books in French from the London printing presses is a more daunting task than for any of the other European languages. French books are by far the most numerous (after English and Latin) for the period up to 1800, as can be measured using statistics from the ESTC project: French books represented one out of every ninety editions printed in London in this period (perhaps 2,500-3,000 in total, with a further 1,000 in Law French), while all the other European languages combined amount to only one in 400.[1] It is not possible to obtain reliable statistics for the nineteenth century but there is little reason to doubt that French predominated in that period too.[2] The challenge is increased by the fact that French was the only foreign language to have been printed in London throughout the period from the fifteenth century through to the nineteenth. Italian, Spanish and Dutch books are found from the sixteenth century, German and Portuguese from the seventeenth century, and other languages only from the eighteenth or nineteenth centuries.

A further complicating factor is the question of 'false imprints'. 'London' (or 'Londres') was often used as a fictitious imprint for clandestine books printed on the Continent. Of these, about three-quarters are in French, according to statistics derived from ESTC, predominantly in eighteenth-

1 Most of the basic research for this chapter for the period up to 1800 was done using searches on the ESTC database and CD-ROM which can be searched for place of publication and language. This should give a reasonably comprehensive view of London-produced French books in that period.

2 For the nineteenth century, there is as yet no equivalent search tool which allows place and language searching; use has been made of the Hand Press Book database (bibliographical material up to 1830, maintained by the Consortium of European Research Libraries) and OPACs such as the catalogues of the British Library, Bibliothèque Nationale de France and COPAC. Although it does not provide searches on language or on imprint, some use has also been made of the *Nineteenth-Century Short-Title Catalogue.*

century books. This makes it difficult to generalise about French-language publishing in London without being constantly on the watch for books which were really printed in Paris or Amsterdam with 'Londres' as the imprint and which were intended for sale in mainland France. There is also a problem with the reverse case: books printed in French in London with the imprint 'à Paris' intended to be smuggled into France to evade the censors or to persuade the buyers of a metropolitan origin for the book. Much work remains to be done on the development of techniques to identify and record these two sorts of false imprints. For French material of the eighteenth century in particular, there is a risk of wrongly including one sort of false imprint and of failing to exclude the other. Fortunately, the situation seems less severe for the nineteenth century (though further work may prove this to be over-optimistic).

Books published in Law French

For the earlier centuries, there is another problem to be faced and disposed of: up to about 1700, most books printed in French were law books printed in 'Law French', a creole based on medieval Anglo-Norman French mixed with English which was used by the common lawyers for their law reports and commentaries. This practice continued into the eighteenth century but more frequently in the form of bilingual editions.

In the fifteenth century, 28 editions were published in Law French in London (18% of the total for the century); for the sixteenth century 700-800 editions (6%), falling to fewer than 200 in the seventeenth century (0.2%). For nearly two hundred years these specialist texts, such as Littleton's *Tenures*[3] and the *Yearbooks*[4] and *Reports* of Lord Chief Justices and others, remained an important niche market for the Stationers' Company and its members. The reign of Charles II saw a new wave of French law reports, both of works from the previous centuries and new reports of contemporary cases, such as

---

3 Sir Thomas Littleton, *Tenures*, first edition: London: J. Lettou and W. De Machlinia, [1482], 2°; STC 15719. STC records 47 editions printed before 1640. From the early seventeenth century they became part of the Stationers' Company's monopolies (Court Book C, p. 16).

4 STC records 15 fifteenth-century editions (STC, I, p. 437). There is a very large number of sixteenth-century editions: see J. H. Beale, *A Bibliography of Early English Law Books* (Cambridge, MA, 1926); *Supplement* by R. B. Andersen, 1943. Modern scholarly editions of the Yearbooks are published by the Ames Foundation at the Harvard Law School.

Court of King's Bench. Les reports du tres erudite Edmund Saunders chivalier, nadgairs Seigniour Chief Justice del bank le roy des divers pleadings et cases en le Court del bank le Roy en le temps del reign sa tres Excellent Majesty le Roy Charles le II. *London: printed by W. Rawlins, S. Roycroft, and M. Flesher, assigns of* R. *and E. Atkins Esquires. For Tho. Dring at the corner of Chancery Lane in Fleetstreet, 1686. Wing S743.* (fig. 1)

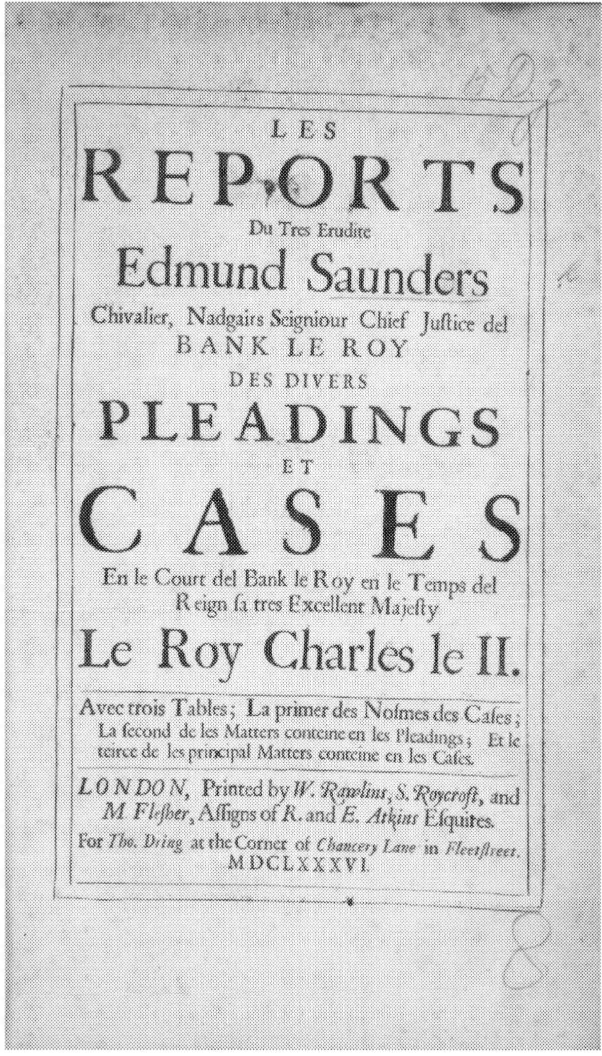

LES

REPORTS

Du Tres Erudite

Edmund Saunders

Chivalier, Nadgairs Seigniour Chief Juſtice del

BANK LE ROY

DES DIVERS

PLEADINGS

ET

CASES

En le Court del Bank le Roy en le Temps del
Reign ſa tres Excellent Majeſty

Le Roy Charles le II.

Avec trois Tables; La primer des Noſmes des Caſes;
La ſecond de les Matters conteine en les Pleadings; Et le
teirce de les principal Matters conteine en les Caſes.

LONDON, Printed by *W. Rawlins*, *S. Roycroft*, and
M. Fleſher, Aſſigns of *R.* and *E. Atkins* Eſquires.

For *Tho. Dring* at the Corner of *Chancery Lane* in *Fleetſtreet*.
MDCLXXXVI.

Fig. 1: *Les reports du tres erudite Edmund Saunders* (London: printed for Tho. Dring, 1686), vol. I, title-page.
British Library pressmark: 512.b.26.

French language textbooks

In contrast to the 28 texts published in Law French in the fifteenth century, only three books are recorded by ISTC[5] as being printed in standard French. These are all bilingual vocabularies for learning French and English:

> **French-English vocabulary**. Frensshe Englissh. Cy commence la table Hier begynneth the table. *Westminster*: [*William Caxton, 1480*]. 2°. STC 24865; Duff 405; Alston 1. Facsimile: *Vocabulary in French and English: a facsimile of Caxton's edition, c. 1480*. With introductions by J.C.T. Oates and L.C. Harmer. Cambridge University Press, 1964.
>
> [Another edition]. Here is a good boke to lerne to speke french. Decy vng bon liure a apprendre a parler fraunchoys. [*London*]: *Richard Pynson*, [*c. 1495*]. 4°. STC 24867; Duff 406; Alston 3.
>
> [Another edition]. Here begynneth a lytell treatyse for to lerne Englysshe and Frensshe. *Westminster: Wynkyn de Worde*, [*c. 1499*]. 4°. STC 24866; Duff 407; Alston 2.

The French volume of Robin Alston's *A Bibliography of the English Language* records over 600 grammars and over 100 dictionaries of French published for the English market before 1801, the great majority of them printed in London.[6] However, the main language of most of these books is English and consequently they do not figure in the statistics of French-language publications retrieved from the ESTC database for this investigation. The popularity of texts such as Claude de Sainliens's *The French Schoole-maister* (Alston 18-38, 1575-1668) and his *The French Littleton* (Alston 39-54, 1566[=1576]-1630) indicates the presence of professional schoolmasters in the capital as well as a market for self-instruction texts. This was a demand which continued throughout the following centuries, slowly at first and with increasing frequency from the second half of the eighteenth century.[7]

---

5 The *Incunable Short-Title Catalogue* (ISTC) is available on-line and on CD-ROM; see the British Library web site for up-to-date details.

6 R. C. Alston, *A Bibliography of the English Language from the Invention of Printing to the Year 1800*, vol. XII, part I: *The French Language: grammars, miscellaneous treatises, dictionaries* (Olney: printed for the author, 1985), p. 3.

7 Kathleen Lambley, *The Teaching and Cultivation of the French Language in England during the Tudor and Stuart Times, with an introductory chapter on the preceding period* (Manchester: University Press; London: Longman and Green, 1920). An overview of the language-learning situation in the STC period is given by H. S. Bennett: for the early Tudor period in *English Books and Readers, 1475-1557*, 2nd edn (Cambridge: Cambridge University Press, 1969), pp. 93-7; for the Elizabethan period in *English Books and Readers, 1558-1603* (Cambridge: Cambridge University Press, 1965); for early Stuart London in *English Books and Readers, 1603-1640* (Cambridge: Cambridge University Press, 1970), pp.137-9.

A seventeenth-century example is

> **Phrases Francoises** fort necessaires pour ceux qui apprennent a parler Francois en forme de question. *Imprime a Londres: Par Richard Field demeurant a la rue de Woodstreet, 1624*. STC 19893a.3.

As well as French textbooks, there was a market for tuition in English for the expatriate French Huguenot communities in London and other towns. An early example is:

> **Jacques Bellot**. Le maistre d'escole Anglois. Contenant plusieurs profitables preceptes pour les naturelz francois, et autres estrangers qui ont la langue francoise pour paruenir a la vraye prononciation de la langue Angloise. *Imprime a Londres: Par Thomas Purfoote, pour Henry Dizlie, 1580*. 8°. STC 1855.[8]

Seventeenth-century examples are George Mason's *Grammaire angloise*, 1633 (STC 17600.7) and Paul Festeau's *Nouvelle grammaire Angloise, enrichie de dialogues curieux touchant l'Estat, & la cour d'Angleterre*, 1675 and subsequent editions (Wing F825A-F825B), and grammars by Guy Miège and by Claude Mauger. At the end of the century an Italian teacher of Italian, French, Spanish and English, dwelling at the sign of the German Academy ('a l'Enseigne de l'Academie Alemande') in Suffolk Street, published his own textbook with very courtly overtones:

> **Francesco Colsoni**. La clef-dor de la langue Angloise, avec laquelle I. On entre dans les entretiens historiques de la paix et la guerre, en campagne ou la campagne de Compiegne II. On ouvre les males des deux couriers des dames de l'Europe, assemblees au conclave de Junon sur tous les mariages des princes et princesses des annees, 1697-8,9. On y a ajoute l'almanach royal, d'Angleterre. [*London: c. 1699*]. 8°. Wing C5422aA.

Colsoni also targeted the leisure market with a London guide book:

> **Francesco Colsoni**. Le guide de Londres dedié aux voyageurs etrangers: il apprend tout ce qu'il y a de plus curieux, notable & utile dans la ville, les fauxbourgs, & aux environs. Troisiéme edition. *Londres: imprimé pour le German Bookseller-shop, 1710*. 8°. Anonymous. By François Colsoni.

The eighteenth century saw dozens of grammars of French, English, Spanish and Latin published in French in London, as well as many educational texts on other subjects.

---

8 Bellot had already produced an English-language French grammar in 1578 (STC 1852).

Liturgical and biblical texts

Given the large proportion of books and pamphlets printed in the early centuries which dealt with religious subjects, it is not surprising that religion features in the French output of the London printing houses. One highly relevant factor here is the presence of a significant population of refugee French Protestants in the capital and elsewhere from the mid-sixteenth century onwards who were given special privileges by the English crown to conduct their religious affairs along Calvinist lines. Many of their needs for printed confessional material were no doubt met by importation from Geneva and elsewhere, but the London book trade attempted to meet their requirements too, especially for those who were assimilated to the Anglican liturgy.

The first record of a French Book of Common Prayer seems to be an edition of 1553 printed for use in the Channel Islands (STC 16430). Another French Prayer Book is recorded in 1616 which had a translation of the Psalms by Pierre de Laune (STC 16431). Many more were produced following the restoration of the monarchy in 1660. As well as *La Liturgie, c'est a dire, le formulaire*, London, 1661 (Wing B3621A), Charles II also had versions of the Book of Common Prayer issued in Latin, Greek, Welsh, Italian and Portuguese. There were at least eight further French editions before the end of the century and over twenty during the course of the eighteenth century. A small group of booksellers specialised in the French liturgical trade: Pierre II de Varennes (1704, 1706, 1719) succeeded by Matthieu de Varennes (1722), Nicolas Prevost (1722, 1729, 1739), Paul Vaillant (1739, 1757) and Jean Nourse (1757, 1780, 1788, 1794). A French translation of the Anglican catechism was also produced, no doubt as part of an attempt to encourage assimilation to the national church:

> **Church of England. Catechism.** Brieve exposition du catechisme de l'eglise anglicane; avec les preuves tirees de la Ste. Ecriture. Par Monseigneur l'eveque de Chichestre, … Traduite sur la dixieme edition angloise. *Londres: se vend chez H. Walwyn,* [*1701?*]. 8°.

There was a similar need in the German territories of the new Hanoverian dynasty a few years later which was documented and later translated into French:

> **Sharp, Thomas**. Relation des mesures qui furent prises dans les années 1711, 1712. et 1713. pour introduire la liturgie anglicane dans le Roiaume de Prusse et dans l'Electorat de Hanover. … Le tout extrait d'un manuscrit qui n'a pas encore été rendu public, contenant des mémoires de la vie du Docteur Jean Sharp, … Traduit de l'anglois par J.T. Muysson. *Londres: imprimé par W. Richardson et S. Clark, 1767.* 4°. Anonymous.

The Calvinist church of course has its own French liturgy and translation of the Scriptures, copies of which were no doubt imported from Geneva since there are none recorded for the sixteenth or seventeenth centuries by STC or Wing. Several later editions of the French metrical Psalms, translated in the mid-sixteenth century by Clément Marot and Théodore de Bèze, were produced in London, such as:

> **Metrical Psalter. French.** Les Psaumes de David. Retouchez sur la version de Marot & de Beze; approuvez par les pasteurs de l'Eglise de Paris. ... avec la liturgie, le catechisme, & la confession de foi. *Londres: pour Jean Cailloüé, & Jaques Levi, 1701.* 12°. With the music.

Slightly later, a new metrical version was produced using the traditional tunes:

> **Metrical Psalter. French.** Les Psaumes de David, sur le chant de ceux de Marot et de Beze. Nouvelle version, ... Mis en rime. Par Paul Beauvais. *Londres: imprimé par A. Pearson, pour l'auteur, 1737.* 8°. With the music.

Another edition declares that it is revised and published with the authority of the Dutch Walloon Synod:

> **Metrical Psalter. French.** Les pseaumes de David, mis en vers françois; revus et approuvez par le Synode Wallon des Provinces-Unies. Nouvelle edition, toute en musique, avec la basse. *Londres: se vendent chez J. Paroissien, 1757.* 8°.

French New Testaments were printed in London in the reign of Edward VI, no doubt in part to cater for French-speaking religious refugees.[9] Few whole Bibles seem to have been printed: 1687 (12°; Wing B2707A), 1688 (4°; Wing B2707B), 1693 (2°; Wing B2707C); ESTC records no eighteenth-century editions, although there are fifteen editions of the New Testament and sixteen of the French Psalter.

In the nineteenth century we find the scholarly publication in French of editions of biblical texts in unusual languages such as the Gospels of Luke and John in the Vaudois dialect, *Les Saints Évangiles de Notre Seigneur Jésus-Christ, selon saint Luc et saint Jean. Li Sént Evangilé de Notre Seigneur Gésu-Christ, counfourma sént Luc et sént Giann. Traduits en langue vaudoise par Pierre Bert* (Londres: Imprimerie de Moyes, 1832) or, more exotically, part of St Luke in Berber: *Extrait d'une traduction ms. en langue Berbère de quelques parties de l'écriture*

9 See STC 2957.6 (1551) and STC 2957.9 (1553). See articles by Bettye Chambers in *Bibliothèque d'Humanisme et Renaissance*, 39 (1977), 143-8, and 41 (1979), 353-8; see also Bettye Chambers, *Bibliography of French Bibles: fifteenth- and sixteenth- century French-language editions of the Scriptures* (Geneva: Droz, 1983).

sainte: contenant XII chapitres de S. Luc (Londres, 1833). Many of these texts were produced for the British and Foreign Bible Society.[10]

Other religious texts

As well as biblical and liturgical texts, the London booksellers also undertook the production of theological works in French, at first translations and later also original compositions. The purpose of these works changes with the contemporary religious context. In the sixteenth century, the earliest examples reflect attempts to define or to defend the early development of Anglicanism or attack contemporary Catholicism, such as

> **Eutichius Myonius** (*pseudonym of Wolfgang Musculus*). Le temporiseur. Avec plusieurs bons conseilz & aduis sus la mesme matiere. Sauoir est comment chascun fidele se doibt maintenir entre les papistes. [Colophon:] *Imprime a Londres: Par moy Estienne Mierdman, 1550.* 8°. STC 18311.

> **Thomas Cranmer**. Defence de la vraye et catholique doctrine du sacrement du corps & sang de nostre sauueur Christ, auec la confutation de plusieurs erreurs concernantes icelle, ... Translatee de la langue Angloyse en francoys, par Francoys Philippe. *Imprime a Londres: par Pierre Angelin, 1552.* 8°. A translation of Cranmer's *Defence of the True and Catholike Doctrine of the Sacrament of the Body and Bloud of our Sauiour Christ.* STC 6003.5.

The seventeenth century saw the publication of controversial and expository works by ministers of the French Protestant churches resident in London, such as Charles de Beauvais and Jean d'Espagne, who was pastor of a Huguenot congregation which met at Somerset House in Westminster. Louis Herault, describing himself as 'Pasteur de l'Eglize Francoise de Londres', published a *Remerciment faict au Roy au nom des eglises estrangeres de ce royaume, pour sa royale protection* (Londres: Chez Octavian Pulleyn le jeune, 1666; Wing H1491) in which he thanked Charles II for renewing royal protection of the foreign churches in London. The members of the French churches in London no doubt followed with care the religious situation in their home country, leading for example to the publication of accounts of the conversion of their adversaries, such as

---

10 A list of these editions in French dialects, based on the holdings of the British and Foreign Bible Society, can be found in vol. II of T. H. Darlow and H. F. Moule, *Historical Catalogue of Holy Scripture* (London, 1903; reprint New York, 1963), pp. 452-458. French-language editions are listed on pp. 376-452.

François de La Motte. Les motifs de la conversion à la religion reformée du Sieur Francois de la Motte, cy-devant predicateur de l'Ordre des Carmes, prononcez, en partie, par luy-même dans l'Eglise de la Savoye le jour de son abjuration. *A Londres: Se vendent chez Moyse Pitt à l'enseigne de l'Ange dans le Cemetiere de S. Paul, 1675.* 4°. Wing L304.

or a slightly later translation of a work by an Anglican author noting the new influx of refugees following the revocation of the Edict of Nantes (1685):

Joseph Stevens. La chaine d'or, pour enlever les ames de la Terre au Ciel. Ou, Considerations importantes sur les quatre fins de l'Homme, la mort, le jugement, l'Enfer & le Paradis. Avec des avis tres-utiles pour bien mourir traduit de l'Anglois du docteur J. Stevens ... Ouvrage ... dedié aux fideles protestans François echapés de la grande tribulation, qui sont refugiés en Angleterre. [*London*]: *Se vend à Londres, par D. Du Chemin, marchand libraire dans le Strand, vis-a-vis Somerset-House, au Sacrifice d'Abraham, 1699.* 12°. Wing S5497A.

This period also saw the publication of further Anglican material such as the French translation of Bishop Stillingfleet's *Discourse concerning the Idolatry Practised in the Church of Rome* (London, 1673; Wing S5672A) or of Thomas Barlow's *Popery*, translated as *Les Principes et la doctrine de Rome sur le sujet de l'excommunication et de la deposition des roys* (London, 1679; Wing B842) with its obvious reflection of contemporary fears about Catholic influence at the English Court.

Works by Catholic authors also appeared in London, sometimes apparently with official consent: Saint François de Sales, *Conduite de la Confession et de la Communion pour les ames soigneuses de leur salut tiree des manuscrits de S. F. de Sales; avec une table tres-utile aux confesseurs & aux penitens. Reueue, corrigee & augmentee* (Londres, chez Henry Hills, 1686; Wing F2068).[11]

One surprising category is works by Quakers published in French, some with the characteristic explanation of their name: 'Publié par ceulx lesquels le monde par mespris appele Quakers, c'est à dire ceulx qui tremblent'. Wing records several examples, mainly translations of books by George Fox. This phenomenon continues into the eighteenth century, when a number of translations of works by William Penn appeared, as well as works originally published in America, such as Anthony Benezet's *Observations sur l'origine, les principes, et l'etablissement en Amerique, de la societé connue sous la denomination de Quakers ou Trembleurs* (imprimé à Philadelphie: et r'imprimé à Londres par Jacques Phillips, 1783). When Voltaire was in London from 1726 to 1728, he was in touch with the Quakers and wrote favourably of them in his *Lettres sur*

11 For the earlier publication of an English translation of Sales, see N. W. Bawcutt, 'A Crisis of Laudian Censorship: Nicholas and John Okes and the publication of Sales's *An Introduction to a Devout Life* in 1637', *The Library*, 7th ser., 1 (2000), 403-38.

les Anglais.[12] Immediately after the French Revolution, the Quakers seem to have had an agent in Paris: several works appeared with the imprint 'Londres: de l'imprimerie de Jaques Phillips. Et se trouve à Paris chez Le Gras'.[13]

French publications in the eighteenth century reflect the growing religious diversity of the age. As well as the Quakers, we find John Welsey's *Le Caractere d'un Methodiste. … Traduit mot à mot de l'anglois* (1743) or a work by his brother and fellow Methodist Charles Wesley (1780), along with Anglican works by Archbishop Cornwallis (1776), editions of Emanuel Swedenborg's *De la nouvelle Jerusalem et de sa doctrine céleste* (1782, 1787) and innumerable sermons of all sorts. And a flood of works by and relating to the new religious refugees from France, the churchmen, noblemen and others fleeing the consequences of the French Revolution.

> **Bareau de Girac, François,** *Bishop of Rennes*. Lettre de Mgr. l'évêque de Rennes, aux prêtres de son diocèse, exilés pour la cause de la foi. *Londres: de l'imprimerie de Baylis, 1796*. Dated: 'Königsworth, le 15 octobre 1795'.

French Catholic clergy were allowed to practise their religion at designated places:

> **Catholic Church. Vicariate Apostolic of the London District.** A messieurs les ecclésiastiques français qui ont obtenu la permission de célébrer la sainte messe dans des chapelles particulieres. [*London, 1798*]. Dated and signed at end: 'Donné à Londres ce 24 Mars 1798. Jean Evêque de Centurie … par Monseigneur Jacques Barnard secretaire'.

and enjoyed the possibility of publishing devotional literature for their flock:

> **Rosary**. Instructions sur le rosaire, avec des paraphrases sur l'oraison dominicale et; [*sic*] la salutation angélique suivies de considerations sur les quinze mysteres qui font l'objet du rosaire. *Londres: chez J. M. Dulonchamp, 1797*.

Not surprisingly the religious diversity of French material printed in London continued into the nineteenth century, as the Royalist exile was prolonged into the period of the Napoleonic Empire. The assassination of the duc d'Enghien was marked by a Catholic memorial service in London:

---

12 For a bibliographical account of Voltaire's publishing activities in London, see Giles Barber, 'Some Early English Editions of Voltaire', *British Library Journal*, 4 (1978), 99-111.

13 Penn, William, *Fruits de l'amour d'un père, ou avis de Guillaume Penn à ses enfans, touchant leur conduite tant en matiere civile, qu'en matiere de religion. Nouvellement traduit … par Edd. P. Bridel.* Londres: de l'imprimerie de Jaques Phillips. Et se trouve à Paris chez Le Gras, 1790.

Bouvens, Charles de, *abbé.* Discours funèbre prononcé dans la chapelle catholique de St. Patrick de Londres, le 26 avril 1804, au service solonnel célébré pour le repos de l'ame de S.A.S. M. le duc de Enghien. *Londres: Cox, 1804.*

Official publications

French was frequently used during the reign of Elizabeth I as a language for the publication of diplomatic and other official documents. For example, a protestation made to the Queen in 1560 by the French ambassador was printed in London in Latin and in French (STC 11309.5 and 11309.7); the Queen's reply was also published in Latin and French (STC 9183 and 9183.5), the two French versions being issued together by Jugge and Cawood. *An official Declaration of the Causes Mooving the Queene of England to Give Aide to the Defence of the People Afflicted and Oppressed in the Lowe Countries* (1585) appeared in translations into Latin, Dutch, French and Italian (STC 9189-9193). An attack by James I on Conrad Vorstius's Arminian writings appeared in London in two French editions (1612) with translations into Latin and English (STC 9229-9233). Use of French for diplomatic propaganda continued into the Commonwealth period (Wing E1336: a translation of a *Declaration* by the Council of State on relations with the Dutch, 1652) and into the reign of the later Stuarts. An interesting ephemeral example is a printed passport form in French issued by Charles II:

Great Britain. Passport. Sauvegarde du roy de la Grande Bretagne, [*London: 1672*], 1 sheet; 'Donné a nostre cour le [blank] jour de [blank] l'an de grace, mil six cents soixante douze, et de nostre regne le vingt quatriesme' (Wing C3604AD).

Eighteenth-century examples include the texts of the treaties of Versailles and Paris in 1783 which ended the War of American Independence and the European conflicts involving Great Britain, France, Spain and the Netherlands. An earlier example saw the publication of a parallel French-English text of documents relating to the outbreak of war with France in 1744:

Louis XV. Ordonnance du Roy, portant déclaration de guerre contre le Roy d'Angleterre; avec une glose ampliative & instructive. The King of France's declaration of war. In French and English. With an ample and instructive explanation thereof. *Hague printed, London re-printed for M. Cooper, 1744.* 4°.

George II. Declaration de guerre de sa Majesté contre le Roi Tres-Chretien. [*London: 1744*]. 4°.

Charles VII. Lettre circulaire que l'Empereur, a envoiée a ses ministres dans les cours étrangeres. The Emperor's circular letter, to his ministers at foreign courts. *London: printed for Joseph Collyer, 1744.* 8°.

Current affairs

We have already seen that the English authorities thought it worth while publicising their actions in French versions of official documents. With a sizeable French-speaking population in the capital, it is not surprising that the booksellers should have sought to supply French-language material on current affairs too, nor that there were pens willing to produce it. During Elizabeth's reign, news consisted mainly of reports on diplomacy and warfare, more or less official publications in fact, by the Cecils and others of Elizabeth's officers.[14]

The marriage of Charles I with Henrietta Maria of France in 1627 was the occasion for the publication of an *Eclogue, ou Chant pastoral sur les nopces des Serenissimes Princes Charles Roy de la Grand' Bretagne, France & Irlande, & de Henriette Marie fille de Henry le Grand, Roy de France, & de Nauarre* (A Londres: 1627; STC 1052) by I. D. B. Even the health of the new Queen's doctor was recorded in verse as he prepared to be operated on for the stone: *L'Adieu au monde de David Echlin, medecin de la Royne, aage enuiron de soixante ans, prost à estre taillé de la pierre, au hazard de sa vie. Auec vne priere pour leur sacrées maiestés. Dedié à la Royne* (A Londres: Chez George Purslowe, 1627; STC 7475) and again following his successful recovery: *Echlin par la grace de Dieu resuscité. Auec la paraphrase Latine, par l'autheur mesme. Dedié à la Royne* (A Londres: Chez George Purslowe, 1628; STC 7477). The visit of the Queen's mother, the French Regent Marie de Medicis, in 1639 was recorded by the French Royal Historiographer, Jean Puget de La Serre: *Histoire de l'entrée de la reyne mere du roy tres-Chrestien, dans la Grande-Bretaigne* (A Londre [*sic*]: par Jean Raworth, pour George Thomason, & Octauian Pullen, à la Rose, au Cimetiere de Sainct Paul, 1639; STC 20488).

The Solemn League and Covenant was published in French translation: *Convenant & alliance saincte pour la reformation & defense de la religion, l'honeur & prosperite du Roy, la paix & seurte de trois Royaumes, d'Angleterre, Ecosse & Irlande, faicte solennellement par les estats & peuple desdits royaumes* ([London], 1643; Wing R23), as were a number of other landmarks of the struggles between Crown and Parliament, including a French version of the *Eikon basilike. Ou portrait roial, de sa Majeste de la Grande Bretagne: dans ses souferances & solitudes. Contenant, ses meditations sacrees, prieres, derniers propos* (Imprimées à La Haye, [*i.e.* London], 1649; Wing E267A) and Milton's officially sponsored reply, *Eikonoklastes, ou Reponse au livre intitulé Eikon basilike … Par le Sr Jean Milton* (A Londres: par

14 E.g. STC 4902-4907, translated into Latin, Dutch, French and Italian; STC 15412-15414.6, translated into French and Italian.

Guill. Du-Gard, imprimeur du Conseil d'Etat, l'an 1652. Et se vend par Nicolas Bourne, à la porte Meridionale de la vieille Bourse; Wing M2116).

The flight of James II and the welcoming of William of Orange were also marked with French translations, no doubt partly for reasons of diplomatic justification abroad. Two examples are official sermons to the Commons and at the Coronation by Bishop Gilbert Burnet:

Burnet, Gilbert. Sermon prononcé devant la Chambre des Communes le trente uniéme de janvier, 1688/9. Jour d'action de graces pour la delivrance de ce royaume de la papauté & du pouvoir absolu, par le moyen de son altesse Monseigneur le Prince d'Orange. Traduit de l'anglois du Reverend Docteur Burnet, chaplain de son altesse. *Londres: imprimé par R.E. pour R. Chiswel demeurant à l'enseigne de la Rose & Couronne dans le Cemetiere de S. Paul, 1689.* 4°. Wing B5911.

— Sermon prononcé au couronnement de Guillaume III et Marie II roy & reine d'Angleterre, d'Ecosse, de France & d'Irlande, deffenseurs de la foy par Monseigneur G. Burnet, eveque de Salisbury, dans l'eglise de Westminster, le 11 d'avril, 1689. *A Londres, imprimé pour J. Delage ... & se vend chez tous les libraires françois de Londres, 1689.* Wing B5910A.

There was clearly a market for news in French in the capital during these troubled times in the seventeenth century. A weekly newsbook *Le Mercure Anglois* appeared between June 1644 and December 1648 (Nelson and Seccombe 258) and a semi-weekly *Gazette de Londres* between November 1666 and December 1696 (Nelson and Seccombe, 165). Both were translations of English newspapers and were followed by other similar ventures in the next century especially following the French Revolution, for example the *Courier d'Angleterre* which appeared from 1805 to 1815.

The events of the Revolution itself were widely reported and commented on among the refugee French population of London. There were several editions of works such as

Calonne, Charles Alexandre de. De l'état de la France, présent & à venir. *Londres: de l'imprimerie de T. Spilsbury & Fils. Octobre, 1790.* 8°.

The execution of Louis XVI not surprisingly was noted in London:

Lenoir, P. V. Éloge funèbre de Louis seize, ... prononcé à Londres, ... 27 mars; ... et le 23 avril, 1793. *Londres: chez l'auteur et chez J. Deboffe, Hookham, Edwards et P. Elmsly,* [*1793?*]. 8°.

as were the subsequent events of the 1790s as the Revolution devoured its own offspring:

Vilate, Joachim. Causes secretes de la revolution du 9 au 10 thermidor, par Vilate, ex-juré au Tribunal Révolutionnaire de Paris, transferré et détenu au Luxembourg. *Londres: se vend chez de Boffe; Owen; et chez Glindon, imprimeur français,* [*1795*]. 8°.

There were exile French communities in England throughout much of the nineteenth century which provided a continuing market for political reporting in French concerning both domestic and foreign affairs in Europe and in North America:

> **France. Treaties.** Actes et mémoires concernant les négociations qui ont eu lieu entre la France et les États-Unis de l'Amérique, depuis 1793, jusqu'à la conclusion de la Convention du 30 Septembre 1800. *Londres: Vogel, 1807.*
>
> **Ivernois, Francis d',** *Sir.* Effets du blocus continental sur le commerce, les finances, le crédit et la prospérité des Isles Britanniques. *Londres: Se vend chez B. Dulau, 1809.* Several subsequent editions in 1809 and 1810.
>
> **France. July Revolution.** La vérité sur la révolution qui a éclaté à Paris au mois de Juillet dernier, sur ses causes et ses conséquences. *Londres: 1830.*
>
> **Gruau, Modeste.** Abrégé de l'histoire des infortunes du Dauphin, depuis l'époque ou il a été enlevé de la tour du temple, jusqu'au moment de son arrestation par le gouvernement de Louis-Philippe … November 1836. *Londres: Armand, 1836.*

Literature

The French-speakers of London were not only concerned with spiritual matters and with political affairs. French literature had always played an important role in English publishing from the time of Caxton's translations of French texts. Literary works published in French are found from the sixteenth century and in considerable quantities in the eighteenth century. Wynkyn de Worde published a French edition of Virgil in about 1525 which he had had printed in Paris (STC Addenda 24827.5). Later in the century, Du Bartas's *Urania* was published by John Wolf in a parallel French-Latin edition translated by Robert Ashley[15] and two French editions of Pierre Boaistuau's *Le Theatre du Monde, ou il est faict vn ample discours des miseres humaines* (A Londres: de l'imprimerie de Edmund Bollifant, 1587; STC 3166; second edition: 1595, STC 3167).

The seventeenth century saw a widening range of literature in French: both occasional verse for royal events and serious matter such as Jonatan de Sainct Sernin's *Essais et obseruations sur les essais du Seigneur de Montaigne* (A Londres: de l'Imprimerie d'Edward Allde, 1626; STC 21551.7) or a translation of Aristotle's *Rhetorica* printed in Amsterdam for sale in London: *La Rhetorique d'Aristote traduite en Francois par feu M. Cassandre. Nouvelle edition. Suivant la copie de Paris* (A Londres: chez Pierre de Varennes, demeurant dans le

15 Du Bartas, Guillaume de Salluste, *L'Uranie ou muse celeste de G. de Saluste Seigneur du Bartas = Urania sive musa coelestis, Roberti Ashelei de Gallica G. Salustij Bartasij delibata.* Londini: excudebat Iohannes Wolfius, 1589. 16 leaves; 4°. STC 21673.

Strand proche la Savoye a la Teste de Seneque, 1698; Wing A3696B. Colophon: 'A Amsterdam, De l'imprimerie de Daniel Boulesteys de la Contie').

Play texts started to become popular from the end of the seventeenth century; an early example is the anonymous *Gabinie, tragedie chretienne, suivant la copie à Paris* (A Londres: chez Jean Cailloue, & Henry Ribotteau, libraires François dans le Strand, 1700. Wing B5221B; first published in Paris in 1699) which was republished fifty years later for performance by the young gentlemen of the Académie d'Hoxton.[16] Many examples are found in the eighteenth century where the texts were sometimes intended for use in educational establishments, either as reading texts or for performance, or else were intended to accompany professional theatrical performances:

> **Procope-Couteau, Michel Coltelli**. Arlequin balourd, comedie italienne, en cinq actes, comme elle a été representée sur le Theatre Roial de Hay-Market. *Londres: chez Henri Ribotteau, 1719.*

In one case they were part of the publicity apparatus of a commercial play-reading venture by the journalist and publicist A. A. Le Texier:

> **A. A. Le Texier.** Recueil des pièces de théâtre, nouvellement lues par M. Le Texier, en sa maison, Lisle-Street, Leicester-Fields. *Londres: de l'imprimerie de Baylis, se trouve chez l'editeur. A. Dulau & Co. Deboffe. L'Homme. Thomas Hookham. T. Boosey, 1799.* This venture started in 1785 and by 1799 had reached its twelfth volume.

Editions of the plays of Molière and Racine appeared in the second half of the eighteenth century. These may have been intended as reading texts of the French classics rather than for performance.[17] This would also be the case with a three-volume collection such as *Chef-d'œuvres* [sic] *dramatiques: ou recueil des meilleures pièces, de Corneille, Racine, Molière, et Voltaire, Crébillon, Destouches* (Londres: chez P. Elmsly, T. Cadell, Leigh et Sotheby, 1782), which was reprinted in the early nineteenth century in a *Nouvelle édition, revue, corrigée, et augmentée* (Londres: Law & Whittaker, 1816. 12°: 2 v.). In the later nineteenth century annotated school editions of individual plays started to appear, the

---

16 *Gabinie, tragédie chrétienne, qui doit être représentée à l'École de Pension d'Hoxton, par les jeunes messieurs de ladite École, le mai, MDCCLI.* Londres: au depens de l'Académie d'Hoxton, [1751]. 8°. Anonymous; by D. A. de Brueys.

17 Molière, J.-B. Poquelin de, *Les précieuses ridicules. Comédie.* Londres: de l'imprimerie de Baylis, et se trouve chez l'éditeur; A. Dulau & Co; L'Homme; Deboffe; T. Hookham, & T. Boosey, 1799. Racine, Jean, *Esther, tragedie tirée de l'Ecriture Ste*, Londres: chez Nourse, 1745; *Athalie, tragedie*, Londres: imprimé pour T. Osborne & J. Shipton, 1756; *Oeuvres de Racine*, Londres: de l'imprimerie de J. Tonson & J. Watts, 1723. Another complete works of Racine is recorded for 1782 but the imprint may be false.

beginnings of a pattern of modern language textbook production which continues today.

French poetry was popular and influential too in the eighteenth century: for example, Boileau's *Oeuvres poëtiques* (1750), *Satires et œuvres diverses … avec les poësies du Pere Sanlecque* (1769); a later edition *Poésies de Boileau-Despréaux, avec des notes historiques et grammaticales, et un essai sur sa vie et sur ses écrits. Par M. de Lévizac* (1800) suggests that he was already being studied as a school author. The same is probably true of La Fontaine, whose *Fables* appeared in two editions (1736, 1798). Other collections of fables such as that of Lewis Chambaud (eleven editions between 1751 and 1797) were expressly aimed 'à l'usage des enfans, et des autres personnes qui commencent à apprendre la langue françoise'. A number of anthologies were also produced, such as François Moysant's *Bibliothèque portative des écrivains françois, ou choix des meilleurs morceaux extraits de leurs ouvrages, en vers* (Londres: chez A. Dulau et Co, 1800) with a parallel volume of prose writers.

The London publishers produced a considerable quantity of prose fiction in French, by authors great and small. The anonymous *L'Heureux Esclave. Nouvelle* (1677) is an early example, printed in Cologne for sale in London.[18] In the eighteenth century, many of the most fashionable authors were published in London (as well as those false imprints which were allegedly published in London): Crébillon, Diderot, Fénelon, Florian, Laclos, Mme de La Fayette, Le Sage, Marmontel, Montesquieu, Restif de La Bretonne, Rousseau, Bernardin de Saint Pierre, and other more minor or more scandalous works. The extent of a fashionable English (or at least England-based) reading public for French fiction can easily be guessed at from this list. In the nineteenth century the trend continued but is complicated by multi-national imprints: books printed in Paris which list outlets in other European cities such as London.

But above all, the London booksellers published Voltaire: the ESTC records about forty separate works by Voltaire appearing with an apparently genuine London imprint during the eighteenth century, some of them in several editions: plays, poetry, history, philosophical and controversial works as well as novels. For example, his collected stories *Romans, ou contes philosophiques … Par M. de Voltaire* appeared in 1772 and 1776. His historical epic poem *La Henriade* was published in London in at least eight editions

18 *L'heureux esclave. Nouvelle.* Imprimé a Cologne, et se vend a Londres, chez Mrs Jaques Magnes & Richard Bentley a la Poste de Russell-street au Covent-Jardin, 1677. [12], 180 p.; 12°. Anonymous; by Gabriel de Brémond. Wing B4352A.

dated 1728, and in later editions of 1789, 1795 and 1800, as well as editions in the nineteenth century.

One could cite Voltaire again as an example of the production of historical writing: his *Histoire de Charles XII. Roi de Suède* was printed by Bowyer in 1731 and 1732 with the false imprint 'Basle: chez Christophe Revis'; further editions appeared in 1756, 1773, 1798 and in the nineteenth century, e.g. *Histoire de Charles XII par Voltaire. Soigneusement revue par Gabriel Surenne … Cinquième édition* (A Edimbourg: chez Oliver et Boyd. A Londres: chez Simpkin, Marshall, et Cie., 1855). History as a popular category included translations of English works such as David Hume's *Histoire de la maison de Stuart sur le trône d'Angleterre* (1766) and his *Histoire de la maison de Plantagenet, sur le trône d'Angleterre, depuis l'invasion de Jules-César jusqu'a l'avénement d'Henri VII* (Londres: et se trouve à Paris, chez la Veuve Desaint. Nyon l'aîné, 1783).

The London book trade clearly found the production of original literary and historical texts in French to be a profitable niche market. Translations from English into French play a much smaller role but nevertheless a significant one. An early example was a 1619 French translation of Bacon's *Essays* published by John Bill (STC 1152). Other cases, such as Thomas Gumble's *Life of General Monck*, translated by Guy Miège as *La Vie du General Monk duc d'Albemarle &c. Le restaurateur de Sa Majeste Britannique, Charles Second* (A Londres: chez Robert Scot, 1672; 12°; Wing G2231) might be more political propaganda than literature. The eighteenth century saw many more examples of English classics offered in French:

Chesterfield, Philip Dormer Stanhope, Earl of. Choix des lettres du Lord Chesterfield, à son fils. Traduites de l'anglois. Par M. Peyron. *Londres: et se trouve à Paris, chez Nyon l'aîné, 1776.*

Defoe, Daniel. Memoires et avantures de Madlle. Moll Flanders, ecrits par elle-meme. Traduit de l'anglois. *1761.*

Goldsmith, Oliver. Le curé de Wakefield. Traduit de l'Anglais, par M. J. B. Biset. *Londres: chez l'auteur; T. Cadell le jeune, & G. Davies, successeurs de M. Cadell; Deboffe; & Tindal, 1796.*

Johnson, Samuel. Rasselas, Prince d'Abissinie. Roman. Traduit de l'Anglois de Dr. Johnson, par le Comte de Fouchecour. *Londres: chez M.M. Lackington, Allen, et Comp, 1798.*

Milton, John. L'allegro et le pensieroso de Milton. Traduits en vers françois. *Londres: chez Messrs. Becket & de Hondt, 1766.* Also a 1792 edition with parallel French and English texts.

Pope, Alexander. Essais sur la critique et sur l'homme. Par M. Pope. Ouvrages traduits de l'anglois en françois. *A Londres: 1737.*

Richardson, Samuel. Pamela: ou la vertu récompensée. Traduit de l'anglois. *A Londres: chez T. Woodward et J. Osborn, 1741.*

Sheridan, Richard Brinsley. L'école du scandale, ou les mœurs du jour, comedie par monsieur Sheridan: traduite en françois par Mr. Bunel Delille. *Londres: imprimé par Galabin. Et se trouve chez Mr. Debrett; chez Mr. Hookham; chez Mr. Southern; chez Bossiere; chez Balcetti, 1789.*

And the trend continued in the nineteenth century with translations such as William Beckford's *Vathek* (Londres: chez Clarke, 1815), though increasingly the supply of translations of the major authors such as Scott or Dickens passed to Continental firms.

Science

A surprising amount of scientific material was published in French, as well as in English and Latin. Sometimes this was because of the nationality of the writer, such as the Huguenot engineer Isaac de Caus, 'ingeneur & architecte a Charles le Premier, Roy de la Grand Bretaigne';[19] sometimes for reasons of maximum publicity for a new invention such as the desalination process of Robert Fitzgerald and Nehemiah Grew, members of the College of Physicians and of the Royal Society, whose books went through numerous editions in English as well as in Latin and French translations.[20] In the eighteenth century many French scientific works were published in London on a wide range of topics: botany, astronomy, electricity, medicine, as well as many texts announcing the invention of scientific equipment such as those of Edward Nairne, who advertised several of his microscopes in French.[21] Scientific activity did not slow up in the nineteenth century; for example:

Bournon, Jacques Louis de. Traité de minéralogie. Première partie. Renfermant l'introduction à la minéralogie en général, la théorie de la cristallisation, l'étude de la chaux carbonatée proprement dite, et de l'arragonite, avec application du calcul cristallographique à la détermination des formes cristallines de ces deux substances. Par M. le comte de Bournon. *Londres: chez William Phillips, 1808.*

Works of popularisation continued, such as:

Calemard, M. N. Abrégé d'astronomie à la portée des jeunes demoiselles. *Londres: W. et C. Spilsbury, 1801* (fig. 2).

---

19 Caus, Isaac de, *Nouvelle invention de lever l'eau plus haut que sa source avec quelques machines mouvantes par le moyen de l'eau*, Londres: imprimé pour Thomas Davies, 1657 (Wing C1529); also his elder brother Salomon de Caus, *La perspectiue, auec la raison des ombres et miroirs. Par Salomon de Caus ingenieur du serenissime Prince de Galles*, Brussels and London, 1611 (STC 4868.7) and 1612 (STC 4869).

20 See Wing F1086 and Wing G1958D.

21 Nairne, Edward, *Description d'un simple microscope; & des machines necessaries* [sic] *à en faire un microscope solaire, … beaucoup perfectionnés pour ces usages par Edward Nairne, opticien & faiseur d'instruments philosophiques & mathematiques.* [London, 1780].

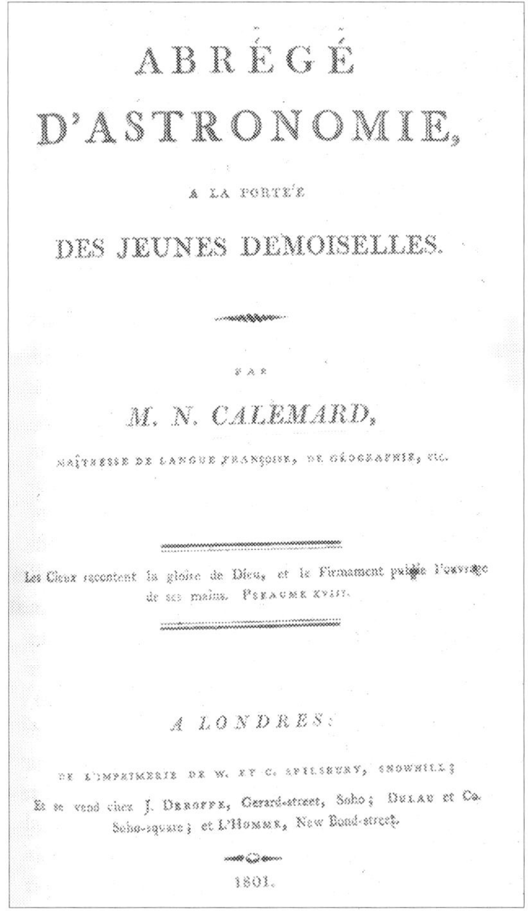

ABRÉGÉ
D'ASTRONOMIE,
A LA PORTÉE
DES JEUNES DEMOISELLES.

PAR
M. N. CALEMARD,
MAÎTRESSE DE LANGUE FRANÇOISE, DE GÉOGRAPHIE, ETC.

Les Cieux racontent la gloire de Dieu, et le Firmament publie l'ouvrage de ses mains. PSEAUME XVIII.

A LONDRES:
DE L'IMPRIMERIE DE W. ET C. SPILSBURY, SNOWHILL;
Et se vend chez J. DEBOFFE, Gerard-street, Soho; DULAU et Co. Soho-square; et L'HOMME, New Bond-street.
1801.

Fig. 2: Calemard, *Abrégé d'astronomie* (London: Spilsbury, 1801), title-page. British Library pressmark: 531.l.17(4).

Book trade

One final topic which should not be overlooked is the activity of the tradesmen who provided books in French for the various markets we have examined. The presence of 'aliens' in the ranks of the London book trade in the early Tudor period is well known.[22] In Elizabeth's reign Thomas Vautrollier, father and son, were active booksellers producing French

22 See E. J. Worman, *Alien Members of the Book-Trade during the Tudor Period* (London, 1906).

material as well as other books. There were also English printers and booksellers who specialised in satisfying the needs of the French-speaking market and who could be approached by an author with a manuscript to be published in French or who would commission translations of English works. John Norton declared himself as 'imprimeur ordinaire du Roy es langues estrangeres' in French books of 1609 and 1612. The number of native French book trade personnel seems to have been highest in the decades around 1700, no doubt owing to the numbers of Huguenot refugees following the revocation of the Edict of Nantes. These French booksellers are not well documented in the Bibliographical Society's *Dictionaries of the Printers and Booksellers Who Were at Work in England, Scotland and Ireland, 1557-1775*,[23] probably because their discovery during the initial compilation of STC and Wing was hindered by the fact that their books were in French. For example, Pierre de Varennes (noticed above as a printer of French Books of Common Prayer) produced French books in 1694, 1695 and 1698; his widow Madeleine in 1699, and Pierre II (their son?) from 1702 to 1719, and a Matthieu de Varennes (or Varrennes or Varenne) in 1722 and 1725. Of these, the *Dictionaries* record only a 'Varens' active in 1711. The Vaillant family (active between 1686 and 1802) is also not fully represented in the *Dictionary*. Daniel Du Chemin produced a number of books between 1688 and 1704 but the *Dictionary* recorded only his widow in 1705.[24]

In addition to this trade in locally published material, there were booksellers who imported modern language texts for sale in London. Strictly these fall outside the scope of the present study, but from quite an early date booksellers issued catalogues in French to advertise wares of this sort. This is mainly an eighteenth-century activity but one earlier example is:

> **Martin, Robert.** Catalogue des diverses liures francoises recueillées dans la France par Robert Martine, libraire de Londres ; aupres du quel ils se vendent, a l'enseigne de Venize, en la rue nommé Old-Bayly. *Imprime a Londres: chez Thomas Harper, 1640.* STC 17511.5.

---

23 H. R. Plomer et al., *Dictionaries of the Printers and Booksellers Who Were at Work in England, Scotland and Ireland 1557-1775* (London: Bibliographical Society, 1977) (reprint of works of 1910, 1907, 1922, 1932).

24 The imprints of entries retrieved from the ESTC database for this study reveal over 80 booksellers or printers with French names active in the production of French-language books up to 1800. Not all French names refer to a French national; the imprint 'A Londre: Ches Robert le Blanc, pour Henry Mortlock, 1673' (Wing S5672A) hides the English printer Robert White. I hope to publish a more detailed study of these French book trade personnel.

In the eighteenth century Paul Vaillant issued an alphabetical catalogue of his French stock, stressing his holdings of novels:

> **Vaillant, Paul.** Catalogue alphabétique des livres François, qui se trouvent & se vendent chez Paul Vaillant, libraire, vis-a-vis Southampton-street dans le Strand: avec un ample catalogue de romans. *1735.*

Towards the end of the century Thomas Hookham in Old Bond Street had a circulating library with a French stock:

> **Hookham, Thomas**. Nouveau catalogue francais de la bibliothèque circulante de Messrs. Hookham, sur un plan beaucoup plus étendu qu'aucun de ceux qui aient parû jusqu'à présent. [*London, 1792*].

and the well-known firm of Dulau which published foreign books in the first quarter of the nineteenth century issued catalogues of foreign-language material:

> **Dulau & Co.** Catalogue des livres François, Italiens, Espagnols, &c. &c. de A. Dulau & Co., libraires, No. 107. Wardour-Street, Soho. *Londres. Avril, 1798.*

The nineteenth century

It has already been pointed out that the absence of a fully coded and searchable database such as ESTC for nineteenth-century books makes it impossible to provide a full analysis of trends in French publishing in London after 1800. As has been stated several times, many of the trends of the eighteenth century are still to be found in the nineteenth. Booksellers continued to issue catalogues of French books:

> **Bossange & Masson.** Catalogue des livres français, italiens, espagnols, grecs, latins, &c. qui se trouvent chez Bossange & Masson, à Londres … à Paris … à Québec et à Montréal, même maison. *Londres: imprimé par Schulze et Dean, 1816.*

The need for educational texts continued to grow, as did demand for literary texts (though the two fields merge into each other). Religious, political and scientific controversies were still publicised in French editions. The topics of political controversy of course changed with the times: first of all, the French Revolution and its aftermath and the European obsession with Bonaparte; later, the various mid-century revolutions and counter-revolutions. A new campaigning topic which used French translations for publicity was the anti-slavery movement. Wilberforce petitioned Talleyrand at the Congress of Vienna in a letter translated into French:

> **Wilberforce, William.** Lettre à son Excellence Monseigneur le prince de Talleyrand Périgord, ministre et secrétaire d'état … au département des Affaires étrangères, … au sujet de la traite des nègres. … Traduite de l'anglais. *A Londres: De l'imprimerie de Schulze et Dean … et se trouve à Paris chez Le Normand, octobre 1814.*

as well as other heads of state:

> **Wilberforce, William.** Lettre à l'empereur Alexandre sur la traité des noirs. *Londres: Imprimé par G. Schulze, 1822.*

The Anti-Slavery Society was quick to use all opportunities to fight for abolition beyond Great Britain. Thomas Clarkson's famous pamphlet *The Cries of Africa* was translated into French, Spanish and Portuguese:

> **Clarkson, Thomas.** Le cri des Africains, contre les Européens, leurs oppresseurs, ou, Coup d'oeil sur le commerce homicide appelé traite des noirs … traduit de l'anglais. *Londres: G. Schulze, 1821.* Further edition: *Londres: Harvey et Darton, 1822.*[25]

Tourism had started to find a place in the Francophone output:

> Description historique de la Tour de Londres, et de ses curiosités. *Londres: Hack*, [c. *1820*].

And finally the Quakers still seem to be of potential interest to the French market:

> **Du Thon, Adèle.** Histoire de la Secte des Amis ; suivie d'une notice sur Madame Fry et la Prison de Newgate, à Londres. *Londres: W. Phillips, 1821.*

Conclusion

Such is the volume of French-language material produced in early modern London that it has only been possible to give a brief indication of the breadth of subjects covered in any one period. This ranged from leisure reading, through popular piety and the liturgical needs of the French-speaking communities, to news and political reporting, and scientific discovery. The striking thing about the market for all this material is the presence of a sizeable French population in the capital: merchants, diplomats, but more numerously the religious refugees of the Huguenot period and the political refugees of post-Revolutionary times. From Caxton's French vocabulary through to the voluminous literary, political and scholarly publication of the nineteenth century, the French language can be seen to be a constant factor in the composition of the capital's book trade.

---

25 See *The Slave Trade: books and pamphlets on slavery and its abolition printed before 1900 in Canterbury Cathedral Library*, compiled by Clare Gathercole, revised by David Shaw, with an Historical Introduction by David Turley, Canterbury Sources, 3 (Canterbury, 2001), no. ST90.

Morna Daniels

A King's Last Days
true and false memoirs of Louis XVI's valet

In the 1790s English society enjoyed the frisson of horror at events across the Channel. There were of course more serious concerns over the war with France, the high price of food and, among the upper classes, fears that Republicanism would spread to England. Emigrés crowded into London. In such an atmosphere, a tremendous stir was created by the publication in London in 1798 of the memoirs of Jean-Baptiste Cléry, the valet of the executed Louis XVI, who shared his last imprisonment in the Temple: *Journal de ce qui s'est passé à la Tour du Temple, pendant la captivité de Louis XVI, roi de France*. Fanny Burney, who was to marry an émigré, wrote to her father that 'M. Cléry's book has half killed us; we have read it together, and the deepest tragedy we have yet met with is slight to it'. She praised the 'evident worth and feeling of the writer' and claimed to have undergone 'a soul-piercing experience'. Cléry himself read the text to audiences and achieved great, but short-lived, celebrity. Six thousand copies were sold in three days, and it was immediately reprinted (fig. 1).

Louis XVI married Maria Antonina (Marie Antoinette), youngest daughter of the Empress Maria Theresa of Austria. Their son, the Dauphin, was theoretically Louis XVII after his father's execution, but died as a child in the Temple prison. After the fall of Napoleon, Louis was succeeded by two younger brothers in turn, the comte de Provence as Louis XVIII and the comte d'Artois as Charles X, deposed in the revolution of 1830. Charles's son the duc d'Angoulême married Louis XVI's daughter, but they were exiled to Scotland in 1830 and had no children.

Jean-Baptiste Cant-Hanet Cléry was born on 11 May 1759, the son of a farmer, within the park of Versailles, and was recommended by the comtesse de Polignac to be valet to the young Dauphin. His journal begins by describing the attack on the Tuileries palace on 10 August 1792, when many of the Royal household and the Swiss guards were massacred. Cléry owed his life to his plain clothes, which led the mob to assume that he was one of them. He quickly threw away his palace pass and made his escape through streets

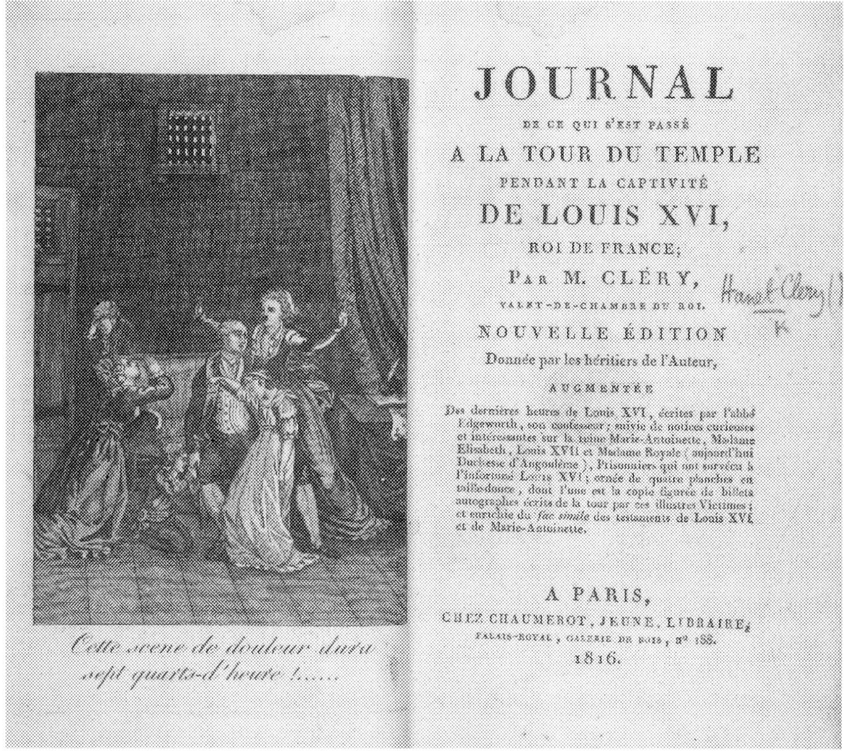

Cette scène de douleur dura sept quarts-d'heure !......

JOURNAL
DE CE QUI S'EST PASSÉ
A LA TOUR DU TEMPLE
PENDANT LA CAPTIVITÉ
DE LOUIS XVI,
ROI DE FRANCE;
PAR M. CLÉRY,
VALET-DE-CHAMBRE DU ROI.

NOUVELLE ÉDITION
Donnée par les héritiers de l'Auteur,
AUGMENTÉE

Des dernières heures de Louis XVI, écrites par l'abbé Edgeworth, son confesseur; suivie de notices curieuses et intéressantes sur la reine Marie-Antoinette, Madame Elisabeth, Louis XVII et Madame Royale (aujourd'hui Duchesse d'Angoulême), Prisonniers qui ont survécu à l'infortuné Louis XVI; ornée de quatre planches en taille-douce, dont l'une est la copie figurée de billets autographes écrits de la tour par ces illustres Victimes; et enrichie du *fac simile* des testamens de Louis XVI et de Marie-Antoinette.

A PARIS,
CHEZ CHAUMEROT, JEUNE, LIBRAIRE,
PALAIS-ROYAL, GALERIE DE BOIS, n° 188.
1816.

Fig. 1: Cléry, *Journal* (Paris: Chaumerot, 1816), title-page and frontispiece. British Library pressmark: 10658.b.27.

littered with naked, decomposing bodies, and, talking his way out of being arrested, reached his home in the country.

He went back to Paris to seek news of the King, and applied to Pétion the mayor of Paris to serve the royal family now imprisoned in the Temple. The Temple was a fortified monastery originally built for the Templars, but used after the dissolution of the order as a state prison, then as a priory for the Hospitallers of St John of Jerusalem before reverting to a prison. It was in the north-east of the old city, now just south-west of the Place de la République. After the Revolution it became a place of pilgrimage for Royalists, but was demolished in 1811, under Napoleon, and only the Square du Temple remains.

Cléry describes the scene when the Queen was forced to see the head of her friend the princess de Lamballe on a pike, 'her blond hair, still in curls floating around the pike', and her heart spiked on a sabre. The mob wanted to bring the princess's body into the Temple, and possibly kill the royal family too, but city officials tied a tricolour ribbon across the entrance. A

'Commissaire' called Daujon harangued the crowd about the rule of law, and told them that justice belonged to all the people of Paris and should be enforced through the courts, which seems to have deterred them. Afterwards an official made Cléry pay 45 sous for the ribbon.

Cléry describes the daily routine. The King rose at six and read until nine. Cléry dressed the hair of all the family, and cleaned the rooms. The King and Queen gave their children lessons, and at midday the ladies changed from their morning dresses and walked in the garden if fine. Cléry encouraged the Dauphin to run about and play. People who were still sympathetic to the royal family would try and glimpse them from nearby windows. Dinner was at two, and the King had a nap at four. Then Cléry taught the Dauphin writing, and played ball games with him. Afterwards the Queen would read history books to the children. Someone came and shouted out items of news outside the tower (he does not say who sent him). Their clothes became worn out, and Madame Elizabeth had to mend the King's clothes while he was in bed. The wife of the English ambassador sent clothes to the Queen.

On 29 September writing materials were taken away, and the King was separated from his family and lodged in the large tower. Cléry went with him. The grief of the royal ladies softened the hearts of their captors, and the family were allowed to dine together and Cléry attended them all.

Cléry's wife brought news, which he tried to whisper to the King while putting on his shoes so that the guards should not hear. On 26 October Cléry was arrested and accused by the Revolutionary Tribunal of passing letters to the King. He was acquitted by the jury as no letters were produced. Then the Dauphin was removed from the Queen, to her great distress, and housed next to the King, with Cléry to look after them. Cléry fell ill with rheumatic fever, as the tower was chilly and airless, but refused to be bled as that would have meant leaving the family, and perhaps not returning. The royal family smuggled him medicines.

All sharp items were removed, including embroidery scissors, and the ladies had to bite their thread. The ante-chamber of the King's room was covered with wallpaper depicting the interior of a prison, with a panel listing the rights of man. Mass was forbidden, so the King read a breviary. He also read travel and natural history books, Tasso, and Hume's *History of England.* The guards even broke open peach stones to see if there were messages inside. The King revised a translation he had made of a book by Horace Walpole on Richard III, which defended Richard's reputation. This was published, as an act of piety, by Lerouge, in 1800. He offered the opinion that Louis, concerned about accusations of tyranny against himself, was sympathetic to another king who had gained a possibly false bad reputation. Louis also read about Charles I.

When the King was separated from his family, the royal ladies arranged for Cléry to pass messages between them with dirty clothes, or to poke them into cupboards where their sympathetic guard could find them. Madame Elizabeth pricked out messages with a pin, and when enough string had been saved from parcels, letters were lowered from the ladies to a window Cléry could get to, for delivery to the King.

The King was very upset at missing his daughter's birthday, and at not being able to shave (for fear he would cut his throat), and eventually he was allowed to shave in front of the guards. In December 1792 he was tried, and finally on 17 January 1793 his defending counsel brought news that he was condemned to death.

Cléry could not bring himself to look at the King, and prepared the King's shaving materials, but when he did eventually catch the King's eye, his knees buckled, and the King went pale, as if suddenly taking in the reality of his sentence. He grasped Cléry's hands and urged him to be brave. He read an account of the execution of Charles I. On the evening of the 20th the family farewells took an hour and three quarters, in sight but not in hearing of Cléry and the guards.

That night the King said it 'wasn't worth' curling his hair. Cléry records the King's words of gratitude to him, his goodness and courage, and his request to look after his son. He entrusted to Cléry his wedding ring to give the Queen and his seal for his son. Cléry was terrified when told he would be required to help the King undress, on the scaffold, and although he steeled himself to perform this last service for the King, he is honest enough to admit his relief when told by the guards the executioner would do this. The King departed with Santerre, head of the National Guard, and an hour later they all heard the salvo of guns which announced his execution.

Cléry served the royal family for a while, but was persuaded to retire to the country and in June he was listed as a 'Suspect' for having carried correspondence between the King and the Girondins. In mid September he was arrested and imprisoned in La Force prison. His family tried every means they could to free him, but as the Terror claimed more victims, Cléry felt it would be better not to remind the authorities of his existence. He remained in prison a year, but at least he survived, and was released only after the fall of Robespierre, on 10 August 1794.

He was very hard up, and managed to get an office job in the City administration, but the pay was low, and the fall in the value of assignats depleted any reserves he may have had, so he had to sell some of his possessions to support his wife and family.

After the execution of his parents, the child Dauphin, known as Louis XVII to the Royalists, was kept in filthy, cramped and dark conditions, in the very room where his father had been imprisoned, and with unsympathetic gaolers. He developed a skin disease, swollen joints and tuberculosis of the bones, and recent DNA tests conclude that he died there. His older sister Marie-Thérèse, Madame Royale, stood up better to captivity, and, as the 'orphan of the Temple', won the sympathy of the Paris crowds, who gathered under her window to sing sad songs. She became an embarrassment to the Government, who exchanged her in December 1795 for a prisoner of the Austrians.

Cléry obtained a post in Strasbourg, but when Marie-Thérèse passed through on her way to Austria, he joined her, accompanying her to the Austrian court in Vienna. Cléry was worried at leaving his own family destitute, but his brother undertook their support. In Vienna Marie-Thérèse was urged by her Austrian relatives to marry the Archduke Charles, brother of the Emperor, and a very able general, with the intention of reclaiming the throne on her behalf, as her brother was dead, and adding France to the Austrian Empire. Her uncle, now calling himself Louis XVIII, wanted to boost his family's claims by marrying her to his nephew, the duc d'Angoulême, son of the comte d'Artois. Cléry argued her uncle's case, and was able to take a letter to him in Verona in January 1796 to say she accepted Angoulême.

Louis urged Cléry to write his memoirs. Cléry returned to Vienna with money for Marie-Thérèse to make her less dependent on her relatives, and was eventually granted a pension by the Austrians, at Marie-Thérèse's request. Cléry visited Louis XVIII in Blankenburg in the Harz mountains, where he had taken refuge, having been expelled from Verona. By this time Cléry had written his memoirs, and Louis was much affected by a reading which Cléry gave.

Cléry was not able to publish his memoirs in any country under Austrian domination, because Napoleon had defeated the Austrians in northern Italy, and signed a peace treaty with them at Campo-Formio in October 1797. Napoleon was of course opposed to the Royalists, not only as a Republican, but because he had ambitions to seize power. The Austrians did not want to anger Napoleon, but Cléry and his publication were welcomed in England, still at war with France, and pro-Royalist, although the British government was not enthusiastic about the characters and conduct of the surviving royal brothers. Britain had declared war on France, ostensibly as a result of the execution of the King, though a desire to free the Low Countries from the French, and a determination to retain supremacy at sea and seize French colonies were probably more important. But of course, such a hagiography of the King and stirring up of feeling against the French was welcome to the government, glad to justify the new income tax which had been imposed to finance the war. So Cléry travelled to London.

Cléry's *Journal de ce qui s'est passé à la Tour du Temple, pendant la captivité de Louis XVI, roi de France*, was published by subscription in London, by Baylis, of Greville St, and was sold 'chez l'auteur, no 29 Great Pulteney St, Golden Square' and at booksellers. The list of subscribers is headed by the King, the Queen, and their numerous offspring. Sixteen octavo pages follow, from the Marquess of Abercorn to J. Zoffany, presumably the artist, and including Mrs Cosway, Mrs Fitzherbert, Lady Elizabeth Foster, the Dukes of Marlborough, Northumberland, many other peers, and William Pitt. The British Library inherited the copies of three of the subscribers, the King (pressmark 182.d.19), Grenville (G.15299) and Cracherode (672.h.12) . The subscription list also features in a fourth copy of this edition (010661.g.46). A later edition from 1798, of which the British Library has a copy, has no subscription list, and gives the author's address as 6, Lisle Street, Leicester Square (1200.h.2(1)). Baylis published in the same year, 1798, translations of Cléry's *Journal* into English, German and Italian. Also in that year the French text was printed in Quebec by John Neilson.

Some historians queried Cléry's authorship, suggesting instead the ex-bishop of Nancy, Nicolas de La Fare, which seems to indicate a snobbish incredulity that a valet could publish a book. Jean Eckard, however, who contributed to the preface to the 1825 edition of the *Journal*, says that he saw the original manuscript, with a note from the comte de Provence (Louis XVIII), and had no doubt it was by Cléry.

Cléry made a considerable amount of money from the memoirs, and then delivered a letter from the comte d'Artois, who was exiled in Edinburgh, but who made visits to London, to Marie-Thérèse in Vienna, urging her to marry his son, whose portrait he carried. Artois lived in Holyrood House on the interesting grounds that, as it had once been an Abbey, he could not be arrested for debt there. Cléry accompanied Marie-Thérèse to Mitau, in Courland, where Louis XVIII had been lent a home by the Tsar, to marry her cousin Angoulême in 1799.

Cléry died on 27 May 1809 at Hitzing, near Vienna, worn out with travelling and grieved at the separation from his children and loss of hope that the monarchy might be restored. On his gravestone was written 'Ci gît le fidèle Cléry'. His wife, née Duverger, who had also served the royal family, died in Paris in 1811. He left two daughters and a son, Charles Cléry de Klufeld, a sub-lieutenant in the Gardes-Wallonnes, who was wounded in the Battle of Zujar (Murcia) on 9 August 1812, taken prisoner, and shot the next day. After the Restoration, the King gave a title of nobility to the husband of Cléry's youngest daughter Madame Grem de Cléry, to honour her father's memory.

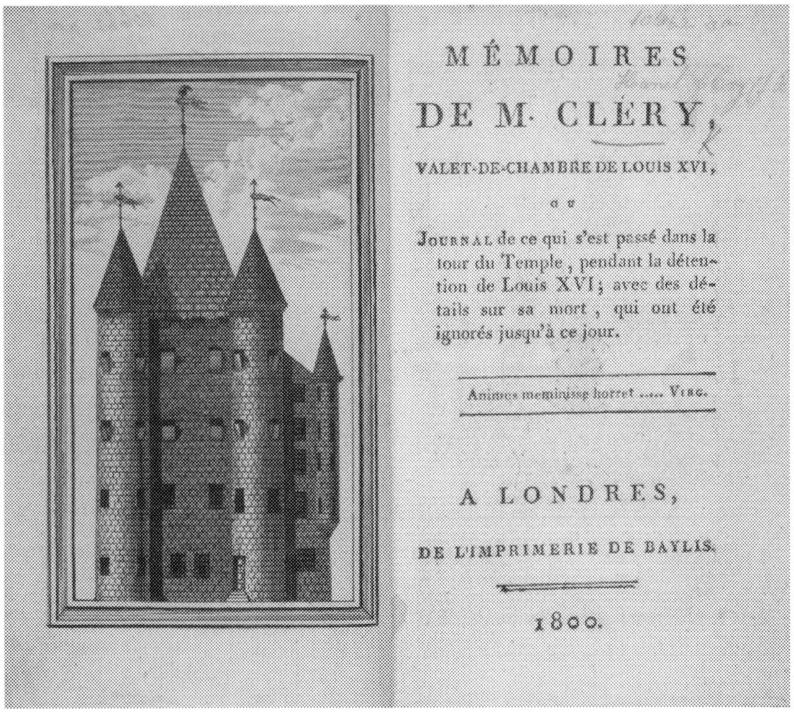
MÉMOIRES
DE M. CLÉRY,
VALET-DE-CHAMBRE DE LOUIS XVI,
OU
JOURNAL de ce qui s'est passé dans la tour du Temple, pendant la détention de Louis XVI; avec des détails sur sa mort, qui ont été ignorés jusqu'à ce jour.

Animus meminisse horret .... VIRG.

A LONDRES,
DE L'IMPRIMERIE DE BAYLIS.
1800.

Fig. 2: Cléry, *Mémoires* (London: Baylis, 1800), title-page and frontispiece. British Library pressmark: 10662.aa.29.

In 1800 there appeared in London what purported to be another edition of Cléry's memoirs also claiming (falsely) to be published by Baylis (BL copy 10662.aa.29) (fig. 2). Although much of the text is copied from the first edition of the memoirs, they are considerably expanded in order to absolve the National Convention, the government of the time, of blame for the execution of the King. Instead the book claims that the King, by his own behaviour and guided by the bad advice of the Queen and Cléry, brought his fate on himself. The false Cléry claims that he was not Royalist, but his 'stupidity and presumption' led to the death of the King. He thought the Germans and Austrians would defeat the French and restore the monarchy, and brought the royal family only good news from outside which made them over-optimistic and arrogant, which irritated their guards and their judges.

The Queen, 'l'autre chienne' ('the other bitch' – instead of *l'Autrichienne*, 'the Austrian') was scheming to be regent, and wanted to keep control of the Dauphin and she, and the King's sister, are constantly attacked by the writer. In fact a footnote deplores the arrogance and bad attitudes of women in general since the Revolution, and their failure to keep to their place, which is to change attitudes by their gentleness and goodness. This is not the fault of the 'tricoteuses', the women who knitted round the scaffolds, but of those from the upper classes, like Olympe de Gouges, who led them astray. Napoleon strongly believed in the subservience of women, and took away all the rights women had gained during the Revolution. He made divorce impossible, except for himself.

The false Cléry claims that he did not tell the King that it was forbidden to wear orders and decorations, and that foreign ones should have been returned to the Convention, and continued to adorn his master with them, thus giving the King an appearance of defiance which led to his condemnation. The King, he says, expected to be deported, and this made him adopt an unwise attitude at his trial. He, Cléry, was too ambitious to follow the King into exile, but wanted instead to serve the Dauphin, a role which would be more important. He also 'confesses' that when the King was refused a razor, he said he should acquiesce, so that he would look more pathetic at his trial, whereas in fact the King did get permission to be shaved. He makes the King seem less brave and suggests that he was expecting to be rescued.

The main drive of the false memoirs is to blame the queen, as an Austrian, for the execution of the King, and to discredit the heroic Cléry and tarnish the saintly image of the royal family. Napoleon seized power in November 1799, being confirmed as First Consul (with two others) in December. He continued the war with Austria declared the previous March and defeated the Austrians at Marengo in June 1800. But England was having great success against the French at sea, blockading French ports; and Napoleon, wanting to re-establish trade and prosperity, was working towards a settlement with England, concluded at the Peace of Amiens on 27 March 1802, after which English tourists flooded across the Channel. It is within this context that we see the writer of the new memoirs attacking the Austrians, Britain's allies, but trying to court British public opinion and excuse the sacrilegious execution of a King.

Cléry vehemently denounced these memoirs as a 'production de la plus raffinée scélératesse' (a production of the most refined wickedness) in the periodical *Le Spectateur du Nord*, February 1801. He rants that he, known for his faithfulness, would hardly publish such a confession of faults, and he had the confidence of the wife of the as yet unrestored Louis XVIII, in whose household he served.

Pierre Ladoué, in his bibliography of panegyrics of Louis XVI, describes these memoirs as the edition of the Commissaires du Temple (commissioners of the Temple). They were re-circulated during the Hundred Days, when Napoleon re-established himself after his escape from Elba, and obviously wanted to denigrate the Royal family who had been temporarily restored. So who was Napoleon's tool?

The British Library catalogue mentions that these false memoirs are sometime attributed to François Daujon. This is the name given in the first 'true' memoirs to the guard who persuaded the mob carrying the head of the princesse de Lamballe to go away, and not to burst in and murder the Queen. Cléry informed the King of Daujon's name, and when the latter returned to his duties four months later the King thanked him. François Daujon was a sculptor, still active in 1809. Goret, a friend, stated in 1816 that he had been dead several years, and that he disliked Bonaparte as a tyrant, though he did have a post in the city administration. A manuscript memoir by him of the Lamballe incident was acquired by Victorien Sardou, and was published by G. Lenotre. He calls the King Capet, and notes the haughty behaviour of his sister. He describes the Lamballe episode in gruesome detail, and his own part in restraining the mob, standing on a chair behind the barrier of a tricolour ribbon. He also urged the mob to take its horrible trophies to the Tuileries garden. He was later congratulated by officials from the Assemblée législative and by the Mayor, Pétion.

In the false memoirs this protector is named as Danjou. The Lamballe episode is narrated in great detail, which suggests an authentic eye-witness account. The heroic orator is described as a man of nearly 60, and his age and authority calmed the mob, who were not Parisians but outsiders, and riff-raff 'thrown up by the dubious policies of France's enemies'. He acted out of respect for the law but did not like the royal family. This could have been Daujon, if he died about 1810, when he would have been about 76, and his name a mistake. On the other hand it seems rather unlikely that Daujon would have got his own name wrong in these false memoirs, unless he never saw the proofs. Also, he was known to be hostile to Napoleon, and considered by his friend to be a forthright sort of chap.

There was a Danjou who could have written the false memoirs. Jean-Pierre-André Danjou (1760-1832) was a deputy from Oise, who was elected to the Council of 500, but was pleased with Napoleon's coup, and became a supporter of his policies. In July 1800 he obtained a government post within the criminal tribunal of Oise, and four years later gained the légion d'honneur. But he was too young to be 'nearly 60', unless he wished to claim glory for his father, or another relative.

Napoleon had already become a skilled self-propagandist in the reporting of his Italian campaigns. As the post of Commissioner of the Temple was only undertaken for short spells, there were a number of former commissioners who could have been encouraged to write this account to justify the treatment of the King and to dispel the saintly glow that Cléry had cast around the royal family.

Bibliography

Kirsty Carpenter, *Refugees of the French Revolution. Emigrés in London, 1789-1802* (London: Macmillan, 1999).

E. H. Daniel, *Biographie des hommes de Seine-et-Oise* (Paris, 1832).

Ernest Daudet, *Madame Royale*, translated by Mrs Rodolph Stawell (London: William Heinemann, 1913).

Pierre Ladoué, *Les Panégyristes de Louis XVI et de Marie-Antoinette* (Paris: Alphonse Picard, 1912).

J. F. E. Robinet, A. Robert and J. Le Chaplain, *Dictionnaire de la Révolution et de l'Empire* (Paris: Librairie historique de la Révolution et de l'Empire, 1898).

Maurice Tourneux, *Marie-Antoinette devant l'histoire*, 2nd edn (Paris: Henri Leclerc, 1891).

Stephen Parkin

Italian Printing in London 1553-1900

Although the number of books published in London in the Italian language over the course of the 350 years of this survey (1553 – the date of the appearance of the first book in Italian – and the end of the nineteenth century) is substantial, as revealed by a preliminary search on the online databases of the *English Short-Title Catalogue* and the *Nineteenth-Century Short-Title Catalogue*,[1] a closer look at the dates and details of the records

1 As of January 2002, a straightforward search of the ESTC combining language of publication ('Italian') and place of publication ('Londra') produced 437 records. For the NSTC 1st series (to 1871) it is not possible to search by language and more roundabout methods using relevant subject headings have to be employed which also retrieve much material printed in English: without a careful analysis of all the data from the NSTC it is impossible to give a precise figure but a rough estimate might be at least double the number in the 327 years covered by the ESTC. But even the ESTC figure can only be a temporary and approximate total: the catalogue is still growing and being amended as bibliographical discovery and research continues. An even more pressing reason why these figures should not be taken at face value is that both catalogues include editions in which London is given as a false imprint (and not always identified as such): here is perhaps the best place to point out that, by definition, such false imprints fall beyond the scope of this essay. The most comprehensive, if still incomplete, listing of publications which use 'Londra' as a false imprint remains Marino Parenti's entry under the place-name in his *Dizionario dei luoghi di stampa falsi, inventati o supposti in opere di autori e traduttori italiani* (Firenze, 1951) and from this (and the ESTC) it is evident that the practice was most common in the eighteenth century. Where the use of false imprints does touch on the subject of this essay is in the degree of plausibility intended in the deceptive use of 'Londra' since its effectiveness clearly depends on the presence of Italian printing in the city being well known. It is usually hard, however, without clear evidence beyond the books themselves, to determine the intention behind the use of a particular place in a false imprint. A relevant case in point is the series of Italian literary classics published by the Livorno printer and bookseller Tommaso Masi, all of which, with minor variants, carry the (half-false) imprint; 'Londra: si vende in Livorno presso Giovanni Tommaso Masi e Compagni'. Guido Chiappini's *L'Arte della stampa a Livorno: note ed appunti storici* (Livorno, 1904) quotes archival documents showing that Masi used this, with the connivance of the secular authorities, in order to avoid having to obtain a licence for printing from the ecclesiastical censors in Tuscany, since some of the texts (but by no means all) might

retrieved shows that the phenomenon is a highly discontinuous and episodic one. The map drawn by these bibliographic resources depicts an archipelago not a single landmass. What we find are single events or at the most short-lived clusters of activity: a prestigious subscription edition comes out, a publisher collaborates with an (Italian) editor on one or a few books, the arrival of an author in the metropolis leads to a short flurry of production. Not until the end of the nineteenth century could it be said that publishing in Italian becomes an institutionalised aspect of London publishing.

This should not be surprising. Publishing books in a foreign vernacular for the domestic market is in the best of circumstances an artificial enterprise, more willed than spontaneous, both in commercial and technical terms. Many of these books respond to a short-lived public interest or the support of particular patrons; some editions, especially in the sixteenth century, appear to have been printed more for private circulation than for public sale. Even with the emergence of a wider readership in the eighteenth century there is intermittent evidence that the commercial path was not always smooth: subscription editions are announced which never get beyond the first volume, while, from the 1790s onwards, the first Italian (or parallel text) periodicals, a form of publishing the economic viability of which depends on a steady and numerous readership, cease publication after only a few issues. In the early nineteenth century, the vain efforts made by Foscolo, newly arrived in London and desperate to make money, to enlist subscribers for a series of Italian classics, to be edited by him, are well known.[2] From a purely technical

be regarded as morally licentious. This 'evidence' raises more puzzles than it solves and in any case the question of why Masi chose London remains unanswered. Were imported books from London a plausible possibility which would bamboozle the Church inspectors, if Masi were found out, and convince them that he was merely an innocent if opportunistic bookseller? Ever since it was founded as a free port, Livorno (Leghorn) had had close and durable commercial links with England; moreover this was a period when the classics of Italian literature, as published by Masi, were in vogue in England. Did such considerations enter Masi's head? Did he think they increased the verisimilitude of the false imprint? Would putting 'Filadelfia', say, have done as well? Examples of the reverse case – of surreptitious printing in London which gives a false imprint elsewhere – are largely confined to the sixteenth century, and particularly to the production of John Wolfe, who appears to have taken an almost theatrical pleasure in using fictional aliases: see Denis B. Woodfield, *Surreptitious Printing in England 1550-1640* (New York, 1973).

2 Even when a sufficient number of subscribers was signed up, the prospects were not secure: Foscolo in a letter to Lord Guilford quotes the publisher John Murray telling him that 'even if five hundred subscribers were found it would still be difficult to find a hundred of them prepared to pay for the book once published' ('quand'anche si trovassero *cinquecento associati*, si stenterebbe a trovare *cento pagatori* del libro') (Francesco Viglioni, *Ugo Foscolo in Inghilterra: saggi* (Catania, 1910), p. 209).

point of view, too, printing in Italian was not a straightforward task for the employees of a London printing house. Many of these publications were seen through the press by Italians resident in London: it was perhaps the only way of ensuring sufficient accuracy in the text. Where such close involvement and surveillance was not exercised, complaints about compositorial errors abound: in the preface to his *Del teatro brittannico* of 1683, Gregorio Leti craves his readers' indulgence for the infinite number of errors in the text ('à hauer compassione degli errori della stampa, che sono infiniti…') because he had not been present ('io lontano, e lo stampatore inglese'); Pickering's 1825 edition of Foscolo's *Discorso sul testo di Dante* was 'so full of misprints that [the poet] was in despair';[3] the (first) *Gazzetta italiana di Londra*, which had a brief life of less than a year in 1871, carries an evidently embarrassed (and repeated) apology for the numerous mistakes in the paper which the editors attribute to the 'innumerable difficulties encountered in printing an Italian newspaper in a foreign country' ('gli innumerevoli difficoltà che abbiamo ad incontrare nel fare stampare un giornale italiano in paese straniero').[4] Even Baskerville (or his compositor) nods: a variant title-page, no doubt quickly discarded and corrected, exists for one of the volumes of the 1771/3 *édition de luxe* he printed (on commission from the London bookseller Pietro Molini) of the *Orlando furioso* (the only book in Italian from the Baskerville press) where the error 'dai trochj', instead of 'torchj', is prominently displayed in the imprint statement itself.[5]

The nature of the activity of publishing Italian books in London as just described suggests that a knowledge of the people involved as much as of the books themselves is important for a full understanding of the phenomenon: the authors, editors, translators, the publishers, printers and booksellers, the patrons and subscribers whose presence, interests and activities can be deduced from the printed volumes. Again, closer analysis of the short-title catalogue data reveals how comparatively restricted their number is: most of the books we have are the result – almost, it might be said, the trace – of the energetic activities of a few individuals who either chose or were obliged to

3 Margaret C. W. Wicks, *The Italian Exiles in London 1816-1848* (Manchester, 1937), p. 57.

4 Wolfe playfully transposes the predicament in the preface to one of his false 'Palermo' imprints, as part of the fiction: 'Per esser eglino siciliani, et per non sapere la favella toscana, con tutta la loro diligenza, non gli hanno potuto schifare' ('as Sicilians, they have not been able to avoid making typographical errors, despite all their care'). Clifford Huffman comments: 'For Palermo, pretty clearly, we are to understand London, and for the Sicilian typesetters ignorant of Tuscan, we are to construe John Wolfe's London typesetters ignorant of Italian in any form' (C. C. Huffman, *Elizabethan Impressions: John Wolfe and his press* (New York, 1988), p. 4).

5 Philip Gaskell, *John Baskerville: a bibliography* (Cambridge, 1959), p. 60.

make a living outside Italy and who undertook a variety of jobs in the process – teaching, translating, writing books and journalism, editing, bookselling[6] – most, however, in various ways exploiting their origin for their careers' sake and in order to disseminate the language and culture of their native country.

Such persons are more or less easy to identify and range from the celebrated exiles – Bruno, Foscolo, Mazzini – to less dramatic intermediaries between the two cultures such as the translator and editor Paolo Rolli, the teacher and journalist (and friend of Johnson) Giuseppe Baretti, the brothers Giambattista and Pietro Rolandi, booksellers and publishers (the former was also an editor and translator). The close-knit internal relations – rivalries as well as alliances – formed within this comparatively limited dramatis personae, especially in the second half of the sixteenth and the first half of the nineteenth centuries, provide in themselves a kind of unity and continuity in the subject. London was a very small society for most of the period under consideration and the Italians who lived and worked in the city knew their contemporaries and fellow expatriates. But there is also a kind of continuity over time. Michelangelo Florio, the pastor of the Italian church in London and the translator of the first book in Italian printed in London, was the father of the celebrated John Florio, translator (most notably of Montaigne's *Essayes*) and lexicographer (he compiled the first English-Italian dictionary, *A Worlde of Wordes...*, printed in 1598); in the following century, the teacher and bookseller Giovanni Torriano refers explicitly to John Florio as a predecessor whose work his own continues and completes.[7] Gregorio Leti claims (with

6 Teaching was the financial mainstay of almost all the Italians mentioned in this essay; many, from John Florio to Panizzi, also published language manuals and readers. For Gabriele Rossetti, mindful of Foscolo's incessant money problems, the priorities on his arrival in England were clear: his writing would support his teaching, 'the author [will] accredit the instructor' (E. R. Vincent, *Gabriele Rossetti in England* (Oxford, 1936), p. 1). For most of the period, teaching took the form of private tutoring, often as a member of an aristocratic household (who would also sometimes be expected to accompany his charges on their grand tour in Italy); in the later eighteenth century we find Italian masters working in institutions such as the city's musical and dancing academies and private schools; in the early nineteenth century the first chairs of Italian in the country were founded at University College and King's College, occupied by the arch-rivals Panizzi and Rossetti respectively. (The initial intake of students was, however, extremely low.) In 1871, the Italian newspaper *La Gazzetta italiana di Londra* lamented the decline both in the general interest in learning Italian and the quality of teaching available, undertaken by men of undistinguished intellect ('uomini di niuna levatura') rather than the scholars and writers of former times.

7 See Giovanni Torriano, *The Italian Reviv'd...* (London, 1689), ff. A2-3. Torriano had produced a new edition of Florio's dictionary: *Vocabolario italiano & inglese, a dictionary Italian & English formerly compiled by John Florio...* (London, 1659).

characteristic inaccuracy – but it was a useful credential) that his 1683 account of Britain, *Del teatro brittannico*, completes the work left unfinished by Charles I's Italian historiographer Giovanni Francesco Biondi. Giuseppe Baretti in *The Italian Library* (1757) urges English grand tourists in Venice to search out Petruccio Ubaldini's manuscript history of Edward VI's reign gathering dust in the Marciana library: in his view, their money would be better spent on getting an edition published of this – a text by a once well-known figure in Elizabethan London – than on yet more paintings.[8] Other types of presence provide continuity too: patrons have already been mentioned. Aristocratic and on occasion royal patronage remains a constant feature of Italian publishing in London, from the Italophile circles which congregated round Philip Sidney in the Elizabethan court to Lord and Lady Holland's support of Foscolo or Panizzi's relations with Thomas Grenville (although the change in social conditions, not to mention the personalities involved, make the latter two cases more complex relationships).

In the survey which follows I have chosen to concentrate on figures such as these (since a mere bibliographical listing, given its potential size and the limits of this essay, would necessarily be incomplete, as well as unillustrative) – on people and on the patterns of collaboration they formed, so shedding light, I hope, on the kinds of circumstances which led to the publication of Italian books in England.

One figure of course is missing from those just listed: the reader. 'To ask the hard question is simple': who read these books? Dedications to patrons and lists of noble and wealthy subscribers testify to the status of 'la lingua toscana' and its literature but not necessarily to the real knowledge and use made of it. A useful distinction may be drawn between (native) Italian readers and readers with a knowledge of Italian. There was no large settled Italian immigrant community in London (or elsewhere in Great Britain) until the middle decades of the nineteenth century (the first newspaper titles aimed expressly at the expatriate community were launched towards the end of the century), and even then 'settled' is a misleading term, since it included an unusually high proportion of people practising itinerant trades (street-vendors, entertainers, and the like).[9] Before this period, with one exception,

8 Giuseppe Baretti, *The Italian Library containing an account of the lives and works of the most valuable authors of Italy* (London, 1757), p. 186.

9 Lucio Sponza, *Italian Immigrants in Nineteenth-century Britain: realities and images* (Leicester, 1988), chapters 1 and 3. Giuseppe Mazzini founded a free Italian school in London in the 1840s for the education of poor immigrant children; for a year (1842-3) it published its own magazine: *Il Pellegrino: giornale istruttivo, morale e piacevole della Scuola Madre Italiana gratuita.*

Italian books published in London do not appear to have been produced for Italian readers in England to buy and read. The exception comes in its own temporal parenthesis at the very beginning of our survey:[10] Michelangelo Florio's translation of John Ponet's Protestant catechism *Cathechismo, cioe forma breue per amaestrare i fanciulli*... was written and printed (in 1553, probably during the political limbo which followed the death of Edward in July – much later, Florio's life of Jane Gray, whose Italian tutor he had been, containing an account of these turbulent days, was printed posthumously)[11] specifically for the small congregation of Italian Protestants in London centred on the so-called Italian Church.[12] However, it also appears to be the case that many books printed in London were also – or primarily – intended for export to Italy. Under interrogation from the Inquisition, Giordano Bruno asserted that the use of false imprints (specifically of 'Venetia', although 'Parigi' had also been used) by the printer John Charlewood for the series of his dialogues published in London between 1583 and 1585 was for reasons of commercial advantage rather than secrecy, 'per venderli piú facilmente ed acciò havessero maggior esito' (i.e. on the Continent).[13] Thirty years later, we find the King's Printer John Bill complaining to the Stationers' Company that 'some great quantities' of copies of books by the exiled renegade archbishop of Spalato

---

10 It had obviously been forgotten nearly thirty years later by the time Wolfe printed Ubaldini's *Vita di Carlo Magno* (1581), which the author claimed was the first Italian book printed in London. Since there continued to be an Italian congregation in London, it is curious that the Anglican liturgy had to wait until 1685 for a published Italian translation: *Il libro delle preghiere publiche ed amministrazione de' sacramenti ... secondo l'uso della Chiesa anglicana*...('appresso Moise Pitt libraro'), done by Edward Browne and Giovanni Battista Cappello. In the early seventeenth century, when an official rupture between the Venetian Republic and Rome looked probable, William Bedell, the English ambassador's chaplain in the city, prepared a translation of the Book of Common Prayer, presumably in readiness for a sudden new flock of converts. Brown knew of Bedell's version, which he says was done at the instigation of Paolo Sarpi ('Padre Paolo di Venezia') and adds that the fact it was never printed has encouraged him to publish his own version.

11 Florio left England in 1554 to escape the Marian persecutions. His *Historia de la vita e de la morte de l'illustriss. Signora Giovanna Graia*... was printed in 1607 (the British Library catalogue gives the place of printing as 'Middelburgh'). It was probably composed in the early 1560s, since it refers to the deaths of Cranmer and Ridley 'six years before'. See Frances Yates, *John Florio* (Cambridge, 1934), pp. 9-12.

12 On the Italian church, see Luigi Firpo, 'La chiesa italiana di Londra nel Cinquecento' in *Ginevra e l'Italia* (Firenze, 1959), pp. 372-91 and *Unity in Multiformity: the minutes of the coetus of London, 1575 and the consistory minutes of the Italian church of London, 1570-1591*, ed. O. Boersma and A. J. Jelma, Publications of the Huguenot Society of Great Britain and Ireland, 59 (London, 1997).

13 Luigi Firpo, *Il processo di Giordano Bruno*, ed. Diego Quaglioni (Roma, 1995), p. 166.

Marco Antonio de Dominis which he had printed had been sent over 'into fforraine Contries by our appointment … ymediatlie upon the first ympression thereof', only for them to be 'seised and confiscated';[14] later in the century, the language teacher Giovanni Torriano writes in the dedication to his great dictionary of proverbs *Piazza universale di proverbi italiani…* (1666) that the book will carry the fame of its dedicatee, Charles II, to Italy where copies will be found ('ove sarà per capitare quest'Opera') and beyond, to all the peoples and nations who understand Italian ('i Popoli e Nationi [che] intendono L'Idioma nostro Italiano'[15] – in fact, the few significant Italian-language publications from the seventeenth century all seem to have been published at least partly with Italy in mind – in so far as their commercial viability was a contributory factor at all). In eighteenth-century Europe the circulation of learned books, like Nicola Francesco Haym's great work of erudition on English numismatic collections *Del tesoro britannico* (1719-20), was part of the inter- or supranational ethos of Enlightenment intellectuals.[16] Subscription lists too from the period usually include the names of a good many Italian 'associati'. Finally the tracts and Bibles published in the nineteenth century by such organisations as the Religious Tract Society and the British and Foreign Bible Society were for distribution in Italy in the cause of Protestant evangelisation.

---

14 *Records of the Court of the Stationers' Company 1602-1640*, ed. William A. Jackson (London, 1957), p. 363.

15 This seemingly hyperbolic claim was echoed by Gregorio Leti twenty years later, when he claims that the Italian language is 'admired and in vogue everywhere, not only in Europe but in Asia' (*Del teatro brittannico*, 1683). But Italian was an important trading language. In the mid seventeenth century, Giovanni Torriano had many 'Turkey merchants' among his pupils. Edward Browne, the translator of the 1685 Italian version of the Book of Common Prayer, writes in the preface that as chaplain to the English ambassador to the Ottoman court in Constantinople he had to learn Italian for his dealings with the Christians who lived there and hold services in the language for a group of French Protestants living in the city, who would otherwise have been without a church they could attend. Even in the early nineteenth century, the British and Foreign Bible Society found that 'copies of [the Italian scriptures, as published by the Society] were found to be very acceptable in different parts of the Mediterranean, and in the Levant' (George Browne, *The History of the British and Foreign Bible Society* (London, 1859), II, 18).

16 We learn from a letter written by Scipione Maffei to his fellow scholar Lodovico Muratori that Haym had sent him a supply of copies ('alcune') to distribute in Italy ('per farne esito in Italia'): he wanted Muratori to try to sell them and specified the exchange rate ('vale 34 Scellini p[rim]o e 2.o volume, che sono in circa 64 Paoli'). Haym had paid for the publication of the volumes himself. See Lowell Lindgren, 'The Accomplishments of the Learned and Ingenious Nicola Francesco Haym (1678-1729)', *Studi musicali*, 16 (1987), 319.

If there were no native Italian readers in England for these books, the intended domestic audience must have consisted of English readers with a knowledge of the language. There were two main motives for acquiring Italian: a practical need to learn the language, mostly for commercial reasons, and the influence of cultural prestige (and its more banal manifestation, fashion). The former reason is certainly strong until the end of the seventeenth century and the shift away from the Mediterranean as the centre of English commercial interests; in the nineteenth century, with the development of new overland routes by railway, it enjoys a revival, with the publication of bilingual manuals of business correspondence and the like, of a recognisably modern type. The teaching of Italian in the eighteenth century on the other hand seems entirely focused, if we are to judge from the published record, on the acquisition of the language as a cultivated attainment – the dedication of one language book (a 1768 edition of Sannazaro's *Arcadia* designed as a reader) 'Alle dame inglesi amanti della lingua italiana' (gender as well as class is characteristic here) could apply to all.[17] As for the latter motive, it is hard to underestimate its potency and durability. Centuries before Italy itself became one country, the renown of its artistic and literary culture and with them its language – what Tullio De Mauro is careful to call 'toscano-italiano'[18] – was widespread. He identifies three other causes active over time for the prestige of the language: Italy's highly developed banking network, the popularity of opera, the international influence of the Catholic church. The Italian language enjoyed fashionable status from the beginning – Roger Ascham, Queen Elizabeth's former tutor and a stalwart Italosceptic ('I was once in Italie myselfe: but I thanke God, my abode there, was but ix dayes') famously complained in his 1570 treatise *The Scholemaster* about the 'Italianated' Englishmen who frequented the Italian church in London 'to heare the Italian tonge naturally spoken, not to heare Gods doctrine trewly preached'.[19] After a lull in the seventeenth century when Francophilia became

17 'Polite' literature and language books could almost be said to merge: a representative example is Vincenzio Martinelli's *Lettere familiari e critiche* (1758) which can be read as one of the collections of miscellaneous essays so popular at the time but is also designed for linguistic instruction.

18 Tullio De Mauro and Massimo Vedovelli, 'La prospettiva degli anni '90', in *La diffusione dell'italiano nel mondo e le vie dell'emigrazione* (Roma, 1996). 'La lingua – or 'l'idioma' – toscana/o' was a normal synonym for 'Italian' up to the end of the eighteenth century.

19 Roger Ascham, *The Scholemaster* (London, 1570), f. 28v. Three centuries later, Protestant missionaries in 1869 reported that the congregation for morning Mass at the recently built Catholic Italian church, St Peter's, in Hatton Garden, 'consisted more of English than Italians' (quoted in Lucio Sponza, op. cit. in n. 9, p. 136).

dominant, it reached a zenith in the eighteenth century with the craze for the exotic import of Italian opera: Addison, like Ascham, distrustful of Continental influences – he tried, unsuccessfully, to promote an 'English opera' to supplant the Italian form – wrote satirically in 1711:

> … our great Grand-children will be very curious to know the Reason why their Forefathers used to sit together like an Audience of Foreigners in their own Country, and to hear whole Plays acted before them in a Tongue which they did not understand.[20]

This cultural prestige took many forms, of which Italian-language publications in England are only a minor one: the social institution of the Grand Tour and the English passion for collecting Italian art are better-known manifestations. But the larger context of Italy's cultural prestige helps us to see – although the task is far beyond the scope of the survey which follows – that these publications are best studied and understood as one aspect or category of a wider, fourfold group, along with: translations from Italian into English, of which there were many hundreds in the period under consideration;[21] books for teaching Italian – grammars, readers, dictionaries and the like, an equally early and long-lasting tradition (William Thomas's *Principal Rules of the Italian Grammar with a dictionarie for the better understanding of Boccacce, Petrarcha and Dante* was published in 1550);[22] and, finally, the distribution, sale and ownership of Italian books (from Italy) in England, an aspect which is as rewarding as it is difficult to reconstruct in depth. These four elements together provide the framework for a detailed picture of Italian books in England.

---

20 In Joseph Addison & Richard Steele and others, *The Spectator*, ed. Gregory Smith (London, 1907), I, 55-6 (Wednesday 21 March 1711, no. 18). Italophilia was confined to the educated classes. Popular xenophobia, in the case of Italians usually reinforced by anti-Catholic sentiment, was widespread: John Florio found the English 'yl manered … towards strangers' (*His Firste Fruites*, 1578) and a few years later Bruno gives a memorable description of it in *Spaccio de la bestia trionfante*. Even within their cultivated, professional circles, and despite their perfect knowledge of English and personal capacity for assimilation, men such as Baretti and Panizzi encountered occasional hostility as foreigners.

21 For the sixteenth century, see Mary Augusta Scott, *Elizabethan Translations from the Italian* (Boston, 1916).

22 A list of publications up to 1657 can be found in R. C. Simonini Jr., 'Italian-English Language Books of the Renaissance', *Romanic Review*, 42 (1951), 241-4.

The second half of the sixteenth century sees the first wave or cluster of Italian-language publishing in London, much of it due to the presence of a large number of Italian Protestants in exile. This was a period when London was one of the most important European centres of refuge from and resistance to Counter-Reformation forces. The printer and publisher John Wolf(e), or Giovanni Volfio, in the Italianised form he used, whose career is discussed by Denis V. Reidy in this volume, is a central figure, if only for the number of editions of Italian books which issued from his press (twenty-three in the decade 1581-91, according to ESTC, the largest number from one printer/publisher until Rolandi in the nineteenth century); even so this was only a small part of his total production – at one time he owned a tenth of all the presses working in the city.[23] He was also unusual, if not unique, among English printers in possessing a fluent knowledge of Italian (he had completed his apprenticeship and practised his craft for a time in Florence). This familiarity and the impression it must have made on the Italians in London, where knowledge of the language was not common outside aristocratic circles,[24] doubtless explains Petruccio Ubaldini's (misplaced) optimism, as expressed in the preface to the *Vita di Carlo Magno Imperadore*, printed by Wolfe in 1581, that Italian books could be printed in London as well as in Italy itself ('l'opere italiane non men si possono stampar felicemente in Londra, che le si stampino altrove...'). But Wolfe, though of primary, indeed essential importance as a 'catalyst',[25] was only part of a network of people involved in the publication of Italian books. Among the most notable and productive of these are Petruccio Ubaldini and Giacomo Castelvetro, both of whom collaborated frequently with Wolfe, but who prefigure more closely than he does the kinds of characters we encounter in later centuries.

Wolfe's first London-printed Italian book was the life of Charlemagne just mentioned; he went on to publish a further two works by Ubaldini: the *Descrittione del regno di Scotia, et delle isole sue adiacenti* in 1588 (an adaptation of a work by Hector Boece) and *Le vite delle donne illustri del regno d'Inghilterra, & del regno di Scotia* (1591). Ubaldini also collaborated closely with Wolfe as an editor

23 See K. T. Butler, 'Giacomo Castelvetro 1546-1616', *Italian Studies*, 5 (1950), 9.

24 John Florio writes in his language book *His First Fruites* (London, 1578), f. 51r: 'When I arrived first in London, I coulde not speake Englishe, and I met above five hundred persons, afore I coulde finde one, that could tel me in Italian, or French, where the Post dwelt'.

25 Huffman's word, translating Giovanni Battista Castiglione's description of Wolfe in his preface to *Una essortatione al timor di Dio* (1580) as 'l'occasione d'un giovane di questa Citta venuto di nuovo d'Italia, ov'ha con molta industria appresso l'arte de lo Stampare' (Huffman, p. 7).

and proof-reader, playing a very similar part in the publication process to that undertaken by fellow humanists in his native country.[26] It is probable, for example, that he wrote the prefaces to Wolfe's editions of Machiavelli and Aretino. Ubaldini was a Florentine, of an older generation than most of the exiles in London, who had spent much of his early career wandering through Europe in search of patronage.[27] It seems he first visited England in 1545 when Henry VIII was still on the throne, returning during his son's reign and again after Elizabeth had succeeded. In 1565 he married an Englishwoman and settled in London. He became a well-known figure, perhaps falling into the common vice of expatriates in becoming a kind of professional foreigner, to judge from Bruno's contemptuous remark about him in *La cena de le Ceneri:* 'There are two false Florentine relics revered in this country: Sassetto's teeth and Petruccio's beard'.[28] Like the polymath humanist he was, his talents and activities were many: historian, poet, moralist, translator and editor – but he is perhaps best known as a calligrapher and illuminator, the one field in which his skills were more than mediocre. His episodic interest and involvement in printing co-existed, apparently without tension, with a continuous production of manuscripts.[29] The latter appears to have been exclusively for his aristocratic and royal patrons, to judge from the distinction he draws in the 'proemio' to the *Descrittione del Regno...*, where he refers to 'le carte semplicemente scritte' (i.e. manuscripts) addressed to the few ('i pochi'), whereas printing enabled his texts to reach the many ('i molti'). But even with works which might seem suitable for the many, he did not always follow the path of publication in print: his account of the Armada composed for Ferdinand of Tuscany was published in 1590 but in an English translation and with an English editor. By the 1590s Wolfe had stopped printing Italian books and, between 1592 and 1597, Ubaldini turned to another printer,

---

26 See Brian Richardson, *Print Culture in Renaissance Italy: the editor and the vernacular text 1460-1600* (Cambridge, 1994) and Paolo Trovato, *Con ogni diligenza corretto: la stampa e le revisioni editoriali dei testi letterari italiani (1470-1570)* (Bologna, 1991).

27 On Ubaldini's life and works, see Giuliano Pellegrini, *Un fiorentino alla corte d'Inghilterra nel Cinquecento: Petruccio Ubaldini*, Studi di Filologia moderna, Università di Pisa, Facoltà di Lettere e Filosofia, n.s., 7 (Torino, 1967), although the book contains a number of mistakes and should be used with caution.

28 'Due son le false e onorate reliquie di Firenze in questa patria [i.e. England]: i denti di Sassetto e la barba di Pietruccia': Giordano Bruno, *La cena de le Ceneri*, ed. Giovanni Aquilecchia, Nuova raccolta di classici italiani annotati, 4 (Torino, 1955), p. 86.

29 Ubaldini was not unusual: the production and circulation of manuscripts was common practice for the whole of the seventeenth century: see H. R. Woudhuysen, *Sir Philip Sidney and the Circulation of Manuscripts 1558-1640* (Oxford, 1996), in which Ubaldini and his calligraphic work are briefly mentioned (p. 41).

Richard Field. Field, Shakespeare's fellow-Stratfordian, the printer of *Venus and Adonis* and connected with Thomas Vautrollier, the French Huguenot printer, who was long thought to be responsible for Bruno's London dialogues, already had experience of foreign-language publishing. The six titles are as miscellaneous as those he published and worked on with Wolfe: *Parte prima delle brevi dimostrazioni et precetti utilissimi ne i quali si trattano diversi propositi morali, politici & iconomici* (1592); *Lo stato delle tre corti* (1594 – on the political situation of Italy); *Scelta di alcune attioni* (1595 – a textbook of *exempla*); his own *Rime* (1596); *Militia del gran duca di Thoscana* (1597 – Ubaldini had started his career as a soldier); and a new edition of the life of Charlemagne (1599). Ubaldini seems to have regarded his printed publications in much the same light as the manuscripts he prepared as gifts for his patrons; these books, especially those printed by Field, appear designed to attract the attention and favour of aristocratic patrons – they repeat the open dedicatory formula 'Al nobile et prudente et si amichevol lettore della real natione inghilese' – and of Elizabeth herself. There is no indication that they had any commercial life outside the restricted Italophile circles of the English court. There is an air of dilettantism about them, an abiding feature of much Italian-language publishing in London, which only serves to highlight further the unusual business acumen and initiative displayed by Wolfe with his Italian editions.

Giacomo (or Giacopo) Castelvetro is in many ways a more interesting figure.[30] He was the nephew of the celebrated classical scholar and editor Lodovico Castelvetro and had followed his uncle at the age of eighteen into Switzerland for religious motives (he himself later gave an outbreak of plague in Modena, where he was born, as the ostensible reason for his departure). He first visited England in 1574 (it is possible that on arriving in Switzerland he would have known Michelangelo Florio, who was by then a pastor in the Grisons). He returned to England again in 1580, this time more or less permanently. Castelvetro, like Ubaldini, worked closely with Wolfe on several Italian and Latin editions, as editor but also as publisher; he also visited the Frankfurt Book Fair on Wolfe's behalf. The editions printed by Wolfe in collaboration with Castelvetro cover, like Ubaldini's books, a surprising and opportunistic variety of subjects, such as *L'historia del gran regno della China*... and, in Latin, della Porta's book on ciphers *De furtivis litterarum notis, vulgo de*

---

30 On Castelvetro see K. T. Butler, op. cit., pp. 1-42; Eleanor Rosenberg, 'Giacopo Castelvetro: Italian publisher in Elizabethan London and his patrons', *Huntington Library Quarterly*, 6 (1943), 119-48; Paola Ottolenghi, *Giacopo Castelvetro: esule modenese nell'Inghilterra di Shakespeare* (Pisa, 1982).

ziferis libri III. The most significant collaboration, however, for our purposes are the two editions which he published of contemporary Italian poetry and drama, the first of their kind. Castelvetro first put up the money for a Latin version of the first canto of Tasso's epic *Gerusalemme liberata* done by Scipione Gentili, a fellow exile and younger brother of the more famous jurist Alberico, who held a chair at Oxford. This was followed two years later by Gentili's Italian *Annotationi* on Tasso's poem. The publication of such a volume without a corresponding edition of the text might suggest that editions from Italy were available in London, since it seems unlikely that Wolfe would have published a commentary if the original poem was not widely known,[31] but if this is the case it would seem to contradict what Castelvetro wrote five years later in his preface to his 1591 edition of Guarini's *Il pastor fido* together with Tasso's *L'Aminta*. Here he explains that it is the difficulty of obtaining Italian books in England which has prompted him to publish these two pastoral dramas so soon after their first appearance in Italy: the pleasure he has taken in reading Guarini's work (in a copy he purchased in Italy) has led him to ask himself if he should not reprint it in London 'because it is so difficult to obtain it in this country' ('se non farei male a farla qui ristampare: si per trovarla dilettevole molto, & anchora per vedere quanto malagevole fosse il poterne havere'). In the edition in the same year of della Porta's work on ciphers, Castelvetro also claimed that it was needed because the text had gone out of print, even though one had been published in Rome the previous year; either he was unable to obtain a copy or – as is more probable – he did not know of its existence.[32] Castelvetro's direct involvement in the printing and publishing world in London seems to have ceased with this edition but he maintained contacts. In the 1590s he went to Scotland where he taught Italian to James VI and his queen, Anne of Denmark, and thus in a sense could be described as an instrumental cause of

31 However, the false imprint 'In Leida' might indicate that this edition was destined for the Continental market (Gentili's commentary in fact enjoyed a long life – it was still being reprinted with editions of the poem in the eighteenth century). 'Leida' (Leiden) might be significant: the humanist circle in the Dutch town had close cultural contacts with English scholars, including Gentili: see J. A. Van Dorsten, *Poets, Patrons, and Professors: Sir Philip Sidney, Daniel Rogers, and the Leiden humanists* (Leiden, 1962). If so, this is another example of Wolfe's allusive use of false places of publication.
The first complete Italian edition of Tasso's epic appeared in 1581; a parallel text edition of the first five cantos was published in London in 1594; the famous Fairfax translation of the poem appeared in 1600.

32 Castelvetro, however, may not be telling the whole story: see Woudhuysen, op. cit., pp. 359-60, for an alternative, hypothetical account of how Guarini's drama came to be published in England.

the 1619 London publication in Italian of Paolo Sarpi's history of the Tridentine council, sponsored by and dedicated to James (and printed by his printer). In fact Castelvetro had close personal links with Sarpi and the English circle round him when after Scotland, he moved to Venice. There he worked as a translator from English for Venetian publishers and, in collaboration with one of them, Giambattista Ciotti, made an unsuccessful proposal to have Tommaso Campanella's works printed back in England. Campanella, like his older contemporary Bruno an ex-Dominican, was imprisoned in Naples for the first two decades of the century for his heterodox writings on religion and politics. Castelvetro's dealings became dangerous and after a spell in the Republic's prisons he eventually returned to England where he ended his days teaching Italian in Cambridge.

Giordano Bruno appears to have come to London with some of the same motives as his other fellow-expatriates: to escape the increasingly oppressive Counter-Reformation persecution in Italy and in the hope of establishing a lucrative career, specifically as a university teacher. But in almost all respects he stands out as an exception: his intellectual stature and independence, his unaccommodating personality, his isolation within the close-knit world of exiles, familiar as he inevitably became with them during his two years in the capital. Most publications covered in this survey are the products of Italians working to disseminate their language and their culture within England; they are transactions between the two cultures. Bruno publishes in London because it offers him the possibility of doing so; if the political and religious circumstances in Paris, from where he came over to London, had allowed him to stay, no doubt he would have published them there (he had in fact published, among other books, the first edition of his play *Candelaio* in 1582 in the French capital). This is not to deny that his London publications show the deep impression made on him by his intellectual contacts and personal experiences in England, but essentially they continue and develop the quite independent trajectory of his thought. Using London as a convenient base, Bruno represents a much rarer type; perhaps the only equivalent among the Italians is Mazzini in the nineteenth century, whose political struggles for a united Italy obliged him to publish his journal *Pensiero ed azione* from exile in London in the 1850s. Bruno's stay in England is merely one episode in a restless series of European travels which end, notoriously, back in Rome.

He arrived in 1583 as part of the newly appointed French ambassador's entourage. His first published works here were the short Latin texts on mnemotechnics with which he had made his reputation and which he no doubt had printed to establish his credentials with potentially useful English contacts. In 1584 his first philosophical dialogue appeared: *La cena de le Ceneri* (in two issues – the second modifies some of the text in response to the hostility it encountered when it was first published), followed over the period of the next few months by *De la causa, principio, et Uno* and *De l'infinito universo et mondi.* Towards the end of 1584, in the wake of the Throckmorton conspiracy, anti-Catholic persecution intensified and although Bruno was excommunicate his nationality made him suspect; he published his own contribution to the violent religious polemic of the time, *Spaccio de la bestia trionfante*, in which he announces his imminent departure in the dedication to Philip Sidney, one of Bruno's most important interlocutors while he was in London. The *Cabala del cavallo Pegaseo* was published in early 1585 and continues the attack on revealed religion; his final book, *De gl'heroici furori*, published in the summer of 1585 (he left in October) is the most literary of these works, drawing on poetry, mythology and emblem literature and ending in praise of Elizabeth as a new Diana. Although Bruno is named as the author on all but the first, these editions do not identify their printer or give London as the place of printing. The French Huguenot printer Vautrollier was for long thought to be responsible, a plausible conjecture, until Harry Sellers of the British Museum Library, applying the technique of painstaking typographical analysis which he had learnt there, established the printer as John Charlewood.[33] Giovanni Aquilecchia, the leading Italian scholar on Bruno's London publications, points out that Charlewood was a curious choice: he had no experience of printing Italian books (these texts were the only ones he printed) or of Latin; and the kind of books he printed tended to be popular rather than learned.[34] It is not obvious why Bruno did not turn to Wolfe, who was still active in this field. If Wolfe was approached, was he unwilling to risk printing these highly heterodox texts? Or did he simply decide that they were unlikely to turn him a profit? Did Bruno distrust the Florentine background of both Wolfe himself and his chief collaborator Ubaldini? His dialogues are notable for the linguistic resourcefulness and energy with which they contravene 'l'idioma toscano' (Bruno was from Nola south of Naples and was commonly known as the Nolan). As Aquilecchia writes, the dialogues 'reveal Bruno's style with its already distinctive and idiosyncratic features'. It is this, together with the remarkable accuracy of the printed texts despite Charlewood's inexperience of printing in a foreign language, 'exceptional for the time and place of printing', which leads

33 'Italian Books Printed in England before 1640', *The Library*, 4th ser., 5 (1924), 105-28.

34 Charlewood seems to have had a hand in the printing of Bruno's Latin text on mnemotechnics; moreover, he was an ally of Wolfe in opposing the monopoly exercised by the Stationers' Company (see Simonetta Bassi, 'Editoria e filosofia nella seconda metà del 500: Giordano Bruno e i tipografi londinesi', *Rinascimento: rivista dell'Istituto nazionale di studi sul Rinascimento*, 2a ser., 38 (1997), 437-58).

Aquilecchia to argue that Bruno's involvement with the printing was 'continuous, scrupulous and exclusive'.[35]

The concentrated activity, the sense of a busy and close-knit network of Italian exiles, aristocratic patrons and printers, dwindles in the seventeenth century and with it the number of publications in Italian. The ESTC records only fifteen editions for the entire century, and two of those – both editions of *Il puttanismo romano* by Gregorio Leti in the 1670s – are probably false imprints from Geneva, where the author was living at the time. In this respect, the figure of Giovanni Francesco Biondi is worth considering: strictly speaking, he is not part of this story at all, having published nothing in Italian in England, but this very absence may be thought (in an admittedly speculative way) to be significant.[36] Biondi belonged to Paolo Sarpi's circle in Venice and used Sarpi's English contacts to gain a foothold in the service of James I. After several visits to England and back to the Continent in performance of the various diplomatic missions with which the English king entrusted him, he was knighted in 1622. Married and with a pension, he settled down in England to become a man of letters, writing a number of literary and historical works. Although he lived in this country until 1638, when he moved to Switzerland, none of these works was published here in the original (although English translations did appear), not even of the opus to which he dedicated most time and effort, *L'Istoria delle guerre civili d'Inghilterra...*, a history of the Wars of the Roses. This was published in Venice in three parts over a period of seven years from 1637 to 1644, the year of Biondi's death; an edition, 'englished by ... Henry Earle of Mounmouth', was published in London in 1641. If the prevailing cultural and economic circumstances had resembled those in the last two decades of the previous century, the English publication of such a text in Italian, despite its considerable length, would surely have been attempted, under the auspices of an appropriate noble or

---

35 Giovanni Aquilecchia, 'Lo stampatore londinese di Giordano Bruno e altre note per l'edizione della *Cena*', *Studi di Filologia italiana*, 7 (1960), 101-62, reprinted in his *Schede bruniane (1950-1991)* (Roma, 1993), pp. 157-207. See also Tiziana Provvidera, 'On the Printer of Giordano Bruno's London Works', *Bruniana & Campanelliana: ricerche filosofiche e materiali storico-testuali*, 2 (1996), 361-7. For a detailed reconstruction of the circulation of Bruno's London dialogues (and a model of the serious use of provenance studies) see Rita Sturlese, *Bibliografia, censimento e storia delle antiche stampe di Giordano Bruno* (Firenze, 1987). This includes the composite volume of four of Bruno's London books bound for Elizabeth I, which came into the possession of the early eighteenth-century English philosopher John Toland, and is now in the Austrian National Library.

36 See the articles on Biondi in the *Dizionario biografico degli Italiani* (Roma, 1960-), X, 528-31 and the *Dictionary of National Biography* (London, 1885-1900), V, 61-2.

royal patron. On the other hand, there is no evidence of a decline of interest in Italian culture – rather the contrary. This was the age which saw the first real flowering of the Grand Tour as an essential part of a gentleman's education, and clearly related to this, from early on in the century, the beginnings of serious connoisseurship and the collecting of Italian art on a large scale. As far as books are concerned, there is some evidence too from booksellers' catalogues of how widespread and well rooted knowledge of Italian had become.[37] In such catalogues as Henry Featherstone's in 1628 and one from an anonymous bookseller (possibly George Thomason) in 1637, there are large sections devoted to 'libri italici'. What is striking in these lists is the range of content: not just literature and history, but books on travel, politics, current affairs and exploration as well as practical guides to such matters as cookery, farming, medicine, horsemanship and engineering. The availability of such books would seem to imply that many of the customers must have had a working competence in the language which they used for ordinary purposes. Certainly teachers continued to work in England: we have already seen the elderly Castelvetro teaching Italian to the sons of the nobility and gentry in Cambridge. The leading teacher of the century, Giovanni Torriano, seems to have started his long career in the university town in the late 1630s (his *New and Easy Directions for the Attaining of the Thuscan Italian Tongue* was printed there) but soon moved to London where he was clearly something of a pioneer in teaching Italian for business purposes: his *The Italian Tutor…* of 1640 includes not only a dedication to an aristocratic patron (Elizabeth, Countess of Kent) but also one to the company of 'Turkey Marchants' ('none affecting the Italian Tongue so much as yours') and is prefaced by laudatory verses from his pupils. He was also a bookseller, located in the City, which meant that his shop and entire stock were destroyed in the Great Fire, including, by his own account, most of the print run of his major work, the *Piazza universale di proverbi…* – in which case the British Library is doubly fortunate in possessing the royal copy, presumably presented to Charles as one of the first copies off the press. In the preface to *The Italian Reviv'd…* of 1689 he refers to the dismal effect this calamity had on the progress of Italian studies in England, which he

37 See Dennis E. Rhodes, 'Some Notes on the Import of Books from Italy into England 1628-1650', *Studi secenteschi*, 7 (1966), reprinted in his *Studies in Early Italian Printing* (London, 1982) and John L. Lievsay, *The Englishman's Italian Books 1550-1700* (Philadelphia, 1969), chapter 2, 'Italian books on English Shelves'. The two catalogues referred to in the text are *Catalogus librorum in diversis locis Italiae emptorum, anno 1628 qui Londini in officina Fetherstoniana prostant venales* and *Catalogus librorum in diversis locis Italiae emptorum anno 1636 … qui Londini in Cœmaeterio sancti Pauli ad insigne rosae prostant venales* (bound together in the British Library copy at C.118.i.5).

describes as 'declining, and almost expiring' for want of appropriate books. The Fire and Plague of the 1660s and the political and social upheavals and conflict throughout the century may well have discouraged (they can hardly have helped) the kind of sustained flowering of Italian studies and publishing in London which we find in the sixteenth and again in the eighteenth centuries. And larger historical causes can be invoked too: the military, political and cultural dominance of France and the contemporary decline in Italy's fortunes throughout most of the century. But perhaps the explanation for the comparative dearth of Italian-language books being printed here is a simple and practical one: alternative channels sufficed. Travel to Italy was easier, better organised and more extensive and travellers brought back books.[38] This together with the greater availability of imported Italian books (despite the hiatus caused by the Great Fire) – in other words, the development of European travel and the Continental book trade – meant that Castelvetro's reasons for publishing Guarini's *Pastor fido* in London in 1590 had been superseded.

But chronological divisions are often artificial: the handful of Italian books printed by John Bill (Giovanni Billio) between 1617 and 1619 belong recognisably to the world of Wolfe and Charlewood and their Italian authors and collaborators. Bill was clearly a suitable choice as a printer of foreign-language books: he was a bookseller (this was his principal activity) with extensive European contacts, which he had had an opportunity of building from the start of his career, when Thomas Bodley commissioned him to buy books on the Continent for his new library in Oxford. Bodley also speaks of him visiting 'the chief cities of Italy [and buying] books to the value of upwards of four hundred pounds'. He regularly attended the Frankfurt Book Fair and published its catalogues back in London.[39]

---

38 See, for example, this dialogue from one of Torriano's language books, as summarised by Frances Yates in 'An Italian in Restoration England', *Journal of the Warburg & Courtauld Institutes*, 6 (1943), p. 219 (books of dialogues were a favourite teaching method – John Florio had used them – combining what would now be called 'role play exercises' with a highly elaborated form of the modern phrase-book. It is the circumstantial detail contained in them which makes them such interesting sources): 'The Englishman in Italy buys the dictionary of the *Accademmia della Crusca* at a bookseller, and discusses with his lodging-house keeper the chances of his getting the Boccaccio and other old books which he has bought at great expense out of the hands of the Inquisitors. He buys all his books unbound and intends to have them bound when he gets home'.

39 See H. G. Aldis et al., *A Dictionary of Printers and Booksellers in England, Scotland and Ireland, and of Foreign Printers of English books 1557-1640* (London, 1910), pp. 31-2.

The tortuous transactions which lay behind his two most significant Italian books make their history far too complex to narrate in detail here: the first edition of Paolo Sarpi's famous history of the Council of Trent and an Italian translation of Bacon's essays. They are important for many reasons but in this bibliographical context it should be pointed out that the 1619 publication of the *Historia del Concilio tridentino*, like Bruno's London books, is, as a first edition, and despite the editor's tampering with the text, of special significance in the long history of this influential book, while the volume of Bacon's essays marks, in J. L. Lievsay's words, 'the first time that a work of English literature (as distinct from propaganda) had been translated into Italian, printed in England, and exported to an Italy already entering upon an era of cultural eclipse'.[40] The publication of both books in London is related to the English circle round the Venetian writer Paolo Sarpi; born in 1552, Sarpi had joined the Servite order at the age of thirteen and had developed a wide range of intellectual interests and contacts. His radical views on the relationship between Church and State were formed in the bitter contest between the Venetian Republic and the Papacy, when he acted as an official advocate for the former's interests; he was excommunicated (and barely escaped assassination) and his writings were condemned, but he remained an important and productive figure in Venice until his death in 1623.[41] Of more immediate consequence, however, was the curious figure of the Italian exile Marco Antonio de Dominis. Of Dalmatian origin, de Dominis was archbishop of Spalato, but had grown disaffected with his Catholic faith; in 1615 he abandoned his post and went to Venice, where he came to know Sarpi, with the intention of converting to Anglicanism and moving to England. His negotiations to the purpose with the English ambassador in the Republic, Henry Wootton, were successful and he reached England in 1616, publishing, with Bill, almost immediately on arrival his *Profectionis consilium*, an account of the reasons for his recantation of Catholicism, in Latin and English. As a celebrated convert, he gave an Advent sermon in 1617, which Bill again printed in Italian (with an English title). And Bill went on to print other works by de Dominis, most notably his *De republica ecclesiastica* which he had brought with him from Italy in manuscript.

That de Dominis knew Sarpi in Venice is certain but the once widely accepted belief that he was responsible for bringing the manuscript of Sarpi's work to London is now thought to be groundless. Over a number of years Sarpi had had frequent contact with English diplomats and visitors to Venice

---

40 John L. Lievsay, op. cit., p. 28.

41 On Sarpi's contacts with England, see John Leon Lievsay, *Venetian Phoenix: Paolo Sarpi and some of his English friends (1606-1700)* (Lawrence, Kan., 1973).

who knew of the project on which he had been working since 1610. After the Venetian authorities had settled their differences with Rome, they would not have wished to provoke the Papacy by licensing its printing in Venice itself, and elsewhere in Italy it was unpublishable; it seems likely that plans to publish the history, once it was completed, in London had already been mooted before de Dominis arrived in Venice. What is certain is that de Dominis as an Italian and a friend of Sarpi was asked to edit the text once he was in England and the manuscript was ready for publication. Sarpi's title for the book was the plain *Historia del Concilio tridentino* (his name on the title-page, with the addition of 'Veneto', was anagrammatised as 'Pietro Soave Polano') but de Dominis expanded this with a fervidly anti-papal subtitle – '*nella quale si scoprono tutti gl'artificii della Corte di Roma, per impedire che né la veritá di dogmi si palesasse, né la riforma del Papato, & della chiesa si trattasse*' ('in which are shown all the practices of the Roman Curia to obstruct doctrinal truth and the reform of the Papacy and of the Church') and added a similarly outspoken dedication to the King (fig. 1).[42] The work's closely argued view that the Council of Trent, far from effecting reform within Catholicism, had been instrumentalised by the Papacy in order to increase its own worldly power was clearly an attractive one for Protestant churches, the more so because it was expounded by a Catholic. The publication of the volume in London was a kind of Anglican propaganda coup but being in Italian the effect must have been muted. In 1620, Bill, this time in partnership with another King's printer Robert Barker, produced an English version (in a translation by Nathaniel Brent who had also known the author in Venice) which went through four editions in the course of the century. In the same year Bill also produced a Latin translation which seems to have been intended for export to other Protestant countries.

De Dominis's contribution to Bill's other significant Italian publication is much less clear and is shared with others. This was an edition, published in 1618, before the Sarpi volume, of Francis Bacon's essays *Saggi morali* which also included an Italian version of his short Latin work *De sapientia veterum* (*Della sapienza de gli antichi*). Bacon's essays in their English form went through three main redactions, the number of essays increasing from ten in 1597 to fifty-eight in 1625. This Italian version comes seven years before the third, definitive English edition (which was published a year before Bacon's death in 1626) and cuts across and contributes to the English sequence by adding an essay *Of Seditions and Troubles* (*Delle seditioni, & turbationi*) which is not included in England until the final collection, indicating that Bacon himself was

42 The second edition of Sarpi's work, published in Geneva in 1629 and 'riveduta e corretta dall'autore', restores the original title.

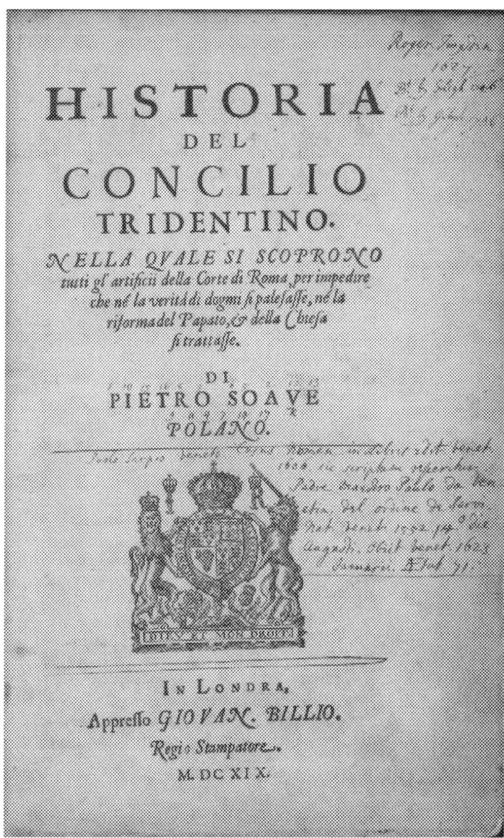

HISTORIA
DEL
CONCILIO
TRIDENTINO.
NELLA QVALE SI SCOPRONO
tutti gl'artificii della Corte di Roma, per impedire
che nè la verità di dogmi si palesasse, nè la
riforma del Papato, & della Chiesa
si trattasse.
DI
PIETRO SOAVE
POLANO.

DIEV ET MON DROIT

IN LONDRA,
Appresso GIOVAN. BILLIO,
Regio Stampatore.
M.DC.XIX.

Fig. 1: Paolo Sarpi, *Historia del Concilio Tridentino* (London: John Bill, 1619): the title-page of the British Library copy which once belonged to the antiquarian Sir Roger Twysden (1597-1672). It is copiously annotated throughout by Tywsden possibly in preparation for his own critical edition of the text.
British Library pressmark: C.55.k.6.

involved with the gestation of the Italian version. The translation has long been attributed to one of Bacon's closest disciples and companions, Tobie Matthew, best known as the first English translator of Augustine's *Confessions*, who wrote the preface to the volume. Matthew knew Italian well: he had spent some years in Florence and elsewhere in Italy, where he had converted to Catholicism, a move which aroused much consternation and scandal in England – his father, also called Tobie, was Dean of Christ Church and had known Bruno during the Italian's ill-fated sojourn in Oxford. The attribution seems plausible but it has been made despite Matthew's own disclaimer in the preface: 'There have recently come into my hands the two works printed here … I found them, already translated, in the possession of Sir William Cavendish, a most noble English knight … who, with the author's blessing, lent them to me' ('Mi sono á questi giorni venute alle mani le due opere qui stampate … e le ho trovate tutte due tradotte in poter del sig.re Guglielmo Candiscio cavagliere inglese nobilissimo … che con il beneplacito dell'autore me le prestò'). It now appears that he was telling the truth of the matter: a close friend of Bacon and with many contacts in Italy, he was indeed merely an intermediary for the publication of the translation. The complex history of the edition has recently been reconstructed:[43] the explanation turns on the discovery of an apparently unique copy in Lambeth Palace Library of an edition predating that of 1618 and bearing a more explicit preface by Matthew.[44] Briefly, the Italian translation was indeed done – to practise his knowledge of the language – by the young English nobleman William Cavendish (i.e. 'Candiscio' – the future second earl of Devonshire) and overseen for the press – much in the same way he had 'prepared' Sarpi's text – by de Dominis, who also added the Italian version of the *De sapientia*. The initial impulse to publish the translation, however, came from Italy, from Fulgenzio Micanzio, Sarpi's fellow-Servite, companion and biographer, who had met Cavendish during the young man's stay in Venice between 1614 and 1615 with his tutor Thomas Hobbes and who maintained a correspondence with him after his return to England. It seems clear that the publication was intended for Italy. In a letter of 1616, which Hobbes translated, Micanzio writes that Bacon's essays in Cavendish's version could not be printed in Italy 'for the evill custome we are fallen into, never to print anything that is good'; he suggests that de Dominis 'understanding the tongue' supervise their printing in England; once the copies are ready, 'a good number of them [can be] sent hither by sea which directed to his Majesties Ambassador here will light safely'.[45] Copies reached Florence too: Matthew had dedicated the volume to Cosimo II of Tuscany and his secretary, Andrea Cioli, was responsible for another edition which was published in the city in the same year, the first of several Italian editions of the essays.

One of Gregorio Leti's Italian biographers calls him an 'adventurer with a pen' and this describes Leti's career and personality well.[46] As a professional

43 By Noel Malcolm in *De Dominis 1560-1624: Venetian, Anglican, ecumenist and relapsed heretic* (London, 1984), pp. 47-54.

44 Although this edition is recorded in ESTC as distinct, the translation itself is still attributed to Matthew.

45 Malcolm, op. cit., p. 50.

46 On Leti, see Luigi Fassò, *Avventurieri della penna del Seicento* (Firenze, 1925); Franco Barcia, *Un politico dell'età barocca: Gregorio Leti* (Milano, 1983). The main bibliography of Leti's works is Franco Barcia, *Bibliografia delle opere di Gregorio Leti* (Milano, 1981).

writer of biographies, histories, polemical tracts, guidebooks and in the unstoppable copiousness of his output, the number of translations and versions and false attributions it generated, and the consequent length and complexity of his bibliography, he resembles his much younger contemporary Defoe. One of the reasons he gives for undertaking the work in the logorrhoeic preface to his account of British history and institutions in *Del teatro brittannico o vero Storia dello stato antico, e presente, corte, governo sprituale e temporale, leggi, massime, religioni, & evvenimenti della Grande Brettagna*, is, disarmingly, his sheer inability to stop writing: writer's itch or 'il prurito ordinario degli Auttori, che quando una volta cominciano non possono più astenersi…'. Leti was born in 1630 and seems to have developed early on both a distaste for the Catholicism of his upbringing, which later hardened into ideological aversion, and for following any settled profession. After a formative encounter with a French Huguenot in Genoa he converted to Protestantism and settled in Geneva, as a teacher and translator, and diplomat for hire. The Calvinist authorities began, however, to suspect him of reverting to Catholic beliefs and he was expelled. In the hope of becoming Louis XIV's historiographer, he went to Paris, where his obtaining the post turned out to be dependent on his reconversion to the Catholic faith, and so on to England in 1680. He was far from unknown in England: the anti-Catholicism and polemical verve of his writings had led to various of his works being translated, e.g. *Il nipotismo di Roma…*, an attack on papal nepotism, which he had written and published in 1667, was translated and published in England two years later as *The History of the Popes Nephews.* Like other exiled Italian writers in search of a living, he was an assiduous and dextrous dedicator of his books, and the sheer number he wrote meant that this form of networking was in his case peculiarly extensive: the King's brother, James, Duke of York, and Christopher Wren had already been recipients long before Leti set foot in London. Charles II appears to have been impressed enough with Leti to offer him a pension and the post of royal historiographer provided he first wrote a history of Britain. The chronological arrangement of *Del teatro brittannico* is a loose framework which Leti fills with lengthy excursuses on British institutions, customs, politics, personalities, legends, etc. His English was apparently poor but he did not regard this as a handicap: he set to work, relying on a promiscuous range of sources, which included contemporary gazettes – the text sometimes reads like one – and court gossip (this was his undoing), and in just over two years he had completed the work in two very large quarto volumes. He also found time to start separate lives of Oliver Cromwell and Elizabeth I and to extract a short book on Geneva from a longer unpublished manuscript for an English version; it seems to have been his habit to keep a stock of unpublished work with him all the time: the lives of Cromwell and Elizabeth were only published in Amsterdam, where he ended his days, ten years later. In the preface to his book Leti gives four reasons for writing it: first, as we have seen, his need to write *something*, secondly, the pressure put on him by others in the English court to write it, thirdly, his belief that accurate information about England was in short supply in the rest of Europe, and lastly, the exemplary greatness of Charles II. He also explains why he thinks it fitting that an Italian should write such a work (and in Italian): a foreigner will take a more detached view and natives will be inclined to confide in him. Since the work was intended to tell the world about England and its greatness, Italian, according to Leti an international lingua franca, was ideally suited. The first volume was dedicated to the King and the second to the Queen Catharine of Braganza and it was printed by the 'mercante libraro' Robert Scott (one of his very few ventures into printing – like John Bill, he was better known as a bookseller with a large stock of Continental books). However, Leti's uncontrollable tongue or pen led him into trouble: he had written an indiscreet passage on the Duke of York's secret first marriage with Anne Hyde as well as passing offensive remarks on other prominent members of the Caroline court. Leti himself attributed his subsequent disgrace to the Duke's displeasure at his prediction of disastrous consequences for the kingdom if James as a Catholic succeeded his brother. However, the fact that he removed the passage on Anne Hyde in the second edition which he published in Amsterdam, where he moved after his expulsion from England, suggests that this was the real reason. The book itself was suppressed: the Tuscan ambassador in London at the time, Terriesi, wrote in a letter home that 320 copies had been taken and destroyed.[47] Since Leti had had to pay for the publication himself (presumably the prospect of the pension made this initial outlay worthwhile) it was a blow to his finances as well as to his pride. Copies had by then gone into circulation – many of course as gifts – but the volumes do appear to be rare: only thirteen copies are known,[48] and, most unusually for a book of this kind, there is only one copy in the British Library.[49]

47 The figure for destroyed copies given in W. H. Hart's *Index Expurgatorius Anglicanus*, V (London, 1878), p. 267, no. 277, is 700 but no source is given; Fassò (op. cit., p. 199) estimates the total print run to have been 500. A curious detail to emerge from Terriesi's letters about the affair is the fact that Leti was also selling copies from his house (see Fassò, p. 197).

48 The ESTC lists only six locations in the UK, USA and Germany; Barcia's bibliography adds seven more.

49 Interestingly, given the scandal surrounding the book, this is a royal copy: not its dedicatee's, but his nephew-in-law's, William of Orange (William III), whose arms are on the binding (195.d.17). It was subsequently included in George III's collection (the King's Library). I am grateful to my colleague John Goldfinch for drawing this to my attention.

The events of three consecutive years at the beginning of the eighteenth century mark a new development in the story: in 1709, the Queen's Theatre (renamed King's after the accession of George I in 1714), the main home of Italian opera in London throughout the century, opened; the first opera in Italian was given there in 1710 and in the following year 'giant Handel' inaugurated his own thirty-year involvement with Italian opera in the city with one of his masterpieces *Rinaldo*, based on Tasso's epic poem. It was the extraordinary success of Italian opera which reawakened English interest in Italian language and literature and on an unprecedented scale. The ESTC gives 413 editions for the period: even when the considerable number of books with London as a false imprint are removed (including many from Tommaso Masi's Livorno press, discussed in note 1) this is a startling increase in the total number distributed incrementally over the course of the century. Printing in Italian begins to appear more widely outside London: isolated examples had appeared in Dublin, Oxford and Cambridge in the seventeenth century, but now we also find Italian books being published, although still in a very sporadic way, in Edinburgh, Glasgow (the Foulis press), Liverpool, Birmingham (Baskerville) and even Calcutta (thirty years after Clive retook the city for the British at the Battle of Plassey).[50]

While miscellaneousness of both subject and occasion is a continuing feature, on the whole these publications fall into distinct genres. One clearly defined category was a direct by-product of opera: printed libretti. Despite the vicissitudes of the opera business and attempts to oppose the cultural invasion, opera in Italian proved a durable phenomenon and it became the native language of the operatic stage. There was a practical reason for this: most of the singers (and musicians) came from Italy (a small colony of them settled in the area round the Haymarket where the King's Theatre was located). But it is also clear that for London audiences the use of a foreign language was an integral and consonant part of the strange and beautiful world created by these works, an aspect of their artifice and expressiveness. Libretti were bought by the audience on going in (many imprints state 'to be

50 This is Thomas Hickey's unfinished *Storia della pittura e la scultura antica* (1788), in a parallel English and Italian text. This is one of only a handful of British books on art and antiquity published in Italian in the eighteenth century: in addition to Haym's volumes on Greek and Roman coins and medals (discussed in the text) others include Bonaventura van Overbeke's *Degli avanzi dell'antica Roma* ... translated from the Latin and edited by Rolli (1739) and the volume of Palladio's designs *Fabbriche antiche*... (1730) with a single engraved plate of text. What might have seemed a leading candidate for a London Italian edition, Francesco Algarotti's well-known *Saggio sopra la pittura*, was published in English translation in several editions in the 1760s. Given that Italian was the international language of connoisseurship, it is a curious absence.

sold at the King's Theatre', the profits going to the librettist) and read – they were the surtitles of their day – during the performance (the candles in the auditorium would have remained lit throughout). They follow an almost invariable pattern: in a standard octavo format, they provide the Italian text, usually with a parallel English version (the translator is not named); the text itself is prefaced with a dedication to a patron (of the performance rather than the text – Italian opera was entirely supported by a subscription system), a cast list with the names of the singers who sang the roles at the performance, a summary of the plot with scene summaries (usually in English only) interspersed in the text. The variety of imprints found doubtless reflects the extreme financial instability of opera management in eighteenth-century London: Thomas Wood of Little Britain printed many of them but some appear to have been printed *sur place* 'in the King's Theatre' or in the 'Opera-Office'.[51]

Two of the most prominent figures in the world of Italian opera, Nicola Francesco Haym and Paolo Rolli, were also active in promoting Italian culture outside the confines of the theatre. Haym was born in Rome in 1678 and came to London in 1701 where he worked as musician (he was a professional cellist), librettist, stage manager and secretary of the Royal Academy of Music, one of the organisations set up to provide opera performances (he succeeded Rolli in this post); it is however his publications outside this sphere of activity which concern us. The *Del tesoro britannico* of 1719-20 has already been mentioned: it was, in the words of the subscription proposal, a description of 'such Greek and Roman antiquities as are to be found in the several cabinets of the Nobility and Gentry of Great Britain'. It appears that Haym not only learnt Greek and Latin for the purposes of compiling this work but also, remarkably, trained himself as an etcher in order to provide the engraved illustrations. In his proposal Haym half apologises for intending to write it in Italian and offers to supply gratis and separately an English 'appendix' for subscribers unfamiliar with the language. Two volumes only were published of this ambitious project, partly because Haym was drawn away to work on others. He cultivated diverse interests and activities but there are only two other main works which he saw published. The first was an edition of Tasso's *Gerusalemme liberata* (1724), which was to be the first in a series of Italian classics published by Jacob Tonson, who

51 The fullest listing of libretti published in London can be found in Claudio Sartori, *I libretti italiani a stampa dalle origini al 1800* (Cuneo, 1990-94), *Indici*, I, 77-81. On opera in London in the eighteenth century, see Sesto Fassini, *Il melodramma italiano a Londra nella prima metà del Settecento* (Torino, 1914); Frederick C. Petty, *Italian Opera in London 1760-1800* (Ann Arbor, 1972).

published Haym's other works. As with Molini's similar series later in the century and Foscolo's plans with Pickering in the 1820s nothing came of this. This was based closely on the Genoa edition of 1590; Haym had the celebrated engravings done for that edition by Bernardo Castello copied, with each one dedicated to a different aristocratic patron. This interest in the antecedent editions of a text leads us to Haym's final and, historically, most significant publication: the bibliography of Italian books *Notizia de' libri rari nella lingua italiana, divisa in quattro parti principali, cioè istoria, poesia, prose, arti e scienze* which he published in 1726, three years before his death, the fruit, as he says in his preface, of many years spent collecting Italian books and visiting public and private libraries. Reprinted in Italy under the title *Biblioteca italiana* (the 1726 version is the only one published in England), this became one of the standard bibliographies of Italian literature until the nineteenth century, an indication of its comprehensiveness and method. It is clear from the title, however, that the work was also intended to serve as a useful guide to collecting early and rare Italian editions and the rarest editions are marked with an asterisk.[52]

Haym's books are diverse but his relatively early death prevented him from adding to them; his fellow expatriate, colleague and rival Paolo Rolli's production is both diverse and prolific.[53] Rolli was ten years younger than Haym and in 1715 at the age of twenty-eight, when he had already established a literary reputation in Italy, had been invited back to London by Thomas Herbert, eighth earl of Pembroke, who had met him while travelling abroad, to serve in his household as an Italian teacher. He enjoyed a highly successful career, becoming royal 'preceptor' in Italian in 1729. He must have been innovative in his methods, to judge from one small book *D'Avverbj, particelle, preposizioni e di frasi avverbiali*... which he published in 1741, shortly before he returned to Italy for good. Rolli soon mastered English and his natural sociability made him well known and liked in musical and literary circles as a poet, librettist, translator and editor. His wide range of contacts among the nobility and gentry must be one reason why he was able to publish so prolifically: in addition to nearly thirty original libretti, he published volumes of his own poetry (the *Rime* in 1717, *Di canzonette e di cantate*... in 1727), editions of Ariosto (the *Satire e rime*, 1716), Boccaccio (*Decamerone*, 1725), works by Francesco Berni and other satirists in what was intended to be a

52 Haym based his research partly on previous published bibliographies: the copy of one of them, Fontanini's *Dell'eloquenza italiana*..., which he used and annotated in his preparation for his own book, is in the British Library (1476.c.7).

53 On Rolli, see George E. Dorris, *Paolo Rolli and the Italian Circle in London 1715-1744* (The Hague, 1967).

replica edition of the mid sixteenth-century Giunti anthology *Opere burlesche* (1721, 1724) and Lucretius's *De rerum natura*;[54] translations of Milton (*Il Paradiso perduto*, completed in 1735), Steele's play *The Conscious Lovers* (as *Gli amanti interni* in 1724), Anacreon's Odes (1739) and Virgil's Bucolics (1742).

But even without the activities of Haym and Rolli, opera by itself stimulated and influenced a wider English interest in Italian literature, the extent of which is shown by the large number of editions which were published during the century (it is by far the largest category).[55] Some of the most successful operas were based on episodes from the epic poems of Tasso and Ariosto and the largest number of Italian-language editions published in London belong to these two authors (as we have seen, Haym and Rolli had a hand in some of them). There are eight editions of the *Gerusalemme liberata* (from 1724 to 1796) and nine of the pastoral drama *L'Aminta* (1726 to 1800). It is surprising that an Italian edition of the *Orlando furioso* had to wait until Baskerville's of 1773; it might be thought that the 'trilogy' of masterpieces on subjects taken from the poem which Handel composed in the space of two years in the mid 1730s would have led to an edition. As it was, more interest was shown in Ariosto's other works: the *Satire e rime* went through four editions between 1716 and 1735, while in 1737 and 1739 Thomas Edlin

---

54 This edition shows that the provenance, publication and circulation of texts in the eighteenth-century European republic of letters was not always straightforward. Rolli's edition is of Alessandro Marchetti's translation. Marchetti's version had circulated widely in manuscript in Italy – where a printed edition of the Epicurean text was out of the question – and a copy was brought back to London by John Molesworth, the English ambassador to Tuscany at the time and a friend and patron of Rolli, to be edited here by the latter (under the transparent pseudonym 'P. Antinoo Rullo') and published by Pickard, with whom Rolli collaborated frequently in these years. But, judging from recent historical scholarship, this 1717 London edition seems to be falling into the paradoxical category of a genuine imprint regarded as a false one: Harold Stone in *Vico's Cultural History: the production and transmission of ideas in Naples 1685-1750* (Leiden, 1997), p. 222, asserts that it is more likely to be an illicit Neapolitan edition with 'Londra' as a false imprint; Jonathan Israel refers to a first edition first appearing 'in November 1718 … as a clandestine publication with "London" falsely given on the title-page' (*Radical Enlightenment: philosophy and the making of modernity 1650-1750* (Oxford, 2001), p. 44, n. 118). Was there a Neapolitan edition which copied the 1717 Pickard publication (which is certainly authentic)? To complicate matters, the London edition was counterfeited, over forty years later, in Lausanne (see Parenti, op. cit., p. 116).

55 Libretti of course were often by good poets and were sometimes regarded as literary achievements: the outstanding example is Metastasio, whose works for the operatic stage transcended their ephemeral status in collected editions and were read in their own right. After Paolo Rolli returned to Italy in the 1740s, he started to publish a collected edition of his libretti in *Componimenti poetici in vario genere…* (Venezia, 1744).

printed separate editions of three plays, *La scolastica*, *Dei suppositi*, and *La lena*. Besides Tasso and Ariosto, there was a marked taste for narrative prose: there were, for example, eleven editions of Boccaccio's *Decamerone*, beginning with Rolli's of 1725. There are also editions of the Renaissance *novellieri* Bandello and Grazzini or 'Il Lasca' which appear to be the results of publishing contacts in Italy. The publisher John Nourse claims to have obtained copies of the latter's *novelle* from 'un letterato fiorentino' to prepare his 1756 edition of the *Prima e seconda cena* and is confident of having done 'cosa grata alla Repubblica delle lettere procurandone una bella e corretta edizione'. The curious 1740 'semi-facsimile' edition of the *Novelle* of Bandello, a painstaking copy of the 1554 Busdrago edition in Lucca, given a disconcertingly discrepant eighteenth-century appearance with wide margins and leading between the lines, was probably printed in Italy, possibly to be published and sold in London ('e di nuovo in Londra, per S. Harding'). The interest in these authors and their texts was on occasion innovative: serious, if undeveloped, bibliographical and even philological concerns guided Haym's edition of Tasso's poem and, later in the century, Vincenzio Martinelli's Boccaccio; Edlin's editions of Ariosto's plays were almost their first appearance in print for 150 years. Edited by Rolli, although his name does not appear, each is dedicated to a different contemporary patroness, but they are clearly intended, like the Bandello volume, to resemble an authentic sixteenth-century Italian edition.[56]

Editions of contemporary Italian writers (not resident in London) are much rarer: a selection of Goldoni's plays was published in 1777 and collected editions of Metastasio's works in 1774 and 1784, two years after his death. These reflected the European fame of the authors; a more idiosyncratic publication is the 1772 edition ('presso Tommaso Brewman') of Zaccaria Seriman's novel *Delli viaggi di Enrico Wanton alle terre australi...* Seriman, a Venetian of Armenian descent, undoubtedly knew Swift's *Gulliver's Travels* which had been translated into Italian and published in Venice as early as 1729 (three years after the first English edition) and modelled his narrative

56 Informed bibliophilia, an important development in the eighteenth century, encouraged by Haym's bibliography (and his Tasso edition), must also lie behind such publications. The edition, among other such projects, of Boiardo's *Orlando innamorato* which Antonio Panizzi undertook in the 1830s with the support of Thomas Grenville and his comprehensive collection of early Italian editions, is the high point of this trend, a true partnership of bibliophilia and philological scholarship. For an account of the history and background of this edition see Denis V. Reidy, 'Boiardo, Panizzi and "Politics"', in *Italy in Crisis 1494*, ed. Jane Everson and Diego Zancani (Oxford, 2000), pp. 175-95.

(first published in 1749) on the same popular genre, in which the author merely claims to be 'editing' a manuscript account which has come into his possession of the travels of an often naïve voyager (Seriman's hero is a young English gentleman). The satirical intention is not lost on the reader who soon realises – in the Italian editions the accompanying engravings make it immediately evident – that, for example, one of the lands visited, inhabited by talking apes, is contemporary Venice and Wanton's wide-eyed account a caustic representation of Venetian society's foibles and failings. It is hard to know whether the printer's preface to the London edition, with its account of how the book came into his hands, is simply adding a further layer of illusion to the game being played by the novel – one which is highly characteristic of the genre – or telling the truth of the matter. D. Maxwell White suggests that the figure of the 'erudito soggetto' who is said in the preface to have sent Brewman the book from abroad with a proposal for publishing it could be George III's librarian Frederick Augusta Barnard who was in Italy in the late 1760s collecting Italian books for the royal library.[57]

There were a number of translations into Italian of English and Latin works, notably of Milton's *Paradise Lost*: Rolli's translation went through various editions until replaced at the very end of the century, first by Felice Mariottini's version and then by Gaetano Polidori's. These may have been intended for Italy, where Pope and later Gray were both published, but they could also have been read by English readers. Many of the literary texts published in the period served a more or less explicitly didactic purpose; while some were accompanied by glossaries and annotations, all displayed the status of Italian (or Tuscan) as a literary language. The translations of Milton's epic may have been intended as further proof of the language's literary dignity and the readers' familiarity with the English original would help them to understand and absorb the new language. Certainly the parallel text edition of John Gay's *Fables* 'with an Italian translation by Gian Francesco Giorgetti' (1773) is quite explicitly designed as a pedagogic aid, the stanzas being carefully matched across the pages. A curious indication of the fashionable status of Italian is the translation of Goethe's *Die Leiden des jungen Werthers* (as *Gli affanni del giovane Werter*) in 1788: according to the translator in his preface, the unique 'dolcezza' of Italian will enhance the sentiment of the story but his version also has the merit of being taken directly from the German original,

57 See D. Maxwell White, *Zaccaria Seriman 1709-1784 and the 'Viaggi di Enrico Wanton': a contribution to the study of the Enlightenment in Italy* (Manchester, 1961). Maxwell White, having found no other books printed by Thomas Brewman and writing in pre-ESTC days, assumes that the name is a pseudonym, but a few other books with his imprint are now recorded.

unlike the previous English translations which had all been based on French editions.

Paolo Rolli is the central figure in the first half of the century; after 1750 no Italian resident in London quite matches his energies, versatility and output. Men like Giuseppe Baretti, Vincenzio Martinelli and Francesco Sastres, while no less Italian than Rolli, are integrated in more effacing ways into the structures of English society.[58] Baretti publishes mostly in English whereas Martinelli, a fellow of the Antiquarian Society, and Sastres, who started out as a teacher – 'Mr Sastres, the Italian master' is mentioned as a beneficiary in Dr Johnson's will – but later became consul for the Kingdom of the Two Sicilies, publish in Italian but on England. These men were interested in the British, their manners, their history, their constitution. Martinelli wrote an *Istoria critica della vita civile* (1752) and also a three-volume history of England (published by the bookseller Pietro Molini in 1770), intended, at its dedicatee Thomas Walpole's suggestion, 'per la curiosità dei miei nazionali'; starting with Caesar's invasion and ending with the accession of George I, it could be described as the dispassionate account (Baretti thought it dull) which Leti had promised and failed to provide a hundred years before. In 1793 Sastres published, at his own expense, the first (and only) volume of his *Saggi sulla Gran Bretagna*... with a survey of Britain and its growing empire, its history and constitution.

Reference to Gaetano Polidori, who can lead us into the nineteenth century, is only to be found in biographies of his son, John William Polidori, author of *The Vampyre* and Byron's physician and companion, and of the Rossettis (his daughter married Gabriele Rossetti, thus making Gaetano the maternal grandfather of Dante Gabriel and Christina).[59] But he is in his own right an interesting and undeservedly neglected figure: enterprising and versatile, like many of his fellow Italians in London, he worked as a teacher, translator, editor, author, bookseller, publisher and printer for over half a century, and his progress from an eighteenth-century world into a mid-Victorian one (he died in 1853) would merit detailed study. He came to London in the 1790s with letters of recommendation from the poet and dramatist Vittorio Alfieri, whose secretary he had been. The works he

58 Like Rolli, Baretti and Martinelli came to London with literary reputations already established in Italy and they maintained close contacts with their homeland. Baretti was initially employed at the King's Theatre, and his first – and now extremely rare – publication in London was a pamphlet in English and French on *A Scheme for Having a New Italian Opera in London, of a New Taste* (1753).

59 He printed on his own press Christina Rossetti's first volume of poems *Verses* (including some in Italian) in 1847 when she was seventeen.

published in the decade after his arrival take us into a small society of foreign printers, publishers and booksellers, many of them Italian, living and working in the narrow streets of Soho behind Oxford Street: Nardini, Duleau (or Dulau), Da Ponte,[60] Zotti, Rolandi, precursors and – some of them – participants over the following decades in a community of political exiles closely resembling that of religious exiles gathered in the Elizabethan city. Polidori occasionally joined forces with them: with Pietro Molini he published an edition of *Il Castello di Otranto* in 1796, and in the following year, with Nardini, an edition of the *Gerusalemme liberata*. Other books – an edition of Petrarch's *Canzoniere* (the first Italian edition of this poet's work to be published in London), the Mariottini translation of Milton's *Paradise Lost*, and a six-volume anthology of *Saggi di prose e poesie de' più celebri scrittori d'ogni secolo…* – appear from 'G. Polidori e Co.'. In 1798 he published the first volume of a reader, cautiously entitled *Saggio di novelle e favole*, which he had written himself and dedicated to the headmistresses of a girls' school in Queen Square where he taught – a rare paratextual glimpse of a bourgeois world. He had a few copies distributed as they came off the press to sound out responses but the venture does not appear to have been a success since only one volume in a planned set of four came out. A year later Polidori returned to the idea of combining moral tales (a fashionable genre at the time, and one which was heavily exploited by the Religious Tract Society, founded in 1799) with linguistic instruction in his edition of Francesco Soave's *Novelle morali* and Luigi Grillo's version of Aesop's Fables. In the early 1800s Polidori appears to have given up his commercial activities as a publisher (at least of other authors' works) and bookseller to concentrate on being a man of letters, producing sacred dramas, tragedies, poems, tales and novels, and translations. Over several decades he worked on a version of Milton's poems (Rolli's classicising eighteenth-century version of *Paradise Lost* had fallen out of favour); in 1840 he printed in his own house in Regents Park the *Opere poetiche* of Milton in an edition of 284 copies, of which 250 were for sale 'presso P.

60 This is Lorenzo Da Ponte, Mozart's most famous librettist, who worked in London for the King's Theatre in the 1790s. However, he also set himself up in business as a printer (of libretti among other things), publisher, and bookseller (with a large stock of both modern and antiquarian Italian books). In his memoirs, he refers both to an expurgated edition of the *Orlando furioso* which he printed (rather than published, as Sheila Hodges writes) for Leonardo Nardini and publishing in his own right an edition of his fellow librettist and poet Giovanni Battista Casti's political satire *Gli animali parlanti*. See Sheila Hodges, *Lorenzo Da Ponte: the life and times of Mozart's librettist* (London, 1985), pp. 158-60.

Rolandi, libraio ed editore in Londra, numero 20, Berners Street, Oxford Street'.

Like Polidori, Pietro Rolandi is a ubiquitous but always marginal reference in the biographies of more celebrated figures, and, as with the older Italian, a more detailed study – or at least a bibliography of his publications – would be welcome. The careers and works of men such as Foscolo, Gabriele Rossetti, Mazzini, Panizzi have been the object of intense study;[61] Rolandi's bookshop and publishing house played an important role in their lives and those of lesser figures in exile in London. Pietro Rolandi arrived in London in 1821 at the invitation of his elder brother Giambattista who, despite being a civil engineer by profession, had left his native Piedmont six years earlier in order to set up a bookshop in London specialising in Italian books and prints; it was at first largely in this second aspect of the business that he was assisted by Pietro, who had trained as an artist. Giambattista died young in 1825, having compiled and published a number of books, including several readers and anthologies of fables and anecdotes, in small format, of a kind which were popular at the time, but also, more unusually, having edited translations of the Bible and the Book of Common Prayer, and Pietro took over, giving a new and lengthy lease of life – his nephew succeeded after he returned to Italy where he died in 1863 and the shop was still in business in the 1880s – to what became known as the 'Libreria Italiana' (fig. 2).[62] It soon became a social centre for the Italian exiles in the city – Mazzini became a regular visitor within days of his arrival in London at the beginning of 1837 – and Rolandi also published many of their books: literature, memoirs, language manuals – such as Rossetti's inaugural lecture as Professor of Italian at King's College London in 1831, Carlo Beolchi's *Saggio della poesia italiana* (1825 and subsequent editions), Carlo Pepoli's *Prose e versi* (1833-6), Guido Sorelli's memoirs *Le mie confessioni a Silvio Pellico* (1836), Felice Albites's *Della lingua italiana in Inghilterra* (1829).

---

61 Viglioni, op. cit., has chapters on Foscolo's stormy relations with his publisher William Pickering, pp. 119-51, and on his Dante edition, pp. 208-50. On Pietro Rolandi, see Mario Nagari, *Pietro Rolandi da Quarona Valsesia, 1801-1863* (Novara, 1959). For the secondary characters, C. P. Brand's 'Italians in England, 1800-1850: a bibliography of their publications', *Italian Studies*, 15 (1960), 84-101, covers a wide range of their writings (not all in Italian). Carlo Dionisotti's essay 'Panizzi esule' in *Rivista storica italiana*, 92 (1980), 384-411, reprinted in *Ricordi della scuola italiana* (Roma, 1998), pp. 179-226, builds round its main subject a fascinating picture of the community of Italian exiles in London in the period.

62 It later became a subscription and circulating library of foreign books (not only Italian), modelled closely on the Gabinetto Vieusseux in Florence. The shop sold both modern and antiquarian Italian books.

Fig. 2: Rolandi's trade card, from Mario Nagari, *Pietro Rolandi da Quarona Valsesia, 1801-1863* (Novara, 1959), facing p. 2.
British Library pressmark: 2713.cs.1.

Rolandi appears to have avoided publishing overt political and religious texts, but the book with which his name will always be associated is a famous symbol of the combined literary, religious and political concerns of the age: Mazzini's completion of Foscolo's abandoned edition of Dante's *Divina Commedia.* As with *L'Historia del Concilio tridentino*, the history of its gestation and publication is complex. Foscolo had intended to produce an edition of the whole poem in five volumes, with an introduction and commentary, which would establish a version of the text free of copyists' distortions and accretions (to this end, he started examining and collecting manuscripts and early printed editions in order to collate variants) and place the poem in a detailed historical context. It would mark a new beginning in the appreciation of Dante's work after the misinterpretations and neglect of the previous century. But Foscolo's lofty conception of the edition and of the scholarly labour involved clashed with the narrowly commercial priorities of his publisher Pickering. Pickering put pressure on Foscolo, who was ill and penniless, to finish the work on his terms: after forcing Foscolo to accept a change of format (quarto to octavo) and a reduced number of volumes, the final break came when in what was intended to be the introduction, the *Discorso sul testo di Dante*, published in 1825, Foscolo slightly exceeded the contractually agreed limit of 400 pages. This was the only part published in Foscolo's lifetime: two years later he was dead and the material and notes he had accumulated in the preparation of the edition were left in Pickering's possession. When Mazzini arrived in London a decade later one of his projects was to write a life of Foscolo and in doing the research for this he came across the trunk containing the poet's Dante papers, forgotten in Pickering's offices. The publisher's character had clearly not changed: when Mazzini attempted to obtain the material he asked for the very large sum of £400. At this point Mazzini called on Rolandi's help: Rolandi was reluctant (it was a larger undertaking than anything he had previously published) but allowed himself, partly for patriotic motives, to be persuaded. The money would have to be raised by subscription and it is interesting that in order to gather 'associati' Rolandi did not turn to potential English supporters but went on an extended tour of Italy distributing a printed advertisement or manifesto written by Mazzini. One of Foscolo's difficulties had been the impossibility of finding enough subscribers in England to finance his publishing projects. This system, so common – although even then not without problems – in the eighteenth century, seems to have been in crisis, at least for foreign-language books, in the early nineteenth century. The lengthy historical essays which had been planned to accompany each *cantica* had to be abandoned but Mazzini used Foscolo's more or less completed textual notes on the *Inferno* (which he also revised) to apply the same methodological criteria to the *Purgatorio* and the *Paradiso*. As a result it is now difficult to distinguish Mazzini's contributions from Foscolo's original drafts. The edition was published in four volumes in 1842 in London, although – it is not clear why – Rolandi had it printed in Brussels. Mazzini's name does not appear: the preface he wrote recounting the history of the edition is signed 'Un'Italiano' in symbolic anonymity: Dante is the supreme poet of Italian nationhood whose poem pre-enacts the country's unity, conveys its profound spiritual message to humanity, and adopts its real language – 'il Verbo della Nazione' – free, as Foscolo had intended, of 'municipal' dialect accretions, even when these were Tuscan.

Much Italian-language publishing in the nineteenth century follows the patterns established in the previous century – literary texts (both in grand and popular editions), translations from English, language books for learners – but on a wider scale for a more extensive middle-class readership, who visited Italy for its art and followed the country's struggle for unification with enthusiasm. I should like to conclude this survey by singling out two distinctive aspects: one reflecting a revival of interest and the other an almost completely new development.

Our predominant image of Anglo-Italian cultural relations is one which is very largely inherited from the Italophilia of the eighteenth century: the important channels open between the two cultures are art, literature and music. Italian-language publications in London in the eighteenth century form, as we have seen, a significant part of this image. Yet seen within the broader sweep of three and a half centuries Italian publishing in the city reveals another, equally striking but more complexly manifested thematic continuity in our relations: the enmities and alliances, attractions and repulsions generated by different religious convictions and church allegiances. The late sixteenth and early seventeenth centuries and the first half of the nineteenth century are the periods which show this most clearly, despite the fact that many of the Italian exiles in the later period, unlike their predecessors, took refuge in England for political not religious reasons. This is largely because nineteenth-century religious publishing in Italian – predominantly tracts and Bibles – is the product of English involvement in and movement towards Italy rather than the reception of Italian influence at home. This is not to say that Italian Protestants and Protestant sympathisers – many of them ex-priests – living in England were not leading contributors to the mood of evangelical fervour: men such as Salvatore Ferretti, who printed the journal *L'Eco di Savonarola* – for a period he called his printing works the 'Continental Protestant Printing Office' – and also wrote articles and books (including a hymnal *Inni e salmi ad uso dei Cristiani d'Italia*), as well as teaching; the polemicist Raffaelle Ciocci, author of, among other titles, *Barbarie praticate a Roma nel secolo decimo nono* (1845); the ex-Capuchin monk G. B. Di Menna, who taught Italian at Eton for a time and tried to start a magazine, *L'Aulico illustre*, there in 1842; Camillo Mapei, whose best-known work was an essay on 'the recent history and present conditions of Italy and the Italians' which concluded with a long and impassioned section on its religious state (this was translated into English and prefixed to various editions, from 1845, of a travel album of Italian views). Gabriele Rossetti, not a Protestant but a fervent anti-papalist and consequently sympathetic towards the evangelical cause, was also a member of this circle. His name serves to remind us that the reawakened interest in religious issues was not confined to tracts and new editions of the Bible and of the Anglican liturgy in Italian versions: Rossetti's own literary criticism – such as his 1832 book *Sullo spirito antipapale che produsse la Riforma e sulla segreta influenza ch'esercitò nella letteratura d'Europa e specialmente d'Italia...* – was much influenced by his religious convictions and the enormous success in early Victorian England, both in Italian and translated editions, of a 'Risorgimento' classic like Silvio Pellico's *Le mie prigioni* (Rossetti wrote the preface to Rolandi's 1836 edition), a narrative of the author's imprisonment in the notorious Austrian prison on the Spielberg, no doubt owed as much to the book's description of the development of Pellico's Christian outlook as to its tale of political oppression.[63]

---

63 The NSTC lists nine Italian-language editions and eight English translations between the 1830s and 1870s. The book was first published in Italy in 1832.

Pietro Rolandi's brother Giambattista appears to have been responsible as an editor for the appearance in England of Giovanni Diodati's renowned seventeenth-century Italian translation of the Bible.[64] Diodati had been a celebrated scholar and teacher from the Calvinist city of Geneva; his family was part of the notable mid sixteenth-century diaspora of Protestants from the Tuscan city of Lucca and were proudly tenacious of their origins and their language. In 1819 an 'edizione londinese' of the translation, revised by Giambattista Rolandi, was published by Priestley of Holborn, the first of many re-editions (the NSTC lists eighteen up to 1867) of what is, with the Authorised Version, the most famous vernacular translation of the Bible. Two years later another London publisher Bensley brought out another Italian version of the Bible, done in the late eighteenth century from the Vulgate, following Benedict XIV's relaxation of the prohibition on reading the Scriptures in the vernacular, by Antonio Martini, later archbishop of Florence, under the auspices of the Piedmontese monarchy (and first published by the 'Stamperia Reale' in Turin in the 1770s). This edition too had been in Giambattista Rolandi's editorial charge. Unlike Martini's version, which had been approved by the Catholic hierarchy, Diodati's version was anathema and had never been published in Italy.

Ten years before Giambattista Rolandi's edition of the entire Bible, the New Testament in Diodati's version had been published for the British and Foreign Bible Society. This organisation had been established in 1804 (five years after the foundation of the Religious Tract Society, with which it shared some evangelical aims).[65] Its principal object was to distribute the Bible (usually complete, although the New Testament, the Gospels and the Pauline Epistles were often issued separately) throughout the countries of the world in their vernaculars, at first by using agents or correspondents who acted as 'colporteurs' and later, if conditions were favourable, by setting up local Bible

---

64 There is a brief account of Giambattista Rolandi in Nagari's biography of his younger brother (see n. 61): the author tells us that, unable to swear an oath of loyalty to the Austrian government, he left Italy, but makes no reference to his edition of the Bible or his religious convictions. He also edited a revised and supplemented edition of Browne and Cappello's 1685 version of the Book of Common Prayer. It seems improbable though not impossible that Giambattista would have undertaken this and the edition of the *Bibbia Diodatina* while still a Catholic (although he may have been interested in Diodati's version for the renowned excellence of its literary style). From other details in Nagari's book it is clear that the Rolandi family was Catholic. Pietro appears to have remained one; as far as I am aware, he never published religious books.

65 The details which follow are taken from George Browne (see n. 15), I, 481-7 and II, 17-21.

societies. Where an approved translation already existed, the Society republished this. In the case of Italian it used both the Diodati and Martini versions.[66] The timely invention of stereotype printing lent added impetus to their efforts: in 1811, the first 'edizione stereotipata', published by Shacklewell 'dai torchj di T. Rutt', of the Diodati New Testament appeared. Within three years they had printed and distributed 11,000 copies in Italy. By mid-century this figure had risen to 174,000, together with 88,000 copies of the complete Bible and 10,000 'portions of Scriptures'; despite these large numbers, the overall assessment of the Society's activities in Italy drawn up by George Browne, their first historian, writing in 1859, was negative since the distribution of the Scriptures had not encouraged a culture of Bible-reading within the country.[67] While the vast majority of these copies were printed and published in London, the Society attempted to print copies within Italy itself. During the turbulent events of 1849, it managed to print editions of the New Testament in Florence, Pisa and even in Rome under the 'Repubblica Romana' when Pius IX had to flee the city. Even so, demand outstripped supply and more copies had to be sent from England. The Roman edition was suppressed on the return of the Pope when he also issued an edict forbidding the establishment of local Bible societies and once again strictly prohibiting the reading of the Bible in translation. There appears to be a similar correlation between the Italian publications (almost all of them translations from already published English texts) of the Religious Tract Society and the opportunities presented by periods of political unrest or change in the country.[68]

---

66 The editions of Italian dialect translations of books from the Bible printed and published privately by Louis-Lucien Bonaparte in London were the product of his linguistic interests and had nothing to do with the Society's activities.

67 After its long suppression, the sale of Diodati's version seems to have excited much curiosity in Italy. The Bible Society's agent in the country noted the number of clergy among his customers. He also remarked on the interest shown by university students and, with evident surprise, on an order for 400 copies '*from a Jew* [his italics] …for the Roman territories'. In this case the purchaser was better informed than the Society's agent: Diodati had made an intensive study of Judaic traditions of textual commentary and scholarship in the preparation of his version (see Milka Ventura Avanzinelli, 'Giovanni Diodati, traduttore della Bibbia' in *La sacra Bibbia tradotta in lingua italiana e commentata da Giovanni Diodati* (Milano, 1999), I, xli-cxlv).

68 To judge from the catalogued contents of one (destroyed) volume in the British Library, the Religious Tract Society published a whole series of tracts in Italian translation in the 1860s, presumably for distribution in the newly unified country: titles include *La buona novella, Una qualche idea della Bibbia, La Bibbia in prigione*, and *Il camerotto Bertino* (a translation of the tale *Bob the Cabin-boy*).

Evangelical fervour was not concentrated entirely on Italy; some attention was paid to the growing Italian immigrant community in London itself, apparently with some success. The first Catholic church in the city, St Peter's in Hatton Garden in Holborn, where the immigrants had settled, was established in 1864 largely in an effort to stop the inroads being made by Protestant missionaries.[69] In 1845 an evangelical journal in Italian was set up, *L'Eco di Savonarola*, which was circulated free in London 'among poor Italians' but was also printed in Paris and Geneva for European distribution. It invited contributions from Italians in Italy, guaranteeing their anonymity if they feared persecution. Despite precarious finances – it appeared irregularly and changed format twice in its first two years (it settled on a smaller format to facilitate postage abroad) – it survived until 1860. Its contributors and editorial board included many prominent Italian Protestants in London – all the men listed above wrote for it (Rossetti contributed poems) – and its articles provided information on the history of Italian Protestant churches in Italy and elsewhere as well as religious edification and anti-papal polemic. In 1856 it started to appear with a parallel English translation 'with a view to increase its usefulness'; this was a period when British interest in the situation in Italy had intensified and the wider political dimensions of Protestant anti-papalism were especially clear.

The new development which the nineteenth century brings to Italian publishing in London is the rise of the periodical.[70] At the end of the eighteenth and beginning of the nineteenth century several attempts had been made to publish an Italian journal in the city: as the first issue of one of them, *L'Italico*, stated (in 1813), it seemed strange to see periodical papers published in London in German, French, Spanish and Portuguese while 'not one existed in the noble Italian language'. The first was *Il Mercurio Italico*, which Francesco Sastres – although neither he nor any other collaborator is named – started in 1789.[71] This came out monthly, with a parallel English and Italian text in double columns on the page and engraved plates; while largely antiquarian in its interests, it also includes some current political information and comment as well as news from Italian cities. Each issue contains a long list of new Italian

69 See Sponza (as in n. 9), p. 22.

70 See Todeas Twattle-Basket [i.e. Tommaso de Angelis], *Note di cronaca, ossia i giornali, gli istituti e gli uomini illustri italiani a Londra durante l'era vittoriana 1837-1897* (Bergamo, 1897), pp. 2-42; Vittorio Briani, *La stampa italiana all'estero dalle origini ai nostri giorni* (Roma, 1977), pp. 48-51 (I am grateful to Monique Vérité of the Bibliothèque Nationale in Paris for providing me with information on this publication).

71 See Luigi Piccone, 'Un altro italiano amico di Samuele Johnson: Francesco Sastres e il "Mercurio Italico" di Londra', *Rivista d'Italia*, 27 (1924), 444-53.

publications arranged by city; in the first issue there is also a section – later dropped – on 'libri rari' (e.g. advertising a Mantuan incunable for sale from the Venetian bookseller Remondini). After one year, it split into two separate fascicules, in Italian and English, but shortly afterwards stopped altogether. In 1796 the Italian bookseller and publisher Pietro Molini issued a volume entitled *Italian Tracts*, which, 'the plan for an Italian magazine having not met with encouragement', gathered together in a single volume the two issues of the abortive journal; eighteen years later *L'Italico ossia Giornale politico, letterario e miscellaneo da una società d'Italiani*, similar to the *Mercurio* in content but with much lengthier articles like the leading British reviews of the period, ceased after less than a year (May 1813-April 1814). In a distinction drawn in the first issue of the weekly *La Gazzetta italiana di Londra* (in 1871) the individual initiative behind the setting up of these titles had not been matched, as it had to be if they were to succeed, by public acceptance. In the period between the failure of *L'Italico* and the appearance of *La Gazzetta italiana di Londra* in 1871, there was, as we have seen, *L'Eco di Savonarola*, as well as Mazzini's patriotic journals *L'Apostolato popolare* (1840-3 – the last two numbers were printed in Paris) and *Pensiero ed azione* (1858-60 – in London only until August 1859, thereafter in Lugano and Genoa), but these derived their energy from the causes they espoused and were, in any case, largely intended for readers throughout Europe.[72] The first editorial of *La Gazzetta* in May 1871 echoed *L'Italico* sixty years before, but with a difference: Italian journalists arriving in the British capital are astounded to find that, whereas Italian-language newspapers are to be found in Germany, France, the United States, 'even Brazil', no such publication exists in London. But the conditions which seemed so propitious – Italy's new European status as a unified country and the establishment of large emigrant communities abroad, including London (the first issues include articles both on emigration and Rome as the new capital) – proved delusive. Within three months it was running into trouble: in July an editorial blamed its lack of success as a 'giornale nazionale' on what it called the 'divisioni municipali' which prevented the Italian colony from uniting and, although the publication had met with good will, this has not translated into financial support ('… we were not born under the gilded roof of Baron Rothschild's Piccadilly mansion'). Over its six months of survival it changes editorial direction: its very first issues bear a marked resemblance to the erudite journals at the beginning of the century, with something of the gravity of political and cultural comment found in a paper like *The Times* (and, perhaps significantly, the advertising which it carries seems to be directed at the gentry); an attempt both to widen and define an Italian readership begins with the serialisation of a story set among the London Italian community in Holborn and an illustrated series on great fellow countrymen (Garibaldi, Pius

IX, etc.). In an article entitled 'La nostra letteratura in Inghilterra' in August 1871 the paper seems to take stock of its initial error: knowledge of Italian used to be regarded only as a cultivated attainment and it is understandable if interest in it has declined in a great commercial centre like London, but now that a unified Italy is a political and economic partner to reckon with, 'the study ... of Italian which even in the still recent past could be regarded as a luxury is today a necessity'. It was in fact the development of commercial and business contacts between the two countries in the next two decades which finally provided a real context within which an Italian newspaper could thrive. *La Posta di Londra* leads the way in 1878-9, with a section on 'Industria e commercio', regular lists of Italian merchant ships and their cargoes currently in the Port of London, and advertisements for Italian hotels, restaurants, shops and services in the metropolis. The extent and stability of these contacts was marked by the opening of an Italian Chamber of Commerce in the capital in 1886 and in the following years various newspapers appeared, the longest lasting of which were a new *Gazzetta italiana di Londra* (1896-1900) and *Londra-Roma* (1888-1920). No longer trying to imitate the mainstream British press, these publications are sustained by a focus on the Italian community in London, its needs, its interests, the associations and events which mark its life.

In 1901 the editor (and owner) of *Londra-Roma* Pietro Rava published a small book, a spin-off from the newspaper: *Guida per il viaggiatore italiano a Londra e in altre parti del Regno unito*. In a section entitled *Ricordi storici di italiani nelle Isole britanniche* Rava reminds his readers of illustrious Italians, their predecessors, who have visited Britain – an odd hall of fame, including St Augustine of Canterbury, David Rizzio, Garibaldi – with not one reference, apart from entries on Mazzini and Foscolo, to any of the numerous writers and teachers mentioned in this essay who lived and worked and contributed to the life and culture of the city. Part of its intended readership were newly arrived immigrants seeking to find their way about the huge metropolis, busier and more crowded than any place they had seen before (Rava helpfully provides them with a list of roads which are particularly dangerous to cross) and to settle there, giving them information on how to register births, marriages and deaths, the addresses and opening times of consulates, etc., but it is also, principally, designed, as its title states, for a new kind of 'Italian traveller' in the capital, the businessman and the tourist. And with the entry of these two essentially modern figures onto the scene, it seems appropriate to conclude this survey.

This essay has brought together a heterogeneous mass of publications under one bibliographical aspect or criterion – their place of imprint – but a broader assessment is called for. In the context of Italy's retrospective national bibliography, these London publications, taken as a whole, form a kind of annexe, a testimony to Italian culture's formidable prestige in England and the lively interest taken in it. From the point of view of the history of Anglo-Italian relations, all these books are significant, but a number take their rightful place in the mainstream record of Italian literature, thought and history: the choice of titles would be open to discussion but, in addition to Haym's important contribution with his *Notizia de' libri rari* to the retrospective bibliographical record itself, the list will include Bruno's philosophical dialogues, the *editio princeps* of Sarpi's history of the Council of Trent, the first appearance in print, edited by Rolli, of what remains one of the finest vernacular translations of Lucretius, the Foscolo-Mazzini edition of the *Divina Commedia*, which marks a new approach to the understanding of Dante, Mazzini's patriotic journalism.

Denis V. Reidy

Early Italian Printing in London

Despite the statement by the author Petruccio Ubaldini in the preface to the second edition of his Life of Charlemagne, *Vita di Carlo Magno*, printed in London by G. Wolfio, that is to say John Wolf, in 1581 (British Library pressmark G.9987) that this was the first book in Italian to be published in England, it is generally accepted that this distinction belongs to a catechism for children: *Catechismo, cioè Forma breve per ammaestrare i fanciulli*, a translation of John Ponet's *Catechismus brevis Christianae disciplinae* (BL C.37.a.3) (fig. 1). The translation of this work, incidentally, was undertaken by Michelangelo Florio. This book was printed by Steven Mierdman in London in 1553 in octavo format. Not a great deal is known about Mierdman except that he was a Protestant refugee from the Continent. He was born in Hoog-Mierde in Dutch Brabant, some forty miles from Antwerp, was employed as a printer in Antwerp from 1542 to 1546 and fled to England, where he lived from 1549 to 1553. He was responsible for printing several Protestant books in various languages before leaving England and resettling in Emden where he continued to practise his craft from 1554 until 1558.

Although Mierdman omitted the imprint in his book, probably because of fear of religious persecution – a fear which proved well founded – there is strong evidence, particularly typographical, that it is his. For example, the initial letter 'S' on A2r was also used in the edition of W. Turner's *New Herball* which Mierdman printed in London two years earlier in 1551. The title-page of the *Catechismo* is not very impressive or particularly memorable, indeed some might even find it a little on the dull side, however it is the title-page of what is generally regarded as not only the first book in the Italian language to have been printed in the British Isles, but also the first book printed in England in a foreign vernacular without an imprint. I am deliberately qualifying my statements somewhat, not through any sense of timidity or uncertainty, but because bibliographical research progresses at such a pace and new discoveries are being made so frequently that it is difficult to keep up with new research in the field – indeed a new discovery or a new attribution could have been made only today – hence the slight caveat to my statement.

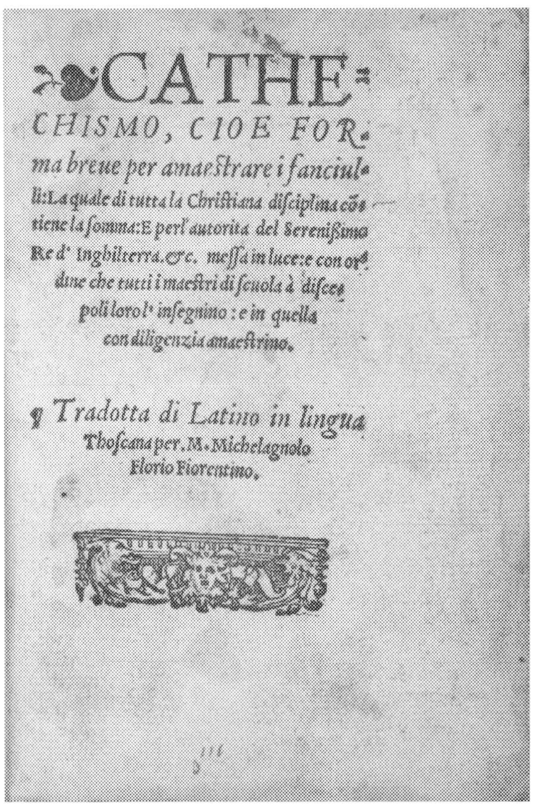

CATHE-
CHISMO, CIOE FOR-
ma breue per amaeſtrare i fanciul-
li: La quale di tutta la Chriſtiana diſciplina cō-
tiene la ſomma: E perl' autorita del Sereniſſimo
Re d' Inghilterra. &c. meſſa in luce: e con or-
dine che tutti i maeſtri di ſcuola à diſce-
poli loro l' inſegnino: e in quella
con diligenzia amaeſtrino.

¶ Tradotta di Latino in lingua
Thoſcana per. M. Michelagnolo
Florio Fiorentino.

Fig. 1: *Cathechismo* (London: Steven Mierdman, 1553), title-page. British Library pressmark: C.37.a.3.

There can be little doubt that the most important and the most prolific English printer of books in the Italian language at this period was John Wolf (1547-1601). In view of the importance of his work as an early printer of Italian texts in London and given the limited space available within the confines of this article, I thought it best to concentrate on Wolf and his printing of early Italian texts in London.

John Wolf was a fascinating character.[1] He first learnt his trade and entered his printing apprenticeship to John Day of the Stationers' Company

1 For further reading on John Wolf see R. B. McKerrow (ed.), *Dictionary of Printers and Booksellers in England … 1557-1640* (London, 1910), pp. 296-7; Harry R. Hoppe, 'John Wolfe, Printer and Publisher, 1579-1601', *The Library*, 4th ser., 14 (1934), 241-88; Dennis E. Rhodes, 'John Wolf in Florence', *British Museum Quarterly*, 33 (1969), 103-5.

in London at the age of 15 on 25 March 1562 where he acquired the art of printing over the next ten years. Being a very shrewd young businessman with an eye to the main chance, who would be regarded as a good entrepreneur in our own age, he seized every opportunity he could of making a tidy profit even if this involved breaking the law by printing an unlicensed book – or even by printing an out-and-out 'forgery', as we will shortly see.

He identified what some today would refer to as a 'niche market' which would soon earn him a good profit in the printing of texts in the Italian language. Between 1569 and 1579 he visited Italy and travelled extensively throughout the peninsula. He certainly must have lived in Italy for a considerable time because he studied printing in Florence. Wolf certainly lived in Florence for a while since in 1576 he published several 'Rappresentazioni' (a genre not dissimilar to our mystery plays) bearing the imprint 'In Fiorenza ad instanzia di Giovanni Vuolfio Inglese'. Fortunately two of these rare works, *La Historia e oratione di Santo Stefano Protomartire* and *Historia et vita di Santo Bernardino* both of 1576, are in the British Library at pressmarks C.34.h.6(35) and C.125.de.1. Wolf appears to have gained an amazingly deep knowledge of Italian printing, Italian types, founts and Italian printers which, as we will see, he was able to put to very good use on his return to London. So knowledgeable was he of Italian printing and the Italian printing scene and so sophisticated was his sense of an Italian or Italianate book that he was able to produce a work in the Italian language which was so convincing that scholars have assumed until fairly recent times that his works were printed in Italy by an Italian – in effect they had been duped by him for almost three hundred years! Indeed it was only a little over a hundred years ago that the celebrated Italian scholar Salvatore Bongi began to question the authenticity of an edition of Machiavelli's *Discorsi* and his *Il Principe (The Prince)* which bore the imprint 'In Palermo, Appresso gli heredi d'Antoniello degli Antonielli a xxviii Gennaio, 1584'. The title-page of this work (fig. 2) looks so convincing and has a very Italian look, design and feel about it and even to the trained eye it can pass quite readily as a typical product of the Italian press of the period. Indeed even Filippo Evola in his literary and typographic history of Sicily praised Wolf's books and accepted them as the product of a genuine Italian printer.[2]

In all fairness to him, Evola did sow the first seeds of doubt in Bongi's mind, by conceding that the name of the printer Antoniello was unknown to the typographical and literary history of Sicily. Evola also admitted not a little

2 Filippo Evola, *Storia tipografico-letteraria del secolo XVI in Sicilia con un catalogo ragionato delle edizioni in essa citate* (Palermo: Stabilimento Tipografico Lao, 1878).

surprise at finding this isolated pocket of publishing of Machiavelli's works in Sicily where he conceded there was not an overwhelming demand for 'good literature' among Sicilians at that time, but was more concerned about the fact that the authorities of Palermo would have permitted the publication of two volumes citing the name of the city and the publisher in 1584 at a time when Machiavelli's works were proscribed in the rest of Italy.

Bongi began to have further doubts: the original vellum bindings of these books seemed to him to be more English than Italian. In his view the vellum was too rich to be Italian and consequently had to be English, which first alerted him to the possibility of a false imprint. He subsequently wrote to Alfred William Pollard at the British Museum, who after painstaking research confirmed that the books indeed were not printed in Palermo, but in London, and on typographical grounds, Pollard ascribed the work to John Wolf.

So why, we may ask, should Wolf print forgeries of Machiavelli's works? Clearly a very lucrative market for these works existed at the time. Niccolò Machiavelli (1469-1527), the Florentine politician, political exile (like Dante Alighieri before him) and the father of modern statecraft, was publicly criticised for his moral principles even in his own lifetime. As Busini, a contemporary writer informs us 'ognuno l'odiava' (everyone hated him), and by 1549 it was prohibited to sell any of Machiavelli's works in Rome. These continued to be read and printed in Italy up until 1559 when all of his works were placed on the Index; they were not openly printed in Italy for a further two hundred years.

Nonetheless, politicians and students of statecraft still wished to consult Machiavelli's works. One of the best ways to promote and advertise a product is to ban it, and this certainly appears to have been the case with Machiavelli's works. Wolf soon realised that there was a considerable demand for Machiavelli and seized his opportunity in responding to and supplying that

IL PRENCIPE
DI NICOLO MA-
CHIAVELLI,
Al Magnifico Lorenzo di Piero
de Medici.
Con alcune altre operette, i titoli delle quali trouerai nella
seguente facciata.

IN PALERMO
Appresso gli heredi d'Antoniello degli Antonielli
à xxviij. di Gennaio, 1584.

Fig. 2: Machiavelli, *Il Prencipe* (Palermo: heredi d'Antoniello degli Antonielli, 1584), title-page. The imprint is false: printed in London by John Wolfe. British Library pressmark: 587.b.9.(2).

demand by providing several counterfeit editions. These heralded the celebrated five 'testina editions' of Machiavelli's complete works printed in the first half of the seventeenth century in Geneva with the false date of 1550. (Incidentally these were and are still referred to as 'testina' editions because of the 'little head' of Machiavelli (in Italian, 'testina') which figures on their title-page.) Wolf's business acumen was second to none and he started to make quite a handsome profit from his Machiavelli texts, nearly all of which were printed without a licence and some with the false place of printing given as Palermo – conveniently right at the far end of the toe of Italy. It took eleven days to sail from London to Naples in the nineteenth century, a journey which must have been even slower in the sixteenth, affording Wolf the protection of distance.

Wolf's Machiavelli editions consist of five small octavo volumes. The first two, *I discorsi sopra la prima Deca di Tito Livio* (*The discourses on the First Ten Books of Livy*) and *Il Principe* (*The Prince*) both bear the imprint 'Heredi d'Antoniello degli Antonielli, Palermo, 1584' (the Heirs of Antoniello degli Antonielli). Antoniello, as we have seen, was purely a figment of Wolf's imagination, and both title-pages bear the device of serpents and a palm-tree which has a motto attached to it 'Il vostro malignare non giova' ('Your malignant speech or thought are to no avail') – perhaps a deliberate and ironic dig at the reader's expense if we bear in mind the circumstances in which the book was printed. This is the first time that Wolf uses this particular device although he did use it on other occasions for other works. Since both books resemble each other very closely, in all probability they were printed together. Not very surprisingly neither book was licensed.

The third of Wolf's Machiavelli items was his edition of *Le Istorie Fiorentine* (*The Florentine histories*), which bears the imprint 'In Piacenza appresso gli Heredi di Gabriel Giolito di Ferrari, 1587' with the statement 'con Licenza de superiori' (with the licence of the authorities). Although this statement is literally true, since the book was licensed by the English authorities, on 18 September 1587, to be precise, it is deliberately misleading since it never received a printing licence from the Italian authorities – yet another case of Wolf being a little 'economical with the truth' or rather bending the truth somewhat.

Wolf uses a device of a phoenix and two satyrs with the initials 'G. G. F.' which, to my mind, is meant to lend credence to the illusion that the work was printed by Gabriel Giolito de' Ferrari although the latter actually printed in Venice. The mottoes contain the words 'Dela mia morte eterna vita i' vivo' (From my death I live an eternal life) and 'Semper eadem' (Always the same). The device is a close copy of one actually used by Giolito and appears here for the first time. Incidentally the device was later copied by several other English printers.

The fourth of Wolf's Machiavellis was the *Libro dell'arte della Guerra* (*The Book of the Art of War*) which also bears the same imprint as the first two of his Machiavelli editions illustrated above, that is to say, 'Palermo, Antoniello degli Antonielli', but there is no date. Curiously enough the British Library copy bears the date 1587 on a cancel title-page, that is to say a subsequent title-page was printed and inserted into the book thereby replacing the original title-page. Unfortunately Wolf committed an error. In the 1584 edition of the *Discorsi* the imprint read 'presso gli Heredi di Antoniello degli Antonielli' (published by the Heirs of Antoniello degli Antonielli) yet in a work published three years later in 1587, Antoniello was still described as living ! – Wolf does make the occasional slip – as the Italian proverb goes 'il diavolo fa le pentole ma non i coperchi' – the devil makes the saucepans but not the lids! Curiously other copies of this work which were intended to be sent to Frankfurt for the book fair did not contain the Palermo imprint, perhaps because Wolf thought that his clientele in Frankfurt was a little more discerning and perhaps a little more sophisticated and might not have been fooled so readily by a Palermo imprint ? It is not surprising that this book was not licensed either.

The fifth of Wolf's Machiavellis is *L'asino d'oro* (*The Golden Ass*) which bears the imprint 'In Roma, MDLXXXVIII – 1588' and contains the device of two goats with the initials 'D. G. F.' and the motto 'Sic semper ero' (I shall ever be thus). The device is copied from part of a device which had been previously used by the Venetian printer Domenico Giglio in Venice in 1552 in an edition of Petrarch's *Canzoniere*, and is used by Wolf for the first time here. This device too was also adopted later by other English printers so we have Wolf to thank for the spread of some Italian ornamentation and devices in England. This work surprisingly was licensed on 17 September 1588. The type used by Wolf in the *Asino d'oro*, incidentally, is identical to that used in his edition of Pietro Aretino's *Commedie*.

Mention of Pietro Aretino brings us very conveniently on to Wolf's editions of this author. Pietro Aretino is generally not as well known as Machiavelli, so a few details about him might not be amiss. As his name suggests, he was born in Arezzo, south of Florence, in 1492. He published numerous plays, penitential psalms and other sacred texts but is principally remembered for writing the occasional obscene, some would say pornographic, work. He was not afraid of criticising the Papal curia openly in print and is often remembered for his sonnets composed to accompany obscene drawings by Raimondi. After settling in Rome he had to flee to Venice where he found a more liberal atmosphere and more tolerant censors. He died suddenly in Venice in 1556.

John Wolf printed three of Aretino's works. The first of these is Aretino's *La prima* [and *seconda*] *parte de Ragionamenti* which as the colophon states, was 'stampata, con buona licenza (toltami) nella nobil citta [sic] di Bengodi, ne l'Italia altre volte più felice, il vigesimo primo d'Octobre, MDLXXXIV (printed with a good licence [probably with the intended pun on the phrase 'licence'] taken from me [that is to say, unlicensed] in the Noble city of Bengodi [which translates as 'enjoy yourself well'] in Italy at other times a happier place, on 21 October 1584). The preface reveals the name of the printer to be 'Barbagrigia' which means Greybeard. The book was considered to be quite pornographic at the time it was printed, but it is relatively mild by modern standards. Wolf certainly knew instinctively what would sell well; his business acumen must have been well rewarded because there are no fewer than three editions of the book which appear to have been published in the same year in the British Library alone! There are at least two other editions of the work. The British Library copy (pressmark 1079.c.5) is certainly printed by Wolf since not only is it printed with his type but it also contains Wolf's tail-ornaments and initials. The BL copy incidentally, also contains Annibale Caro's *Commento di Ser Agresto*, another pornographic book. As with most of Wolf's Machiavelli editions, this book was not licensed either. The second of Wolf's editions of Aretino was *Quattro Commedie* (The *Marescalco, Talanta, Cortegiana* and *Hipocrito*) published in 1588 with no place or printer's name. This uncommon book contains a rather attractive medallion portrait of Pietro Aretino which is inscribed with the words 'Petrus Aretinus Flagellum Principum' (the scourge of princes). The type is the same used by Wolf in his edition of Machiavelli's *Asino d'oro.*

The third of Wolf's editions of Aretino was *La terza, et ultima parte de ragionamenti* and bears the imprint 'Appresso Gio.[van] Andrea del Melagrano, 1589'. The printer's name Melagrano ('pomegranate') is obviously fictitious. Wolf's preface is dated 'Di Valcerca ne la gia [sic] libera Italia a 13. di Gennaio. 1589' (In Valcerca, in already liberated Italy, 13 January 1589). Surprisingly the book was licensed on 14 October 1588. This edition also contains a medallion portrait of the author.

Restrictions of space prevent me from looking at a few other works in the Italian language printed by John Wolf – however, I feel I should point out Wolf's edition of Marco Antonio Pigafetta's *Itinerario (da Vienna a Costantinopoli)* (London, 1585) (BL pressmark C.32.f.28) which is extremely rare (there are also copies in New York Public Library and at Yale). The binding of the British Library copy contains the Royal Arms surrounded by a border bearing the badges of Henry Prince of Wales and may also have been in the possession of King James I along with the works of other contemporary London printers of Italian language works.

Another important figure in the history of Italian printing in London is John Charlewood, who died in 1592. He was responsible for printing six works in the Italian language by the Renaissance scholar and philosopher, Giordano Bruno of Nola (1548-1600), who has been described as one of the most modern thinkers of the Renaissance. Despite having entered the Dominican order at the tender age of sixteen, he soon fell foul of the Inquisition in 1589 and was imprisoned in Rome for eight years until his execution at the stake on 17 February 1600. Charlewood printed six of Bruno's works in London, all small octavos: first *La cena de le ceneri* (*The Supper of Ash Wednesday*), with no imprint, in London in 1584 ; *De la causa, principio, et vno* with the false imprint Venice, 1584; *De l'infinito vniuerso*, also with the false imprint Venice, 1584; *Spaccio de la bestia trionfante*, with the false imprint Paris, 1584; *Cabala del cauallo Pegaseo* with the false imprint Paris: by Antonio Baio, 1585; and *De gl'heroici furori*, also with the false imprint Paris: by Antonio Baio, 1585. Clearly Charlewood too found a ready market for Bruno's equally influential works.[3]

Space is not sufficient here to add more than this postscript. It is sincerely hoped that there will be a repetition of the very successful one-day symposium on printing in London held in the British Library in 1999 at some time in the not too distant future when we could be afforded a further opportunity to examine the work of John Charlewood and other printers in more detail.

---

3 Giovanni Aquilecchia, 'Lo stampatore londinese di Giordano Bruno e altre note per l'edizione della *Cena'*, *Studi di filologia italiana, Bollettino dell'Accademia della Crusca*, 7 (1960), 101-62.

Barry Taylor

Un-Spanish Practices
Spanish and Portuguese Protestants, Jews and liberals, 1500-1900

In this survey I shall ask three main questions: Who were the printers of Spanish and Portuguese books in London? Where in London were these Spanish and Portuguese communities? And where were the intended readers of these books: here in England or there in the Old Country?

I feel that a general survey is appropriate here because, to a large extent, this will be the same story told several times over, with different actors. It seems to me that until very late in our period – possibly only the mid nineteenth century – authors published Spanish and Portuguese books in this country because they could not be printed in the Peninsula or its empire: hence my title.[1] In the sixteenth to seventeenth centuries the motive is religious: Protestantism. The seventeenth century also sees the arrival in this country of Spanish and Portuguese-speaking Jews. And in the first half of the nineteenth comes the influx of a number of Spanish and Portuguese liberals.

It also emerges from this survey that although a fair number of books were printed in London in Spanish and Portuguese, the printers themselves are – with, I believe, the solitary exception of Marcelino Calero – unfailingly English, even though some of them may have Hispanised their names: Ricardo del Campo, who printed in Spanish from 1594 to 1600, is really Richard Field; G. A. Claro del Bosque who in 1863 printed the Protestant Juan de Valdés's *Ziento y diez consideraziones* is Spottiswoode [BL pressmark 3902.f.13/17]. The motive of the former was certainly deception; the latter could be a *jeu d'esprit*.

---

1 'Spanish practices' were the Jesuitical wiles which figured so large in the negative image of the Spaniards abroad.

Elizabethan Protestants

Of the twelve editions which Gustav Ungerer identifies as Elizabethan British imprints in Spanish four are on political topics and eight religious.[2] The first two books printed in England in Spanish were printed at Oxford: Alfonso de Valdés, *Dialogo en que particularmente se tratan las cosas acaecidas en Roma* ('Paris', [i.e. Oxford: Joseph Barnes,] 1586) and Antonio del Corro, *Reglas gramaticales para aprender la lengua española y francesa, confiriendo la una con la otra* (Oxford: Joseph Barnes, 1586).

Of the twelve editions which Ungerer describes for the period 1586-1600, seven are from the press of Richard Field, Ricardo del Campo as he appears in the imprints. According to the *English Short-Title Catalogue*, Field printed about 266 books between 1588 and 1624 of which eighteen are surreptitious editions in foreign languages: French, Italian, Spanish and one in Dutch.[3] The term surreptitious indicates that the place of printing is either falsified, or, as in Field's case, deliberately omitted; in Spain at the time, the law required the place of publication to be stated.[4] Field seems to have printed books of all sorts. During the period of his Spanish books he lived at Blackfriars. His last Spanish book appears to be of 1600, yet he worked on to his death in 1624. The seven books he printed in Spanish are a tiny part of his output.

One of these is Antonio Pérez, *Pedaços de historia, o relaciones* (1594). It passes itself off as 'Leon' (presumably to be taken as Leon in Spain rather than Lyons). This is a clear example of political propaganda. Pérez was Philip II's secretary of state, who being in the habit of selling state secrets and growing too fond of assassination as a tool of government was sacked in 1579 and imprisoned. In 1590 he took refuge in Aragon, where the King's powers were more restricted, and in the following year attempted to lead a revolt. These events are recounted in the *Pedaços*. He was in England in 1593-5. The edition we know was subsidised by the English government, and copies are reported

---

2 Gustav Ungerer, 'The Printing of Spanish Books in Elizabethan England', *The Library*, 5th ser., 20 (1965), 177-229; *Catalogue of Books Printed in Spain and of Other Spanish Books Printed Elsewhere in Europe before 1601 now in the British Library*, 2nd edition, ed. D. E. Rhodes (London: British Library, 1989), pp. 237-94; *Short-Title Catalogue of Spanish and Portuguese Books, 1601-1700, in the Library of the British Museum (the British Library – Reference Division)*, ed. V. F. Goldsmith (Folkstone: Dawsons, 1974), p. 241.

3 *English Short-Title Catalogue* <http://www.rlg.org/estc.html>; Denis B. Woodfield, *Surreptitious Printing in England 1550-1640* (New York: Bibliographical Society of America, 1973).

4 Jaime Moll, 'Problemas bibliográficos del libro del Siglo de Oro', *Boletín de la Real Academia Española*, 59 (1979), 49-107, at p. 52.

to have been sent to Aragon to foment revolution, and sent to the Low Countries for distribution. 'A newsletter written in Flanders at the beginning of 1595 stated the the *Relaciones* had been printed at the expense of the Queen of England and that a great number of copies had been conveyed into Aragon to incite that kingdom to rebellion' (Ungerer 196). William Nichols wrote to Sir Peter Hollins from the Low Countries: 'I pray you use all diligent means to get so many as ye can of those books that Anthony Perez hath made. They shall be well paid for and distributed here…' (Woodford 37)

All Field's other Spanish books appear without a place and are written or translated by the Protestant Cipriano de Valera, including the Spanish New Testament and Calvin's *Institutions* in Spanish. Valera, born c. 1532, had been a Hieronymite in the monastery of San Isidro del Campo in Seville; accused of heresy, he fled Spain in 1557, going first to Geneva and later London, where in 1583 he lived in 'Candelweeke Street Warde'.[5] In the Geffrye Museum in London there is a rather poor portrait of 'Judith de Valera, daughter of the Spanish pastor'. In the books, Valera is either (i) unnamed or (ii) identified by initials in the prefatory matter or (iii) uniquely, named as the translator of Calvin. In 1602 he was on the Continent, publishing the complete Bible in Spanish in Amsterdam. Nothing is known for sure about his whereabouts after that. As the disappearance of Valera from history coincides with the end of Field's Spanish career, we may wonder if the printer was motivated by an exclusive arrangement with Valera.

We should not, I think, infer a special relationship between Britain, land of the free, and the Spanish dissidents. The Spanish Protestant diaspora found homes in equal or greater numbers in the Protestant Low Countries, Germany and Switzerland. The Spanish Protestant community was small, and despite a brief period when they had their own chapel in St Mary Axe were obliged to lodge with the Italian Protestants (Ungerer 216).

Who were the readership for these books? The natural inference is that they were intended for export, i.e. smuggling, to Spain and its Empire. As we saw, there is evidence of these books being taken over to the Spanish Netherlands (Ungerer 189, 190).

The seventeenth century accounts for some nine Spanish books printed in London by eleven printers: again, the sort of book produced here is much in the line of the preceding century. As we have seen, the British establishment was prepared to publish in Spanish for propaganda purposes. The year 1623 saw the publication of *Liturgia inglesa. O libro del rezado publico*

---

5 A. Gordon Kinder, 'Cipriano de Valera, Spanish Reformer (1532? – 1602?)', *Bulletin of Hispanic Studies*, 46 (1969), 109-19, at p. 116.

(Augustae Trinobantum [i.e. London: printed by Bonham Norton and John Bill]) [C.25.i.2]. This was a translation of the Book of Common Prayer, put into Spanish by Fernando de Tejeda, like Valera a former monk, whose other London publications are in English, such as *Texeda Retextus: or the Spanish monk his bill of divorce against the Church of Rome* (1623). The liturgy was produced at the time the future Charles I as Prince of Wales was courting the Infanta Maria and the translation was aimed at encouraging her to convert.[6]

The matrimonial alliance between Charles II and Catherine of Braganza was the occasion for what may well be the first piece of Portuguese printing in London: Sebastião da Fonseca, *Relaçam das festas de palacio, egrandesas* [sic] *de Londres, dedicada amagestade da serenissima Rainha da Gran Bretanha* (Londres: na officina de J. Martin, Ja. Allestry & Tho. Dicas, 1663) [C.125.c.2(3)], a celebratory poem dedicated to the Queen. Some doubt attaches to Salvador do Spirito Sancto, *Sermam da cinza, pregado na corte de Londres, na capella da Real Magestade da Serenissima rainha da Gran Bretanha, em oito de Fevereiro de 1665* (impresso por mandado de Sua Magestade) [C.125.c.2(6)] (fig. 1). There is no imprint, but Wing S2623A gives it to London, and the British Royal coat of arms (rather crudely rendered) appears on the title-page; however, typographically this could well be a Portuguese product: the text proper begins on quire A, while, according to Sayce, B as first text signature 'is a characteristically English feature'; and there exists an explicitly Portuguese reprint: Coimbra: na officina de Rodrigo de Carvalho Coutinho, 1673 [C.125.c.2(7)]. Frei Salvador was preacher to Kings John IV, Alphonso VI and Peter II of Portugal, and was summoned to London by Queen Catherine to lead the Franciscan house which she founded there.[7]

This pattern persists into the eighteenth century.[8] We may note that no London printer seems to have specialised in Spanish books: none appears to be responsible for more than three items. Henry Woodfall published three

---

6 On Tejeda, see Marcelino Menéndez y Pelayo, *Historia de los heterodoxos españoles* (Madrid, 1880-2); rpt as *Edición nacional de las obras completas de Menéndez Pelayo*, vols 35-42 (Santander: Aldus, 1946-48), IV, 184-7. This remains the most extensive study of the Spanish dissidents, despite the author's blatant lack of sympathy for his subject. John Stoughton, *The Spanish Reformers, their Memories and Dwelling-places* (London: Religious Tract Society, 1883), pp. 294-300, mentions the Spanish exiles in England.

7 R. A. Sayce, ' Compositorial Practices and the Localization of Printed Books, 1530-1800', *The Library*, 5th ser., 21 (1966), 1-45, at pp. 17-18; on Frei Salvador, see Innocêncio Francisco da Silva, *Diccionario bibliographico portuguez*, VII (Lisboa: Imprensa Nacional, 1862), p. 194.

8 For this period, the ESTC is supplemented by *Short-Title Catalogue of Eighteenth-Century Spanish Books in the British Library*, ed. H. G. Whitehead (London: British Library, 1995), III, 113.

editions of two works by Antonio Palomino (1655-1726), *Las vidas de los pintores y estatuarios eminentes españoles* (Londres: impresso por Henrique Woodfall, a costa de Claude du Bosc & Guillermo Darres, en el Mercado de Heno, 1742) [688.d.16]; 2nd edn (Londres: impresso por Henrique Woodfall, a costa de Sam. Baker, en Russel-Street, Covent Garden, & T. Payne, en Round-Court in the Strand, 1744) [1044.e.7] and *Las ciudades, iglesias y conventos de España, donde ay obras de los pintores y estatuarios eminentes españoles* (Londres: impresso por Henrique Woodfall, 1746) [1044.c.29]. The audience for these publications is obscure: Palomino's work had been published previously in Spain and so was politically acceptable to the Spanish regime; equally strangely, they were in Spanish although intended for the foreign visitor.

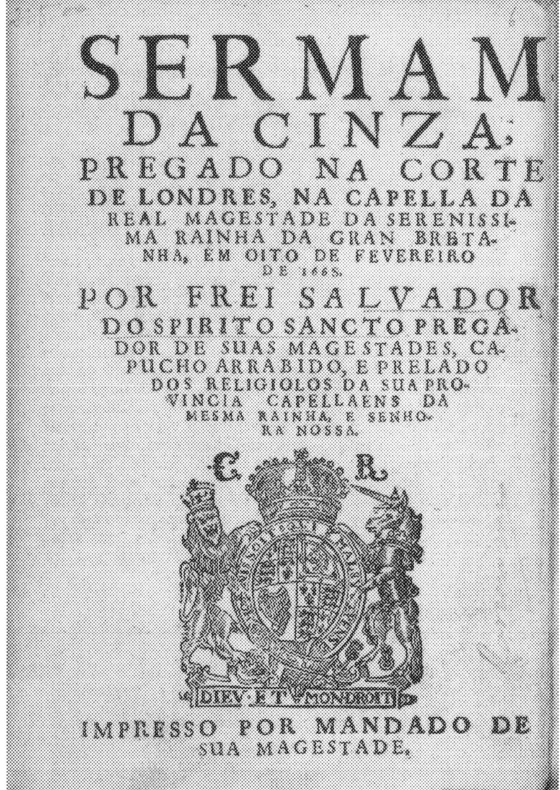

SERMAM
DA CINZA;
PREGADO NA CORTE
DE LONDRES, NA CAPELLA DA
REAL MAGESTADE DA SERENISSI-
MA RAINHA DA GRAN BRETA-
NHA, EM OITO DE FEVEREIRO
DE 1665.
POR FREI SALVADOR
DO SPIRITO SANCTO PREGA-
DOR DE SUAS MAGESTADES, CA-
PUCHO ARRABIDO, E PRELADO
DOS RELIGIOLOS DA SUA PRO-
VINCIA CAPELLAENS DA
MESMA RAINHA, E SENHO-
RA NOSSA.

IMPRESSO POR MANDADO DE
SUA MAGESTADE.

Fig. 1: Salvador do Spirito Santo, *Sermam da Cinza* (London?, 1665?), title-page. British Library pressmark: C.125.c.2(6).

Sephardic Jews

The Sephardim are the Jews of Spain and Portugal. Driven out by the Inquisition in 1492, the first generation of exiles settled in North Africa, Italy and the Low Countries. Following approaches from Menasseh ben Israel, rabbi of Amsterdam, Cromwell allowed these Jews into England in 1656, where they were permitted a degree of religious freedom. The Bevis Marks synagogue in the City of London dates from this period. A monument of Sephardic Jewry is the Old Cemetery in Mile End Road, which opened in 1657, followed in 1733 by the New Cemetery, which is now enclosed by Queen Mary College. Those who came over seem to have done so via Italy or the Netherlands. One of the more prolific Sephardic authors, David Nieto, hailed from Livorno.[9]

In a classic study, Cecil Roth catalogued sixty-nine publications in Spanish or Portuguese printed between 1649 and 1820.[10] All the London publications of Hispanic Jewry address the Jewish community: they are sermons, calendars and works of polemic among Jews. It is of course possible that they were intended for export to communities in the Low Countries or, I suppose, even in Spain, but many look parochial. David Nieto, Rabbi from 1701 to 1728, is a figure who looms large in the publications of the London Sephardic Jews. To quote Roth:

> One sabbath, at the close of 1703, it seems, the Rabbi delivered in the synagogue a sermon in which he expressed certain views which appeared to some of his audience to savour of pantheism. A storm broke out in the community: petitions, addresses, and counter addresses were prepared; foreign rabbis were canvassed for their opinions; and both sides committed their views to paper – none in English, a minority in Hebrew, most in Spanish. Thus James Dover, in Tower Hill, and Thomas Ilive, in Aldersgate St, had their first experience of the Spanish printing which must have provided them with a slender income for some years to come; for London was not like Amsterdam, where Jews early entered the printing business and monopolized synagogal custom (Roth 120).

Another work of Nieto's is an example of Sephardic printing in London for consumption abroad. In 1705 an *auto-da-fé* was held in Lisbon, with a sermon in which the Archbishop of Cranganor execrated the Jews. Nieto replied to this in a pamphlet in Portuguese with the false imprint Turin, but really London, 1709: the use of Portuguese (as opposed to what had been the norm

---

9 Meyer Kayserling, *Biblioteca española-portugueza-judaica* (Strasbourg: Trübner, 1890), p. xv.

10 Cecil Roth, 'The Marrano Typography in England', *The Library*, 5th ser., 15 (1960), 118-28.

of Spanish) suggests very strongly that it was intended to circulate in Portugal (Roth 121).

Of the 69 publications in Spanish or Portuguese listed by Roth, Spanish easily accounts for the majority: only twelve were printed in Portuguese. The inference is that after that date the languages of the Peninsula fell into disuse among the London Sephardim: it is significant, I think, that the records of Bevis Marks synagogue were kept in Portuguese until 1819 and in English after that.[11]

Liberals

It was Spanish politics of the early nineteenth century which gave the world the political term 'liberal'.[12] The period from the Napoleonic invasion of 1808 to the end of the First Carlist War in 1838 was particularly turbulent in both Spain and Portugal, with rapid alternation between liberal and conservative regimes. The main periods of influx into London were the reactionary reigns of Ferdinand VII of Spain of 1814-20 and 1823-33. The exiles settled very near the present site of the British Library, in Somers Town. They were vividly recalled by Thomas Carlyle:

> In those years [the 1820s] a visible section of the London population, and conspicuous out of all proportion to its size or value, was a small knot of Spaniards, who had sought shelter here as Political Refugees. 'Political Refugees': a tragic succession of that class is one of the possessions of England in our time. Six-and-twenty years ago, when I first saw London, I remember those unfortunate Spaniards among the new phenomena. Daily in the cold spring air, under skies so unlike their own, you could see a group of fifty or a hundred stately tragic figures, in proud threadbare cloaks; perambulating, mostly with closed lips, the broad pavements of Euston Square and the regions about St Pancras new Church. Their lodging was chiefly in Somers Town, as I understood; and those open pavements about St Pancras Church were the general place of rendezvous. They spoke little or no English; knew nobody, could employ themselves on nothing, in this new scene. Old steel-grey heads, many of them; the shaggy, thick, blue-black hair

---

11 *Bevis Marks Records, Pt VI: The Burial Register (1733-1918) of the Novo (New) Cemetery of the Spanish & Portuguese Jews' Congregation London*, ed. Miriam Rodrigues-Pereira and Chloe Loewe (London: The Spanish & Portuguese Jews' Congregation, 1997), p. xv.

12 OED, *liberal,* B 1 b. José Alberich, *Bibliografía anglo-hispánica 1801-1850* (Oxford: Dolphin, 1978), gathers the London publications of many of these exiles. There is much useful data in the book reviews which appeared in Bello's *Repertorio americano* of 1826-7: see Pedro Grases, *Tres empresas periodísticas de Andrés Bello: bibliografía de 'La biblioteca americana' y 'El repertorio americano'* (Caracas, 1955), pp. 44-8. A rich source for the London publications of this period is the *Catálogo colectivo del patrimonio bibliográfico español* <www.mcu.es/ccpb>, henceforth ccpb.

> of others struck you; their brown complexion, dusky look of suppressed fire, in general their tragic condition as of caged Numidian lions.[13]

They certainly did not intend to stay: in the words of one, they 'kept their bags packed' (Llorens 36).

Antonio Puigblanch published two books in London: *Opusculos gramatico-satiricos* (Londres: en la Imprenta de Guillermo Guthrie, 1832-28) [12942.aaa.17] and *Prospecto de la obra ... intitulada Observaciones sobre el origen y genio de la lengua castellana* (Londres: en la Imprenta Española de M. Calero, 1828) [12942.aaa.16] . His most famous book was, however, in English: *The Inquisition Unmasked* (1813), a translation of the Cadiz original of 1811-13.

Another liberal was Vicente Salvá (1786-1849), bibliophile and bookseller. As he wrote in 1826, 'the political changes of Spain in 1823 drove me for shelter to this happy land of Civil and Religious Liberty'. He took refuge in Paris and London, where he ran a 'Spanish and Classical Library' (more properly a bookshop), at 124 Regent Street. In 1825 he published the *Obras* of Moratín father and son, printed by the Imprenta Española de M. Calero, 17, Frederick Place, Goswell Road. Marcelino Calero Portocarrero, a liberal exile from La Coruña, was a supplier for Salvá's bookshop who printed in London from 1825 to 1829, when he returned to Spain.[14]

Two waves of Portuguese Jacobins and masons came in 1823 and 1829-31. Some of the refugees landed at Plymouth, where they were able to print patriotic proclamations.[15] The most famous of these is Almeida Garrett (1799-1854), poet, essayist in the English style, diplomat and politician.[16] (He

---

13 Thomas Carlyle, *The Life of John Sterling*, ed. W. Hale White (London: Henry Frowde, 1907), I, ix, pp. 66-7, cited by Vicente Llorens, *Liberales y románticos: una emigración española en Inglaterra (1823-1834)* (Mexico: Nueva Revista de Filología Hispánica, 1954), p. 36. Dickens, *Bleak House*, published in 1852-3 but set some time earlier, mentions them too: 'He [Harold Skimpole] lived in a place called the Polygon, in Somers Town, where there were at that time a number of poor Spanish refugees walking about in cloaks, smoking little paper cigars' (Chapter 43): see Susan Shatto, *The Companion to 'Bleak House'* (London: Unwin Hyman, 1988), pp. 4, 242-3.

14 On Salvá, see Carola Reig Salvá, *Vicente Salvá: un valenciano de prestigio internacional* (Valencia: Institución Alfonso el Magnánimo, 1972); on Calero, see Pedro Ortiz Armengol, *El año que vivió Moratín en Inglaterra, 1792-1793* (Madrid: Castalia, 1985), plate XXIII. For other books printed in London by Calero see Appendix I below.

15 For example, *Proclamação à nação portugueza* (Plymouth: na imprensa de Edvardo Nettleton, 1828) [RB.31.b.151/3]. José Baptista de Sousa, 'Catão em Plymouth: controvérsias acerca da representação da tragédia em Inglaterra – 1829', in *De Garrett ao Neo-Garretismo: actas do colóquio* (Maia: Câmara Municipal de Maia, 1999), pp. 75-90.

16 Carlos Estorninho, 'Garrett e a Inglaterra', *Revista da Faculdade de Letras* (Lisbon), 21 (1955), 40-75; Vitorino Nemésio, *Exilados 1828-1832: história sentimental e política do liberalismo na emigração* (Lisboa: Bertrand, 1946).

owes his second surname to his Irish grandmother.) In 1823-4 and 1828-31 he spent two periods in exile in England, staying at no. 13 Oxendon St, Haymarket, using the libraries of Richard Heber and the British Museum, and dining in Liberal circles at Holland House.[17] (Lord Holland was a notable Hispanophile, who wrote a life of Lope de Vega; Lady Holland kept a *Journal* of her travels in Spain in 1802-9.) Garrett continued his literary career, publishing nine books and two journals with the publishers Boosey (1); Sustenance & Stretch (4); Greenlaw, 39 Chichester Place, Grays Inn Rd (3); and C. S. Bingham, 5 Wilmot St, Russell Sq. (Estornino 73-4). And like so many of the exiles, when the political situation had cooled down at home, back he went, to a distinguished political career, dying a peer of the Portuguese realm.

London presses, such as those of Greenlaw, were occupied in printing topical political material in Portuguese, be it propaganda or translations of British parliamentary debates on Portuguese matters.[18] The surgeon António de Almeida (1761-1822) published his *Tratado da inflammação*... in London (H. Bryer, 1812-13). A clear example of a book printed in Britain for export, it is dedicated to the Portuguese Regent (later John VI). Almeida was soon to return to Portugal, where he published on scientific topics in 1815 and 1825.

To put the work of the liberal emigrés in London in context, England was not their only refuge, nor Spanish their only language. Several of the exiles mentioned here also spent time in France and published in French. On the linguistic side, some authors published mainly in English during their time here: Pascual de Gayangos, for example, author of the *Catalogue of Manuscripts in the Spanish Language in the British Museum* (1875-93), seems only to have published in English, while José Blanco y Crespo published in London in Spanish only at the beginning of his career, becoming so naturalised as to rename himself Joseph Blanco White. António de Vieyra (floruit 1779), Regius Professor at Trinity College Dublin, who is believed to have gone into exile for religious reasons, published in English or Latin.

Two works by Mariano Moreno, *Vida y memorias del Dr Dn Mariano Moreno, Secretario de la Junta de Buenos Ayres..., con una idea de su revolucion, y de la de Mexico, Caracas, &c.* (Londres: Imprenta de J. McCreery, 1812) [615.i.20] and *Coleccion de arengas en el foro y escritos* (Londres: Jaime Pickburn, 1836) [20012.f.1]

---

17 Lia Noemia Rodrigues Correia Raitt, *Garrett and the English Muse* (London: Tamesis, 1983), p. 9.

18 There is some useful raw data in 'Obras de alguma forma relacionadas com países de língua portuguesa', *Revista de Estudos Anglo-Portugueses*, 5 (1996), 9-26. For some Portuguese political pamphlets see Appendix II below.

are rare examples of the work of a Spanish American politician published in London. Pickburn is not known to have printed anything else in Spanish.[19]

Probably the most notable of the Latin American exiles in London was Andrés Bello, the Venezuelan-Chilean politician and writer who spent some nineteen years in London from 1810 to 1829.[20] Among his most important publications are two journals: *La biblioteca americana o Miscelánea de literatura, artes y ciencias, por una Sociedad de Americanos* (Londres: en la Imprenta de Don G. Marchant, Ingram Court, 1823) and *El repertorio americano* (Londres: en la libreria de Bossange, Barthés y Lowell, 14 Great Marlborough Street, 1826-27; en la imprenta de G. Schulze, 13 Poland-Street).

London also played an important role in the history of the press in Brazil. The Portuguese had prohibited printing in Brazil, and the first Brazilian newspaper was the *Correio braziliense* (Londres: Officina de W. Lewis, 1808-22), edited by Hipólito da Costa. The title itself is indicative of the editor's growing consciousness of a separate Brazilian identity.[21]

Academic and literary publishing

This category overlaps considerably with the previous three, as many of these academic authors came to Britain for political or religious reasons. One of the earliest English-Spanish grammars of known authorship is by a Protestant. Juan de Luna left Spain in 1612 for France, where he settled and studied in the Protestant centre of Montauban.[22] He published a Spanish-French grammar, *Arte breve, y compendiossa, para aprender, a leer pronunciar, escreuir, y hablar la lengua Española*, in Paris in 1615. Also in Paris in 1620 he published his continuation of the picaresque novel *Lazarillo de Tormes*. In 1621 the Protestant stronghold of La Rochelle fell to Louis XIII, the Declaration of Niort reduced Protestant rights and Luna moved to London, settling in Cheapside, where he continued to make a living as a teacher of Spanish. He reissued his Spanish grammar for an English readership, *Arte breve ... A Short and Compendious Art for to Learne ...*

19 Alberich, *Bibliografía anglo-hispánica* (cited in n. 12), pp. 122-43, lists very few publications by Latin American exiles in his section on 'Hispanoamérica y Filipinas'.

20 Horacio Jorge Becco, 'Bibliografía analítica de las publicaciones de don Andrés Bello en Londres', in *Bello y Londres: segundo congreso del bicentenario* (Caracas: Fundación La Casa de Bello, 1980), II, 283-321.

21 Barbosa Lima Sobrinho (ed.), *Antologia do 'Correio Braziliense'* (Rio de Janeiro: Cátedra, 1977). For the various London pamphlets printed in response to articles in the *Correio*, see Rubens Borba de Moraes, *Bibliographia brasiliana*, 2nd edn (Los Angeles: UCLA Latin American Center Publications, 1983), pp. 47-48, 156, 234, 561, 892.

22 *Anónimo, Segunda parte del Lazarillo, edición de Amberes, 1555; Juan de Luna, edición de París, 1620*, ed. Pedro M. Piñero (Madrid: Cátedra, 1988), pp. 67-73.

the Spanish Tongue (Londres: Juan Guillermo [i.e. William Jones], 1623) [C.33.a.45] and in 1623 he was preaching at Mercer's Chapel in Cheapside. He is thought to have died in England.

One of the masterpieces of Spanish printing in London is the Carteret *Don Quixote* (Tonson, 1738). Strangely, this is the first critical edition of Cervantes's novel, predating that of the Spanish Academy by twenty-two years. The patron of the edition was Lord Carteret (John Carteret, Earl Granville, 1690-1763), for whom in the phrase of a contemporary it was printed 'at his expense and for his entertainment' ('a su costa i por su diversion'), his intention being to 'cultivate the Spanish tongue in this country' ('cultivar la lengua española en esta tierra').[23] The text was prepared by Pedro Pineda, described by Menéndez y Pelayo (V, 121) as a 'judaizante' ('inclined to Judaism') who also published London editions of such novels as the *Diana enamorada* of Gil Polo (Londres: por Thomas Woodward, 1739) [245.e.1] and the *Fortuna de Amor* of Antonio de Lo Frasso (Londres: por Henrique Chapel, 1740) [89.a.18-19], which he chose to publish because Cervantes had praised them in the scrutiny of Don Quixote's library (see the prologues to the *Diana* and Book II of the *Fortuna*). In the latter case, according to Menéndez y Pelayo, he failed to detect the true meaning of the arch-ironist's praise. The edition also included a life of Cervantes by Gregorio Mayans y Siscar. Mayans was the Spanish Royal Librarian, an establishment figure, with no need to publish abroad. He was approached by Carteret via the British ambassador Benjamin Keene. The Tonson edition has engravings after drawings by J. Vanderbanck. Carteret expressed some reservations about these, as they were 'invented by foreigners who were incapable of capturing the customs and distinctive qualities of Spain' ('inventadas por forasteros incapaces de acertar en las costumbres y algunas particularidades de España') (Mestre xliv). Indeed, Mayans thought worthy of criticism errors 'in the chimney in Don Quixote's bedroom' ('en la chimenea en el quarto de D. Quijote'), 'the Priest's three-cornered biretta and collar and Sancho Panza's shoes and hat' ('en el bonete de tres esquinas y en la balona del cura, en los zapatos i sombrero de Sancho Panza…') (xlv). The Carteret *Don Quixote* is a turning point in the history of Spanish printing in London, as for the first time we see a work of a non-pedagogical nature produced for the interested English Hispanophile reader.

---

23 Gregorio Mayans y Siscar, *Vida de Miguel de Cervantes Saavedra*, ed. Antonio Mestre (Madrid: Espasa-Calpe, 1972), pp. xlii, xliv; *Tesoros de España: ten centuries of Spanish books* (Madrid: Dirección General del Libro y Bibliotecas, 1985), pp. 296-8.

The *Cancionero de obras de burlas provocantes a risa* (En Madrid: por Luis Sanchez, 1841) [G.10949] is an anthology, originally printed in 1519, of obscene poetry. The imprint is false: Sánchez was a real printer, but active in Madrid 1590-1627. The text was edited by Luis de Usoz.[24] Born in 1806, he became a Quaker after reading Robert Barclay's *An Apology for the True Christian Divinity* in the Spanish translation of Félix Antonio de Alvarado, *Apologia de la verdadera theologia christiana … trasladada …ahora en Castellano por Antonio de Alvarado … por el Bien de Todos, Especialmente de la Nacion Española* (Londres: J. Sowle, 1710) [855.i.6]. He came to London in 1839 but, like many another, returned to Spain. Although the book itself looks convincingly Spanish, it is known from Usoz's correspondence that the publisher is Pickering of London.[25] Pickering and his associate the printer Whittingham were adept at this sort of mimetic printing. Doubtless one of the appeals of the book for Usoz was that it was full of anticlerical verse.

The Spanish liberal exiles produced fourteen journals from 1810 to 1851 (Alberich, 22-3); the Portuguese liberal exiles twenty journals from 1808 to 1832.[26] One such is the *Ocios de los emigrados españoles*, a literary journal which ran from 1824 to 1827 (Londres: se vende en casa de los SS. Dulau y Compañia; y Treuttel y Wurtz, Soho-Square; Boosey e Hijo, Old Broad-Street). 'Ocios' is the Latin *otia*, meaning both 'leisure' and 'literary activity'. The editor, José Blanco White, explains that his contributors were making good use of their enforced idleness in exile to write things they would never have had time for back home. I see the *Ocios* as the forerunner of the sort of journal produced by cultural attachés' offices which explain Spanish culture to the interested British reader. In its first year it included articles on 'Spanish proverbs', and on orientalism in Spain, as well as current political comment rather than news.

The figure of George Borrow deserves mention, if only to explain why his bibliography lies outside this study. He was a traveller, philologist and student of Romany life who visited Spain and Portugal in 1835-40 with the backing of the British and Foreign Bible Society, distributing cheap Bibles. The reason I

---

24 Menéndez y Pelayo, VI, 319-25; *Cancionero de obras de burlas provocantes a risa*, ed. Pablo Jauralde Pou and Juan Alfredo Bellón Cazabán (Madrid: Akal, 1974), pp. xiv-xxi.

25 Bernard Warrington, 'William Pickering', in *British Literary Publishing Houses, 1820-1880, Dictionary of Literary Biography*, 106 (Detroit: Gale, 1991), pp. 245-50. As Graham Jefcoate shows in his article in this volume, Whittingham was capable of printing in *fraktur*.

26 Félix Walter, *La Littérature portugaise en Angleterre à l'époque romantique* (Paris: Revue de Littérature Comparée, 1927), p. 130.

exclude him is that, remarkably, he managed to have these Bibles printed for him by Borrego in Madrid.[27]

When the London colleges were founded in the 1820s, they included Spanish on the curriculum. An early example of a publication for the university audience is J. de Alcalá, *A Grammar of the Spanish Language for the Use of the Students in King's College* (London: Whittaker, 1830) [627.b.25].[28] The first professor of Spanish at University College London, Antonio Alcalá Galiano, and of Spanish at King's College London, Pablo Mendíbil, came to Britain as liberal exiles. The chairs date from 1827 and 1829 respectively. Jiménez de Alcalá was the second professor of Spanish at King's College. Besides publishing his *Grammar*, he was also principal editor for Ackermann.[29] From the beginning of the century, we commonly see the names of Ackermann, Boosey and Dulau on Spanish and Portuguese books. Longman already appear in some pre-1850 books. (Nelson and Harrap, by the way, seem not to have entered the market for Spanish school-books until 1912 and 1920 respectively.) None of these publishers dealt exclusively in Spanish and Portuguese. Some of the books of this period are clearly for the British market: Iriarte, *Fabulas*, ed. A. L. Josse (Londres: Dulau, 1809) [11453.a.6], for instance, has a vocabulary appended.

Ackermann, in contrast, was 'the leading publisher of books written principally for the emergent republics in Latin America' (Ford, 'Culture and Commerce', p. 137) (fig. 2). One example of a book expressly intended for export is Sir Walter Scott's *The Talisman* (1826) here published anonymously, in Spanish translation: *El Talisman: cuento del tiempo de las cruzadas. Escrito en ingles por el autor de "Ivanhoe", "Waverley", &c.* (Publicalo R. Ackermann, en Londres, Repositorio de Artes, 101, Strand, y en su establecimiento de Megico, 1826). [12604.cc.20] (The translation is anonymous because the original was also anonymous.). The availability of the book in Mexico serves

---

27 George Borrow, *The Bible in Spain*, ed. Peter Quennell (London: Macdonald, 1959), pp. 186-8.

28 José María Jiménez de Alcalá, *A Grammar of the Spanish Language for the Use of the Students in King's College (London [: Dulau and Co.], 1833) reproduced in facsimile from the second edition (1840) with an introduction by David Hook* (London: King's College London, Department of Spanish & Spanish-American Studies, 1998).

29 On Ackermann, see John Ford, 'Rudolph Ackermann: Publisher to Latin America', in *Bello y Londres* (as in n. 20), I, 197-224, and 'Rudolph Ackermann: Culture and Commerce in Latin America 1822-1828', in *Andrés Bello: the London Years*, ed. John Lynch (London: The Richmond Publishing Co. Ltd for the Venezuelan Embassy, 1982), pp. 137-52. For a selective list of Spanish books published by Dulau, Ackermann and Boosey, see Appendix III.

as a reminder that one reason why Britain backed Latin American independence was that it opened up markets to British trade.

LONDRES:
LO PUBLICA R. ACKERMANN, STRAND,
Y EN SU ESTABLECIMIENTO EN MEGICO:
ASIMISMO EN
COLOMBIA, EN BUENOS AYRES, CHILE, PERU, Y GUATEMALA.
1825.

Fig. 2: J. J. de Mora, *Gramatica latina* (London: Ackermann, 1825), title-page, detail.
British Library pressmark: 12934.b.7.

Charles Wood and Son were active as printers in Spanish from 1824 to 1857, working for Ackermann from 1824 to 1829; Wood also printed one book for Salvá: Perico de los Palotes (pseud.), *Don Termópilo ó Defensa del Prospecto del Doctor Puigblanch* (Londres: Librería de V. Salvá; Imprenta de Carlos Wood e Hijo, 1829).[30]

The minority languages of Spain have a small presence in London printing in our period. They were of course represented in the publications of the British and Foreign Bible Society from 1806.[31] Outside this area, I believe

30 For Wood's Spanish books see Appendix IV.

the earliest book printed in London in Catalan to be a bilingual Catalan-English edition of the *Consolat de Mar*, *The Black Book of the Admiralty* (London: Longman and Trübner, 1874) and the earliest in Basque *Dialogues basques: guipuzcoans, biscayens, par don A. P. Iturriaga, le P. J. A. de Uriarte* ... (Londres, 1857) [12907.c.1], privately printed by W. H. Billing for the philologist Prince Louis-Lucien Bonaparte: both of them clearly academic publications.[32]

Conclusions

In the light of this survey, we can say that at least up to 1800 no London printer seems to have specialised in Spanish, with the small exception of Richard Field. Looking back, there is a long and reasonably homogeneous history of London printing in Spanish and Portuguese, much of it due to the Inquisition. We can distinguish two periods: in the earlier, our Spanish and Portuguese have a refugee mentality, writing for their religious and political comrades either within an enclosed community of outsiders or for those they left behind in the Old Country. Towards the end of our period, we find books aimed at the interested English reader. And both these traditions survive to our own day.[33]

Appendix I
Some books printed in London by Calero

C. B. Depping, *Colección de los más célebres romances antiguos españoles, históricos y caballerescos* (1825) [G.18145]

Real Academia Española, *Ortografía de la lengua española* (1825) [12942.aa.29]

Anonymous, *Ensayo sobre las libertades de la iglesia española en ambos mundos* (1826) [3902.cc.29]

Evaristo San Miguel, *Elementos del arte de la guerra* (1826) (ccpb000381723)

---

31 T. H. Darlow and H. F. Moule, *Historical Catalogue of the Printed Editions of Holy Scripture in the Library of the British and Foreign Bible Society* (London, 1911), list editions in Spanish of 1806 (no. 8491), Catalan 1832 (no. 8650); Basque 1838 (no. 1946), and Asturian 1861 (no. 8645).

32 Julien Vinson, *Essai d' une bibliographie de la langue basque* (Paris: Maisonneuve, 1891), no. 232b; see also Table des lieux d'impression (I, 440), s.v. Londres.

33 I am pleased to acknowledge the help of Elizabeth James, Nigel Roche, David Shaw and Geoff West.

Revista del antiguo teatro español (1826) [11725.aa.22(3)]

José Canga Argüelles, *Diccionario de hacienda para el uso de los encargados de la suprema dirección de ella* (1826-7) (ccpb000241050)

Alvaro Flórez Estrada, *Reflexiones acerca del mal extraordinario que en el día aflije a la Inglaterra y que más o menos incomoda ya a las naciones más industriosas de la Europa* (1827); 2nd edn, 1827 [8276.bb.7]

Flórez Estrada, *Curso de economía política* (1828) (ccpb000313339)

Canga, *Observaciones sobre la historia de la guerra de España que escribieron los señores Clarke, Southey, Londonderry y Napier* (1829-30) [1060.k.14]

Canga, *Breve respuesta a la representacion de los comerciantes de Londres, y varios artículos ... del honor del monarca español: insertos en el periodico "El Times", sobre el reconocimiento de la independencia de las Américas Españolas* (1829) [1389.g.43(1)]

Appendix II
Some Portuguese political pamphlets printed in London

José Anselmo Correa Henriques, *A revoluçam de Portugal: tragedia, dedicada à inseparavel memoria dos portuguezes pellos seus legitimos senhores e reys da Caza de Bragança* (Londres: na Impressam de Cox, Son e Baylis, 1808) [11726.cc.21]

Copia da carta, que hum amigo escreveu de Lisboa ... copiada do Correio Braziliense, numero de mayo de 1817 (Londres: L. Thompson, 1819) [C.189.a.17]

Clemente Alvares d'Oliveira Mendes e Almeida, *Correspondencia entre C.C. de O.M. e Almeida, Consul Geral do Imperio do Brasil em Portugal e os Ministros dos Negocios Estrangeiros de Sua Magestade Fidelissima* (Londres: L. Thompson, 1827) [RB.31.b.156]

Protesto dos plenipotenciarios de Sua Magestade o Imperador do Brasil contra a usurpação, feita ao mesmo Senhor, da Coroã de Portugal (Londres, em 8 de Agosto de 1828) [RB.23.b.4066]

Joaquim António de Magalhaes, *Breve exame do assento feito pelos denominados estados do reyno de Portugal congregados em Lisboa aos 23 de Junho do anno de 1828* (Londres: impresso por R. Greenlaw, 36 Holborn, 1828) [8042.cc.22(1)]

Debates no Parlamento Britanico sobre os negocios de Portugal, em sessão do 1º de Junho na Camara dos Communs, e de 19 do mesmo mes na Camara dos Pares ... (Londres: R. Greenlaw, 1829) [RB.23.a.20140; RB.23.a.20157]

Joaquim António de Magalhaes and Francisco da Gama Lobo Botelho, *Analyse as Observaçoens do General Saldanha. Publicadas em Paris com a data de 13 de Novembro 1829* (Londres: impresso por R. Greenlaw 1830) [8042.g.32]

Heleodoro Jacinto de Araujo Carneiro, *Algumas palavras em resposta ao que certas pessoas tem ditto e avançado à cerca do governo portuguez ...* (Londres: Typografia de G. Schulze, 1831) [Cup.408.tt.27]

José Liberato Freire de Carvalho, *Reflexoens sobre um paragrapho do manifesto do Senhor Dom Pedro Duque de Bragança datado a bordo da fragata Rainha de Portugal aos 2 de Fevereiro de 1832* (Londres: Bingham, 1832) [8042.aaa.24]

Rodrigo Pinto Pizarro, *Speculum justitiae* [an account of his ill treatment by Dom Miguel] ([Londres:] Impresso por R. Greenlaw, 39, Chichester Place, King's Cross, [1832]) [8042.cc.24(3)]

idem, *Justiça de mouros* ([Londres:] Impresso por R. Greenlaw, 39, Chichester Place, King's Cross, Londres, [1833]) [8042.cc.26(11)]

idem, *Appellação do Coronel Rodrigo Pinto Pizarro para o tribunal dos seus concidaõs* [London? 1833] [1414.h.26(2)]

Appendix III
Some Spanish and Portuguese books published by Dulau, Ackermann and Boosey

Agustín Luis Josse (ed.), *El tesoro español, o Biblioteca portatil española, que contiene poesias escogidas de los mas celebres poetas castellanos con notas para la ilustracion y mayor claridad de las voces y sentencias que hubieran podido ofrecer alguna dificultad* (Londres: se hallará en la Libreria de Dulau y Comp., Quadro de Soho, 1802) [95.i.12]

J. B. [Boosey?], *La Floresta española, o piezas escogidas, en prosa, sacadas de los mejores autores de España … select passages, in prose, extracted from the most celebrated Spanish authors* … (London: printed for T. Boosey, No. 4 Old Broad-Street, Near the Royal Exchange, 1807) [1161.c.8]

Le Sage, *Aventuras de Gil Blas de Santillana*, ed. F. Fernandez (Londres: a expensas de F. Wingrave; T. Boosey; Lackington, Allen y Co.; y Dulau y Co., 1808) [1073.i.53]

Tomás de Yriarte, *Fabulas literarias*, ed. A. L. Josse (Londres: Dulau, 1809) [11453.a.6]

Antonio de Solís, *Historia de la conquista de Mexico*, ed. A. L. Josse (Londres: en la imprenta de R. Juigne … a expensas del dicho editor, se hallara, en su casa … y en las de B. Dulau, y Co., … T. Boosey, … White, … De Conchy, … Wingrave … Longman y Rees … y Lackington y Allen …, 1809) [9771.cc.15]

Jacome Ratton, *Recordaçoens de J. Ratton … sobre occurrencias do seu tempo em Portugal* (Londres: H. Bryer, 1813) [1201.c.18]

Samuel Johnson, *Ráselas, príncipe de Abisinia*, tr. Felipe Fernández (Londres: Henrique Bryer á expensas de Francisco Wingrave, y de dicho rev. traductor 1813) [12614.aa.2]

Cervantes, *Don Quixote de la Mancha*, ed. Felipe Fernández (London: expensas de Lackington, Allen y Co … F. Wingrave … T. Boosey … Longman y Co … C. Law y Co … Dulau y Co … y dicho editor, 1814) [12491.b.12] (The BL copy, acquired in 1869, has the label of 'P. Rolandi, Foreign Bookseller, Circulating Library, 20, Berners St, London'.)

William Wilberforce, *Perspectiva real del cristianismo practico*, tr. José Muñoz de Sotomayor (Londres: en la Imprenta de J. Bowman, 1827) [4407.ccc.17]

William Henry Pyne, *Descripcion abreviada del mundo. Inglaterra, Escocia e Irlanda*, tr. Pablo de Mendíbil (Londres: R. Ackermann, 1828) [C.107.bb.110]

José Urculu, *Catecismo de mitología* (Londres: R. Ackermann, 1825?) [T.129*(5)]

Catecismo de gramatica castellana (Londres; Megico: R. Ackermann, s.a.) (University College London, R 214 B 122 CAT)

Francesco Saverio Clavigero, *Historia antigua de Megico* ... (Londres; Megico: R. Ackermann, 1826) [1061.k.17, 18]

Cayetano Moro, *Reconocimiento del istmo de Tehuantepec*... (Londres: en casa de Ackermann y Compa, 1844) [10480.g.16(2)]

Alvaro Flórez Estrada, *Representacion hecha a S.M.C. el señor don Fernando VII* (Londres: impreso por Enrique Bryer ... se vende en la libreria de T. Boosey e Hijos ... 1818) [1141.i.13(3)]

Alvaro Flórez Estrada, *Examen imparcial de las disensiones de la America con la España* ... (Londres: en la imprenta de R. Juigne ... se halla de venta en casa de Dulau y Compañia, ... en casa de Johnson, en casa de Boosey, ... y en casa de Deconchy, ... 1811) [8180.f.7]

Luis Vélez de Guevara, *El diablo cojuelo* (Londres: expensas de T. Boosey, 1812) [12490.a.8]

Damián López de Tortajada, *Floresta de varios romances sacados de las historias antiguas de los hechos famosos de los doce pares de Francia / Ancient Spanish ballads* (London: Boosey; Rodwell and Martin, 1821) [1064.k.24]

Hipólito José da Costa Pereira Furtado de Mendonça, *Historia de Portugal*... (Londres: na offic. de F. Wingrave; T. Boosey; Dulau e Co. e Lackington, Allen e Co., 1809) [1196.b.35-37]

El espejo de señoritas: manual de preceptos morales, artes de recreacion, ejercicios elegantes, y entretenimientos domesticos; adornado con muchos grabados, 2a ed. (Londres: Ackermann y comp, 1835) (ccpb000379078)

Ibarra, José Joaquín de, *No me olvides: coleccion de producciones en prosa y verso, originales, imitadas y traduzidas por José Joaquín de Ibarra* (Londres: R. Ackermann, 1825) (ccpb0003800082)

Ibarra, José Joaquín de, *No me olvides: coleccion de producciones en prosa y verso, originales y traducidas por José Joaquín de Ibarra* (Londres: R. Ackermann, 1826) [Half tp: *No me olvides: recuerdo de amistad para el año de 1826*] (ccpb0003800083)

Ibarra, José Joaquín de, *No me olvides: coleccion de producciones en prosa y verso, originales y traducidas por José Joaquín de Ibarra* (Londres: R. Ackermann, 1827) [Half tp: *No me olvides: recuerdo de amistad para el año de 1827*] (ccpb0003800084)

Mendibil, Pablo de, *No me olvides: coleccion de producciones en prosa i verso, orijinales, imitadas i traduzidas para MDCCCXVIII* (Londres: R. Ackermann, [impreso por] Carlos Wood e hijo, 1828) (ccpb0003800081)

Mendibil, Pablo de, *No me olvides: coleccion de producciones en prosa i verso, orijinales, imitadas i traduzidas para MDCCCXXIX* (Londres: R. Ackermann, [impreso por] Carlos Wood e hijo, 1829) (ccpb0003800080)

Appendix IV
Some Spanish books printed by Charles Wood

William Davis Robinson, *Memorias de la Revolución de Megico* ..., tr. José Joaquín de Mora (Londres: R. Ackermann; impreso por Carlos Wood, 1824) (ccpb000304856)

José de la Riva Agüero, *Exposicion de Don José de la Riva Agüero acerca de su conducta política en en tiempo que ejerció la Presidencia de la República del Perú* (C. Wood, 1824) [1202.i.23]

Ignacio Núñez et al., *Noticias históricas, políticas y estadísticas de las Provincias Unidas del Río de la Plata; con un apéndice sobre la usurpación de Montevideo por los gobiernos portugués y brasilero* (Londres; Megico: publicado por R. Ackermann; impreso por Carlos Wood, 1825) (ccpb000372999)

José Joaquín de Mora, *Gramatica latina dispuesta en forma de catecismo* (Londres: lo publica R. Ackermann, Strand, y en su establecimiento de Megico: asimismo en Colombia, en Buenos Ayres, Chile, Peru y Guatemala, 1825) [12934.b.7]

José Joaquín de Mora, *Cuadros de la historia de los árabes* ... (Londres: R. Ackermann, Strand; impreso por Carlos Wood, 1826) (ccpb000329788)

Perico de los Palotes (pseud.), *Don Termópilo ó Defensa del Prospecto del Doctor Puigblanch* (Londres: Librería de V. Salvá; Imprenta de Carlos Wood e Hijo, 1829) (ccpb000325471)

Agustín de Argüelles, *Apéndice a la sentencia pronunciada en 11 de mayo de 1825 por la Audiencia de Sevilla contra sesenta y tres diputados de las Cortes de 1822 y 1823. Por Don Agustín de Arguelles, uno de los comprendidos en la sentencia* (Londres: Imp. de Carlos Wood e Hijo, 1834) [1509/1332]

Agustín de Argüelles, *Exámen histórico de la reforma constitucional que hicieron las Córtes generales y estraordinarias desde que se instalaron en la Isla de León el día 24 de setiembre de 1810, hasta que cerraron en Cadiz sus sesiones en 14 del propio mes de 1813* (Londres: Imp. de Carlos Wood e Hijo, 1835) (ccpb000076122)

Niel Arnott, *Elementos de física*... , tr. Manuel Saenz de Buruaga (Londres: Carlos Wood, 1837) (ccbp000079640)

Agustín de Argüelles, *Apelación a los habitantes de Europa sobre la esclavitud el tráfico de negros. Publicado en nombre de la sociedad religiosa de amigos de la Gran Bretaña* (Londres: Imp. Española de Wood, 1839) (ccpb000077555)

Riego, Miguel del (ed.), *Coleccion de obras poeticas españolas: unas casi enteramente perdidas, otras que se han hecho muy raras y todas ellas merecedoras de ser conservadas en el Parnaso Español* (Londres: impreso por Carlos Wood, Poppin's Court, Fleet Street, 1842) [11451.g.27]

Mayoral, Francisco, *Historia verdadera del sargento Francisco Mayoral natural de Salamanca, fingido Cardenal de Borbon en Francia escrita por el mismo y dada a luz por D. J. V.* (Londres: imprenta de Wood, 1846) (ccpb000379399)

Mariano Torrente, *Memoria sobre la esclavitud en la isla de Cuba* ... / *Slavery in the island of Cuba* ... (Londres: Imprenta de C. Wood, 1853) [8155.b.73] (Wrapper: London: H. Baillere)

Manuel Martínez de Morentín, *Estudios filológicos, ó sea Exámen razonado del uso de los verbos ser y estar* … (Londres: Trübner y Cie; [impreso por] C. Wood, 1857) (ccpb000290426)

Chris Michaelides

Greek Printing in England, 1500-1900

I. A survey

Unlike Venice, Florence, or Paris, London has never been one of the major centres of Greek printing. The vast majority of Greek books printed in England during this period were devoted to the classical Greek writers, the Bible, the Church Fathers, Church history or religious controversy. There were, however, two periods – the first half of the seventeenth century and the nineteenth century – during which the output of Greek books presents special interest either because of the circumstances of its production or its variety.

The first book in which Greek types were used in England was printed rather late, in 1521. They occur in four maxims at the end of an edition of Lucian of Samosata's *De Dipsadibus* printed in Cambridge by John Siberch.[1] This was followed in 1524 by Thomas Linacre, *De emendata structura Latini sermonis*, printed in London by Richard Pynson.[2]

The first book with a complete Greek text was published several years later, in 1543. It was an edition of two homilies of St John Chrysostom with a Greek transcription by Sir John Cheke followed by their Latin translation.[3] It was printed by Reginald (or Reynald) Wolfe, whose device of a German shield

---

1 *Lepidissimum Luciani opusculū...Περὶ διψάδων... H. Bulloco interprete. Oratio ejusdem, cum...annotatiōibus.* Cantabrigiæ: J. Siberch, 1521.

2 *Thomae Linacri ... De emendata structura Latini sermonis libri sex.* Apud R. Pynsonum: Londini, 1524. Both the Siberch and Pynson types are reproduced in Frank Isaac, *English and Scottish Printing Types 1501-35 [and] 1508-41*, Facsimiles and illustrations issued by the Bibliographical Society, no. 2 ([Oxford]: Oxford University Press, 1930). I am grateful to Dennis E. Rhodes for allowing me to use this information contained in his 'The First Use of Greek Type in Spain, France, the Low Countries, and England', paper given at the conference The Greek Book, 15th-19th century (Delphi, 16-20 May 2001).

3 *Τοῦ ἐν ἁγίοις Ἰωάννου τοῦ Χρυσοστόμου ὁμιλίαι δύο νύν πρῶτον ἐντυπωθεῖσαι καὶ πρός τόν τῆς Ἀγγλίας ἐπιφανέστατον Βασιλέα Ἑνρίκον ὄγδοον εἰς Ῥωμαίαν γλῶσσαν μεταγραφθεῖσαι ὑπό Ἰωάννου Κήκου Κανταβριγιέως. D. Ioannis Chrysostomi homiliæ duæ, nunc primum in lucem æditæ, et ad Sereniss. Angliæ Regē latinæ factæ, a Ioanne Cheko Cantabrigiensi.* Londini: apud Reynerum Vuolfium, 1543.

with two boys and a banderole inscribed 'Charitas' appears on the title-page. Wolfe was the first printer in England to have a complete Greek character set and the first to be granted a patent as printer to the King in Latin, Greek and Hebrew.[4] His Greek types are of Italian provenance (either made in Italian workshops or by Italians settled in England). After Wolfe's death in 1573 his Greek characters were acquired by Henry Bynneman, who planned to print a New Testament in Greek and a Greek and Latin edition of Homer (which never materialised).[5] After Bynneman's death, in 1583, his press passed to the syndicate of printers – Arnold Hatfield, John Jackson & Ninian Newton, and Edmund Bollifant – who established, in 1584, Eliot's Court Press.[6] Melchisedec Bradwood joined the group after Bollifant's death, and it was Bradwood who was the printer of Sir Henry Savile's monumental 8-volume edition of the works of St John Chrysostom (1610-13) usually ascribed to John Norton.[7] Most of the Greek printing in England during the first half of the seventeenth century was carried out by one of the member printers of Eliot's Court Press.

During this period the publication of works in Greek was given added impetus by Greeks visiting England for a variety of reasons. Christophoros Angelos was the first of these visitors.[8] He was born in Peloponnesus c. 1575

4 *Dictionary of National Biography*, LXII, 304.

5 K. Sp. Staïkos, ''Η ἐξάπλωση τῆς Ἑλληνικῆς στόν Βορρά', *Θησαυροί τῆς Ἐθνικῆς Βιβλιοθήκης* (Ἀθήνα: Ἐθνικὴ Βιβλιοθήκη τῆς Ἑλλάδος, 1999), p. 181.

6 H. R. Plomer, 'The Eliot's Court Printing House, 1584-1674', *The Library*, 4th ser., 2 (1921), 175-84.

7 *Τοῦ ἐν ἁγίοις πατρός ἡμῶν Ἰωάννου ΄Αρχιεπισκόπου Κωνσταντινουπόλεως τοῦ Χρυσοστόμου τῶν εὑρισκομένων...ἐπιμελείας κ[α]ὶ ἀναλωμάτων Ἑρρίκου τοῦ Σαβιλίου ἐκ παλαιῶν ἀντιγράφων ἐκδοθέντα*. Etonae: in Collegio Regali, excudebat Ioannes Norton in Graecis, &c Typographus Regius, 1610-1613. Norton often employed other printers to work for him. See R. B. McKerrow, ed., *A Dictionary of Printers and Booksellers in England, Scotland and Ireland, and of foreign printers of English books, 1557-1640* (London: Printed for the Bibliographical Society, 1910), p. 203. In 1610 he also published two other books in Greek:
John, Mauropous, Archbishop of Euchaita *Joannis Metropolitani Euchaitensis Versus Iambici in principalium festorum pictas in tabulis historias atque alia varia compositi; nunc primum in lucem editi cura M. Busti*. J. Norton: Etonae, 1610 and Gregory, of Nazianzus, Saint, Patriarch of Constantinople *S. Gregorii Nazianzeni in Julianum Invectivæ duæ. Cum scholiis Græcis nunc primum editis, et ejusdem authoris nonnullis aliis … Omnia edidit* R. *Montagu*. J. Norton: Etonæ, 1610.

8 On Christophoros Angelos see S. I. Makrymichalos, 'Χριστόφορος Ἄγγελος, ὁ Ἑλληνοδιδάσκαλος τῆς Ὀξφόρδης', *Πελοποννησιακὰ*, 2 (1957), 219-46 and Strickland Gibson, 'Christopher Angel, Teacher of Greek' in *The Glory that is Greece*, compiled and ed. Hilda Hughes (London: Hutchinson, 1944), pp. 57-61. For general surveys of the history of the Greek community in Great Britain see Vasos Tsimpidaros, *Οἱ Ἕλληνες στὴν Ἀγγλία* (Ἀθήνα: Ἐκδόσεις Ἀλκαῖος, 1974) and Charles Mettes, *Οἱ ρίζες τοῦ Παροικιακοῦ Ἑλληνισμοῦ τῆς Μεγάλης Βρετανὶας* (Ἀθήνα: Ἐκδόσεις Ἀθήνα, 2001.)

and travelled widely in mainland Greece and the islands. In Athens he was denounced as a Spanish spy, arrested, savagely beaten when he refused to renounce his Christian faith and, condemned to death, was saved at the last moment. Angelos arrived in Yarmouth in 1608 and was received by the Bishop of Norwich who sent him to Trinity College Cambridge to pursue his studies. He stayed at Cambridge until 1610 but, as the climate did not suit him, he moved to Oxford where he studied at Balliol College. Loosely associated with Balliol, he lived in Oxford and taught Greek for the next twenty years. His popularity was increased by his scars which he would display to sympathetic listeners as a proof of his sufferings. He died at Oxford in 1638.

Angelos published four pamphlets which are perhaps the first works in Modern Greek written and printed in England. The first of these was:

> *Πόνησις Χριστοφόρου τοῦ Ἀγγέλου, Ἕλληνος τοῦ πολλῶν πληγῶν καὶ μαστίγων γευσαμένου ἀδίκως παρά τῶν Τούρκων διά τήν Χριστὸν πίστην.* At Oxford: Printed by Iohn Lichfeild and William Wrench printers to the famous Vniuersitie, 1617.

An English translation of this work was also issued the same year:

> *Christopher Angell a Grecian, who tasted of many stripes and torments inflicted by the Turks for the faith which he had in Christ Jesus.* At Oxford, printed by Iohn Lichfeild, and William Wrench, 1617. [9]

Both versions contain two woodcuts after Angelos's primitive drawings,[10] showing the tortures inflicted by the Turks, the first showing him bound to a frame and being beaten by two Turks (fig. 1) and the second an emblematic representation of England and the protection it offered to Greeks fleeing from persecution.[11] It is the first illustrated book printed at Oxford.[12] Angelos's reason for publishing this work was not only to show the plight of Greeks under Turkish rule but also to raise money for himself as one who had suffered for his refusal to renounce his faith. This was supported by the various letters of recommendation from Cambridge, Oxford, and the bishop of Salisbury which he included in the English translation of his work. It has been suggested that in the two years following the publication of his work Angelos went on a tour in order to collect contributions though nothing is

9 Émile Legrand, *Bibliographie hellénique ou description des ouvrages publiés par des Grecs au dix-septième siècle* (Paris: Alphonse Picard et fils, 1894), I, no. 91 and no. 92.

10 The original drawings are on the proof-copy in the library of Corpus Christi College, Oxford. See Percy Simpson *Proof-reading in the Sixteenth, Seventeenth and Eighteenth Centuries* (London: Oxford University Press, Humphrey Milford, 1935), pp. 80-2.

11 Gibson, p. 60.

12 Ibid, p. 59.

known about the identity of the people who may have helped him. Moreover, in 1620 he printed another edition of the work in English which included a letter supposedly written by his family in Greece who, after Angelos's escape, were tortured and imprisoned and were in urgent need of £300 to regain their freedom. Though this edition has an Oxford imprint, it was probably printed in London.[13]

Fig. 1: Christophoros Angelos, *Πόνησις Χριστοφορου τοῦ Ἀγγέλου, Ἕλληνος τοῦ πολλῶν πληγῶν καὶ μαστίγων γευσαμένου ἀδίκως παρά τῶν Τούρκων διά τήν είς Χριστὸν πίστην* (Oxford: Iohn Lichfeild and William Wrench, 1617), Greek text, p. A4r.
British Library pressmark: G.8893(2*).

13 Makrymichalos, p. 229. Makrymichalos has questioned the authenticity of the letter and Angelos's motives for printing it.

Angelos's second pamphlet was:

> *Ἐγχειρίδιον περὶ τῆς καταστάσεως τῶν σήμερον εὑρισκομένων Ἑλλήνων. Πόνος Χριστοφόρου τοῦ Ἀγγέλου Ἕλληνος*. Ex Officina Cantrelli Legge, Academiæ Cantabrigiensis Typographi, 1619.[14]

A Latin version (*Enchiridion de Institutis Græcorum*) was also published in 1619. The work was very popular as little was then known about the condition of the Greeks under Turkish rule. It was later published in various editions (in Latin and German) and was also included in other works on Greece and Turkey between 1655 and 1679.

The third pamphlet was:

> *Ἐγκώμιον τῆς Ἐνδοξοτάτης Μεγάλης Βρεττανίας* ... (*An Encomion of the famous Kingdom of Great Britaine, and of the two flourishing Sister-Universities Cambridge and Oxford. Written by Christopher Angel a Græcian borne, in token of his thankfulnesse to his charitable worthy friends and benefactors in both Universities*). At Cambridge printed by Cantrel Legge, Printer to the famous Universitie, 1619 (in Greek and English on opposite pages). Probably printed by William Stansby in London.[15]

His last pamphlet was a theological treatise in Greek and Latin

> *Περὶ τῆς ἀποστασίας τῆς Ἐκκλησίας, καὶ περὶ τοῦ ἀνθρώπου τῆς ἁμαρτίας δηλαδὴ τοῦ Ἀντιχρίστου* ... Ἐκδόθη ἐν λοντίνῳ ͵αχκδ' [W. Stansby], 1624.[16]

Metrophanes Kritopoulos (later Patriarch of Alexandria) was a student of Angelos at Balliol.[17] He was the first ecclesiastical student sent to England for further study by Kyrillos Loukaris, since 1620 the Patriarch of Constantinople. Loukaris was concerned about the inability of the Greek Orthodox Church to counter, either through a well-educated clergy or through its own publications, the Catholic propaganda pursued in the East by the Jesuits.[18] He sought to remedy this situation by the provision of better

---

14 Legrand I, no. 100.

15 Ibid., no. 102.

16 Ibid., no. 132.

17 Kritopoulos (1589-1639) arrived in England in 1617 and, after studying at Gresham College in London, he went to Balliol from 1620 to 1622. After the completion of his studies he stayed in London until 1624 incurring the wrath of Archbishop Abbot but little is known about his activities during this period. Kritopoulos later published numerous works which included a translation of the New Testament into Modern Greek, a travel journal (Περιηγηματικὸν) describing his journey from England to France, Switzerland and Germany, epistles discussing current church politics, and theological works. His library in Alexandria was renowned for the wealth of foreign books which he collected during his travels in England, Germany, and Italy.

18 The Jesuits had been permitted, by the Peace of Vienna in 1615, to keep their establishments in the Ottoman Empire and their activities were encouraged by the

higher education for the clergy and for this purpose he cultivated contacts with Protestant theologians. Through Sir Thomas Roe, the English Ambassador at Constantinople, he corresponded with George Abbot, the Archbishop of Canterbury (1562-1633).[19] At the suggestion of King James I, Abbot invited Loukaris to send appropriate students for advanced study in England.[20]

Loukaris seems also to have been an influence on the activities of Nikodemos Metaxas, the first Greek printer in England.[21] Metaxas (1585-1646) was born in Cephalonia into a leading family which had settled on the island after the fall of Constantinople in 1453. Between 1614 and 1620 he met Theophilos Korydaleus who was then teaching in Athens. He came to London c. 1622-3 to visit his brother Iakovos, a merchant connected with the Levant Company. In London he conceived the idea of studying the art of printing in order to serve his church which was without resources for printing books.[22] He worked at Eliot's Court Press as an apprentice and also published two books:

> Theophilos Korydaleus [Theodosios, Metropolitan of Naupaktos and Arta] *Τοῦ Σοφωτάτου Κυρίου Θεοφίλου, τοῦ Κορυδαλέως. Περί ἐπιστολικῶν τύπων* [and *Ἔκθεσις περὶ ῥητορικῆς*]. Londini: Ex Oficina G. S. Typographi, at the shop of William Stansby, London, in 1625.[23]

Some copies of the work (in the British Library and the Ethnike Vivliotheke tes Hellados) have a letter of dedication by Nikodemos Metaxas

Congregatio de Propaganda Fide founded in Rome in 1622. See Michael Strachan, *Sir Thomas Roe, 1581-1644: a life* (Salisbury: Michael Russell, 1989), p. 171. While he was in Poland between 1596 and 1601, as the exarch of the Patriarch of Alexandria, Loukaris was associated with a printing press producing works of religious instruction and controversy. He was probably also engaged in the dissemination of letters of exhortation and instruction written by Meletios Pegas (then Patriarch of Alexandria) to the Orthodox in Poland and Russia.

19 On the relations between Loukaris and Roe and the latter's support for Loukaris against Jesuit plotting to depose him see Michael Strachan, pp. 170-5.

20 This trend continued even after the assassination of Loukaris in 1638 with Nathanael Kanopios (or Conopius), later (1651) Metropolitan of Smyrna. Kanopios was sent to Balliol by the Archbishop of Canterbury (Dr William Laud) in 1639. As well as being a man of learning and a composer, Kanopios, like Angelos, had the ability to attract the attention of his contemporaries, in his case by his coffee-drinking, some thirty years before the habit became common in England.

21 Evro Layton, 'Nikodemos Metaxas, the First Greek Printer', *Harvard Library Bulletin*, 15 (1967), 140-68 and R. J. Roberts, 'The Greek Press at Constantinople in 1627 and its Antecedents', *The Library*, 5th ser., 22 (1967), 13-43.

22 Layton, p. 145, suggests that Metrophanes Kritopoulos met Metaxas in London and that he may have helped the young printer and also written to Loukaris about his interest in establishing a printing press.

23 Legrand, I, no. 144 (I, 194-200). Stansby had also printed, in 1624, Christophoros Angelos's *Περὶ τῆς ἀποστασίας τῆς Ἐκκλησίας*.

addressed to John Williams (1582-1650), Bishop of Lincoln; in it Metaxas speaks of Williams's generosity to the unfortunate Greeks; other copies have a letter of dedication addressed to Pachomios Doxaras, Bishop of Cephalonia and Zante. The work was designed for educational purposes and included a selection of letters of contemporaries (Ἐπιστολαὶ μεταγενεστέρων καὶ καθ' ἡμᾶς ἡκμασάντων). The inclusion of letters by Loukaris and Maximos Margounios (Loukaris's teacher) lends weight to the supposition that Metaxas's book was prompted by Loukaris.[24]

The Loukaris connection also appears in the second Metaxas book, also printed in 1625:

> *Βιβλίον τοῦ ὀρθοῦ λόγου, βεβαίωσις καλούμενον. Τυπωθέν διά δαπάνης καὶ ἐπιμελείας τοῦ θεοφιλέστατου ἐπισκόπου, πρώην Μαΐνης κυρίου Ἰερεμίου.* Ἐν Λωνδώνῃ, παρά Ἰωάννη τω Ἄβιλανδ, κατά τό ͵αχκε´ ἔτος τῆς ἐνσάρκου τοῦ Σωτῆρος ἡμῶν οἰκονομίας [1625].[25]

The work has on the title-page a woodcut of the royal arms of England and includes a dedication from Païsios Metaxas to Theophilos Korydaleus, a letter from Hieremias, bishop of Mani, to Loukaris and a section entitled Ἀναστασίου τοῦ Ἁγιωτάτου πατρὸς ἡμῶν Πατριάρχου Ἀντιοχείας καὶ Κυρίλλου ἔκθεσις σύντομος τῆς Ὀρθοδόξου πίστεως.[26]

Metaxas left London in 1627, having decided to transfer his operations to Constantinople, taking his press and a number of characters and ornaments with him. It has, however, now been established that two books previously thought to have been printed by Metaxas in Constantinople were in fact printed in London. Both are collections of bibliographically separate items always bound together in the same order. They have neither imprint, date, nor signed preface; they both contain Orthodox polemic against Roman Catholicism. The first volume, which Roberts calls 'the Gregory Palamas volume' contains the following three works:

> Gregory Palamas, Archbishop of Thessalonica *Λόγοι ἀποδεικτικοί δύο*; Gennadios II, Patriarch of Constantinople [Georgios Scholarios] *Τὸ Σύνταγμα ἐπιγραφώμενον Ὀρθοδόξου καταφύγιον*; Maximos, Bishop of Cythera [Michael Margounios] *Διάλογος*.[27]

---

24 Roberts, p. 16.

25 Legrand, I, no. 143.

26 See Roberts, p. 17. 'The names of those concerned in the book and its very nature as a book partly the office of a saint [Gerasimos Notaras, a Cephallonian saint] ... and partly a vehicle for the doctrines of Cyril and his circle, leave very little room for doubt over the connection of this book with Metaxas'.

27 Legrand, I, no. 167. Legrand suggests that the volume was printed by Metaxas in Constantinople c. 1627.

The device, an anchor wreathed with foliage and carrying the motto 'Floreat in æternum', and a number of initial letters and other types are English and can be linked with the London press of William Jones in the years 1627-37. Roberts concludes that the book was printed for Metaxas, perhaps by William Jones, in 1626 or early in 1627, that the edition was a large one of which a fair number of copies were distributed to sympathetic English clergy and statesmen and that the remaining copies were taken to Constantinople and distributed from there.[28] Layton has also identified the ornaments and initials of this work as those of the printer William Jones.[29]

The second volume, which Roberts calls the 'Meletios Pegas' book, consists of the following:

> Meletios Pegas, Patriarch of Alexandria *Περὶ τῆς ἀρχῆς τοῦ Πάπα*; Georgios Koresios *Διάλεξις μετὰ τινός τῶν Φράρων*; Nilus [Kabasilas], Metropolitan of Thessalonica *Βιβλία δύο. τὸ πρῶτον περὶ τῶν αἰτιῶν τῆς ἐκκλησιαστικῆς διαστάσεως. Τὸ δεύτερον περὶ τῆς ἀρχῆς τοῦ Πάπα*; Gabriel, called Severus, Archbishop of Philadelphia *Ἔκθεσις κατά τῶν ἀμαθῶς λεγόντων καὶ παρανόμως διδασκόντων, ὅτι ἡμεῖς οἱ τῆς Ἀνατολικῆς Ἐκκλησίας γνήσιοι καὶ Ὀρθόδοξοι παῖδες ἐσμὲν σχηματικοὶ* [sic] *παρά τῆς Ἁγίας καί καθόλου Ἐκκλησίας.*[30]

Layton has established that the volume was printed not in Constantinople but in London at the Eliot's Court Press under the editorship of Nikodemos Metaxas.[31]

Later in the century, another Greek author had a distinguished career in Restoration England. Konstantinos Rhodokanakis (1635-89) was born in Chios.[32] Little is known about his early life other than that he came to England in 1654 and after studying medicine in Dublin, Cambridge and Oxford he became a physician ('Chymist') in the court of Charles II. He published various works, the most popular being the treatise *Alexicacus, Spirit of Salt of the World*[33] (i.e. a remedy against all evil), which ran into various

---

28 Roberts, pp. 20-1.

29 Layton, p. 156.

30 Legrand, I, no. 168.

31 Layton, p. 155.

32 K. Amantos, ***Κωνσταντίνος Ροδοκανάκης*** ('Αθήνησι: Τύποις Παρασκευᾶ Λεώνη, 1937). See also Joannes Gennadius, 'Introduction' in Edwin W. Fletcher, *Hellenism in England* (London: The Faith Press, 1915), pp. 40-5.

33 *Alexicacus Spirit of Salt of the World, which vulgarly prepar'd is call'd the spirit of salt. Or, The transcendent virtue of the true spirit of salt long look'd for, and now philosophically prepared and purified from all hurtfull or corroding qualities, far beyond any thing yet known to the world: being both safe and pleasant for the use of all men, women, and children. By Constantine Rhodocanaces, Grecian of the Isle Chios, and one of his Majesty's chymists.* London: Printed by R. D., in the year 1644.

editions. Rhodokanakis's only work in Greek published in England – *Carmina Græca Rythmica Gratulatoria*, a volume of poems celebrating the restoration of King Charles II to the English throne – was written while he was still a student at Oxford and it may have secured him his future employment.[34] An edition of the work was published by Émile Legrand in 1873.[35] Legrand's introductory biographical note should, however, be read with caution as it was based on a largely fictional account of Rhodokanakis's life published a year earlier by a supposed descendant of his. The self-styled 'Prince' Demetrios Rhodokanakis was one of the great nineteenth-century literary forgers, the sole object of his deceptions being to prove that he was a descendant of the seventeenth-century physician and, more importantly, the legitimate heir to the throne of Byzantium. To achieve this he published sumptuously produced books in which he concocted bogus genealogies the veracity of which he backed by quoting non-existent publications: the study of the life and writings of Konstantinos Rhodokanakis was one of these.[36] The fact that he managed to hoodwink a bibliographer of the calibre of Émile Legrand bears testimony to his great skill. Legrand later took his revenge by denouncing Rhodokanakis's frauds in a minutely researched, 205-page monograph.[37]

Konstantinos Rhodokanakis was probably a member of the Greek community which had formed in London by the middle of the seventeenth century, mostly merchants trading with the Levant or Greeks fleeing from Turkish persecution. The 1670s saw an influx of Greek refugees and the building of the first Greek church in Soho dedicated to the Dormition of the Virgin. The claim by Demetrios Rhodokanakis that these refugees were invited to England by his powerful 'ancestor' has been discredited. It seems that Joseph Georgirenes, Metropolitan of Samos (d. 1686), who was himself expelled from his island by the Turks before settling in London, may have

34 *Carmina Græca Rythmica Gratulatoria de Reditu Serenissimi, sacratissimi & Θεοφυλάκτου Principis Caroli II … Composita à Constantino Rodocanacide Chiensi, tunc commorante in Celeberrima Academia Oxoniensi.* Oxoniæ: Typis A .& L. Lichfield, Acad. Typogr., Anno Dom. 1660.

35 *Le Retour de Charles II roi d'Angleterre, poème grec du prince Rhodocanakis publié, d'après l'édition de 1669 par Émile Legrand*, Collection de monuments pour servir à l'étude de la langue grecque pendant le moyen âge et dans les temps modernes, no. 1 (Paris: Maisonneuve, 1873).

36 Demetrios I. Rhodokanakis, *Life and Writings of Constantine Rhodokanakis, a Prince of the Imperial Houses of Doucas, Angelus, Comnesius, Palaeologus and honorary physician to Charles II* … (Athens, At the Printing House of the Journal of Debates, 1872).

37 Émile Legrand, *Dossier Rhodocanakis: étude critique de bibliographie et d'histoire littéraire* (Paris: Alphonse Picard et fils, 1895).

organised this move. He was certainly the driving force behind the building of the church, travelling about England to collect funds, and he was appointed priest of the community.[38]

By the beginning of the nineteenth century the Greek merchant community in London and other cities like Manchester and Liverpool had grown. Greek ships dominated trade in the Black Sea, the Aegean and the Mediterranean, and trade with England flourished.[39] By the middle of the century Greek families like the Rallis (one of many families that came to England from the island of Chios) and the Ionides amassed enormous wealth and their members played an important role in British commercial and, occasionally, cultural life.

The early years of the century saw an upsurge of philhellenic spirit in England.[40] Publications in English included appeals and addresses to the people of England in the cause of the Greeks, histories of modern Greece, thoughts on the Greek revolution, reflections on the state of Greece, letters from Greece, Lord Byron's visit to Greece and his death at Missolonghi, portraits and biographical accounts of the protagonists of the war, the text of the Greek Constitution, collections of Greek folk songs, and modern Greek grammars.[41] Perhaps not surprisingly very few publications in support of the Greek War of Independence were printed in England in Greek since most such works were directed to an English audience. It seems, moreover, that the attitude of the Greek community in London was less than enthusiastic as they feared that the war might harm their commercial interests in the Levant.[42]

The following seem to be the only English imprints in Greek:

> *The Greeks at Tripolitza (Οἱ Ἕλληνες κατὰ τὴν Τριπολιτσὰν).* London: printed for John Hatchard and son, 1822. (Droulia 225)

> *Canares, a poem in Modern Greek, by Nicholas Maniakes, student of Trinity College, Cambridge. To which is added a Paean, or Greek War Song, translated from the English by the same author. (Κανάρης, ποίημα ἁπλοελληνικὸν ὑπὸ Νικολάου Μανιάκου, μαθητεύοντος ἐν Λυκείῳ τῆς Ἁγίας Τριάδος παρὰ τοῖς Κανταβριγινοῖς πρὸς ὃ ἐτέθη καὶ ἑλληνικὸς Παιὰν).*

---

38 Tsimpidaros, pp. 27-39. See also Gennadius, pp. 46-7. The church was later sold to the parish of St Martin-in-the-Fields but Greek Street in Soho is still a reminder of the Greek church in the area.

39 Gennadius, pp. 51-4.

40 C. M. Woodhouse, *The Philhellenes* (London: Hodder and Stoughton, 1969).

41 For a full bibliography of philhellenic literature, listing 2085 works, see Loukia Droulia, *Philhellénisme: ouvrages inspirés par la Guerre de l'Indépendance Grecque, 1821-1833: répertoire bibliographique*, Centre de recherches neo-helléniques de la Fondation nationale de la recherche scientifique, 17 (Athènes, 1974).

42 Tsimpidaros, pp. 54-61.

Cambridge, J. Smith, 1823. (With a dedication to Frederick North, 5th Earl of Guilford.) (Droulia, 379).

The Provisional Constitution of Greece, translated from the second edition of Corinth, accompanied by the original Greek... London: John Murray, 1823. (Droulia, 445).

Edward Blaquière *Διήγημα περὶ τῆς παρούσης καταστάσεως τῶν Ἑλληνικῶν πόλεων καὶ περὶ τοῦ πῶς κατὰ δίκαιον εἶσιν ἄξιαι τῆς βοηθείας πάντων τῶν Χριστιανῶν*. Ἐν Λονδίνῳ ἐκ τῆς τυπογραφείας Ρικάρδου Τάιλορ, 1823. (Not in Droulia)[43]

Συνεισφοραὶ ἑνὸς στρατιωτικοῦ (Contributions d'un militaire). [London: Richard Taylor], 1825. 2 pamphlets. (Droulia, 718, 719)

Modern Greek Interpreter being a Translation of Mad[e] Genlis' and other Dialogues into Modern Greek, English and Italian by Mesd[lles] M. C. [Marianna Catinga] *and T. Macri of Athens.* Printed for the translators, and published by Messrs Souter and Co ... and Messrs G. and T. Underwood, [s.d.] (Droulia, 819).

Πρὸς τοὺς Γερμανοὺς καὶ τὰ λοιπὰ τῆς Εὐρώπης ἔθνη Πρόσκλησις, εἰς βοήθειαν Ἑλλήνων ὑπὸ κ. Μινωΐδου Μηνᾶ τοῦ ἐξ Μακεδονίας (Appel à la nation allemande et aux autres peuples de l'Europe, en faveur des grecs). Paris: Bossange père; Londres: Treuttel et Wurtz, 1826. (Droulia, 932).

Παραδείγματα Ῥωμαϊκῆς ποιητικῆς (Specimens of Romaic lyric poetry: with translation into English, to which is prefixed a concise treatise on music) by Paul Maria Leopold Joss. London: printed for Richard Glynn, 1826. (Droulia, 1171)

Θεωρία περὶ τῆς Ἑλληνικῆς γραμματικῆς τε καὶ γλώσσης ὑπὸ κ. Μινωΐδου Μηνᾶ (Théorie de la grammaire et de la langue grecques). Londres: Bossange, Barthès et Lowel, 1827. (Droulia, 1382)

The year 1841 saw the first edition of a work by one of the few Greeks to have visited England in the sixteenth century. Nikandros (or Andronikos) Noukios was born in Corfu but after the pillage of the island by Suleiman the Magnificent in 1537 and the death of his wife he settled in Venice where he worked as a scribe, copying numerous manuscripts several of which are now in the Escorial. Noukios also wrote an account of his travels which provides geographical and historical information about the various countries he visited first in the service of Gerardus van Veltwijck (an envoy of the Emperor Charles V), and later as a mercenary. Noukios joined Veltwijck's mission to Constantinople in 1545 and later to Flanders and England where he left his service, joining the English troops of Henry VIII. After fighting in Scotland and France he returned to Italy. His work is in three books and has survived in

43 A translation of Blaquière's *Report on the Present State of the Greek Confederation, and on its claims to the support of the Christian world*, a lecture delivered at the Greek Committee of London, of which Blaquière was the secretary, on 13 September 1823 in which he gives an account of things he saw in the Morea (Peloponnesus) during his first of three visits between 1823 and 1824. On Blaquière and the London Greek Committee see Woodhouse, pp. 61-2, 77-85.

three manuscripts, at the Bodleian Library (Books I and most of Book II), the Ambrosiana (part of Book II and Book III) and the Escorial (Books I and II). It remained unpublished until 1841 when the second of its three books, which includes detailed notes about things Noukios saw in England, was published by the Camden Society in a bilingual edition.[44] The author's descriptions and observations have the directness of a more famous near-contemporary travel journal, that of Michel de Montaigne. Noukios is, for example, impressed by the commercial life of London and by the large quantities of meat the English consume and he comments on the habit of men kissing women on the mouth in public. He also discusses politics and religion.

Prominent among nineteenth-century London Greek publications are the works of three young Greek writers – Andreas Kalvos, Demetres Vikelas, and Georgios Vizyenos – who came to England for a variety of reasons when they were still young and who later achieved literary fame in their own country.

Andreas Kalvos (1792-1869) is one of the greatest Greek poets of the first half of the nineteenth century and, with Dionysios Solomos, Greece's national poet. He first came to London in 1816 as secretary and companion of Ugo Foscolo, the exiled Italian poet, and lived in London until 1820, moving in Philhellenic circles and teaching Greek and Italian. His output was accordingly cosmopolitan, ranging from translations to works on language, literature, ecclesiastical history and controversy.[45] *Le Danaidi*, a tragedy in the style of Alfieri, was his first publication, in 1818.[46] It was also included in part III of *Italian Lessons* published two years later.[47]

---

44 *The Second Book of the Travels of Nicander Nucius, of Corcyra. Edited from the original Greek Ms in the Bodleian Library, with an English translation by the rev J. A. Cramer* (London: printed for the Camden Society, 1841). A critical edition of the entire text with an introduction which includes a biography of Noukios and his works and an examination of the three manuscripts of the text of his travels (Νικάνδρου Νούκιου Ἀποδημιῶν Λόγος [Α-Γ]) was published in 1962. See Nicandre de Corcyre, *Voyages*, ed. J. A. de Foucault, Nouvelle collection de textes et documents (Paris: Les Belles Lettres, 1962).

45 Kostas Andreiomenos, *Βιβλιογραφία Ἀνδρέα Κάλβου· 1818-1988* (Ἀθήνα: Ἑταιρεία Ἑλληνικοῦ Λογοτεχνικοῦ καὶ Ἱστορικοῦ Ἀρχείου, 1993). For a detailed chronology of Kalvos see Leukios Zapheiriou, 'Χρονολόγιο Ανδρέα Κάλβου', *Σημείο*, 1 (1992), 113-34.

46 *Le Danaidi, tragedia di Andrea Calbo*. London: printed for the author by Boyle and Callaghan, 1818.

47 *Italian Lessons, in four parts. Part I.-The synopsis of the Italian grammar, with exercises. Part II.-Translation of the first book of Robertson's History of the reign of the Emperor Charles V. Part III.-Saul, tragedia di Vittorio Alfieri. Le Danaidi, tragedia di A. Calbo. Part IV.-Extracts from Tasso, Ariosto, Petrarca, and Dante.* 4 pt. Alexander Black: London, 1820. The work was published shortly after the poet's departure from London.

In 1818 Kalvos also published his *Remarks on a Passage in Eusebius's Ecclesiastical History*, a contribution to a theological debate between Frederick Nolan and Thomas Falconer. Falconer had claimed that Eusebius was a 'corrupter and editor of the Holy Scripture', a claim refuted by Nolan. Kalvos's work is in favour of Falconer.[48] In 1820 Kalvos's Modern Greek translation of the Book of Common Prayer was published by Samuel Bagster. It was reprinted in 1826 and was also included in an eight-language edition of the work published in 1821.[49] Kalvos's last work before his departure from England was the section on the grammar of the Modern Greek language in F. Nolan's *A Harmonical Grammar of the Principal Ancient and Modern Languages*.[50] Kalvos returned to England in 1852 with Charlotte Augusta Wadams whom he married the following year. From 1857 the couple ran a girls' school in London and later one in Louth (Lincolnshire) where they moved in 1865. Kalvos had by then stopped writing poetry[51] and the only works he produced during this period were translations of works of ecclesiastical history.[52]

Demetres Vikelas was born in Syros in 1835 into a merchant family. He came to London in 1852 at the age of seventeen and worked in his uncles' wheat importing company (A[phoi] Mela)[53] for twenty-four years, first as a clerk

---

48 F. Nolan, *Remarks on a passage in Eusebius's Ecclesiastical History with translations in Modern Greek and Italian (Communicated by M. Calvo to the Rev. F. Nolan)*. London, [1818].

49 *Βιβλίον τῶν Δημοσίων Προσευχῶν καὶ τῆς ὑπηρεσίας τῶν Μυστηρίων καὶ ἄλλων Ἐκκλησιαστικῶν θεσμῶν καὶ τελετῶν, κατὰ τό ἔθος τῆς Ἡνωμένης Ἐκκλησίας Ἀγγλίας καὶ Ἰβερνίας ᾧ προσετέθη τὸ Ψαλτήριον τοῦ Δαυίδ καὶ αἱ μετὰ τᾶς Συναπτᾶς Ἐπιστολαὶ καὶ Εὐαγγέλια.* Μεταφρασθὲν ἐκ τῆς 'αγγλικῆς εἰς τήν κοινὴν τῆς Ἑλλάδος διάλεκτον ὑπό Ἀνδρέα Κάλβου Ἰωαννίδου. London: Samuel Bagster, [1820].

50 F. Nolan, *A Harmonical Grammar of the Principal Ancient and Modern Languages*. London: Printed for Samuel Bagster, no 15 Paternoster Row, 1822. (Kalvos's *Γραμματικὴ τῆς Νεοελληνικῆς Γλῶσσας* is on pp. 79-84.)

51 Kalvos is famous chiefly for a single collection of poems, *Ἡ Λύρα*, which was first published in Geneva in 1824.

52 *Περί δογμάτων, διοικήσεως καί Ἱερουργιῶν τῆς Αγγλικῆς, πονημάτιον Κοσίνου Ἐπισκόπου Δυνέλμου* [i.e. J. Cosin, Bishop of Durham]. Oxford, London: Parker, [1856]. In 1861 appeared his translation of James Meyrick's *Papal Supremacy Tested by Antiquity* (1855) [*Ποία κατά τοὺς Ἀρχαίους ἡ κυριαρχία τοῦ Πάπα*].

53 The Melas family included various distinguished members. Leon Melas (1812-79), Vikelas's uncle, had been a minister of justice in Greece during the reign of king Otto. Disillusioned with politics he moved to London in 1848 where he joined his brother's merchant business. He was the author of various improving works including one of the most famous nineteenth-century Greek novels, *Ὁ Γεροστάθης*, which was written in London but first published in Athens in 1863. Vikelas gives an affectionate biographical sketch of Leon Melas in his autobiography. See D. Vikelas, *Ἡ ζώη μοῦ* (Ἐν Ἀθήναις: Κατάστημα τοῦ Συλλόγου πρὸς Διάδοσιν Ὠφελίμων Βιβλίων, 1908), pp. 216-39.

and later as a partner. In 1862 his first collection of verses was published by Taylor and Francis.[54] The same firm also published, in 1871, the text of a lecture on Medieval and Modern Greek literature which Vikelas delivered at the Hellenic College of London (Hellenike Schole); the same volume also included Vikelas's poem *The Ancient Greeks* (*Οἱ Ἀρχαίοι*) and his verse translation of extracts from Goethe's *Faust* and Homer's *Odyssey*.[55] Similarly, the text of three lectures on Byzantine Greek influence on medieval culture in Europe which he delivered at the Greek Union of Marseilles were published by Williams and Norgate in 1874.[56] The financially independent Vikelas later relinquished his job, moved to Paris and concentrated on his literary activities which included the writing of *Loukis Laras* (1879), his best known work,[57] as well as metrical translations of Shakespeare (*Hamlet*, *Othello*, *Romeo and Juliet*, *The Merchant of Venice*). In 1894 he campaigned for Athens to be the site of the First International Olympic Games in 1896. Vikelas described his life in London and the Greek community of the city in his autobiography, published in 1908.[58]

Giorgos Vizyenos (1849-96) was another young man who, like Vikelas, published a collection of poems in London and also later became better known as a prose writer. Unlike Vikelas, though, Vizyenos was in London only briefly, in 1883. He was preparing a doctoral dissertation on the philosophy of Plotinus and had already begun to write his short stories (one of them – *Τό ἁμάρτημα τῆς μητρός μου* – was published in French in the *Nouvelle Revue* in 1883 and others were published in the Greek literary review *Ἑστία* in the same year). The publication of *Ἀτθίδες Αὖραι* [Athenian Breezes] [59] was munificently sponsored by Georgios Zariphes, a well-known patron and philanthropist, whose financial support had enabled Vizyenos to study philosophy and psychology in Athens and Leipzig and also to cultivate his literary interests in Paris and London. Thanks to his benefactor the poet moved among the best circles of the Greek community, as can be seen from the fact that his book has as a frontispiece an etching by Alphonse Legros,

54 *Στίχοι*. Taylor & Francis: Ἐν Λονδίνῳ, 1862.

55 *Περὶ Νεοελληνικῆς. Δοκίμιον*, etc. Taylor & Francis: Ἐν Λονδίνῳ, 1871.

56 *Περὶ Βυζαντινῶν. Μελέτη*. Williams & Norgate: Ἐν Λονδίνῳ, 1874.

57 *Loukis Laras. Reminiscences of a Chiote Merchant during the War of Independence. Translated from the Greek, with an account of the author, by J. Gennadius*. Macmillan & Co.: London, 1881. The protagonist of the work was inspired by Loukas Ziphos, who had migrated to England after the massacres at Chios and who, like Christophoros Angelos, used to relate the trials of his youth.

58 *Ἡ ζώη μοῦ* (see n. 53 above).

59 *Ἀτθίδες Αὖραι. Συλλογὴ ποιημάτων*... [with an etching by Alphonse Legros]. Trübner & Co.: Ἐν Λονδίνῳ, 1883.

professor of Fine Art at the Slade School and a close friend of the Ionides family, the wealthy collectors and pillars of the Greek community in Victorian London. The work is dedicated to Zariphes and various poems in it are also dedicated to him or his wife. The poet also thanks Legros and the Greek community of London for encouraging him to publish his book. It was reprinted twice in 1884, a year marked by the death of Zariphes and Vizyenos's return to Greece.

Apart from those by Vikelas mentioned above, there was a dearth of translations into Modern Greek of other European literatures. The only exceptions were translations of two of the greatest works of Italian literature. The first was a translation of the first canto only of Torquato Tasso's epic poem *Gerusalemme liberata*;[60] the second was of Dante's *Divine Comedy*, its three *cantica* published separately in 1882, 1883 and 1884.[61] The Dante translation was by Musurus Pasha (Konstantinos Mousouros), the Turkish ambassador in London. A second edition was published (in one volume) in 1890.

The publications of an unconventional figure also deserve mention. Constantine Simonides (1820-67) achieved great notoriety as a forger of Greek manuscripts which he managed to sell to museums and libraries throughout Europe. His claim that he himself had written the Codex Sinaiticus, the fourth-century manuscript discovered in 1840 by Constantin Tischendorf in the Mount Sinai Monastery (now in the British Library), created a stir in literary and theological circles and was widely reported in the British and European press.[62] Simonides also alleged that he had discovered important biblical manuscripts in Joseph Mayer's Egyptian Museum in Liverpool including a portion of the Gospel according to St Matthew dictated to Nicolaus the Deacon in 48 AD.[63] Simonides published various books describing his 'discoveries'. A list of his published works up to 1864 includes forty-two titles published in Moscow, Constantinople, Smyrna, and London. The items he published in London publicising or defending his forgeries were:

---

60 *Τορκουάτου Τάσσου Ἱεροσολυμηΐδος Ὠδὴ Πρώτη*. Ἐν Λονδίνῳ παρὰ Williams and Norgate, 1875.

61 *Dante's Inferno translated into Greek verse by Musurus Pasha (Δάντου ὁ Ἅδης. Μετάφρασις Κωνσταντίνου Μουσούρου)*. [With Dante's Purgatorio and Dante's Paradiso]. 3 vols. London & Edinburgh: Williams & Norgate, 1882[-1885.]

62 J. K. Elliott, *Codex Sinaiticus and the Simonides Affair*, *Ἀνάλεκτα Βλατάδων*, 33 (Θεσσαλονίκη: Πατριαρχικὸν Ἵδρυμα Πατερικῶν Μελετῶν, 1982). See also James Bentley, *Secrets of Mount Sinai: the story of the Codex Sinaiticus* (London: Orbis, 1985).

63 In *Facsimiles of Certain Portions of the Gospel of St Matthew, and the Epistles of SS. James & Jude, written on papyrus in the first century, and preserved in the Egyptian Museum of Joseph Mayer, Esq. Liverpool.* London: Trübner & Co, 1861.

Ἐγκώμιον Κωνσταντίνου Ἀκροπολίτου εἰς Ἅγιον Κωνσταντῖνον τὸν Μέγαν... London: Longmans & Co, 1853.

Ὀρθοδόξων Ἑλλήνων θεολογικαὶ γραφαὶ τέσσαρες [*includes: Νικολάου ἐπισκόπου Μεθώνης Λόγος πρὸς τοὺς Λατίνους...; Γενναδίου τοῦ Σχολαρίου τὸ περὶ ἐκπορεύσεως τοῦ Παναγίου Πνεύματος Ἐπιστολιμαῖον πρῶτον βιβλίον...*; Gregory Palamas, Archbishop of Salonika *Ὁμιλία περὶ πίστεως...*; Georgios Koressios *Συντομία τῶν Ἰταλικῶν ἁμαρτημάτων* ...]. London: David Nutt, 1859.

Ἐπιστολιμαία περὶ ἱερογλυφικῶν γραμμάτων διατριβὴ (A brief dissertation on hieroglyphic letters). London, 1860.

Λείψανα ἱστορικὰ... Ἐν Λιβερπούλῃ, [1864]. (Describing the 'discoveries' in the Egyptian Museum).

The Periplus of Hannon, King of the Karchedonians, concerning the Lybian parts of the earth beyond the Pillars of Herakles ... London: Trübner & Co, 1864. (In English and Greek).

In the early 1860s two attempts were made to publish newspapers for the Greek community in England. Both papers also aimed to have a wider readership in other centres of the Greek diaspora. *Ἄγγελος τῶν Βυζαντινῶν Λαῶν, Γραικῶν, Σλαβώνων, Δάκων, Καυκασίων καὶ Αράβων. Ἐφημερὶς Πανελληνίου Ἑώας καὶ Ἑσπερίας* ran between 5 December 1861 and 27 February 1862. It was published weekly and edited by Nikolaos Theodoros Koresios. Its aim (as stated in its first number) was to unite the Greeks of Europe, Asia and Africa. Its coverage included the latest news, a selection of reports from Greece, Constantinople, and from English, French, German, and Russian newspapers, commercial and financial news, cultural news and reviews, and announcements. It was supportive of King Otto I, a Bavarian prince who had ruled over independent Greece since 1833 and was soon to be deposed in 1862. In contrast, its rival, *Ὁ Βρεττανικὸς Ἀστὴρ*, was vehemently anti-Othonian. Though the coverage of the latter was much the same it was an altogether more ambitious and expensive undertaking. Unlike *Ἄγγελος*, it was lavishly illustrated and was printed by presses specially imported by its owner Stephanos Xenos. A man of letters, a businessman and an industrialist, Xenos was, like Demetrios Rhodokanakis and Simonides an unconventional figure among the Greek community and *Ὁ Βρεττανικὸς Ἀστὴρ* was short-lived, becoming the victim of political controversy – it ran for just under two years, between 9 July 1860 and 26 June 1862. Both the newspaper and its owner deserve a closer look.

II. Stephanos Xenos, a Greek Publisher in Nineteenth-century London

Stephanos Xenos was one of the most fascinating figures of the Greek community of London in the nineteenth century.[64] He was a man of many talents – a businessman who repeatedly made and lost fortunes, but also a man of wide cultural interests and a prolific writer whose output included novels, plays, books and articles on politics and commerce. He was one of the great cosmopolitan figures of his time but one who always had Greece and Hellenism uppermost in his mind. He was born in Smyrna [Izmir] in 1821, from where his family had to flee at the outbreak of the Greek War of Independence a few weeks after his birth. He was always vain about his ancestry, claiming descent on his mother's side from the Palaeologus family (the last emperors of Byzantium) and also, perhaps less exaltedly but more likely, from Apostolo Zeno, the prolific eighteenth-century Italian playwright. After Greece became independent his father returned to Smyrna in 1834 as the first Greek Consul. At the age of fourteen Xenos entered the military school in Athens and graduated eight years later. He decided, however, not to follow a career in the army and, after travelling widely in Greece, Constantinople, and throughout Europe he came to England in 1847, settling in London where he worked for a while for the Ionides family, to whom he was related.[65] Xenos soon established his own business exporting British textiles to the Levant and in 1857 he formed his own steam shipping company, the Greek Oriental Steam Navigation Company, running from London to the Levant and the Black Sea.

In parallel to these commercial activities, Xenos began his publishing career. His first book was a three-volume novel, *The Devil in Turkey; or, Scenes in Constantinople*, translated into English from his Greek manuscript.[66] The title-page bears the motto **Ξένε ξένιζε καὶ σὺ ξένος ἔσῃ** (Xenos, be hospitable to strangers because you are a stranger yourself), playing on his

---

64 Zephyros Ath. Kaukalides, *Στέφανος Ξένος· σκηνὲς ἀπὸ τὸ δράμα τοῦ Ἑλληνισμοῦ σὲ Ἀνατολὴ καὶ Δύση* (Ἀθήνα: Ἐκδόσεις Καστανιώτη, 1998) is a detailed account of Xenos's life and work, with an excellent description of the social and political background. Xenos's years in England are on pp. 80-340.

65 The Ionides were one of the great nineteenth-century Greek dynasties in London, and noted patrons of the arts – Constantine Alexander Ionides bequeathed his wide-ranging collection of oil paintings, watercolours, drawings and prints (over 1,000 items) to the South Kensington Museum (now the Victoria & Albert Museum).

66 *The Devil in Turkey; or, Scenes in Constantinople. Translated from the author's unpublished Greek manuscript, by Henry Corpe Member of the College of Preceptors.* London: Effingham Wilson, Royal Exchange, 1851. 3 vols.

name Xenos, 'stranger'. Xenos also published a Greek edition of this work in 1862 as: *Ὁ Διάβολος ἐν Τουρκίᾳ*.[67]

In his preface Xenos explains that he began writing the work on the shores of the Bosphorus and that his object was to make known to Greeks who had never visited Turkey the conditions, customs, and sentiments of the different tribes of that Empire. He sees his role as that of a traveller and a social historian who chooses fiction as 'the best mode of exhibiting truths in the clearest light'.[68] He also hopes that the novel will excite the curiosity of his fellow Greeks, who during centuries of slavery were plunged into ignorance, and that it will lead to the study of works of a more classical kind. His decision to publish it in English is explained by his belief that foreign visitors to the Levant are incapable of depicting 'the habits and character of, not only Turks, but also Jews, Greeks, and Armenians bound together by common interests, and resembling a large family, the members of which differ only in their religion'.[69] The novel, which is a series of interconnected episodes used to create a vast fresco of Ottoman society in the first decades of the nineteenth century, was a great success.

In 1861 Xenos published a second historical novel, this time in Greek, called: *Ἡ ἡρωῒς τῆς Ἐπαναστάσεως, ἤτοι σκηναὶ ἐν Ἑλλάδι ἀπὸ τοῦ ἔτους 1821-1828* [The heroine of the Greek Revolution, or scenes from the Greece of 1821-1828].[70] An adventure story set against the background of the Greek War of Independence, it was among the most popular Greek works of the second half of the nineteenth century.

Eighteen fifty-two, the year after the publication of *The Devil in Turkey*, saw the publication of another work of a different type and on a lavish scale, *Ἡ Παγκόσμιος Ἔκθεση τοῦ Λονδίνου τοῦ 1851*,[71] a description of the Great Exhibition of 1851, the first exhibition of the Products of Industry of All Nations, held at the Crystal Palace in 1851. The text was based on articles Xenos originally published in the newspapers *Ἀμάλθεια* (in Smyrna) and *Ἀθηνὰ* (in Athens). The publication includes a list of over 500 subscribers which constitutes a Who's who of Greek communities in England (including London – which has, naturally the greatest number of names – Manchester and Liverpool), Greece (Athens, Piraeus, Magnesía [in Thessaly], and

67 *Ὁ Διάβολος ἐν Τουρκίᾳ*. Ἐν Λονδίνῳ: Τύποις τοῦ Βρεττανικοῦ Ἀστέρος, 1862.

68 *The Devil in Turkey*, vol. I, iv.

69 Ibid, p. vii.

70 *Ἡ ἡρωῒς τῆς Ἑλληνικῆς Ἐπαναστάσεως, ἤτοι σκηναὶ ἐν Ἑλλάδι ἀπὸ τοῦ ἔτους 1821-1828.* Ἐν Λονδίνῳ: Τύποις τοῦ Βρεττανικοῦ Ἀστέρως, 1861.

71 Xenos, *Ἡ Παγκόσμιος Ἔκθεση τοῦ Λονδίνου τοῦ 1851*. Printed by K. K. Wertheimer, London, Wall Street, 1852.

Hermoupolis [in Syros]), Asia Minor (Smyrna – numerous, as this was the author's birthplace –, Kydonies, and New Ephesus), Ismailion and Galazion (or Galatz, in Romania), Bucharest, Vienna, Alexandria, Beirut, Trieste, Messina, and Marseilles.

London subscribers include: E[ustratios] K[onstantinos] Ionides (five copies), Eustratios Rallis, I[oannes] G[eorgiou] Kavaphes (a doctor and uncle of the poet), Leon Melas, Leonidas Rhodokanakis, Georgios P. Laskarides (Xenos's candidate as representative of the Greek community of London to Greece) and other prominent figures of the Greek community. The work has 392 illustrations and its twenty-three chapters describe all types of artefacts displayed at the exhibition. Two chapters are dedicated to the displays of Turkey and Greece.[72] In his description of the Greek contribution, Xenos recounts how on his first visit to the Greek room in the exhibition, in the company of Charles Strong, Oxford professor of Greek but better known as a poet and for his collection of *Sonnets from the Most Celebrated Italian Poets* (1827), the elderly professor sighed: 'Poor Greece, you have come to this splendid wedding in rags; and yet you are the Mother of this whole wide world'. Xenos proceeds to castigate the Greek Government for the meagreness of its display, saying that, once it had accepted the invitation to participate, it should have attempted to provide something better. As a result, for example, a miniature wooden cross made by a Greek monk with 85 reliefs of Saints, which Xenos describes in some detail, was dwarfed in the midst of the profusion of artefacts from other countries. He also laments the lack of modern sculpture next to the few examples of classical sculptures shown (there were only two copies of the Parthenon sculptures), and also the absence of agricultural products. He praises, however, the display of Greek folk costume (worn at the exhibition by a young Englishman!).

Another lavishly produced publication came out in 1859, this time of a more personal nature, *Ἡ κιβδηλεία ἤτοι μία ἀληθὴς ἱστορία τοῦ καιροῦ μας* (*Coining, i.e. a true story of our time*).[73] Here Xenos sets out to disprove the accusations of counterfeiting made against his father (who was still, at the time, the Greek Consul at Smyrna) which led to his imprisonment for eleven months before he was tried and found innocent. The book is also a diatribe against contemporary Greek politics and the government of King Otto. Demetres Vikelas, who knew Xenos in London, commented that the exaggerated tone of the book did more harm than good to Xenos's father's

---

72 Ibid, chapters 21, 22, pp. 157-67.

73 *Ἡ κιβδηλεία ἤτοι μία ἀληθὴς ἱστορία τοῦ καιροῦ μας*. Ἐν Λονδίνῳ: τύποις Wertheimer, 1859. 2 vols.

reputation.[74] Like the volume on the Great Exhibition, this work has hundreds of plates and illustrations in the text. The British Library copy has a dedication from the author – on headed papers of The Greek Oriental Steam Navigation Company – addressed to the Librarian of the British Museum. It also contains, bound in the first volume, a very large dossier of manuscripts (which includes letters, receipts, bills and other material). Xenos described elsewhere his habit of taking notes and keeping a diary of all important transactions in which he was engaged and of never destroying letters or documents so that, in case of necessity, he could refer to them or reproduce them.[75]

Xenos's most remarkable achievement, however, was the publication of *Ὁ Βρεττανικὸς Ἀστὴρ* (*The British Star*), the weekly Greek illustrated newspaper he published in London between 9 July 1860 and 26 June 1862. Xenos's business at the time was in the ascendant, and he had ample means with which to launch a newspaper. The scope and lavishness of the paper were unheard of in the context of Greek publishing in London. Xenos said that the favourable reception of his books on the Great Exhibition and on coining, especially the comments on their illustrations, suggested to him the idea of establishing an illustrated Greek newspaper in London. His reasons for publishing the paper were to introduce English institutions and the civilization of Western Europe to the Greeks in various parts of the Ottoman Empire believing that such information would eventually replace Russian influence in the East with English. He also wanted to use the paper as a mouthpiece for opposition to the Government of King Otto of Greece, as well as advancing the interests of the Greek and Oriental Steam Navigation Company. Its presses were also used for the publication of Xenos's literary works – both the Greek translation of *The Devil in Turkey* and his new novel *Ἡ ἡρωῒς τῆς Ἑλληνικῆς Ἐπαναστάσεως* came out in 1861 under the imprint of *The British Star* and were publicised in its pages.

These aims are reflected in the masthead of the paper (fig. 2) which shows a landscape depicting the architectures of various countries with a Greek population – including Hagia Sophia at Constantinople, the Pyramids in Egypt, and the Acropolis in Athens. Curiously, the English S was mistakenly used in the lettering for the title of the paper in the first issue. This was corrected in later issues and, the following year, the illustration was further elaborated by the inclusion of St Paul's Cathedral, which dominates the scene,

---

74 Vikelas, *Ἡ ζώη μοῦ*, p. 361.

75 *Depredations; or, Overend, Gurney, & Co., and the Greek and Oriental Steam Navigation Company*. London: published by the author, at no 9, Essex Street, Strand, 1869, p. [iii].

and the allegorical figures of Britannia (on the left, with the lion) and Greece, on the right, with her shackles broken (which can be interpreted either as freedom from the Turk or the Bavarian). Below the masthead there is a list of the agents of the newspaper in the various cities, and countries where it was distributed – Constantinople, Salonika, Patras, Syros, Alexandria and Cairo, Beirut, Manchester, Liverpool, Cork, Smyrna, Varna, Galazio, Bucharest, and Trieste.

The paper was divided in two sections. The main part had articles on art (mainly wood engravings of contemporary paintings accompanied by a commentary), culture, literature (short stories, poetry, sayings), reports of important contemporary trials, commercial and financial information, and advertisements. Its second component was a political supplement. This consisted of an editorial (or leader), followed by reports of the week's news from various European countries, but also from China and India. Occasionally, there was also a letter from the paper's correspondent in another country, or the texts of official proclamations. The articles were not signed and were mostly gleaned from other publications. The translations were provided by a team of ten professional translators Xenos brought from Athens. For the production of the paper Xenos also brought Greek printers to London and imported Greek type faces. The literary style of the paper was described by *The Times* as 'a favourable specimen of the laboured and artificial language young Athens imagines to be a return to Classical Greek'. (This use

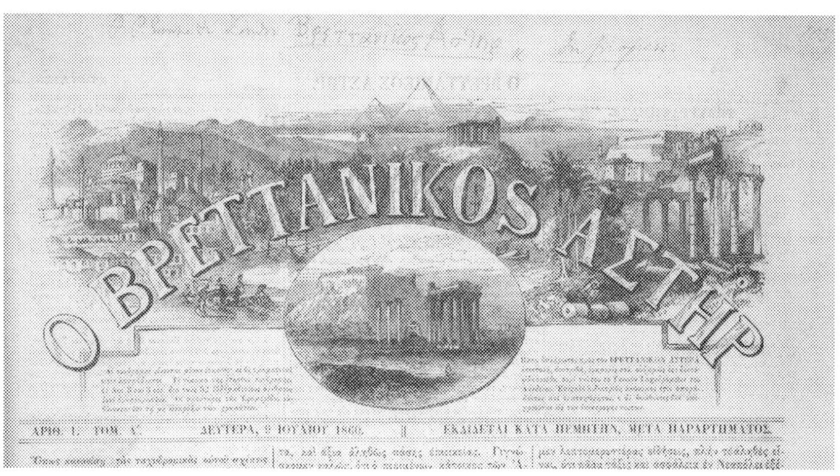

Ο ΒΡΕΤΤΑΝΙΚΟΣ ΑΣΤΗΡ

ΑΡΙΘ. 1. ΤΟΜ. Α΄ ΔΕΥΤΕΡΑ, 9 ΙΟΥΛΙΟΥ 1860. ΕΚΔΙΔΕΤΑΙ ΚΑΤΑ ΠΕΜΠΤΗΝ, ΜΕΤΑ ΠΑΡΑΡΤΗΜΑΤΟΣ.

Fig. 2: *The British Star*, 9 July 1860
The British Library Newspaper Library.

of what has also been described as 'hyper katharevousa' is a problem for the modern reader, as is Xenos's tendency in all his works to translate names of persons and places. *The Times* newspaper is, for example, called *Chronos*, while an illustration captioned (I translate) 'A view of Kerameikos and Omonoia Square' is not, as one might imagine, a view of Athens but of the Tuileries and Place de la Concorde in Paris.)

The paper contained both general cultural material and also special features. Examples of the former included a report, on 9 July 1860 (the paper's first issue), on the restoration of paintings of the Dome of St Paul's (the caption explaining that Sir Christopher Wren had originally wanted mosaics, but as this proved too expensive, paintings by James Thornhill depicting scenes from the life of St Paul were executed instead) and the review, on 9 August 1860, of a performance of Meyerbeer's *Le Prophète* at Covent Garden. It took the opportunity to provide an illustration of the new auditorium of the recently rebuilt and re-opened Opera House, and also of the old auditorium which had burned down in 1856.

Special features about topical issues were also frequent. In the three numbers published between 4 and 18 October 1860 the paper printed articles on Rome. It was widely expected at the time that Pope Pius IX would succumb to pressure and relinquish his temporal rule to Victor Emmanuel II. In the event Italy would be unified in 1860 but without Rome and Venice, and Rome would remain under papal rule for another ten years before becoming the capital of Italy in 1870. The three articles in the paper, which occupied twenty-two pages, examined the history and the topography of Classical and Christian Rome. They were accompanied by numerous illustrations depicting sights of the Eternal City – the Quirinal, the Spanish Steps, the steps of the Campidoglio and those of Santa Maria in Aracoeli. In the issue printed on 11 October the paper published a huge fold-out showing a panoramic view of Rome seen from the Janiculum by the Gate of San Pancrazio, with S. Pietro in Montorio and the Fontana Paolina in the foreground. At the time Rome was occupied by French troops who can be seen in the foreground. In the political supplement of the same issue the paper contained coverage of the latest political and military developments in Italy.

It was the political element, of course, and not the cultural information it provided that was to be the paper's undoing. To quote *The Times* dated 21 June 1862:

> The Christians [in Turkey] are growing active and curious, and take a great interest in anything that relates to Western Europe. In no society would a description of the great Exhibition, or the last improvements in Paris, or the Derby Day … be read with more zest than among some of the subjects of the Sultan. But as Mr Xenos is a Greek, it is needless to say that this paper does not content itself with science and art, but treats of Eastern politics with a

> strong revolutionary bias. We presume that the writers must have been guilty with more than the usual rhodomontade which distinguishes the journalists of their race, for it appears that the Turkish Government actually applied to our own that the British Star should not be distributed to Constantinople through the Embassy Post Office.

The Turkish Government's complaint was that the paper contained anti-Turkish propaganda. According to the arrangements which still prevailed in Turkey at the time, the British Embassy had mailbags of its own which, as a special privilege granted by the Porte, entered the country and were distributed without any examination by the Turkish authorities. Any letters or newspapers could be sent from England in this way. The Foreign Office accepted the Turks' request and the paper was refused distribution. Xenos objected to this decision and suggested that the paper should continue to be distributed with its political supplement removed. This request was refused. The matter was the subject of heated discussion in the House of Commons and there was considerable sympathy for Xenos but, as *The Times* put it in its editorial of 20 June 1862, though the Christian subjects of the Sultan would be deprived of a very fair medium of instruction, the Porte was, nevertheless, within its rights to request a formal requisition of the paper. That proved to be the demise of *The British Star*, as it could not survive without its subscribers in the Ottoman Empire. Its last issue was published on 26 June 1862. Xenos lost a lot of money as a result, not least from the wood engravings already produced showing views from the Exposition Universelle in Paris which remained unused. At least he had the pleasure of seeing, later in the same year, the deposition of his *bête noire*, King Otto, from the Greek throne, an event to which his paper had, to a certain extent, contributed. We have for this the judgement of Demetres Vikelas who, for this very reason, considered *The British Star* to be Xenos's greatest success.[76] In his farewell note Xenos says that the publication of the paper is temporarily suspended but will resume in the near future. This was not to happen until 1891 and not in London but in Athens (though it curiously retained its original title) and without success. The closure of *The British Star* was the end of Xenos's Greek printing in London.

He remained in London for another fifteen years which saw his gradual alienation from the Greek community in London, the collapse of his navigation company, and his involvement in other enterprises which also failed. During these years he published two more works in English: *East and West, a diplomatic history of the annexation of the Ionian Islands to the Kingdom of*

76 Vikelas, ibid. p. 363.

Greece[77] and *Depredations; or, Overend, Gurney, & Co., and the Greek and Oriental Steam Navigation Company.*[78] This is a polemical account of the formation and collapse of his company and also of his other business undertakings, including *The British Star.* The book, though one-sided, gives an interesting picture of financial life and the Greek merchant class.

Xenos returned to Greece in 1877, was involved in a number of political scandals, re-launched *The British Star* in Athens in 1891, wrote numerous novels and plays, and finally died penniless in Athens in 1894. He is chiefly remembered today for his historical novel *The Heroine of the Greek Revolution* [79] but also by his life which was more adventurous than the plot of many a novel.

---

77 *East and West, a diplomatic history of the annexation of the Ionian Islands to the Kingdom of Greece.* London: Trübner & Co, 1865. The Ionian Islands were annexed by Greece in 1864 on the election of King George I to the throne of Greece.

78 *Depredations*, op. cit.

79 A critical edition of this work was published in 1988. See *Ἡ ἡρωΐς τῆς Ἑλληνικῆς Ἐπαναστάσεως, ἤτοι σκηναὶ ἐν Ἑλλάδι ἀπὸ τοῦ ἔτους 1821-1828. Γενικὴ ἐποπτεία Ἀπόστολος Σαχίνης*; φιλολογικὴ ἐπιμέλεια Βικτώρια Χατζηγεωργίου-Χασιώτη (Ἀθήνα: Ἵδρυμα Κώστα καὶ Ἑλένης Οὐράνη, 1988).

Kate Sealey Rahman

Russian Revolutionaries in London, 1853-70
Alexander Herzen and the Free Russian Press

The opening passage of the section of Alexander Herzen's memoirs which describes his life in Britain reads:

> When at daybreak on the 25th August 1852, I passed along a wet plank on to the shore of England and looked at its dirty white promontories, I was very far from imagining that years would pass before I should leave those chalk cliffs ... The idea with which I had come to London, to seek the tribunal of my own people, was a sound and right one ... I had had my own people once in Russia, but was [now] completely cut off in a foreign land; I had at all costs to get into communication with my own people ... Letters were not allowed in, but books would get through of themselves ... I would print; and so little by little I set to work upon ... setting up a Russian printing-press.[1]

With these words, Herzen not only embarks on an account of his life in England, but also, in effect, begins the history of Russian-language printing in London. This history is surprisingly short. In theory, the prospects for Russian-language printing in Britain were good. Russians have been present in England from as early as the twelfth century.[2] Moreover, Heinrich Ludolf's *Rossiiskaia grammatika* [Russian Grammar], variously described as the first Russian grammar ever printed and the second book ever printed in the Russian vernacular language (the first being the *Ulozhenie* or Code of Laws)

---

1 *My Past and Thoughts: The Memoirs of Alexander Herzen*, translated by Constance Garnett, revised by Humphrey Higgins, with an introduction by Isaiah Berlin, abridged, with a Preface and Notes by Dwight Macdonald (London: Chatto &Windus, 1974), pp. 445, 448.

2 It is generally considered that the first Russian in England was Rabbi Isaac from Chernigov, who arrived in England in 1181. See Joseph Jacobs, 'The First Russian in England', *The Academy*, XXXIV, no. 868 (22 Dec. 1888), 404-5.

was printed in Oxford by Oxford University Press in 1696.[3] Yet despite this, research to date has uncovered almost nothing printed in London in Cyrillic type prior to Herzen's arrival in Britain. On initial view, an English-Russian commercial dictionary, compiled by Adam Kroll and printed by Thomas Plummer of Seething-Lane in 1800, seems promising. However, a glance at the preface reveals that the cited purpose of the work is 'to enable the English trader to render himself intelligible to the Russian, without having to resort to … the laborious and difficult task of learning the RUSSIAN characters, which would appear so formidable to his imagination, that he would be deterred from making the attempt'. The preface goes on: 'to obviate this difficulty, the Author has substituted ENGLISH Characters, in a manner that he conceives … will enable the Reader to speak plain enough for a RUSSIAN easily to understand him'.[4] And indeed, the Russian words have been transliterated into Roman characters.

Exploration to date, while far from exhaustive, has uncovered only two works containing Cyrillic script published in London prior to Herzen's arrival in Britain. The first, a work by John Bowring entitled *Rossiiskaia antologiia* [Russian anthology]: *specimens of the Russian poets*, was printed in 1821 by R. A. Taylor of Shoe Lane. Although this is almost entirely in English, the title itself appears in Cyrillic script, as does a short quotation from a poem by Batiushkov – although this is lithographed, rather than printed.[5] The second work to contain some Cyrillic type is a volume by Robert Lyall, entitled *The Character of the Russians and a detailed history of Moscow, with a dissertation on the Russian language*, printed in 1823 by A. & R. Spottiswoode of New Street Square. This again, whilst almost entirely in English, contains a table showing the Russian alphabet.[6]

---

3 See B. O. Unbegaun, 'Russian Grammars before Lomonosov', *Oxford Slavonic Papers*, 8 (1958), p. 100. In the preface to his work, Ludolf himself describes his grammar as the second ever Russian book (cited in *The Athenaeum*, no. 1419, 6 Jan. 1855).

4 Adam Kroll, *A Commercial Dictionary in the English and Russian Languages with a full explanation of the Russian trade etc. etc.* (London: printed for S. Chappel, Royal Exchange by T. Plummer, Seething-Lane, [1800]), p. 1.

5 *Rossiskaia antologiia: specimens of the Russian poets*, translated by John Bowring (London: printed for the author, 1821).

6 Robert Lyall, *The Character of the Russians and a Detailed History of Moscow, with a dissertation on the Russian Language and an appendix…* (London: printed [by R. & A. Spottiswoode] for T. Cadell, in the Strand and W. Blackwood, Edinburgh, 1823), p. 13. It seems probable that other works containing details of the Russian alphabet would have been printed in London prior to Herzen's arrival in England, although, to date, I have been unable to find other examples.

So, a very meagre output indeed. However all this was to change with the arrival in London of Herzen and the establishment, under his direction, of the *Vol'naia russkaia tipografiia*, or Free Russian Press.

Herzen has been variously described as a novelist, essayist, memoirist, political theorist and journalist. He was born in Moscow on 6 April 1812, the illegitimate son of a wealthy Moscow nobleman Ivan Yakovlev and a fifteen-year old German girl, Luiza Haag, whom Yakovlev had met while travelling in Europe. The name Herzen, from the German word for 'heart', was given to him by his father, although opinions differ as to whether this was intended cynically or affectionately.[7] Herzen is described as having had an isolated childhood, 'spoilt by the servants of the household ... but isolated from companions of his own age'.[8] He took refuge in his father's extensive library, where he became familiar with the works of the major European writers of the eighteenth century. At seventeen, he entered Moscow University, and it was at this time, heavily influenced by both Hegel and French Utopian Socialism, that he began to formulate the political ideas that were to dominate his thinking throughout his life – in particular a belief in individual liberty, opposition to serfdom, to autocratic government and to censorship of the press. As he himself put it, 'a deadly hatred for slavery in any form and for any tyranny'.[9] (He later summed up his work in three slogans: Freedom for Russia, Land for the serfs, and Independence for Poland.)[10] Herzen finished university in 1833, and within the year was arrested on a charge of 'dangerous free-thinking' and sentenced to internal exile. He was to spend most of the next decade exiled to various provincial towns within Russia, before finally leaving Russia altogether in 1847, ostensibly for reasons of ill health. He arrived in Paris on the eve of the 1848 Revolution. After the failure of that revolution, he moved to Switzerland and then to Italy, becoming acquainted with most of the prominent members of the European exile community, among them Mazzini, Garibaldi and Louis Blanc.

Descriptions of Herzen by his contemporaries emphasise his energy and intelligence. The English radical and republican William Linton described him as 'a rich-blooded barbarian, impulsive, child-like, carried away by

---

7 See Colin Ward, 'Introduction' to Alexander Herzen, *Childhood, Youth & Exile: Being Parts I & II of My Past and Thoughts*, translated by J. D. Duff, introduction by Colin Ward (London: The Folio Society, 1983), p. 10.

8 Ibid, p. 10.

9 See the Preface to Alexander Herzen, *Who is to Blame? A novel in two parts*, translated by Margaret Wettlin (Moscow: Progress Publishers, 1978), p. 11.

10 *Desiatilietie vol'noi russkoi tipografii v londonie: sbornik eia pervykh listov, sostavlennyi i izdannyi L. Chernetskim* (London: Vol'naia russkaia tipografiia, 1863), p. xx.

enthusiasm where his feelings were concerned, … wise and diplomatic; … a profound and subtle thinker, [whose] choice of speech was ready, clear and concise, as well as impressive, with a remarkable power of apt illustration, witty … , and a "lord of irony"'.[11] Jane Carlyle, in a letter to her husband, Thomas, put it more simply: 'He is a brave and energetic man, Herzen, but with a basis of barbarian. His tawny eyes have a hungry animal look that makes me feel as if he might easily spring at me and eat me.'[12]

Herzen arrived in England in 1852 with the intention of paying a brief visit to Mazzini in London. However the brief visit was to stretch to a thirteen-year stay, during which time he established one of the most successful and prolific of all the émigré presses which appeared in Europe in the mid-nineteenth century.

Herzen himself stated that he had first considered setting up a Russian printing press as early as 1849,[13] but it was not until his arrival in London that he was able to realise this aim. This was largely due to his contact with the Polish Democratic Society, an émigré Polish republican organisation, which had moved its base to London in 1849. Herzen had first become acquainted with the Central Committee of this society in Paris in 1847, and soon after his arrival in London, he renewed his acquaintance with Stanislaw Worcell, then one of the three principal members of the Central Committee. In his memoirs Herzen describes Worcell as 'the first man with whom I discussed the founding of a Russian printing-press', stating, 'after listening to me the sick man grew animated, seized a pencil and paper and began making calculations, reckoning how much type we should require and so on.'[14] Later, in a piece written following Worcell's death in 1857, he described how Worcell, holding in his hand the first page printed by the Press, declared: 'My God, my God! A free Russian printing press in London! How many terrible moments … are wiped out by this scrap of paper, smeared with printer's ink!'[15]

The Polish Central Committee had already established a Polish printing press at 38 Regent Square, where they were printing their journal *Demokrata Polski* [The Polish Democrat]. (They published also a second edition of one of

11 W. J. Linton, *European Republicans: recollections of Mazzini and his friends* (London: Lawrence and Bullen, 1893), p. 275.

12 Monica Partridge, *Alexander Herzen: collected studies*, second enlarged and revised edition (Nottingham: Astra Press, 1993), p. 105.

13 Aleksandr Gertsen (Iskander), *Vol'noe ruskoe knigopechatanie v londonie* (London, 21 fevralia, 1853), [p. 3].

14 See *My Past and Thoughts: The Memoirs of Alexander Herzen*, translated by Constance Garnett, revised by Humphrey Higgins, with an introduction by Isaiah Berlin, III (London: Chatto & Windus, 1968), p. 1136.

15 *Desiatilietie vol'noi russkoi tipografii v londonie*, p. *159*.

Herzen's works, *Du Développement des idées révolutionnaires en Russie* [On the Development of Revolutionary Ideas in Russia], written under his pseudonym, Iskander, in 1853.) Herzen was asked to contribute funds towards the upkeep of the press, and it is perhaps this that gave him the final impetus towards establishing a Russian printing press. An agreement was reached whereby a Russian press would be set up alongside the Polish press at the Regent Square premises. Herzen would pay the costs of rent and labour, and provide paper and type. In return, the Polish Central Committee would use their system of contacts to smuggle papers and pamphlets into Russia. Second-hand Cyrillic type was purchased from the Paris firm, Didot, and the Free Russian Press was born. In April 1853, Herzen wrote to a friend: 'There will be a press, and if I do nothing else, then this initiative for open discussion within Russia, will one day be valued.'[16]

Herzen's relationship with the Polish émigrés appears to have been a mixed one. In his memoirs he recounts arguments with the younger members of the Central Committee, particularly Zienkowicz, and complains of their attempts to get money from him above and beyond the terms of their agreement.[17] Yet when, forced by fears that Zienkowicz's failure to pay his debts would lead to the seizure of the press, Herzen decided to move the Russian printing press into its own premises – first at Number 2 and then Number 82 Judd Street, and later to premises on the Caledonian Road – he took with him the Polish émigré Ludwik Czerniecki. Czerniecki was to manage the Free Russian Press throughout its existence. He and his family lived in the press's premises on the Caledonian Road and apparently became so enamoured of the place that, when in 1865 Herzen moved the press and its entourage to Geneva, Czerniecki was described as pining for 'the open skies of King's Cross and the broad horizon of Tottenham Court Road'.[18]

On 21 February 1853 a pamphlet, lithographed from copperplate handwriting and signed with Herzen's pseudonym Iskander, was issued (fig. 1). Addressed 'To my brothers in Russia', it asks 'Why are we silent?' and notes 'Up to this hour nobody has printed anything in Russian outside of Russia, because nowhere was there a free Russian press.'[19] It goes on to announce that from 1 May 1853 there would be such a press, and invites

---

16 Letter to M. K. Reichel, 8 April 1953. See Z. P. Bazilova, *'Kolokol' Gertsena: (1857-1867 gg)* (Moskva: OGIZ, 1949), p. 22.

17 See *My Past and Thoughts*, III, 1142.

18 Cited in Edward Hallet Carr, *The Romantic Exiles: a nineteenth-century portrait gallery* (London: Victor Gollancz, 1933), p. 255.

19 Aleksandr Gertsen (Iskander), *Vol'noe ruskoe knigopechatanie v londonie* (London, 21 fevralia 1853).

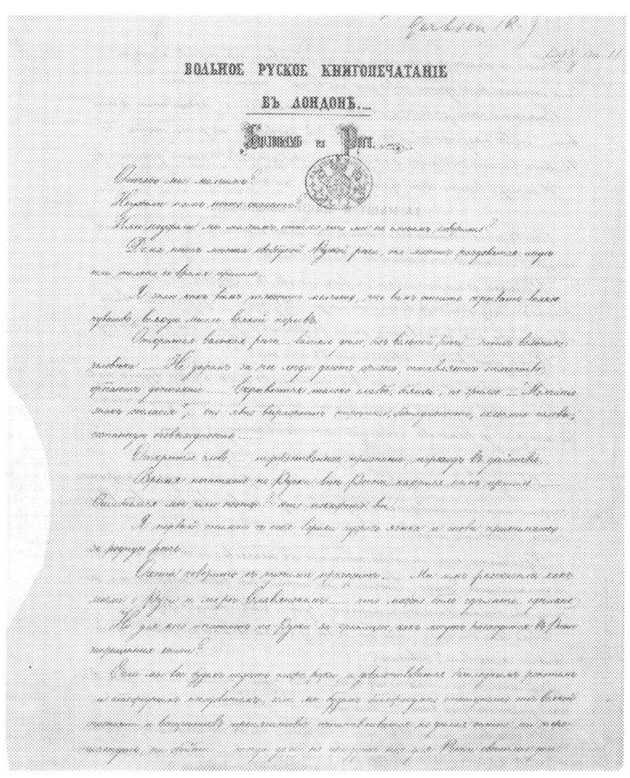

ВОЛЬНОЕ РУСКОЕ КНИГОПЕЧАТАНІЕ

ВЪ ЛОНДОНѢ.

Fig. 1: 'Iskander' (i.e. Alexander Herzen), 'To My Brothers in Russia', lithographed pamphlet announcing the foundation of the Free Russian Press (21 Feb. 1853)
British Library pressmark: 1298.m.11(8).

people to send in manuscripts. A similar announcement appeared in *Demokrata Polski*, where, in a letter to the editors, Herzen famously declared that 'the establishment of the Russian printing office in London is the most revolutionary action a Russian can take today.'[20]

Notices in the English press were scarce,[21] although a short article appeared in William Linton's paper, *The Leader*, on 11 June 1853. Under the headline 'A Russian Democratic Printing Office in London', it declared

20 *Demokrata Polski*, 25 May 1853, p. 55.

21 For a more comprehensive discussion of Herzen and the English press see Monica Partridge, 'Herzen and the English Press', in her *Alexander Herzen: collected studies*, pp. 19-35.

proudly that 'London is becoming daily more and more the centre of the intellectual movement of the world.'[22] A later article, printed in the *Athenaeum* in January 1855, and co-authored by the editor, W. H. Dixon, and by Thomas Watts, then an assistant in the Department of Printed Books at the British Museum, noted:

> Are many of our readers aware that there is a Russian press in London? We do not mean an Anglo-Russian press ... but a veritable Russian press, – printing Russian books in the Russian language, for the purpose of circulation in Russia? Such is the fact. This press is active, vigilant and prolific. Moreover it is free. No censor suggests its issues, no police controls its types. It prints what it pleases; and it circulates what it can. In a word, the Russian Free Press in London is a Democratic Press.[23]

The first Russian language publication to roll off the press in May 1853 was the pamphlet, *Iur'ev den'!* [St George's Day!], so called because historically this was the day when the free peasantry in Russia would hire themselves out to work on a year-by-year basis. Addressed 'To the Russian Gentry', it called for the emancipation of the serfs. (Incidentally, the *Athenaeum* reviewers, cited above, referred to *Iur'ev den'!* as 'the first Russian publication ever issued in England'. They were mistaken in this, although their error is perhaps indicative of how little Russian-language printing there had been in Britain up until this date.) *Iur'ev den'!* was followed in July by another pamphlet, *Poliaki proshchaiut' nas!* [Poles forgive us!], which discussed the issue of Polish independence; and then by *Kreshchennaia sobstvennost'* [Baptised property], again on the issue of serfdom.

Despite Herzen's efforts, the initial years of the press were unsuccessful – in the first five years of its life, it produced just fifteen publications. The response from within Russia was unenthusiastic and indeed one friend – the actor, Mikhail Shchepkin – came to London expressly to advise Herzen against the venture. Herzen's pleas for contributions brought just one response – a poem by Viazemsky called *Russkii Bog!* [The Russian God!] – and he was forced to rely largely on his own works. He later recounted his despondency in a piece written to celebrate the tenth anniversary of the press, noting that 'we printed for three years, not only selling nothing, but unable even to send into Russia a single copy of anything except the first leaflets despatched by Worcell and his friends in Warsaw.'[24]

---

22 *The Leader*, 11 June 1853.

23 *The Athenaeum*, no. 1419, 6 Jan. 1855.

24 *Desiatilietie vol'noi russkoi tipografii v londonie: sbornik eia pervykh listov* (as in n. 10), p. x.

Fortunes began to turn in 1855, when two events in Russia – the death of Tsar Nicholas I and his succession by the more liberal Alexander II; and the announcement in the April Budget of the abolition of the stamp duty on newspapers and other periodical publications – prompted Herzen to publish a journal.[25] The first issue of the journal *Poliarnaia zvezda* [The Polar Star] went on sale in August 1855 at a price of 8 shillings (fig. 2). The title was carefully chosen, as it imitated that of a short-lived journal published in Russia in the 1820s by the leaders of the failed 1825 Decembrist uprising. The repression of this uprising was one of the first acts of Nicholas I's reign and the front

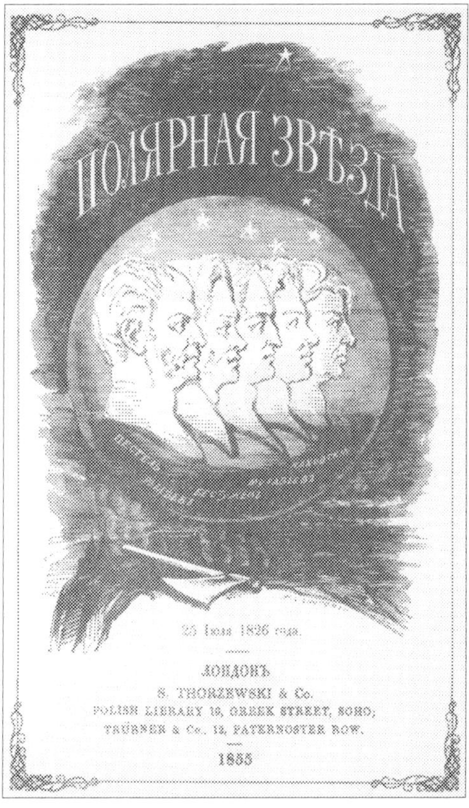

Fig. 2: *Poliarnaia zvezda* [The Polar Star] (London: Thorzewski, August 1855), cover.
British Library pressmark: P.701/980.

25 Carr suggests that it was perhaps the abolition of the stamp duty that provided the greater impetus, noting that more than a hundred new journals were founded in England during the months following the budget (see *The Romantic Exiles*, p. 207).

cover of the journal – illustrated by an engraving by William Linton – depicts the five Decembrists who were hanged for their participation in the uprising. On the title-page, a quotation from Pushkin reads 'Hail reason!'. By this, Herzen was not only welcoming the new, more reformist regime anticipated by the accession of Alexander II, but also firmly aligning himself with the liberal ideals of the Decembrists.[26]

Issues of *Poliarnaia zvezda* appeared infrequently, with only seven appearing between 1855 and 1862. Initially, Herzen succeeded in getting only a small number of copies into Russia via his Polish contacts. However, with the appearance of the second and third numbers in 1856 and 1857, interest in both *Poliarnaia zvezda* and the other publications of the press grew rapidly.[27] It was at this time of increasing success that Herzen's most influential publication, *Kolokol* [The Bell], was founded (fig. 3). The idea for *Kolokol* came from the poet Nikolai Ogarev, a life-long friend of Herzen's, who had joined Herzen in exile in London in 1856. *Poliarnaia zvezda* was a weighty and expensive journal, the sheer cost of which prevented it from gaining wide circulation. By contrast, *Kolokol* was intended as a cheaper, more frequent newsletter, designed to keep pace with the changing events in Russia. As Herzen and Ogarev stated in their introduction to the first issue of the journal: '*Poliarnaia zvezda* comes out too rarely, we do not have the means to publish it more frequently. In the meantime, events in Russia are speeding ahead, they need to be caught rapidly, discussed immediately. For this we are launching a new periodical publication ... under the title *Kolokol*.'[28]

The first issue of *Kolokol* went on sale, priced sixpence, on 1 July 1857, and for the next ten years it was to appear regularly, at first on a monthly and then a fortnightly basis. During this period 245 issues appeared, the first 196 of which were published in London, the rest in Geneva. The impact of *Kolokol* was phenomenal. It achieved remarkable popularity, and was read remarkably widely, even, so it is said, reaching the Tsar himself. It became accepted as the mouthpiece of Russian public opinion, despite the fact that, as the critic Marc

26 Colin Ward, in his introduction to J. D. Duff's translation of Parts I & II of *My Past and Thoughts*, notes the famous passage in Herzen's memoirs where he describes how, following the hanging of the Decembrist conspirators in 1826, he and Nikolai Ogarev climbed the Sparrow Hills outside Moscow and 'vowed to devote their lives to the struggle for liberation'. *Poliarnaia zvezda* could be seen as the embodiment of that vow (see Ward, p. 11).

27 Bazileva notes that in a letter to Fokht on 9 April 1857, Herzen wrote: 'My books are selling wonderfully ... For example: the third volume of *Poliarnaia zvezda* comes out on 15 April. Orders have already been placed for 300 copies, and I calculate that there will be 200 more by 1 May' (Bazileva, p. 55-6).

28 *Kolokol*, 1 July 1857, p. 1.

Slonim has stated, it came from London and was published by émigrés.[29] With a first edition print run of two and a half thousand, it frequently ran to a second edition. This was, as E. H. Carr suggests, 'a stupendous circulation for a journal produced and circulated by two exiles in a country where not one man in ten thousand had the faintest understanding of the subjects which it treated or the language in which it was printed.'[30]

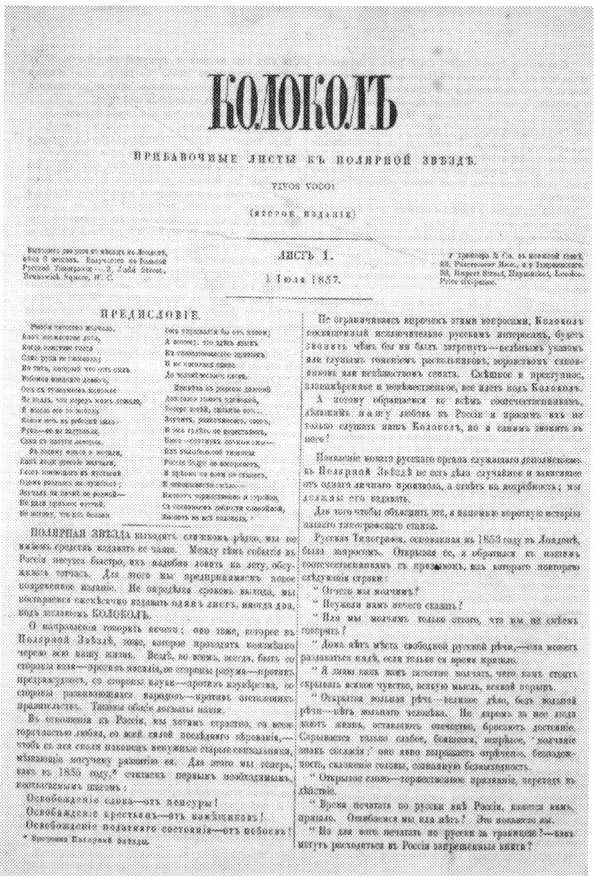

КОЛОКОЛЪ

ПРИБАВОЧНЫЕ ЛИСТЫ КЪ ПОЛЯРНОЙ ЗВѢЗДѢ.

VIVOS VOCO!

(второе изданіе)

ЛИСТЪ 1.

1 Іюля 1857.

ПРЕДИСЛОВІЕ.

Fig. 3: *Kolokol*, no. 1 (1 July 1857)
British Library pressmark: C.127.k.4.

29 See Ward, p. 15.
30 Carr, p. 252.

Central to the success of the Free Russian Press was the issue of distribution. Much of Herzen's despondency in the early years of the Press resulted from his inability to get his material back to its intended readership in Russia. This too formed part of the disillusionment he felt with the younger members of the Polish Committee, whose ability to distribute his material fell short of the expectations he had held on first entering into agreement with them. However, as Monica Partridge has shown, Herzen had, right from the inception of the Press, taken care to notify a number of London and Continental booksellers of its existence – among them, Brockhaus in Leipzig, Franck in Paris, and in London, Franz Thimm and David Nutt.[31] Another key figure was that of the Polish émigré Stanislaw Tchorzewski, who ran the Polish Library in Soho at premises in Greek Street and later Macclesfield Street.

By far the most significant bookseller involved with the Press, however, was Nicholas Trübner.[32] Trübner not only became the principal supplier of the Free Russian Press's publications, but also, after purchasing the copyright from Herzen, took over the publication of all second editions of the Press's works. When the demand for the Press's publications outstripped Ludwik Czerniecki's ability to keep up, Trübner installed a Russian press in the office of another Polish émigré, Zeno Swiętosławski, who had set up his Universal Printing Establishment at premises in High Holborn. There he published, under the Trübner trademark, not only the works of the Free Russian Press, but also other Russian works, among them a series of memoirs of prominent Russian figures. (Incidentally, Swiętosławski is one of the few émigré printers who complied with the 1799 Seditious Societies Act requiring printers to register their presses with the County Clerk. The letter he wrote registering his presses – one of which was presumably Trübner's – is held in the London Metropolitan Archives.)

As well as printing material, Trübner played a significant role in smuggling the Free Russian Press's material into Russia, using the Association of German Booksellers and Publishers [the Börsenverein] to despatch Free Russian Press material into Russia under his own label. Trübner aside, Herzen had a network of contacts who delivered material for him, among them figures such as Lionel Rothschild and Joseph Cowen, as well as the English MP, Charles Wentworth Dilke, who made use of his diplomatic immunity to

31 See Partridge, *Alexander Herzen: collected studies*, p. 193.

32 For a more comprehensive discussion on the relation between Trübner and the Free Russian Press, see Monica Partridge, 'The Free Russian Press and Trubner & Co.' in her *Alexander Herzen: collected studies*, pp. 193-215.

carry material into Russia. As he stated in his diary, by making use of his diplomatic passport he was able to take into Russia 'the most extraordinary collection of books that was probably ever put together in that country, unless in the office of the censorship of the police'.[33] Yet the process of getting material into Russia remained a hazardous one. Herzen and his acquaintances were under constant surveillance by the Russian secret police, or Third Section – and indeed one of Trübner's employees, a Pole named Michalowski, was later discovered to be in the pay of the Third Section.[34]

Anecdotal evidence about the means used to smuggle publications into Russia comes from an anonymous article (probably written by William Linton's wife, Lynn) which appeared in the *Saturday Review* on 27 June 1863. The article provides a vivid eyewitness account of the workings of the Press and thus is worth quoting at length. It begins:

> Not far from King's Cross Station, at the end of one of the blocks of building facing the Caledonian Road, stands a small house with a workshop attached to it, decorated with a doorplate bearing the words 'Volnaia Russkaya Tipografiya' written in Russian characters. With the exception of this strange inscription, there is nothing remarkable in its appearance, but it possesses considerable interest for those who are aware that it is the office of the 'Free Russian Press'.

It goes on:

> The presses which work [there] ... furnish little which is intended for home consumption. Their sheets are adapted for Russian eyes alone, and the rooms which they occupy are pervaded by so thoroughly Slavonic an air that a visitor might imagine he had suddenly been transported to Moscow or St Petersburg. Russian books occupy the shelves, Russian proof-sheets cover the tables, and Russian manuscripts are being set up by compositors whose speech is Russian or Polish.

Regarding distribution, the author speaks of the 'no small difficulty and no slight risk' to the bearers 'who carry this material across the Russian frontier', noting that:

> not long ago, a traveller was nearly compromised by the fact of his plaid jacket becoming unstitched and all but disclosing the sheets of the *Bell* with which it was stuffed ... At another time, an English lady, the wife of a Russian gentleman, was arrested at the frontier and discovered to be in possession of a

33 Cited in Partridge, p. 108. Again, for a more comprehensive discussion of Herzen's English contacts, see Partridge's *Alexander Herzen: Collected Studies.*

34 Herzen vents his disgust at Michalowski in his memoirs, describing him as 'a cringing, ugly, drunken, [but] efficient Pole ... [who] had every qualification for the calling of a spy'. (See *My Past and Thoughts*, vol. III, 1375).

> number of copies of the dreaded journal. But [happily] she boldly set at defiance the General before whom she was brought, calling upon him to point out the precise law by which the introduction of this particular newspaper was forbidden, and so puzzling him that he ended his doubts as to how he ought to deal with her by allowing her to continue her journey in peace.[35]

Despite the somewhat humorous pictures conjured up by these descriptions, carrying publications of the Free Russian Press into Russia was indeed a risky business. A number of couriers were arrested and imprisoned.

Between 1857 and 1865, the Press devoted itself to the publication of *Kolokol* and its two supplements, as well as printing a series of works by Herzen, among them his memoirs, *Byloe i dumy* [My Past and Thoughts]. Yet by the time of Herzen's move to Geneva in 1865, the popularity and influence of the Press had already begun to decline. The last issue of *Kolokol* appeared in July 1867 and Herzen himself was reaching the end of his life. He was to die, three years later, in 1870.

Herzen's legacy, however, was lasting and profound. In addition to the publications of the Free Russian Press itself, Herzen inspired a wave of Russian émigré publishers, among them members of his own staff, such as the Ukrainian Ahapii Honcharenko. A typesetter at the Free Russian Press and contributor to *Kolokol* (who worked for a while in the numismatics department of the British Museum), Honcharenko went on to establish the first Russian émigré press in America.[36]

In the last decades of the nineteenth century, figures such as Petr Lavrov, Sergei Stepniak and Feliks Volkhovsky were all actively printing in London. Stepniak – who arrived in London in 1884 having assassinated the notoriously brutal St Petersburg Chief of Police six years earlier – was particularly influential in increasing British understanding of and sympathy for the Russian revolutionary movement. (Indeed perhaps more so than any other Russian émigré of the time.) He and Volkovsky were closely associated with the Russian Free Press Fund, a group of émigrés who had established a Russian printing press and bookshop at premises at 15 Augustus Road, Hammersmith. Their principal publication, the periodical *Letuchie listki* [Leaflets], edited by Volkhovsky, first appeared in 1894. By 1900, it had run to forty-six issues. Also printing was Vladimir Burtsev, who was the first Russian to write a comprehensive description of the Russian collections of the British Museum Library, and who distinguished himself by being arrested in the

35 *Saturday Review*, 27 June 1863.

36 For further information on Ahapii Honcharenko, see S. Svatikov, *Agapii Goncharenko - osnovatel' russkoi pechati v Amerikie* (Paris, 1938).

Round Reading Room.[37] Outside London – at first in Maldon, Essex, and then in Christchurch, Hampshire – the Chertkovs were publishing the works of Tolstoy at their *Svobodnoe slovo* [Free Word] press.

Indeed the list of Russian émigré publications being produced in England at this time far belies the modest beginnings of Russian-language printing in Britain. In London alone, there were as many as twenty-four different periodical titles published in Russian between 1855 and 1905 – and the number of books and pamphlets published in the Russian language has yet to be calculated.[38]

Among the periodical publications was the output of a certain Russian Social Democratic Labour Party, which, between 1901 and 1905, printed seventeen issues of its journal, *Iskra* [The Spark] in London. Closely involved in this was a certain Vladimir Il'ich Ulianov, otherwise known as Lenin. But that is to embark on another story altogether.[39]

---

37 His arrest was at the request of the Russian government. For a fuller discussion of the arrest, see R. Henderson, 'Russian Political Emigrés & The British Museum Library', *Library History*, 9: 1- 2 (1991), 59-68.

38 For details of periodical publications, see Helen Williams, 'Russian-Language Periodical Publishing by the Radical Emigration 1855-1900', *Solanus*, N. S., 12 (1998), 12-33.

39 The author gratefully acknowledges the support of the British Academy, whose current funding of a Post-Doctoral Fellowship enabled her to work on preparing this article for publication.

Janet Zmroczek

Poetry and Polemics
the Polish book trade in London, 1836-67

When invited to participate in the seminar on foreign printing in London, I had no idea of the wealth of Polish material to be studied and the many fascinating themes which would emerge. Initially, I experienced some disappointment at how little material in Polish had been printed in London before the nineteenth century, especially given the well-documented cultural links between Poland and Great Britain from the sixteenth century onwards.[1] To date, I have found only two examples of Polish texts in London imprints prior to 1836, the date of the first Polish book printed in London, a London *Oratio dominica* (a polyglot collection of texts of the Lord's Prayer) printed by D. Brown and W. Keblewhite in 1700 and a few examples in John Bowring's *Specimens of the Polish Poets* printed in London in 1827 by Richard Taylor. However, it soon became clear that the history of Polish printing in London in the nineteenth century would provide ample material, the emerging picture of Polish society in London at that time becoming ever more intriguing. Who were these Poles? Why were they here? Why did they feel driven to commit their words and those of their community to print, often at the expense not only of everyday comforts but also their health and all their meagre funds? My interest in these questions has led me to embark upon a long-term research project on Polish printing, publishing and bookselling in nineteenth-century England – this article should be viewed as a brief overview of my research so far. Rather than attempting a general survey of the output of Polish printers in nineteenth-century London, which for the non-specialist might appear as a

1 See, for example, Urszula Szumska, *Anglia a Polska w epoce humanizmu i reformacji* (Lwów, 1938); Edward Mierzwa, *Anglia a Polska w pierwszej połowie XVII w.* (Warszawa, 1986); Zofia Libiszowska, *Życie polskie w Londynie w XVIII wieku* (Warszawa, 1972); Aniela Kowalska, *Echa ciągłe żywe: o kulturze i sprawie polskiej w Anglii przed i po powstaniu listopadowym* (Warszawa, 1982); Jan Dąbrowski, *Polacy w Anglii i o Anglii* (Kraków, 1962); Stanisław Kot, *Anglo-polonica: angielskie źródła rękopiśmienne do dziejów stosunków kulturalnych Polski z Anglją* (Warszawa, 1935).

frustrating list of unfamiliar names, incomprehensible titles and obscure political parties, I have chosen to limit myself to a brief introduction to the lives and work of three individuals: Jan Marcin Bansemer (1802-40), Aleksander Radwan Rypiński (1811/12-86) and Bartłomiej Beniowski (c. 1800-67).

Polish life in nineteenth-century London

Since the Second World War London has been considered a major centre of Polish émigré life and publishing, but few people are aware that this was the continuation of a tradition established in the nineteenth century. Following the Third Partition in 1795, Poland ceased to exist as a unified sovereign state, her lands divided between Russia, Prussia and Austria.[2] The unsuccessful uprising in Warsaw against Russian rule in November 1830 and further insurrections in 1831 led to the exodus of about 8,000 educated Poles, known as the Great Emigration.[3] The destination of the greatest number, about 3,500, was France, which soon became the epicentre of Polish émigré politics and culture. However, around 700 Poles found their way to Britain. In the period 1831-57, there were estimated to be about 2,700 Poles in Great Britain of whom about 1,000 became permanent residents,[4] the remainder either returning to Europe or leaving for the Americas. The majority of the first wave of Polish émigrés to Britain were political exiles, but later economic migrants predominated. The census of 1871 recorded 4,229 Poles living in London,[5] many of whom were Jewish economic migrants employed in the East End. How were the needs of the Polish community for reading matter in their own language met? Certainly Poles took advantage of the library facilities which were available to them. Some sample searches through the records of admissions to the British Museum Reading Room in the period 1820-79, carried out as part of another research project,[6] show a steady stream of Polish readers applying for tickets, amongst them many famous names.

2 For more information in English see: Jerzy Lukowski, *The Partitions of Poland* (London, 1999); Jerzy Lukowski and Hubert Zawadzki, *A Concise History of Poland* (Cambridge, 2001).

3 Stanisław Kalembka, *Wielka emigracja* (Warszawa, 1971), p. 58.

4 Tadeusz Radzik, 'Działalność oświatowa emigracji polskiej w Wielkiej Brytanii w latach 1852-1939', *Przegląd historyczno-oświatowy*, 27: 1 (103) (styczeń-marzec 1984), 163-82.

5 Ibid., p. 173.

6 Janet Zmroczek, 'A National Library for the Poles in Exile: the development of the Polish Collections of the British Museum Library in the nineteenth century', *Solanus*, N.S. 15 (2001), 17-34.

The importance of the British Museum in the intellectual nourishment of the Polish refugees is also noted elsewhere, such as in the *Report of the Seventh Annual General Meeting of the Literary Association of the Friends of Poland* (London, 1839) in which thanks are recorded 'to Sir Henry Ellis, A. Panizzi Esq ... of the British Museum, for facilities continued to be afforded to the Refugees in the prosecution of their studies and researches in that establishment' (p. 31). During the early part of this period, the Polish collections of the British Museum were not large, consisting mainly of items which had come into the Library as part of the foundation collections, and an additional bequest of eighty books on Polish affairs and Polish literary classics donated by Prince Adam Jerzy Czartoryski in 1832. Collecting of Polish material really took off only in the late 1840s, under the stewardship of Antonio Panizzi and his able assistant Thomas Watts working with the bookseller Adolphus Asher. In addition, references have been found in memoirs to small libraries being available for the use of the émigrés in various clubs and societies. Nonetheless, there was clearly enough demand, both in London and on the Continent and back in Poland itself, for a sizeable group of Polish émigrés to undertake to publish in London material both in Polish and in English in support of the Polish cause. So far, I have identified about thirty Poles engaged in printing, publishing and bookselling in nineteenth-century London. One should note, however, that the first Polish-language titles published in the United Kingdom in the nineteenth century were actually printed in Portsmouth, where, in 1834, 212 displaced Polish soldiers, mainly simple peasants and NCOs, had arrived and settled. By the following year, Polish-language publications were being published in Portsmouth by the socialist organisation the Grudzią Commune.[7] Other important Polish émigré publishing centres were to be found in Jersey, Edinburgh and Glasgow.

There is no complete listing of the output of nineteenth-century Polish printers and publishers in the United Kingdom. The British Library has only a part of their output: some of the printers clearly abided by the legal deposit regulations and deposited a copy of their publications at the British Museum; others did not, probably because the Polish Library in Paris functioned as a Polish national library in exile and therefore, for many Polish émigré printers, would have had first call on their publications. A union catalogue of nineteenth-century UK Polish imprints is clearly called for: none of the major Polish libraries appear to have substantial collections of this material, though

7 For more information see Peter Brock, 'Polish Democrats and English Radicals 1832-1862', *Journal of Modern History*, 25 (1953), 139-56.

they hold titles which are not in the British Library collections; access to the catalogue of the Polish Library in Paris is, at the time of writing, problematic but one might expect its holdings to be the most comprehensive.

A listing by the bibliographer Stanisław Zieliński published in 1935 contains twenty-eight Polish periodical titles published in the United Kingdom in the nineteenth century of which all but four were published in London.[8] Most were short-lived, surviving for only a few issues before folding, usually owing to lack of funds. So far, about seventy-five books and pamphlets printed in Polish in London have been identified in the British Library collections and about twelve more elsewhere, but considerably more are probably waiting to be discovered in collections not yet explored.

Three case studies: Bansemer, Rypiński and Beniowski

A series of brief case studies seems the most appropriate method to give a flavour of the diversity of early Polish publishing in London. The individuals selected for consideration represent different political views, Bansemer being associated with the conservative Czartoryski camp, Rypiński steering a middle path and Beniowski representing anarchist tendencies, but they are also bound together by certain common themes: they all played an active part in the 1830-1 Uprising, but having been forced to leave their country, did not confine themselves to narrow émigré circles; each, in his own way, found a role in British society. They were all interested in language and its codification, as befitted educated Central Europeans of their generation, a normalised national language being considered one of the pre-requisites of nationhood in its nineteenth-century sense. The subject was of particular interest to Bansemer, Rypiński and Beniowski because they were all from the eastern lands of what is now Belarus, an area of complex, shifting, cultural identities, a melting pot of Polish, Belarusian, Lithuanian, Ukrainian and Russian. All three represent the earlier phase of Polish émigré printing in London which is characterised by a wide variety of output including imaginative literature and memoirs, whereas in the later part of the nineteenth century the publications of the Polish émigrés were more exclusively political.

Jan Marcin Bansemer was the publisher of the first Polish book printed in London in 1836.[9] Born in 1802, he was a graduate of Warsaw University. After the failure of the 1830 Uprising, he distinguished himself as a

8 Stanisław Zieliński, *Bibliografia czasopism polskich zagranicą 1830-1934* (Warszawa, 1935).

9 See *Słownik pracowników książki polskiej* (Warszawa, 1972), p. 31; *Polski słownik biograficzny* (Kraków, 1935), I, 266.

benefactor of dispossessed Polish soldiers in Prussia and set up an émigré academic centre in Leipzig. It was here that he began his publishing career before moving to London.

In 1832, influential English supporters of Poland including the poet Thomas Campbell and the MP Lord Dudley Stuart (1803-54) founded the Literary Association of the Friends of Poland, based at 10 Duke St, St James's.[10] In 1834, the Association appointed Bansemer as an adviser on the distribution of funds to needy Poles. That year, a bill introduced in Parliament by Lord Dudley Stuart, and carried unanimously, had allowed for the setting aside by the government of £10,000 as a relief fund for Polish refugees, who at that time numbered about 460.[11] Similar sums were voted annually until 1850, though, as the number of émigrés in need of financial assistance grew, the relief fund was increasingly inadequate to meet their needs. Bansemer, having gained respect in London intellectual circles, soon occupied himself again with publishing. In 1836, using his own imported Polish types, he published the first Polish language book printed in London, Antoni Malczewski's *Marja: powésć ukraińska* (*Maria: a Ukrainian tale*), at the printing works of Thomas Russell Drury at Johnson's Court off Fleet St (fig. 1). Why did Bansemer choose this work, first published by Malczewski in Warsaw in 1825? *Maria* was the first Polish verse novel, heavily influenced by Scott and Byron.[12] The Polish poet and Nobel laureate Czesław Miłosz described it thus: ' … its place in Polish literature is exceptionally high. It is written in a verse which is still classical and that contrasts with its content which is pervaded by moods of nostalgia and gloom … The plot is based on a real event of the eighteenth century: Count Potocki, a Polish aristocrat residing in Ukraine, enraged by his son's marriage to Gertruda Komorowska, of noble, but not aristocratic parentage, had the girl drowned in a pond. Malczewski moved the action back to the seventeenth century when the Ukraine was constantly harrassed by Tartar raids.'[13] Its themes of love, loss and sentimental attachment to the 'kresy' (the Ukrainian, Belarusian and Lithuanian lands of the historic commonwealth of Poland-Lithuania) were

10 For more information see the recently published monograph about Stuart: Krzysztof Marchlewicz, *Polonofil doskonały: propolska działalność charatatywna i polityczna lorda Dudleya Couttsa Stuarta* (1803-1854) (Poznań, 2001); *Dictionary of National Biography*, LV (London, 1898), 76-7.

11 Ludwik Zieliński, *Emigracja polska w Anglii w latach 1831-46* (Gdańsk, 1964), p. 129, n. 52.

12 See article on Antoni Malczewski (1793-1826) in *Literatura polska: przewodnik encyklopedyczny*, I (Warszawa, 1984), 629.

13 Czesław Miłosz, *The History of Polish Literature*, 2nd edn (Berkeley, 1983), p. 248.

issues very much alive for the Polish exiles in London and Paris at the time of printing. It was 'printed according to a new orthography based on the Czech' (according to the title-page), further evidence of Bansemer's interest in the codification of Slavonic languages. The book is dedicated to Klaudyna Potocka[14] to whom Bansemer writes 'I am indebted for the idea of printing this work, conceived in another country, and printed in England with the first Polish type'. Potocka, daughter of one of Poland's most prominent families, the Działyńskis, and a leading patriotic philanthropist in emigration, had worked closely with Bansemer in distributing material aid to displaced Polish soldiers in Prussia.

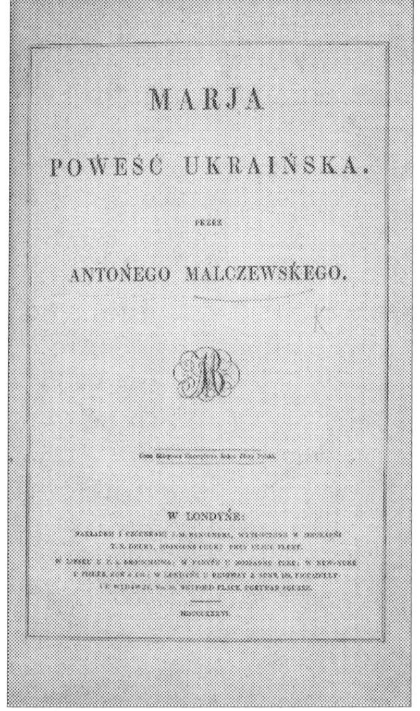

MARJA

POWEŚĆ UKRAIŃSKA.

ANTOŃEGO MALCZEWSḰEGO.

Antoni Malczewski, *Marja: poweść ukraińska* [Maria: a Ukrainian tale] (London: at the printing works of Thomas Russell Drury at Johnson's Court off Fleet St, 1836), title-page.
British Library pressmark: 1163.c.21.

Most Polish printers produced material both in Polish and in English. One can assume that their motivation was twofold. First, the Polish readership in Britain was too small to guarantee even short-term economic survival. Many of the books and periodicals they published did find their way abroad, but they had to publish in English also to ensure a more reliable income. Second, there was support for the cause of Poland amongst a wide

14 See article on Potocka in *Polski słownik biograficzny*, XXVII (Kraków, 1983), 743-4.

cross-section of English society, from aristocrats to working people, and it was natural that Polish patriots in exile should seek to inform and influence this audience too. In addition, Polish printers were heavily involved with the establishment of Herzen's Free Russian Press in London, studied by Kate Sealey Rahman in this volume.

Bansemer was no exception, his other contribution to the development of émigré publishing being his 1837 *Atlas Containing Ten Maps of Poland exhibiting the political changes that country has experienced during the last sixty years from 1772 to the present time*. He edited the *Atlas* with Piotr Falkenhagen-Zaleski, another Polish refugee.[15] It was published by James Wyld, Geographer to the King, and also printed by T. R. Drury, in 150 copies. The *Atlas* was dedicated to 'the Literary Association of the Friends of Poland in Testimony of High Esteem and Gratitude for its zeal and exertion in favour of the cause of Poland'. As well as the maps showing the partitions, adjacent countries and their religions and languages, it included a 'geographical, historical, political, chronological, literary and commercial table'. The only extant copy so far located in the UK is held by the Royal Geographical Society, though others are to be found at the Biblioteka Narodowa in Warsaw and at the Library of Congress in Washington DC. Bansemer was never to return to his native land, dying from tuberculosis in London in September 1840, aged 38.

The next short case study is devoted to Aleksander Radwan Rypiński, who arrived in London in 1846 with the intention of learning English (fig. 2).[16] Born around 1812 in what is now Belarus, Rypiński became a devoted collector of Polish, Ukrainian, Belarusian and Russian folk-songs. As well as writing his own poetry, in 1827 he translated Pushkin's *Rusalka* into Polish, one of the earliest translations of Pushkin into any language. He took part in the 1831 Insurrection in Lithuania and, after its collapse, made his way to France. He settled in Paris, where he took an active part in émigré cultural and political life, moving in circles close to the Polish national bard Adam Mickiewicz, with whom he shared his Romantic attachment to Lithuania and Belarus. In 1840, in Paris, Rypiński published his own work *Białoruś* (the Polish form of Belarus). A translation of its subtitle reads (most contentiously to the modern ear): 'a few words about the poetry of the simple people of this Polish province, their music, song and dance'. Once in London, unlike most of his fellow Polish printers and publishers, who congregated in central areas around Bloomsbury such as Judd St, Burton Crescent (now Cartwright

15 See article on Falkenhagen-Zaleski in *Polski słownik biograficzny* (Kraków, 1948), VI, 358.

16 See Franciszek German, 'Aleksander Rypiński', *Etnografia Polska*, 6 (1962), 267-80.

Fig. 2: Portrait of Aleksander Rypiński, from his *Three short Polish poems on the last war with Russia* (London, 1856). British Library pressmark: 11585.a.37.

Gardens), Thanet St and Grafton Place (next to the present Euston Station) or slightly further afield in Westminster, Covent Garden and the Strand, Rypiński settled in Tottenham, to the North East of London. In the mid-nineteenth century, Tottenham was still a green and leafy village, the site of a number of schools to which Londoners sent their sons to partake of the clean and healthy air.[17] Polish émigrés, it would seem, were well suited to teaching, themselves well educated and multi-lingual. In Tottenham alone there was a small community of Polish teachers: a Mr Przyjemski (known to his pupils as Shem as presumably his real name was too perplexing!) taught French and German at Grove House School. In the 1840s, the progressive Bruce Castle School, run by the father of Rowland Hill, the inventor of the postage stamp, employed at least two Poles: Father Stanisław Poncyan Brzeziński, the first Chaplain of the Polish community in London, and a certain Karol Jaworski, who taught languages and history.[18] A search in the British Library catalogue for more information about these characters yielded only one entry. This was *A Sermon, Preached by the Rev. S. P. Brzezinski…, on the 29th November, 1846, the Sixteenth Anniversary of the Polish Revolution*, printed in London by Eugene Detkens, another Polish printer, in 1847, but destroyed by bombing during the Second World War. However this disappointment was soon allayed by the discovery, when consulting an outwardly uninspiring tract volume for an example of the work of a Westminster-based Polish pamphlet printer Stanisław Milewski, that the

17 See Guy Picarda, 'Polish and Byelorussian émigrés in old Tottenham' (1964). Unpublished paper, held at Bruce Castle Museum, Lordship Lane, London N17.

18 Ibid. p. 2.

volume was, in fact, Brzeziński's own, including an index written in his own hand.[19]

By 1849, three years after his arrival in England, Rypiński had joined this band of expatriate teachers and had found a position at Eagle House School in Tottenham. In 1851, he is recorded as 'occupying a small cottage at 3 Chancers Row with Stanisław Rutkowski' and is described as a 'batchelor [sic], lieutenant of the Polish Army, now artist, painter, Professor of French, German and Drawing'.[20] Once established in England, Rypiński returned to printing and publishing. The Poznań monthly *Przegląd Poznański* in 1852 carried an article which began as follows:

> Perhaps the finest but least known contribution of Polish émigrés is the work at which they unceasingly and modestly toil, denying themselves even a crust, not for show or to better their own fate but for the benefit of their far off homeland. An admirable example of such devotion reaches us now from England. Two émigrés have established there a modest printing house in which they serve as typesetters, publishers, and even authors of the books they print...[21]

These 'two émigrés' were in fact Rypiński and his fellow Pole Ignacy Jackowski and the 'modest printing house' the Drukarnia Polska (Polish Printing Press) which they established in Tottenham in 1852. A preliminary review of Rypiński's publications has been facilitated by the fact that of all the Polish printers in London he seems to have been the most enthusiastic about depositing his publications at the British Museum. Twenty-five titles from his press have so far been identified in the British Library collections, on a wide range of subjects including contemporary history and events, poetry and memoirs (including his own and Jackowski's works) and political tracts, all of which came into the collections by legal deposit. He printed publications reflecting the entire émigré political spectrum, from early issues of the *Demokrata Polski*, the organ of the Polish Democratic Society to the publications of the pro-Czartoryski Literary Association of the Friends of Poland. He often illustrated his books with his own drawings and lithographs and was an early exponent of the use of photography as illustration. A search at the National Library in Warsaw yielded a copy of his *Catalogue nr 1* from around 1853 which shows that he also ran a bookshop from his premises at 5 Grove Place, Tottenham, selling émigré books and journals from other

19 British Library shelfmark 9475.c.32.

20 The collection at Bruce Castle contains a prize certificate drawn by Rypiński for one of his pupils, a Master E. Thorn who won second prize for pencil landscape drawing in 1850.

21 See 'Książki Drukarni Polskiej w Londynie', *Przegląd Poznański*, 15 (1852), 370-2.

publishing houses as well as his own. When Jackowski left the business in 1855, Rypiński continued alone until 1857. In a letter to a friend he describes the hardship of his life in London, working as 'an author, compositor, corrector, editor, printer, binder and even bookseller – all this in addition to my duties as a teacher. It was all too much for me alone and thank God that it didn't do for me altogether, though it certainly exhausted all my funds.'[22] He consequently sold his printing press to Zenon Świętosławski (1811-75), a Polish émigré writer, socialist activist and printer, based first in Jersey and later in London at 52 Greek St and then 178/9 High Holborn where he set up his Universal Printing Establishment. Rypiński's old equipment was probably amongst that used by Świętosławski to publish the works of the Free Russian Press under the Trübner trademark.[23] In 1859 Rypiński returned to his estates in the Vitebsk region (now Belarus) following an amnesty, to pursue his literary and ethnographical interests until his death in 1886.

But for whom were all these sacrifices made? Who read these books apart from the Polish émigrés in Britain? They were certainly distributed in other European centres of the emigration such as Paris, Brussels and Leipzig. Many publications contain names and addresses of booksellers in these cities from whom they could be obtained. Despite varying levels of censorship and control on the import of books and periodicals in the three Partitions, many of the books also found their way to Poles at home, where they were enthusiastically received, as proven by the article in *Przegląd Poznański* quoted earlier.[24]

The final brief case study is of a figure little concerned with the Polish market at home or in emigration, but who merits inclusion as a publisher in English and for his work on the mechanisation of printing. Bartłomiej Beniowski was born around 1800 to a wealthy Jewish family in the Grodno region (now Western Belarus) and studied medicine at the University of Wilno.[25] After participating in the 1830 Uprising he emigrated to France,

22 See letter from Rypiński to Plug (Pietkiewicz) in *Księga pamiątkowa A. Mickiewicza*, I (Warszawa, 1899), 255-7.

23 See *Słownik pracowników książki polskiej* (Warszawa, 1972), p. 844; Kate Sealey Rahman, 'Russian Revolutionaries in London, 1853-70: Alexander Herzen and the Free Russian Press' in this volume.

24 For more information about the reception of émigré works in partitioned Poland see also Alina Barszczewska-Krupa, 'Z badań nad cenzurą państw zaborczych wobec nielegalnej literatury emigracyjnej w kraju, 1831-1863', *Rocznik Łodzki*, 21 (24) (1976), 171-86; Alina Barszczewska, 'Z badań nad rozpowszechnianiem nielegalnej literatury emigracyjnej w kraju, 1832-62 (pośrednictwo firm kupeckich)', *Acta Universitatis Lodziensis. Zeszyty Naukowe Nauki Humanistyczno-Społeczne*, Ser.1, zesz. 18 (1978), 31-41.

25 See *Polski słownik biograficzny* (Kraków, 1935), I, 429.

already at the rank of Major in the Polish Army. He hoped to be accepted into the School of the General Staff in France, but meeting with rejection, found his way to England, probably arriving for the first time in 1836. Indeed, the British Museum Register of Admissions to the Reading Room lists Beniowski as having received a reader's ticket for the first time on 29 April 1836 and gives his address as 57 Newman St.[26] He soon began to participate in English politics and became involved with the most radical leaders of the Chartist movement,[27] encouraging Polish radical émigrés to identify themselves more closely with the struggles of the English working classes. Beniowski himself was elected Chairman of the East London Democratic Association and had close links with the London Working Men's Association.[28] In Polish circles, he became one of the most aggressive opponents of the conservative Czartoryski faction and its supporters. On 30 November 1838, a meeting had been planned to commemorate the 1830 Uprising. The meeting, attended by both liberals and democrats, commenced at 1.00 in the afternoon with Lord Dudley Stuart presiding. Contemporary reports suggest that Beniowski seized the platform and, greeted by the cries of a group of Chartists accompanying him, protested against the meeting being held during ordinary working people's working hours and in general against the political and social status quo. For some twenty minutes attempts were made to remove Beniowski from the platform and in the ensuing struggle Lord Dudley Stuart was nearly sent flying from his chair![29] He thus earned the reputation, according to the contemporary émigré press, of a man whose name was inseparable from every political row and disturbance. In 1839 Beniowski became a regular contributor to the Chartist newspaper, the *London Democrat*, writing columns entitled 'The Polish Revolution' in which he showed himself to be a staunch advocate of Jewish emancipation and 'On military science'. The latter began with the following paragraph:

> The military science is simply that which teaches you how to maim and kill as many of your opponents as possible and also how to protect yourself against a similar propensity of your opponents. If those who reduced this 'glorious' wholesale murder to rules had no end in view but to gratify the beastly passions of the few, they were abominable monsters ... but if their intention was the defence of the enslaved, the oppressed and starving millions, to curb

26 British Museum Archives: *Admissions to the Reading Room.*

27 See, for example, James Epstein, *Lion of Freedom: Feargus O'Connor and the Chartist movement 1832-1842* (London, 1983), pp. 182-207; David Goodway, *London Chartism 1838-1848* (Cambridge, 1982), p. 34.

28 Peter Brock, *Z dziejów Wielkiej Emigracji w Anglii* (Warszawa, 1958), p. 23.

29 For a fuller description of this incident see Krzysztof Marchlewicz (as in note 10), pp. 190-3; Ludwik Zieliński (as in note 11), pp. 75-6.

> ambition or to oppose the claims of incomprehensible rights, mankind ought to erect altars to their memory...[30]

Beniowski did not intend to confine himself to mere theorising: when the split between the pacifist and militant sections of the Chartist movement became manifest, he sided with the 'physical force group'. He appears to have taken an active part in the Newport Rebellion of November 1839. Some 7,000 coalminers and ironworkers marched on Newport at the beginning of what was to have been a rising in the Welsh Valleys to capture key towns and establish a republic. Letters and reports in police files suggest that Beniowski acted as a military adviser, helping to drill and arm the militant Welsh workers, and had been charged with taking command in the Welsh mountains if the rebellion had taken hold.[31] Contemporary letters and reports also link him to later plans to plant bombs and to raise fires in London in January 1840.[32] Needless to say, knowledge of these activities did not leave him in good favour with the government nor the Literary Association of the Friends of Poland, charged with distributing funds to needy Poles. He was no stranger to the Police – the first reference found to his physical appearance is in a Home Office Police report, which describes him as 'tall, well-looking, slim'.[33] The issue of the *London Democrat* for Saturday 8 June 1839 (p. 68) carried the following announcement:

> We have this moment learned that Major Beniowski has been refused the government allowance (£40 per year) as a Polish exile for writing in the *London Democrat* and taking part in the Chartist movement. He is, this moment, without any means of subsistence whatsoever.

The need to earn a better living was probably one of the reasons why he turned to publishing and teaching, propagating his ideas on orthography, 'phrenotypics' (a system of mnemonics), and the mechanisation of printing. As previously explained, all three printers chosen as case studies were interested in orthography, as befitted educated Slavs of their time. Beniowski, however, took a different angle, proposing not reform of the Polish system of spelling, but the English! In 1844 he published *The Anti-Absurd or Phrenotypic Alphabet and Orthography for the English Language*, in which he declares 'the English spelling book an abominable absurdity ... a most tyranically ridiculous nonsense' (pp. 1, 9) (fig. 3). High levels of illiteracy were the logical result of English spelling rules which thus 'retard and often stop the progress

30 *London Democrat*, Sat. 27 April 1839, p. 21.

31 David V. Jones, *The Last Uprising: the Newport insurrection of 1839* (London, 1985), p. 99.

32 Goodway (as in note 27), p. 34.

33 H.O. 40/44, police report of 13 May 1839.

of beneficial improvements – social, moral, religious and political … But all is not lost Britons, alter your alphabet, alter your orthography, make your language easy, speak to the world, be intelligible, and you shall conquer and liberate nations without bloodshed and you will gain friends without expense.' He styled himself: 'Major Beniowski, the Author of the system of artificial memory designated phrenotypics' (title-page). Pseudo-scientific systems of memory-enhancement were popular at the time and Beniowski was certainly competing with others, and not averse to making exaggerated claims. In his *Phrenotypics*, published in 1842, which laid down the principles of his system, he claimed that 'to know nothing of a real language in the morning and be master of all its words used in common conversation (about 1,000), before the clock strikes midday, is with phrenotypers a matter of amusement'.[34] The title-page stated that 'these feats of memory, with specimens of phrenotypically acquired knowledge may be witnessed and scrutinized at the Royal Adelaide Gallery, Lowther Arcade, Strand every Friday at ¼ past 9 and every

ii

Shape.	*Represents the initial sound of the word spelt* — *Absurdly*	*Anti-absurdly*
a	ape . .	ap
ʌ	apple .	ʌpl
ʌ́	arm . .	ʌ́rm
b	babe . .	bab
ch	chamber	chamber
d	dog . .	dog
ɐ	eel . .	ɐl
e	egg . .	eg
f	face . .	fas

iii

Shape	*Represents the initial sound of the word spelt* — *Absurdly*	*Anti-absurdly*
g	gig . .	gig
h	hat . .	hʌt
y	eyes . .	yz
i	ink . .	ink
j	jar . .	jʌ́r
k	cat . .	kʌt
l	lamb .	lʌm
m	man .	mʌn
n	napkin	nʌpkin

Fig.3: Bartłomiej Beniowski, *The anti-absurd or phrenotypic alphabet* (London, 1844), pp. ii-iii.
British Library pressmark: 12985.aa.17.

34 Bartłomiej Beniowski, *Phrenotypics: a detailed description* … (London, 1842), p. 2.

Saturday afternoon at 3.' Advertisements appeared on the back of many of his publications, for example 'Classes for Gentleman and Ladies are continually forming at the Author's Residence, 8 Bow St, Covent Garden at half a guinea the course (three lessons) embracing the phrenotypical principles and their application to languages, sciences and arts. Classes for working men 5 shillings the course.' Not only did he publish all his own works on orthography and phrenotypics, but also found time to publish works for the blind in a Braille-like format such as his *Catechism of the Church of England for the Blind in Major Beniowski's or Phrenotypic Orthography* (London, [c. 1850]) and later turned his mind to the mechanisation of printing, based on a logotype system. His 1854 *Improvements in Printing* includes an illustration of his 'authoriton' or automatic composing apparatus and his design for a printing machine. His own books usually give as the printer either Thomas Hatton, Phrenotypic Printing Office, 14 Hart St, Covent Garden or William Read, 16 Hart St. These printers were his near neighbours, Hart St running perpendicular to Bow St.

Beniowski died in London on 29 March 1867 from heart disease, aged sixty-seven. He remained enigmatic to the last: his obituaries are somewhat at odds with each other. *The Times* stated the bald facts and declared him 'valued and respected by all who knew him'.[35] The Polish émigré newspaper, *Głos wolny* (*Free Voice*), was less reserved, stating that 'the anarchism of his behaviour made it impossible for him to cooperate with anyone and made him universally unpopular'.[36] There are suggestions that he renounced his radical beliefs and participated in conservative émigré circles. Rumours circulated throughout his life that he was really a Russian spy. There is clearly still much work to be done on unravelling fact from myth in the life of the redoubtable Major Beniowski!

I hope to have succeeded in persuading the general reader, with little knowledge of Poland or the Polish language, that the history of nineteenth-century Polish printers in London is of interest. My own interest in printing and printers is not a technical one: rather, I approach printing from the point of view of people and their commitment to the transmission of ideas. These nineteenth-century asylum-seekers, while maintaining close links with their own culture and language, each in different ways, made their mark in Britain. Thanks to their commitment to printing and publishing, they have left behind all the pieces of a complex jigsaw of the world they inhabited. It remains for me and other interested researchers to track down all these pieces, and eventually to put them all together.

---

35 *The Times*, Tuesday 2 Apr. 1867.

36 *Głos wolny*, 136 (20 Apr. 1867), 550.

Bridget Guzner

The Beginnings of Hungarian Printing in London

Cultural contacts between Hungary and England go back to the second half of the sixteenth century, a time when visitors' interests and preoccupations already varied considerably. As Protestant clergymen or theologians, Hungarians studied in Wittenberg and Heidelberg and arrived in England via Leiden. Their peregrinations included London, Oxford, and Cambridge, either visiting for shorter periods or more extensively, taking degrees. As a result of their endeavours, on their return to Hungary, a number of significant religious works were translated into Hungarian. Hungarian authors were published in England from as early as 1593, but the contribution of Hungarian visitors to English culture until the nineteenth century was very small indeed.[1]

It was the author, linguist and diplomat Sir John Bowring (1792-1872) who first devoted much time to the study of the languages and literatures of Eastern Europe. Having been to Hungary and learned Hungarian to a reasonable standard, he became the first English translator of Hungarian poetry. His *Poetry of the Magyars* (London, 1830) played an important role in arousing interest in Hungarian culture and making it accessible to Victorian England. An informed essay on the Magyar language and Magyar literature introduced an anthology of some 100 poems and 65 popular songs. Although his translations were often inexact, at times even misleading, Bowring's anthology saved Hungarian poetry from sinking into oblivion. Ferenc Kazinczy and Ferenc Kölcsey's poetry received laudatory reviews, as did Dániel Berzsenyi's for his delightful use of classical metre. Hungarian authors for the first time realised they were not only addressing their own countrymen, but foreign audiences beyond their own borders. By the mid-nineteenth century English booksellers were flooded with pamphlets and books written about the 1848-9 revolution and its Hungarian leader Lajos

1 Szegedi Kis István, *Tabulae Analiticae*... (Schaffhausen, 1592; 2nd edn London, 1593).

Kossuth. In the presence of a growing émigré readership there was an increasing need for a Hungarian grammar, to assist those interested in the study of the language. Two such works were published almost simultaneously in mid-nineteenth-century London.

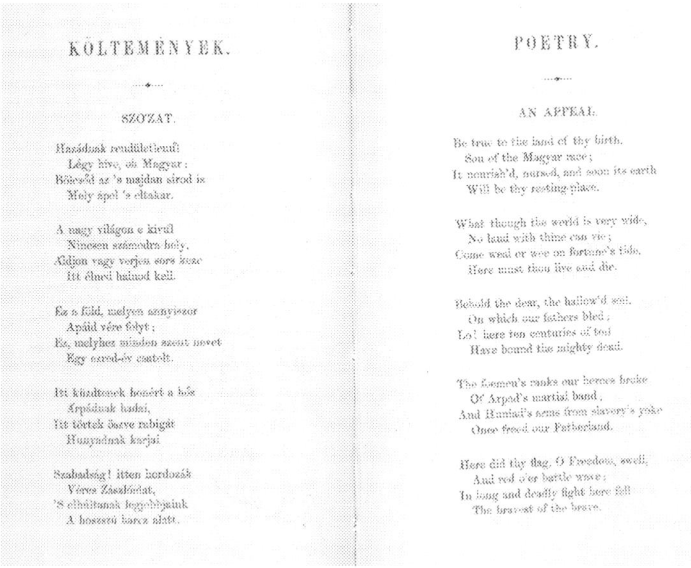

KÖLTEMÉNYEK.

SZÓZAT.

Hazádnak rendületlenül
Légy híve, oh Magyar:
Bölcsőd az 's majdan sírod is
Mely ápol 's eltakar.

A nagy világon e kivül
Nincsen számodra hely,
Áldjon vagy verjen sors keze
Itt élned halnod kell.

Ez a föld, melyen annyiszor
Apáid vére folyt;
Ez, melyhez minden szent nevet
Egy ezred-év csatolt.

Itt küzdtenek honért a hős
Árpádnak hadai,
Itt törtek össze rabigát
Hunyadnak karjai.

Szabadság! itten hordozák
Véres Zászlóidat,
'S elhúltanak legjobbjaink
A hosszú harcz alatt.

POETRY.

AN APPEAL.

Be true to the land of thy birth,
Son of the Magyar race;
It nourish'd, nursed, and soon its earth
Will be thy resting-place.

What though the world is very wide,
No land with thine can vie;
Come weal or woe on fortune's tide,
Here must thou live and die.

Behold the dear, the hallow'd soil,
On which our fathers bled;
Lo! here ten centuries of toil
Have bound the mighty dead.

The foemen's ranks our heroes broke
Of Arpad's martial band,
And Huniad's arms from slavery's yoke
Once freed our Fatherland.

Here did thy flag, O Freedom, swell,
And red o'er battle wave;
In long and deadly fight here fell
The bravest of the brave.

Fig. 1: Sigismund Wékey, *Grammar of the Hungarian language with appropriate exercises, a copious vocabulary, and specimens of Hungarian poetry* (London: Trelawny Saunders; New York: John Wiley, 1852), pp. 124-5. British Library pressmark: 12962.f.12.

The first was written by Sigismund Wékey, a lawyer and officer in the Hungarian army, who later emigrated to England and became secretary to the committee of Hungarians in exile.[2] His *Grammar of the Hungarian Language with appropriate exercises, a copious vocabulary, and specimens of Hungarian poetry* was published by Trelawny Saunders of Charing Cross and John Wiley of New York in 1852 (BL 12962.f.12) (fig. 1). From a glance at the short preface Wékey strikes the reader less as a linguist and more as a patriot, hoping 'to convey to those interested in Hungary a clearer idea of the real character of its oppressed people'. He then gives a traditional outline of Hungarian grammar, starting with the alphabet followed by examples, in Hungarian and English, of

2 Szinnyei's *Magyar írók élete és munkái*, XIV, 1055-6, gives further details of Wékey's life and works.

the phonetic characteristics and morphological structure of Hungarian. After sketchy notes on syntax there follow remarks on orthography and a list of Latin grammatical terms with their amusingly dusty Hungarian translation. Progressive reading exercises on parts of the body, human life, the earth and the air, followed by anecdotes, fables and letters include some stilted prose but the vocabulary reassures today's reader that Hungarian has always been a rich enough language to render the use of foreign loan words unnecessary. The inclusion of an extensive list of military expressions could be justified by the political events preceding this publication. The volume ends with an announcement of a related publication in preparation: *A Complete Hungarian-English and English-Hungarian Dictionary*. Regrettably this did not materialise.

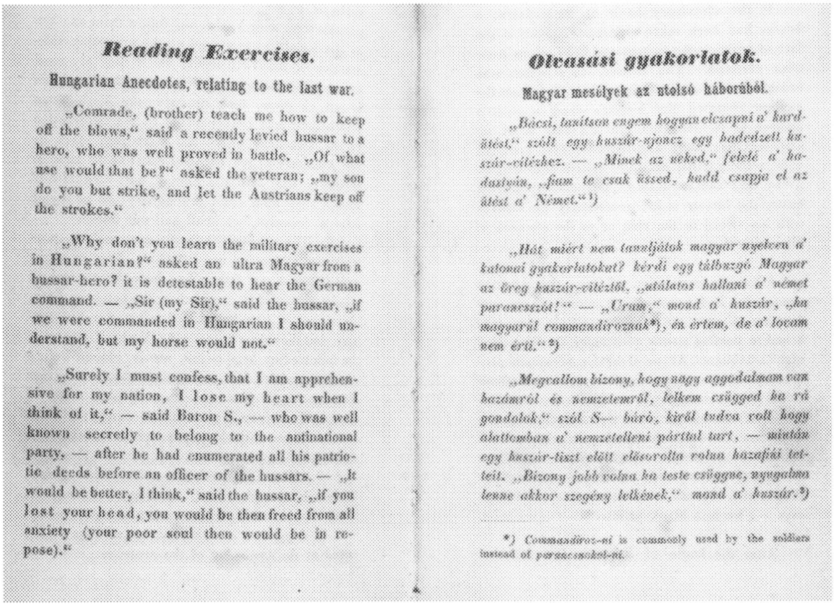

Reading Exercises.

Hungarian Anecdotes, relating to the last war.

„Comrade, (brother) teach me how to keep off the blows," said a recently levied hussar to a hero, who was well proved in battle. „Of what use would that be?" asked the veteran; „my son do you but strike, and let the Austrians keep off the strokes."

„Why don't you learn the military exercises in Hungarian?" asked an ultra Magyar from a hussar-hero? it is detestable to hear the German command. — „Sir (my Sir)," said the hussar, „if we were commanded in Hungarian I should understand, but my horse would not."

„Surely I must confess, that I am apprehensive for my nation, I lose my heart when I think of it," — said Baron S., — who was well known secretly to belong to the antinational party, — after he had enumerated all his patriotic deeds before an officer of the hussars. — „It would be better, I think," said the hussar, „if you lost your head, you would be then freed from all anxiety (your poor soul then would be in repose)."

Olvasási gyakorlatok.

Magyar mesélyek az utolsó háborúból.

„Bácsi, tanítson engem hogyan elcsapni a' kardütést," szólt egy huszár-ujoncz egy hadedzett huszár-vitézhez. — „Minek az neked," felelé a' hadastyán, „fiam te csak üssed, hadd csapja el az ütést a' Német." [1])

*„Hát miért nem tanuljátok magyar nyelven a' katonai gyakorlatokat? kérdi egy túlbuzgó Magyar az öreg huszár-vitéztől, „utálatos hallani a' német parancsszót!" — „Uram," mond a' huszár, „ha magyarúl commandiroznak**), *én értem, de a' lovam nem érti."* [2])

„Megvallom bizony, hogy nagy aggodalmam van hazámról és nemzetemről, lelkem csügged ha rá gondolok," szól S— báró, kiről tudva volt hogy alattomban a' nemzetellenes párttal tart, — miután egy huszár-tiszt előtt elősorolta volna hazafiúi tetteit. „Bizony jobb volna ha teste csüggne, nyugalma lenne akkor szegény lelkének," mond a' huszár. [3])

*) *Commandirozni* is commonly used by the soldiers instead of *parancsolni*.

Fig. 2: János Csink, *A Complete Practical Grammar of the Hungarian Language, with exercises, selections from the best authors and vocabularies, to which is added a historical sketch of Hungarian literature* (London: Williams and Norgate 1853), pp. 280-1.
British Library pressmark: 0122977.a.2.

The second Hungarian grammar, written by János Csink, a Hungarian schoolteacher from Késmárk, today in Slovakia, was a more comprehensive offering: *A Complete Practical Grammar of the Hungarian Language, with exercises, selections from the best authors and vocabularies, to which is added a historical sketch of Hungarian Literature*, published by Williams and Norgate of Henrietta Street,

Covent Garden, 1853 (BL 012977.a.2 and 02976.bb.2) (fig. 2).[3] The work is divided into three main sections: a phonological introduction, including articulations, sounds and characters; compositions, with practical and theoretical subdivision into grammatical forms and syntax; and finally, reading exercises and a vocabulary to the compositions.[4] The entire work is far more substantial than Wékey's. Its structure may appear cumbersome in parts, but covers more detail than most modern Hungarian grammars. A review in *The Athenaeum* of 10 December 1853 acknowledged Csink's work as a good introduction to the language and literature of Hungary, but maintained it would have better served an English readership had it been carefully supervised by a methodical English editor.

Both grammars contain excerpts from Hungarian literature. Wékey introduces parallel Hungarian and English texts of poems by Mihály Vörösmarty, Sándor Petőfi, József Bajza, and József Eötvös. Csink's sketches of the history of Hungarian literature followed by a selection of Hungarian classics is equally distinguished and much more substantial. These however do not include English translations. In Csink's selection of Hungarian poetry Vörösmarty is also introduced as one of the first Hungarian translators of Shakespeare, with an extract from Act III, Scene 2, of *Julius Caesar*. The prose selections from Hungarian classics include fables by András Fáy, József Kármán, Ferenc Kazinczy, an oration by Kölcsey commemorating Kazinczy, and József Péczely's history of the reoccupation of Buda. These are demanding texts that even fluent Hungarian speakers would find difficult reading. Both works made a laudable effort to introduce knowledge of the Magyar language and literature to their 'favoured and hospitable nation'.

Available evidence offers little to explain how a small London publisher like Trelawny and Saunders came to issue Wékey's grammar. A mere handful of imprints dated between 1850 and 1852 have been identified in miscellaneous works, mostly in the fields of transport, trade and commerce on British territories.

Conversely, Williams and Norgate's catalogues for 1865 reveal a great variety of themes: Greek and Latin Classics, Theological Books in foreign languages, Natural History Catalogue, Bibliotheca Indica, Medical Catalogue, etc. Their *Linguistic Catalogue* is a classified list of books on and in European Languages, ancient and modern (fig. 3). The 1853 London edition of Csink's

---

3 Ibid.

4 For a detailed analysis of Wékey and Csink's grammars see G. F. Cushing, 'The Two Earliest Hungarian Grammars for English Students', *Hungarian Studies in English* (Debrecen, 1977).

Greenland] LINGUISTIC CATALOGUE. [Icelandic 25

FABRICIUS (O.) Grönlandske grammatica. 8vo. *Copenh.* 1801 5s

GOSPEL-HARMONY in Eskimo. 12mo. *Barbime* 1804 6s 6d

GROENLAND'S historiske Mindesmaerker, *vide* Icelandic.

KLEINSCHMIDT (S.) Grammatik der Grönländischen sprache mit theilweisem einschluss des Labrador-dialects. 8vo. *Berl.* 1851 8s

PENTATEUCH in Esquimaux. 12mo. *Sheep* 4s 6d

ISAIAH in Esquimaux. 12mo. *Sheep* 3s 6d

TESTAMENT in Esquimaux. *Sheep* 4s

HUNGARIAN.

ACS (K.) Conversations in Hungarian, German, Italian, Wallachian, Bohemian, Slovac and Servian. 12mo. *Boards*, *Pesth* 1859 4s 6d

BALLAGI (M.) Wörterbuch der Deutschen und Ungarischen Sprache. 2 vols. 8vo. *ib.* 1857-62 18s

BLOCH (M.) Vollständiges Ungarisch u. Deutsches Wörterbuch. 2 vols. 8vo. *ib.* 1857 12s

CASSEL (S.) Magyarische Alterthümer. 8vo. *Berl.* 1888 5s

CSINK'S Complete Practical Grammar of the Hungarian Language, with Exercises, Selections from the best Authors, and Vocabularies; to which is added a Historical Sketch of Hungarian Literature. 300 pages, 8vo. (*Cloth boards.*) *London* 1853 (8s) 4s

CZUCZOR (G.) es FOGARASI (J.) A Magyar nyelv Szotara. (Dictionary of the Hungarian Academy.) Vol. I. II. Roy. 8vo. *Pesth* 1862-64 20s

DALLOS (G.) English-Hungarian Dictionary. Vol. I. 8vo. *Pesth* 1860 6s

EÖTVÖS (T. A.) Falû Jegyzöje. Regény. (The Village Notary.) 3 vols. 8vo. *Pest* 1845 9s

EXERCISES, Hungarian and German. 12mo. *ib.* 1s 6d

FREREYCH (E.) Hungarian and English Dialogues for the use of travellers and students. 8vo. *Pesth* 1851 2s

JOSIKA (M.) Masodik Rákóczy Ferencz. Regény. 6 vols. 12mo. *ib.* 1861 12s

KARADY (F.) Dictionnaire Français Hongrois et Hongrois Français. 12mo. *Leips. and Pesth* 1848 10s

MARTON (J.) Lexicon trilingue. Latino-Hungarico-Germanicum. 4 vols. 8vo. *Vien.* 1818 (47s) 24s

OLLENDORFF'S Methode zur Erlernung der Ungarisch. Sprache, v. F. Ney. 12mo. *Pesth* 1857 4s—Key. 12mo. *ib.* 1s 6d

PETÖFI (S.) Költeményei. 1842-46. 2 vols. 12mo. *ib.* 1847 7s 6d

——— Ujabb Költeményei 1847-49. 2 vols. 12mo. *ib.* 1858 7s 6d

RIEDL (A. M.) Magyarische Grammatik. 8vo. *Wien* 1859 5s 6d

——— Leitfaden f. den Unterricht in der magyarischen Sprache. 8vo. *ib.* 1859 2s

——— Magyar Hangtan (Hungarian Etymology). 8vo. *Prag* 1859 3s 6d

SAJNOVICS (J.) Demonstratio, Idioma Ungarorum et Lapponum idem esse. 4to. *Tyrnau* 1770 4s

STRAHLHEIM (J.) Finnische Sprachlehre mit Beziehung auf d. Ungarische Sprache, finnische und ungarische Mythologie. 8vo. *Petersb.* 1816 9s

TESTAMENT, New, in Hungarian. 12mo. 3s

TOMPA (M.) Népregek, Népmondák (Popular Tales, Proverbs). 8vo. *Pesth* 1846 3s

ICELANDIC. Old Norse.

A.M.—Arnaemagnaean Fund.
R.S.N.A.—Roy. Society of North. Antiquaries.

ALEXANDERS SAGA, af Philip Gautier latinske Digt Alexandreis, udgiven af C. R. Unger. 8vo. *Christ.* 1848 4s 6d

ANALECTA Norraena, *vide* Möbius.

ANECDOTON Historiam Sverreri regis Norvegiæ illustrans. ed. M. Werlauff. 8vo. *Havniæ* (*A.M.*) 1815 4s 6d

ANNALER, Antiquariske, udgivne af den kgl. Comm. til Oldsagers Opbevaring. 27 plates. 4 vols. 8vo. *Copenh.* 1812-27 24s

——— for Nordisk Oldkyndighed og historie. 1836 to 1860. 18 vols. 8vo. (*Numerous plates.*) (*R.S.N.A.*) *Copenh.* 1837-64 Each Volume 7s

ANTIQUARISK Tidsskrift. 1852-60 (*woodcuts.*) 3 vols. 8vo. *Copenh.* (*R.S.N.A.*) 1854-61 21s

ANTIQUITATES AMERICANÆ, sive scriptores septemtrion. rerum Ante-Columbianum in America, studio C. C. Rafn. (*R. S. N. A.*) Folio. *Havn.* 1845 48s

ANTIQUITÉS Américaines d'après les monuments historiques des Islandais et des anciens Scandinaves, publiées par C. C. Rafn. 8vo. *Maps.* *ib.* 1845 12s

ANTIQUITÉS Russes, d'après les monuments historiques des Islandais et des anciens Scandinaves editées par la Soc. Roy. des Antiq. du Nord. Vols. I. II. folio. *Beautifully printed.* *Copenh.* (*R.S.N.A.*) 1850-52 £6.

ARNASON (J.) Islenzkar Thjódsögur og Aefintyri. 2 vols. Roy. 8vo. *Leipz.* 1864 28s

ARWIDSSON (A. I.) Förteckning öfver Kongl. Bibliothek. i Stokholm Isländska Handskrifter. 8vo. 1848 4s

ASBJOERNSEN u. Grässe. Nord und Süd. Ein Märchen-Strauss. 8 *woodcuts.* *Dresd.* 1859 3s

ATLAS DE L'ARCHEOLOGIE du Nord, representant des Echantillons de l'âge de Bronze et de l'âge de fer publié par la Société Royale des Antiquaires du Nord. 15 *plates.* *folio.* *Copenh.* 1858 30s

——— de l'Archeologie du Nord—Texte explicatif. 8vo. *ib.* 1860 3s

BANDAMANNA Saga *vide* Nord. Oldskrifter, 10.

BARDARSAGA, Snaefellsass, Viglundarsaga &c. ved G. Vigfusson. (Nord Oldskr. 27.) 8vo. *Kiöb.* 1860 3s

BARLAAMS ok Josaphats Saga, overs. paa Norsk af Kong Hakon Sverressön udg. af R. Keyser og Unger. 8vo. *Christ.* 1851 10s

BERGMANN (F. G.) Les Chants de Sól (Só-

20, South Frederick Street, Edinburgh.

Fig. 3: *Williams and Norgate's Linguistic catalogue*, no. 5 (Jan. 1865), p. 25. British Library pressmark: 11903.h.28.

grammar is still listed in the Hungarian section, together with some twenty other works of Hungarian interest imported from Tyrnau, Pest, Leipzig, Berlin or Vienna. Williams and Norgate's stocks were remarkably rich and varied considering the relatively small number of the émigrés living in London at the time. The revolutions of 1848-9 awakened interest in languages and cultures of European nations, much as current political turmoil inspires British readers today.

David J. Shaw

Statistics of Foreign-Language Publishing in London

For the period up to 1800 it is now relatively easy to calculate statistics for the publication of each of the European languages published in London century by century, thanks to the existence of the *English Short-Title Catalogue.* Originally called the *Eighteenth-Century Short-Title Catalogue*, this project has recently extended its coverage to include books printed before 1701 from the records of the Bibliographical Society's *Short-Title Catalogue of Books Printed in England, Scotland, & Ireland and of English Books Printed Abroad, 1475-1640* (STC)[1] and Donald Wing's *Short-Title Catalogue of Books Printed in England, Scotland, Ireland, Wales, and British America, and of English Books Printed in Other Countries, 1641-1700.*[2]

These data exist as a searchable computer database and so it is in principle possible to search for all the books printed in each European language which were printed in London. This involves creating a search like

Place = 'London' AND Language = 'French'

Additionally an extra clause

Country = 'England'

would ensure that 'false imprints' are excluded.[3] The addition of a search clause for a date range like

Date > 1700 AND Date < 1801

enables statistics to be tabulated on a century by century basis.

---

1 (London: The Bibliographical Society, 1976, 1986, 1991), 3 vols.

2 2nd edn, revised and enlarged (New York: Modern Language Association of America, 1994–1998).

3 A 'false imprint' is where a book is printed abroad with a title-page claiming that it is printed in London. For a discussion of false imprints in French books, see my 'French-Language Publishing in London to 1900', in this volume.

Unfortunately, the version of the ESTC CDROM issued in 1998 is incomplete: it has about 65% of the entries in the printed volumes of STC and about 50% of the Wing entries.[4] Equally unfortunately, the coding of elements such as 'language' and 'country of publication' does not always prove to be accurate. The statistics in the accompanying table are presented as offering an approximate picture of the volume of foreign-language publishing in London up to 1800. Figures for the fifteenth century have been taken from the *Incunable Short-Title Catalogue* (ISTC) database and can be considered as being very accurate. (The ISTC figures include books printed in Westminster as well as in London.) This is also the case for the eighteenth century, since ESTC's coverage for that period is very extensive. For the sixteenth and seventeenth centuries, the figures derived from the ESTC database searches have been scaled up by appropriate factors representing the shortfall in coverage for the STC and Wing periods.[5] It is not possible to provide similar statistics for the nineteenth century as there is no comparable database; the *Nineteenth-Century Short-Title Catalogue* does not provide language codes for its records.

It will be seen from the table that books in English predominate, representing 56% of the total for the fifteenth century and rising to over 95% for the seventeenth and eighteenth centuries. Books in Latin form the next largest group, falling from 36% of the London incunables to 1·4% by the eighteenth century. It can be seen that books in modern foreign languages have never formed more than a small proportion of the output of the London presses: about 1·5% overall and only significantly more in the fifteenth and sixteenth centuries when the numbers are artificially swollen by the category of law books printed in Law French (7.5% of the incunables, 6% in the sixteenth century, declining to a tiny fraction in the eighteenth century).

The 'genuine' foreign-language books amount to an estimated 2,945 editions (excluding Latin, Law French, and Welsh, Irish and Gaelic) or just under 1% of the total production up to 1800. The earliest and most numerous are books in French: 3 in the fifteenth century and 0·8% of the total. This represents 81% of all the foreign-language books. Next most frequent are the

---

4 The on-line versions of the ESTC files are somewhat more complete but unfortunately did not provide convenient access to all the search terms needed.

5 The scale factors are 1·525 (36662 / 24034) for the STC period and 2·039 (97456 / 47806) for the Wing books. For the seventeenth century, the two scale factors are combined in the proportion 40 :: 60 (1·833), representing the years before and after 1640. These factors are likely to be fairly crude approximations. It is quite possible that the proportion of books in English on the ESTC database is higher than the proportion of books in foreign languages.

books in Italian (11%), found from the sixteenth century onwards. Also recorded from the sixteenth century are books in Spanish (2·2%) and Dutch (1·3%). The only other significant numbers are for books in German (2·6%, starting in the seventeenth century).

Book Production in London to 1800 Analysed by Language

	15th century		16th century			17th century			18th century		TOTAL	
	ISTC	%	ESTC	estimate	%	ESTC	estimate	%	ESTC	%	estimate	%
TOTAL	**372**		8,568	**13,070**		54,097	**99,177**		**190,513**		**303,132**	
English	**208**	55.9	6,941	**10,588**	81.0	51,933	**95,209**	96.00	**184,984**	97.10	**290,989**	95.994
Not English	**164**	44.1	1,627	**2,482**	19.0	2,164	**3,967**	4.00	**5,529**	2.90	**12,142**	4.006
Latin	**133**	35.8	997	**1,521**	11.6	1,786	**3,274**	3.30	**2,659**	1.40	**7,587**	2.503
French	**3**	0.8	30	**46**	0.4	136	**249**	0.25	**2,109**	1.11	**2,407**	0.794
Law French	**28**	7.5	503	**767**	5.9	97	**178**	0.18	**0**		**973**	0.321
Italian			36	**55**	0.4	10	**18**	0.02	**255**	0.13	**328**	0.108
German			0	**0**	0.1	4	**7**	0.01	**70**	0.04	**77**	0.026
Spanish			9	**14**	0.1	3	**5**	0.01	**45**	0.02	**64**	0.021
Dutch			11	**17**		7	**13**	0.01	**10**	0.01	**40**	0.013
Portuguese			0	**0**		1	**2**	0.00	**15**	0.01	**17**	0.006
Danish			0	**0**		0	**0**		**6**	0.00	**6**	0.002
Swedish			0	**0**		0	**0**		**5**	0.00	**5**	0.002
Icelandic			0	**0**		0	**0**		**1**	0.00	**1**	0.00
Welsh			7	**11**	0.1	36	**66**	0.07	**131**	0.07	**208**	0.069
Irish			0	**9**		5	**9**	0.01	**3**	0.00	**12**	0.004
Gaelic			0	**0**		0	**0**		**2**	0.00	**2**	0.001

Notes on Contributors

Graham Jefcoate has been Director General of the Berlin State Library (Staatsbibliothek zu Berlin – Preußischer Kulturbesitz) since March 2002. He was formerly Head of Early Printed Collections at the British Library. He has published widely on topics relating to Anglo-German book trade relations in the eighteenth century. His bibliography of books printed in German (or printed or published by Germans) in London between 1680 and 1811 is due to appear in autumn 2002.

Susan Reed is the British Library's Curator of Early German Printed Books, responsible primarily for the Library's extensive holdings of books printed in the German-speaking countries between 1501 and 1850. Her recent areas of research among the collections include material relating to the 1848 Revolution in Berlin and a newly-acquired collection of early twentieth- century proto-fascist esoterica. She co-edits the *German Studies Library Group Newsletter.*

Anna E. C. Simoni was born in Leipzig; fled to Britain after three years' study in Italy; took an honours degree in Classics at Glasgow University; and served in the WAAF as a flight mechanic, 1943-6. In 1950 she joined the Department of Printed Books, British Museum, retiring as head of Dutch in 1981. In 1998 she was made Knight of the Nederlandse Leeuw and in 2000 received an honorary doctorate at the University of Genoa. Her publications on early and World War II Dutch bibliographical subjects include *Publish and Be Free* (The Hague: Nijhoff, 1975) and *Catalogue of Books from the Low Countries 1601-1621 in the British Library* (London: British Library, 1991).

Peter Hogg was formerly printed-books curator in the British Museum Library 1961-73 and subsequently the British Library 1973-99. His forthcoming short-title catalogue of the Library's early Scandinavian holdings is described in his 'The Development of the pre-1801 Scandinavian Printed Collections in the British Library', *British Library Journal*, 25 (1999), 144-63.

David J. Shaw has recently been appointed Secretary of the Consortium of European Research Libraries, having retired as Senior Lecturer in French at the University of Kent at Canterbury. He has written extensively on the history of the book in fifteenth- and sixteenth-century France and was Editor-in-Chief of the Bibliographical Society's Cathedral Libraries Catalogue. In Early Printed Collections at the British Library he is preparing a typographical catalogue of the Library's books printed in France between 1501 and 1520.

Morna Daniels is a curator in the French Section of the British Library. Her publications include *Victorian Book Illustration* (London: British Library, 1988) and the volumes on Burundi and Cote d'Ivoire in the World Bibliographical Series (Oxford: Clio Press, 1992 and 1996); 'A Memento of Napoleon', *British Library Journal*, 17 (1991), 104-8 and 'French Newspapers and Ephemera from the 1848 Revolution', *British Library Journal*, 24 (1998), 219-33.

Stephen Parkin is a curator in Early Printed Collections, with responsibility for the Italian printed collections 1501-1850. His interests include the development of the Library's historical holdings of Italian books, and in particular the Colt Hoare collection, assembled by Sir Richard Colt Hoare during visits to Italy in the 1790s and given to the British Museum Library in the 1820s. He has also collaborated on a project to catalogue the manuscripts and printed items largely relating to Italian diplomatic and papal history which belonged to the library of Frederick North, 5th Earl of Guilford, and were purchased by the Library in the 1830s.

Denis V. Reidy is Head of the Italian and Modern Greek Section at the British Library. His most recent publications include *The Risorgimento Collection: full texts of rare historical and political materials relating to the unification of Italy* (London: K. G. Saur, 1992); *The Italian Book 1465-1800: studies presented to Dennis E. Rhodes on his 70th birthday* (London: The British Library, 1993); *Antonio Panizzi: tre lezioni sul mondo cavalleresco* (Brescello, 1998); *The Digital Library: challenges and solutions for the new Millennium*, ed. Pauline Connolly and Denis Reidy (London: IFLA, 2000).

Barry Taylor is Curator of Hispanic Collections 1501-1850 at the British Library and is also responsible for Portugal, Brazil, Portuguese-speaking Africa and the Southern Cone of South America. His books include *Cultures in Contact in Medieval Spain: historical and literary essays presented to L. P. Harvey*, ed. David Hook and Barry Taylor (London: King's College, 1990); *Andorra*, World Bibliographical Series (Oxford: Clio Press, 1993); (with Geoffrey West) *Medieval Love Poetry: course guide* (London: University, External

Programme, 1995); *Latin and Vernacular in Renaissance Spain*, ed. Barry Taylor and Alejandro Coroleu (Manchester: Department of Hispanic Studies, 1999).

Chris Michaelides is a curator in the Italian and Modern Greek Section of the British Library. He has published articles and reviews on French, Italian and Modern Greek art and literature. His publications include the Clio Press World Bibliographical Series volumes *San Marino* (1996; with Adrian Edwards), and *Rome* (2000); 'Three Early Cavafy Items in the British Library', *British Library Journal*, 19 (1993), 83-104, and 'Between "La peinture archéologique" and "la poésie de la vie": Eugène Carrière, 1876-1879, and the British Museum sketchbook', *Gazette des Beaux-Arts* (Déc. 1998). In 1995 he organised an exhibition on Torquato Tasso.

Kate Sealey Rahman, formerly a curator in the Slavonic and East European Collections of the British Library, is a British Academy Post-Doctoral Research Fellow in the School of Slavonic and East European Studies, University College London. Her current research interest is the Russian dramatist Aleksandr Ostrovsky, on whom she has written a number of publications, including the monograph *Ostrovsky: reality and illusion* (Birmingham Slavonic Monographs, 1999).

Janet Zmroczek is Curator of Polish and Baltic Collections at the British Library. Her research interests include the development of the British Library Polish and Baltic collections, the Polish book trade in nineteenth-century Britain and Polish state publishing policy and underground publishing in the communist era. Her recent publications include: '"A National Library for the Poles in Exile": the development of the Polish collections of the British Museum Library in the nineteenth century', *Solanus*, 15 (2001), 17-34; 'Lietuvišku knygu rinkinys Britu bibliotekoje (The Collection of Lithuanian Books at the British Library)', *Knygotyra* 32 (1996), 249-89; 33 (1997), 114-53 (with Dr Aušra Navickiene).

Bridget Guzner is Curator of Hungarian and Romanian Collections at the British Library. Her interests include all aspects of Hungarian and Romanian culture and the recent history of Central and Eastern Europe. She has published: contributions to the Bibliographic Studies section of the serial publication *The Eighteenth Century: a current bibliography* (New York: AMS Press, 1986-9); (joint compiler) *Hungary 1956: a catalogue of British Library holdings* (London: The British Library, 1995); *Hungarian Studies, a brief guide to reference sources in the British Library* (London: The British Library, 2000). She is currently working on a short-title catalogue of Romanian books printed before 1900 in the British Library.

Index of Printers, Publishers and Booksellers